Consuming the Romantic Utopia

Consuming the Romantic Utopia

Love and the Cultural Contradictions of Capitalism

Eva Illouz

UNIVERSITY OF CALIFORNIA PRESS
Berkeley · Los Angeles · London

University of California Press
Berkeley and Los Angeles, California

University of California Press, Ltd.
London, England

©1997 by
The Regents of the University of California

Library of Congress Cataloging-in-Publication Data

Illouz, Eva, 1961–
    Consuming the romantic utopia : love and the
cultural contradictions of capitalism / Eva Illouz.
        p.   cm.
    Includes bibliographic references and index
    ISBN 978-0-520-20571-0 (pbk. : alk. paper)
    1. Love.   2. Capitalism.   I. Title.
HQ801.I64   1996
306.7—dc20   95-44241

Printed in the United States of America

12   11   10   09   08   07   06
11   10   9   8   7   6   5   4   3

The paper used in this publication meets the minimum requirements of
ANSI/NISO Z39.48-1992 (R 1997) (*Permanence of Paper*).

This book is dedicated to Elchanan Ben-Porath

Do you hear the neighing of the horses, the blaring of the trumpets, and the rattle of the drums?
I hear nothing, answered Sancho, but the bleating of the sheeps and lambs.

Cervantes, Don Quixote

Contents

Acknowledgments

This book owes many debts to many people. Contrary to custom, I would like to thank my husband, Elchanan Ben-Porath, at the very beginning. The two years during which I wrote this book coincided with the first two years of our marriage and saw the successive births of our sons, Nathan-El and Immanuel. That I managed to complete this book in such hectic times is mostly due to his hard domestic work, his thorough critiques of the manuscript in its various stages, and his unwavering support.

A number of institutions have played an important role in the writing of this book. A student fellowship from the Annenberg School for Communications helped me defray the costs of interview transcriptions. A Fulbright Fellowship defrayed my travel costs. A fellowship from the National Museum of American History, at the Smithsonian Institution, supported me during the writing of chapters 1 and 2 of this book. The Rachi Foundation in Paris provided a generous grant that enabled the purchase of equipment and defrayed the costs of secretarial assistance.

I would like to thank the faculty of social sciences at Tel-Aviv University for a grant that helped defray the costs of editing. Finally, I would like to thank the secretarial staff of the Department of Sociology at Northwestern University, where I visited during the last year spent writing this book, for the efficiency of their assistance.

My intellectual debts go way back.

First and foremost is Larry Gross, my adviser at the Annenberg School of Communications at the University of Pennsylvania, who has been a model of intellectual rigor and generosity. Intensive discussions with

Charles Bosk provided the important milestones in the conception of this project. At the Smithsonian Institution, Charlie McGovern helped me find my way in the maze of studies on the early American twentieth century. Michele Richman has played a key role in my intellectual development in general. Her unfailing warmth and love of knowledge sustained me more often and in many more ways than she suspects. Amy Jordan, Christine Hoephner, and Luba Vikhanski read and corrected an embarrassing number of pages. I feel fortunate to have benefited from their abilities. Discussions with Arjun Appadurai were crucial in the early development of my thoughts. My gratitude goes to Paul DiMaggio for supporting this project at its inception and for sharing with me a rarely encountered depth of knowledge.

The second stage of writing this book owes its most significant debt to Michele Lamont. Her generosity of mind and heart and her incisive critiques significantly contributed to the quality of this manuscript. Francesca Cancian's meticulous and thought-provoking critique helped me bring some critical clarifications in the structure of the argument. An anonymous reader at the University of California Press provided critiques of unexpected thoroughness and breadth. I am grateful to him or her for a careful and insightful reading. Haim Hazan and Sacha Weitman read the completed manuscript and offered constructive critiques with their usual warmth and acumen.

Erika Büky, William Murphy, and Naomi Schneider at the University of California Press have assisted me in the sometimes hazardous process of turning the manuscript into a book. I thank them for their unfailing responsiveness throughout our electronic relationship.

My deep gratitude goes to the men and women who were interviewed for this study.

A cohort of friends and colleagues helped me overcome the self-doubts often involved in the writing of such a book. Philippe Zard has never failed to give me the warmth and intellectual challenges that make his friendship a rare one. Philippe Corcuff has been and continues to be a source of sociological inspiration. At an early stage, Gideon Kunda voiced constructive criticism of an early draft of the book prospectus. Haurit Hermann-Peled and Yohav Peled read chapters 1 and 2 and made perceptive critiques. Cathy Preston and Moira McLoughlin made important suggestions on ways to improve chapter 3. Michele Richman read chapter 4 and contributed important insights on the role of expenditure. Nurit Bird-David, José Brunner, Avi Cordova, Shlomo Deshen, Sigal Goldin, and Moshe Shokeid read and reread early drafts of chapter 5.

Their patient criticism and bibliographical suggestions contributed much to this chapter. Discussions with Philippe Corcuff and Claudette Lafaye helped me conceive of the ideas of chapter 6. Philippe Corcuff, Yuval Yonai, and Yehuda Schenhav made enlightening suggestions about chapter 7, and all three directed my attention to the idea of multiple rationalities.

Last, I would like to express my gratitude to my parents, brothers, and sister, whose presence sustained me through the writing of this book.

Introduction to
the Sociology of Love

We would shiver a little at the coldness, severity, and calculating clarity of such a noble concept of marriage as has ruled in every healthy aristocracy, in ancient Athens as in the eighteenth century, we warm-blooded animals with sensitive hearts, we "moderns"! Precisely this is why love as a passion—in the great meaning of the word—was *invented* for the aristocratic world and in it, where constraint and privation were greatest.

Nietzsche, The Will to Power

Romantic love, we are told by some, is the last repository of the authenticity and the warmth that have been robbed from us by an increasingly technocratic and legalistic age. To others, it represents an ideology that enslaves women, a symptom of the demise of the public sphere, or a flight from social responsibility.

This book does not intend to be another voice celebrating the virtues of love or lamenting its failings. Rather, it aims to highlight the terms of this debate by examining how romantic love relates to the culture and class relationships of late capitalism. While many studies have examined the impact of capitalism on the self and on human relationships, this book addresses more seriously the question of how the encounter of love and capitalism occurred. This focus on the "how" is then about understanding the forms and the mechanisms through which romantic emotions intersect with the culture, the economy, and the social organization of advanced capitalism.

Capitalism is a notoriously Janus-like entity: to the extent that it promotes the incorporation of all social groups into the market, it has created a powerful common symbolic space unified by the twin spheres of consumption and mass media. But capitalism does not only unify; in its industrial phase it has brought about intense class conflicts; in its postindustrial phase it has fragmented social classes into ever-smaller communities of consumption or lifestyle groups. Capitalism makes possible the participation of everyone in the economic and symbolic sphere of consumption, yet sustains and reproduces itself through the concentration of wealth and the legitimation of social divisions.

This book argues that the modern definitions and practices of romance are intertwined with this duality of consumer capitalism. Romantic love has become an intimate, indispensable part of the democratic ideal of affluence that has accompanied the emergence of the mass market, thereby offering a collective utopia cutting across and transcending social divisions. Concomitantly with that process, however, romantic love has espoused as it were the mechanisms of economic and symbolic domination at work in American social structure. The broad thesis of the book then is that romantic love is a collective arena within which the social divisions and the cultural contradictions of capitalism are played out.

ROMANTIC LOVE AS A CULTURAL PRACTICE

As an economic system, capitalism "involv[es] the production and exchange of commodities with the aim of accumulating a surplus value, that is, profit, with some part of this profit being re-invested in order to maintain the conditions of future accumulation."[1] Beyond this technical definition, however, capitalism is characterized by an entire cultural mind-set, in that "exchange relationships, that of buying and selling, have permeated most of the society."[2] In capitalism, two parties come together explicitly on the basis of self-interest and mutual economic benefit; transactions are justified by calculating their effects on the "bottom line" of the balance sheet. In romantic love, by contrast, two individuals are bound together by the "capacity to realize spontaneity and empathy in an erotic relationship."[3] In the marketplace, trading partners are ultimately interchangeable; relationships shift with economic circumstances. In romantic love, the person we love and feel united with is unique and irreplaceable; furthermore, "love is the most important thing in the world, to which all other considerations, particularly material ones, should be sacrificed."[4] Romantic love is irrational rather than rational, gratuitous rather than profit-oriented, organic rather than utilitarian, private rather than public. In short, romantic love seems to evade the conventional categories within which capitalism has been conceived. In popular culture and "common sense," as well as in scholarship, romantic love stands above the realm of commodity exchange and even against the social order writ large.

Until the 1960s, anthropology, sociology, and history implicitly sub-scribed to this view.[5] Conceiving of culture as a public and collective practice, these disciplines equated emotions with subjective, physio-logical and psychological experiences, thus ultimately excluding them from the study of collective and symbolic life. Romantic love was in-evitably relegated to the sociologically awkward sphere of private life rather than discussed in terms of public rituals, social conflict, or class relationships.

In the last two decades, however, new voices in anthropology and psychology have insisted that emotions are influenced and even shaped by the volatile "stuff" of culture: norms, language, stereo-types, metaphors, symbols.[6] But if most disciplines of the social sci-ences are willing today to profess a link between culture and emotion, they are more reluctant to acknowledge a connection between love and economy. Like art and religion, love "is the site par excellence of the denial of the social world" especially when this world takes the murky face of economic interest, and, like art or religion, romantic love denies its social basis through its claim to transcend or overturn it.[7] How then are the links between emotion, culture, and economy to be conceptualized?

"Emotions" are the complex conjunction of physiological arousal, perceptual mechanisms, and interpretive processes; they are thus situ-ated at the threshold where the noncultural is encoded in culture, where body, cognition, and culture converge and merge.[8] As a cultural prac-tice, then, romantic love is subject to the twin influence of the economic and political spheres; unlike other practices, however, romantic love im-plies an immediate experience of the body.

The social psychologists Schachter and Singer have offered a com-pelling account of just how and when a physiological arousal might be-come "love."[9] They suggest that emotions are activated by a general and undifferentiated state of arousal, which becomes an emotion only when appropriately labeled. For example, the same general state of arousal could trigger either fear or infatuation, depending on environmental cues.[10] If this is indeed the case, we can then expect culture to play a con-siderable role in the construction, interpretation, and functioning of emotions. Culture operates as a *frame* within which emotional experi-ence is organized, labeled, classified, and interpreted.[11] Cultural frames name and define the emotion, set the limits of its intensity, specify the norms and values attached to it, and provide symbols and cultural scenarios that make it socially communicative.

In the evolution of sexual arousal to the codified sentiment of love, culture plays at least three roles. First, it provides meaning to physiological arousal by labeling it. For example, depending on one's cultural tradition (e.g., Christian, Romantic, scientific), sexual arousal can be variously construed as "recognition of two souls destined for each other," "love at first sight," "infatuation," "lust" (either a sin or a somewhat pleasurable irritant), or just "hormonal disorder." Similarly, the physiological arousal associated with jealousy may be interpreted as a sign of romantic passion, an expression of personal insecurity, or an attempt at control. Second, labels contain meanings embedded in bodies of norms, prescriptions, and prohibitions. For example, same-sex friendships might be interpreted as homosexual passions or as spiritual attachments, depending on the range of authorized interpretations. Furthermore, not only does the normative context determine the definition of a given emotion, but people can manage and control their emotions in order to conform to cultural norms, a process that has been called "emotion work" by sociologist Arlie Hochschild.[12]

Third, cultural values stipulate how to evaluate the intensity of physiological arousal. For example, the Romantic tradition would most likely privilege its initial and most intense stage, whereas realist traditions might favor its declining intensity and less turbulent manifestations as exemplifying "true" love. In contemporary culture, two equally powerful repertoires are used to make sense of, express, or control the various stages of the romantic bond: in the main, the initial stages of attraction and the romantic sentiment are expressed in the cultural institution of "dating" and are imbricated with the hedonist values of postmodern culture. On the other hand, the stability and longevity procured by a slow-paced, incremental, and long-lasting love are associated with the institution of marriage and are framed in a blend of therapeutic and economic terms.

Fourth, culture provides symbols, artifacts, stories, and images—symbolic "snapshots"—in which romantic feelings can be recapitulated and communicated. These symbols are often literally photographs—for example, the "romantic" photograph summarizing a couple's vacation or honeymoon and picturing them closely embraced on the beach at sundown—or the memory of past love might take the form of a letter or gift, or a story capturing the vivid uniqueness of the relationship.

The repertoire of images, artifacts, and stories offered by contemporary culture is varied but limited, and some of these cultural symbols are more readily available than others. This is precisely my point of interrogation: How does one cultural vocabulary of sentiments become more visible and more publicly available than another? Why is the image of a couple walking hand-in-hand along the sea more prevalent than the image of a man and a woman casually watching television? Why do most people remember short-lived and intense affairs more easily than slow-paced relationships? Why does a long conversation convey more aptly feelings of "intimacy" and "romance" than attending a basketball game?

Such questions form the backbone of this study and already give clues as to what this book is *not* about. It is not about the phenomenology of love, insofar as it does not interrogate romantic love from "inside," as a reality sui generis, and does not decompose it into categories constitutive of its experience (e.g., "the encounter," "the first kiss," "the caresses," "the communication," "the sexual bond," et cetera). This also explains why the issue of sexuality is obliquely rather than frontally addressed. While it is an undoubtedly crucial element of contemporary romantic experiences, sexuality is subordinated to the same cultural discourses of self-realization, hedonism, and self-knowledge that form the backbone of our culture of love. This book is also not about romantic love as it is usually, and narrowly, defined by cultural historians, that is, as a passionate and absolute longing for someone cast in the language of religious devotion. The material explored here is more diffuse and volatile than such attempts to delimit it would suggest.

This book places in a critical context the multifarious feelings implied in the expression "to be romantically involved with somebody." Although it studies many of the stages of "romantic involvement"—initial attraction, dating, marriage—it does not do so chronologically, for my interest is not in telling the story of contemporary love. Rather, it is in bringing love within the traditional business of cultural sociology and submitting it to questions of which tacit meanings and symbols organize our romantic experience and why precisely these and not others.

Definitions of culture somewhat muddle rather than clarify this issue. One definition, provided by anthropologist Clifford Geertz and now almost canonical, suggests that it is a "historically transmitted pattern of meanings embodied in symbols, a system of inherited conceptions expressed in symbolic forms by means of which men [sic] communicate, perpetuate, and develop their knowledge about and attitudes toward life."[13] This definition purposely refuses the question of the "ultimate"

causes of these cultural patterns and instead confines itself to an imma-
nent interpretation of the given frameworks of knowledge within which
men and women make sense of their world, act on it, and communicate
with one another. Such an approach to culture broadly informs my view
that love is a complex emotion interweaving stories, images, metaphors,
material goods, and folk theories and that people make sense of their romantic experiences by drawing on collective symbols and meanings.

The drawback of such an approach, however, is that it ultimately remains silent on the constitution of cultural meaning—where do these
meanings "come from," what other purposes do they serve beyond making sense? While there is much to be said for Geertz's attention to the
complex and rich texture of meaning, one is tempted to retort to him
that history informs us not only of the relative persistence of cultural categories, but also of the ways in which meanings serve as weapons in the
struggles of social groups to secure and further their interests. Culture
thus is a matter of shared meanings, but it is not only that: it is also one
of the ways in which exclusion, inequality, and power structures are
maintained and reproduced. Linking love to culture in the context of
advanced capitalism, then, demands that we understand how love *at one
and the same time* binds and divides, unites and separates.

To grasp this duality of love in turn requires that we move away from
the self-defeating question of whether economy determines culture or vice
versa.[14] As many sociologists have increasingly come to acknowledge,
culture and economy reciprocally constitute each other; this book hopes
to contribute to these new attempts at synthesis by showing how romantic emotions intersect with the link between culture and economy.[15]
Thus, my primary question is not how romantic love embodies a self-
contained pattern of meanings; the question is how to *frame* the relationship between love and late capitalism. As Randall Collins put it, the
problem of social analysis is not only how to explain social phenomena
but also how to conceive them.[16] This book focuses on *how* romance,
culture, and economy connect with one another, that is, on the mechanisms and the cultural forms through which culture and economy meet
and intersect in love.[17]

ROMANTIC LOVE AS A UTOPIA OF TRANSGRESSION

The idea that romantic love is at the cornerstone of the culture of capitalism is not new. In his *Origin of the Family, Private Property and the
State,* a sweeping critique of the family from Greek civilization to the

bourgeois era, Friedrich Engels condemned the family for subjugating women to men and for preserving private property (through laws of inheritance). For Engels, the monogamous bourgeois "affectionate" marriage is a hypocritical illusion, conditioned by class rather than sentiment, and remains ultimately a marriage of convenience rather than love. Only in the working classes, who have no material wealth to gain or lose, can "true" romantic love flourish. Therefore, as Engels and Marx concluded in the *Communist Manifesto,* only in a communist society, liberated from private property and the profit motive, would the family and love be freed from the relations of domination and interest. The political utopia envisioned by Marx and Engels clearly implied a total separation between commodity and sentiment, interest and love, as a precondition for authentic, fully human relationships.

Combining Marxian and Freudian doctrines, some members of the Frankfurt School refined this critique of capitalism, contrasting it to a social utopia in which love occupied a place of honor. Marcuse argued that erotic desires could and should be liberated from the psychic demands of the capitalist system of production. For him, the "reality principle" that animates capitalism subjugates desire to the iron law of productivity.[18] Erich Fromm echoed Marcuse's critique but offered a different analysis of the relationship between capitalism and love. In his 1956 book, *The Art of Loving,* Fromm argued that modern love had come to be conceived in the same terms as capitalist economic exchanges. The modern romantic couple had become a "working team" and thus adopted the values and the forms of reasoning of modern economic relationships. Both Marcuse and Fromm cast the relationship between society and love as a political issue, thus opening the path to a *political* critique of sexuality, desire, and love.

Despite the wide-ranging influence that these critics have exerted in academic scholarship and, more ephemerally, on the student movements of the 1960s, their vision has failed to transform the popular representations of love in any significant way. Love remains one of the most important mythologies of our time.[19] I would therefore like to start this inquiry with the following question: Why do romantic love and its attendant mythologies have such a powerful grip on our collective imagination? In the first half of the book I argue that the long-lasting power of love is explained—if only partially—by the fact that love is a privileged site for the experience of utopia. In capitalist societies, love contains a utopian dimension that cannot be easily reduced to "false consciousness" or to the presumed power of "ideology" to recruit people's desires. Instead, the

longing for utopia at the heart of romantic love possesses deep affinities
with the experience of the sacred. As Durkheim has suggested, such experience has not disappeared from secular societies but has migrated from
religion proper to other domains of culture.[20] Romantic love is one site
of this displacement.[21]

Paradoxically enough, this "sacralization" of a secularized love occurred at the same time that romance was being stripped of the meanings it had long borrowed from institutional religion. At the turn of the
twentieth century, romantic love ceased being an "altar" to which lovers
"consecrated" a cult conceived in the terms of Christian devotion. In the
process of becoming secular, romance took on the properties of *ritual:* it
started drawing on themes and images offering temporary access to a
powerful collective utopia of abundance, individualism, and creative
self-fulfillment, and these utopian meanings were experienced through
the cyclical performance of rituals of consumption. (The first five chapters of this book illuminate these utopian themes and their connection
to the experience of ritual.)

The themes that make up the romantic utopia preceded the rise of
capitalism per se. Many authors have observed that in most societies,
including premodern Europe, romantic love was perceived as a subversive force threatening the legal and moral order.[22] But nowhere is
this observation more relevant than in Western culture, where romantic love has been imbued with an aura of transgression, while being
elevated to the status of a supreme value. The figures that haunt our
romantic imagination affirm the inalienable rights of passion, defy the
normal arrangements and divisions by gender, class, or national loyalties.[23] One reason romantic love is perceived as so destabilizing is that
it challenges an essential regulatory mechanism of any social group, kinship. As the anthropologist Claude Lévi-Strauss has argued, contained
in the universal taboo of incest is the norm that groups create and maintain relations of reciprocity and obligation through the exchange of
women.[24] In many societies, the exchange of women is supervised and
tightly controlled by agents of authority who ensure that rules of endogamy are carefully observed.

To the extent that romantic love affirms the choice of a mate by the
individual, often against or outside the rules of endogamy, it explores
the limits of the rules maintaining the group. As William Goode, in a
classic paper on love, put it, "To permit random mating would mean
radical change in the existing social structure."[25] Yet even if such a
radical transformation has not taken place, at the level of symbolic rep-

resentation romantic love has articulated a *longing for and a utopian model* of the sovereignty of the individual above and often against the claims of the group.[26] Long before the possessive individualism of commercial and industrial capitalism, romantic love celebrated moral individualism, a value of paramount importance to the worldview of industrial capitalism.[27]

Furthermore, in premodern Europe, endogamic rules not only confined the autonomy of the individual but also regulated the exchange of wealth. Members of the landed aristocracy married people of similar or superior birth and fortune in order to maintain and increase their patrimony and social status. The historian Theodor Zeldin suggests that until the beginning of the twentieth century, marriage was considered by members of all levels of society (except for the lowest, who could not afford the ceremony) to be one of the most, if not the most, important financial operations of their lives. Far from the modern idea of love, the ideal marriage of this era was one in which "the fortunes of both partners where perfectly equilibrated: the ideal marriage was an equitable bargaining."[28] Zeldin notes that in such an atmosphere "love was, for parental authority, the great enemy, the rebel likely to cause disasters for all its projects."[29] Romantic love was perceived to oppose strategies of social reproduction normally safeguarded by the institution of marriage. It stood for such values as disinterestedness, irrationality, and indifference to riches. Ironically, however, in popular literature, love was supposed to magically bring economic security, and abundance, without cold-hearted calculation.

Romantic love, then, precedes capitalism per se but articulates two leitmotifs that will later resonate with capitalism's central ideological themes. One concerns the sovereignty of the individual vis-à-vis the group, such sovereignty being affirmed in illicit sexual choices and in the lovers' refusal to conform to the rules of endogamy set by the group. The other concerns the distinction central to bourgeois ideology between interest and sentiments, selfishness and selflessness, embodied respectively in the public and private spheres. In this division, romantic love asserts the privilege of sentiments over social and economic interests, of gratuity over profit, of abundance over the deprivations caused by accumulation. In proclaiming the supremacy of human relationships governed by the disinterested gift of oneself, love not only celebrates the fusion of individual souls and bodies but also opens the possibility of an alternative social order. Love thus projects an aura of transgression and both promises and demands a better world.

However, in and of itself, a mere representation such as the ideal vision of romantic love does not have the power to win such pervasive and long-lasting devotion. To last and prevail, it must articulate itself through certain categories of experience. From my Durkheimian premises, I will argue that the utopian dimension of romantic love derives from a particular category of the religious, the one that anthropologist Victor Turner calls "liminality."[30] According to Turner, the "liminal" is a category of ritual in which the hierarchies of the regular order are inverted and communal energies liberated and fused together in an organic bond. The liminal is an exploration of the limits of the permissible, controlled and ritually sanctioned by the group. It therefore contains elements of transgression as well as a mechanism designed to reestablish the "normal" order of things. Romantic love has been and continues to be the cornerstone of a powerful utopian vision because it reenacts symbolically rituals of opposition to the social order through inversion of hierarchies and affirms the supremacy of the individual. But saying this is not saying much if one does not specify the social conditions and institutions that make romantic liminality operate in specific contexts. The task that lies before us, then, is to show not only that romantic love carves out the emotional space for the experience of the liminal and the access to utopia, but further that this experience is shaped by the symbols, values, and class relationships of capitalist American society.

Paradoxically, in contemporary culture the liminal inversion of the social order and the opposition to utilitarian values affirmed by romantic love are shaped by the market.[31] In particular, meanings contained in the consumption of leisure temporarily overturn the conditions set by work, money, and exchange. Through its incorporation in the sphere of leisure, contemporary romantic love remains deeply entrenched in the tradition affirming the disorderly individual against the well-regulated group, only now this affirmation is expressed in the consumerist idiom of postmodern culture. As I show in chapters 1–5, the postmodern culture of late capitalism articulates a powerful utopia of love promising transgression through the consumption of leisure and Nature. Romantic practices include transgressive rituals that oppose the values of the productive sphere and celebrate personal freedom, but these rituals are ultimately based in the market.

In line with Durkheim's and Turner's suggestion that social life alternates between "hot" moments of fusion with the sacred and the "cold" moments of pragmatically oriented, everyday action, my analysis shows that the ritual enactments of the romantic utopia coexist with an experience of love as rational, utilitarian, and laborious. Chapters 6–8 show that this mode of relationship demands a careful and rationalized monitoring of the self, which puts this mode on the "profane" end of the romantic experience. This realm of the profane is not sociologically neutral, however: rather, it is suffused with the values and discourses of capitalist *production.*

Romantic love is an exemplary case for the sociology of late capitalist culture because it joins and condenses the contradictions of this culture: between the sphere of consumption and the sphere of production, between a postmodern disorder and the still-powerful work discipline of the Protestant ethic, between the classless utopia of affluence and the dynamic of "distinction." My point of departure is Daniel Bell's evocative and, I believe, still relevant observation that the culture of capitalism is self-contradictory, demanding that people be hard workers by day and hedonists by night.[32] The cultural contradiction between the sphere of consumption and that of production is at the heart (so to speak) of the modern meanings of romantic love; romantic practices simultaneously draw from the pervasive but conflicting cultural idioms of hedonism and work discipline. How such a contradiction came about and how it is reflected in contemporary romantic practices is the topic of this book.

OVERVIEW

In approaching the connection between love and late capitalism, I first examine the part played by commodities in the constitution of romantic experience. At the turn of the century, cultural entrepreneurs and established industries began promoting commodity-centered definitions of romance to further their own economic interests (chapters 1 and 2). Since then, consumption and romantic emotions have progressively merged, each shrouding the other in a mystical halo. Commodities have now penetrated the romantic bond so deeply that they have become the invisible and unacknowledged spirit reigning over romantic encounters. In tracing the early history of this "commodification of romance," I draw on a heterogeneous sample of texts from the 1900s to the 1930s, covering four main cultural codes within which romantic love is prominent: narrative (novels and movies), visual (advertising and movies), musical (songs), and prescriptive (etiquette books, magazine advice columns, self-help books).

Capitalism is characterized by the fantastic production of goods as well as by their circulation through the market; both play a central role in the formation of social and cultural identity. The penetration of commodities into the romantic bond is not enough to account for the particular form of romance in late capitalism. As I show in parts 2 and 3, the personality of the contemporary lover is at once that of the postmodern consumer and that of the rational worker. The postmodern sphere of consumption and the still "modern" ethos of the sphere of production undergird cyclical shifts in the individual between romance as a ritual of inversion and romance as hard work. Parts 2 and 3 examine the evolution of the romantic formula that gelled during the opening decades of the century within the context of late capitalist culture. Because a postmodern romantic sensibility was already latent in the cultural and economic transformations of the turn of the century, parts 2 and 3 are to be read as extending and developing the historical section. The material for analysis includes, first and foremost, interviews with fifty working-class, middle-class, and upper-middle-class people, as well as a sample of advertising images and articles from middle-class women's magazines.[33]

Although postmodernity is conventionally said to begin with the passing of the 1960s, a postmodern romantic sensibility was latent in the culture of the first decades of the century and became explicit after World War II.[34] As Marxist scholar Frederic Jameson puts it, a cultural change is less a matter of content than a restructuring of relationships between subordinate and dominant elements.[35] Cultural forms that were only beginning to emerge early in the century became dominant in the context of advanced capitalism. To this extent, postmodern culture represents neither a new stage of capitalism nor an overcoming of its basic structure, but rather its culmination.

Late (often called "advanced") capitalism is characterized by a number of features, the most relevant for this study being the prominence of the service and information sectors of the economy, the move from mass production and mass consumption to flexible production and specialized consumption ("post-fordist" capitalism), the centrality of lifestyle in class groupings, the fragmentation of the working class, and the extraordinary growth of the culture and leisure spheres.[36] The shift to an economy of information was accompanied by changes in the occupational structure. The "old middle classes," as C. Wright Mills called them, were replaced by corporate and bureaucratic elites with high levels of technical and professional expertise who assist propertied owners. The bureaucratic elites and knowledge experts, as well as the new specialists of "culture" people working in advertising, public relations, and the media, have come to dominate the cultural and social scene. The term "techno-capitalism" has been coined to capture the centrality of information, specialized knowledge, and the media in this new economy. In techno-capitalism, new sources of profit have moved to the economic center stage, where corporations struggle for their control: large-scale information systems, disseminated through technologies of reproduction; the private realm of leisure, now structured by the twin spheres of consumption and mass media; and the "culture industry" (advertising, mass media, publishing, education, etc.). To take an example relevant to this study, large corporations now devote enormous resources and marketing research to the commercial design of mass-mediated love stories (e.g., Harlequin romances, photo-novellas, women's magazines, "relationship" columns, comic books such as "Jackie"). Romantic love is not only a theme of contemporary culture but also an economically autonomous cultural field with its own heroes, genres, theories, and artifacts.[37] This, in turn, makes romantic love the example par excellence of the "postmodern condition," in which economy has been transmuted into culture and culture into the transient and disposable world of goods.

Although the meanings perpetuated by the postmodern romantic utopia are inclusive, populist, transgressive, and egalitarian, and although the romantic utopia cuts across social divisions, it contains and reproduces these divisions because it demands the cultural and, secondarily, the economic capital of the new classes who have come to dominate the social scene. Romantic practices are intertwined with the meritocratic, work-oriented, and rational outlook of the sphere of production, and this outlook ultimately helps reproduce social divisions.

ORGANIZATION OF THE CHAPTERS

Chapter 1 examines what happened to the theme of romantic love and the image of the couple as they moved to center stage in the newly expanding mass markets of leisure and as the vision of utopia they conveyed quickly expanded from individual to collective. The romantic utopia echoed and sustained another equally powerful utopia, publicized not only by social activists but—ironically enough—by advertisers as well, both of whom were promising or demanding the same Eldorado: leisure for all. Movies and advertising in newspapers, magazines, and billboards presented a flow of images with strong democratic overtones, offering to all the utopian vision of relationships free of gender and class divisions and combining the thrills of leisure with those of romance. In the utopia where love and leisure reign, romance, it is still believed, can and should find permanent form in marriage, but romance is also swept up in the new emphasis on beauty, youth, fame, and glamour. This change signaled not only transformations in the definitions of marriage but also the progressive disappearance of "courtship" as a preparatory phase. Instead, as is documented in chapter 2, dating supplanted the practice of "calling on a woman" at her parents' home and relocated the romantic encounter to the public sphere of consumption: restaurants, movie theaters, and dance halls. By inscribing the romantic encounter into the consumption of leisure, the practice of "dating" marked the symbolic and practical penetration of romance by the market. This shifted the focus of the romantic encounter from marriage as a permanent and unique union to the fragmented but repeatable pursuit of pleasurable experiences.

This new romantic formula, based in consumption, was made possible by the democratization of certain goods and services hitherto reserved to the elites (for example, touring in a car) and by the middle classes' adoption of such working-class entertainments as movie attendance. Although the adoption of practices from both higher and lower classes spanned the whole range of social groups, this democratic utopia of romance and leisure remained within class divisions that had intensified with economic expansion. Although its rhetoric was all-inclusive, it reflected the worldview of emerging factions of the bourgeoisie—knowledge experts, culture people—their lifestyle, tastes, and cultural competence. At the same time that the market appeared to transcend social differences within a common sphere of leisure consumption, the transformations in the definition and practice of love acted out novel perceptions of class relationships. The new romantic utopia gave voice to newly found mass access to goods but also to the different class identities and relationships implied in the use of such commodities. Thus the same process that, in loading romantic love with associations of money and commodities and the new technologies of leisure, cut through traditional class divisions at the same time reorganized class identities around this newly emerging definition of love.

Following my hypothesis that love enacts the utopian properties of liminal rituals, I concentrate on the *liminal* properties of postmodern culture.[38] Although the theme of liminality is particularly highlighted in chapter 4, it runs throughout chapters 3, 4, and 5, which variously show that in postmodern culture, the nexus of romance and consumption is embodied in diverse symbolic forms of liminality, for example, in contemplating the spectacle of nature (chapter 3), in traveling (chapter 4), or in having "affairs" (chapter 5). Another feature of postmodern culture relevant to romantic love is what can be called the *penetration of everyday life* by images, technologies, and commodities, a process that entails a threefold transformation of representations studied in chapters, 3, 4, and 5.

One aspect of this transformation is the privileging of the image, a feature of the postmodern era that distinguishes it from the premodern and modern eras, based respectively on orality and print.[39] This development, as shown in chapter 1, began at the beginning of twentieth century, as movies and advertising images codified romance in visual vignettes of erotic intimacy, luxury, and leisure. Chapter 3 uses eighty advertising images collected between 1989 and 1991 and an analysis of interviewees' reactions to photographs and advertising images of romance to map the postmodern romantic imagination. I argue that visual clichés associating romance with travel and nature now dominate advertising images of romance. These images offer the utopian vision of an organic bond, free of the inequalities of the public sphere of production, and mix nineteenth-century bucolic traditions with a postmodern aesthetic sensibility.

The second feature characteristic of postmodern culture is the privileging of a *Dionysian aesthetic*. Already during the 1920s, working-class pleasures and styles irrupted on the middle-class scene and were appropriated, albeit reluctantly, within a hedonist commercial formula of romance. Chapter 4 examines the full-blown expression of this formula in contemporary postmodern culture. On the basis of respondents' reports about their "romantic moments," I try to elucidate the process by which goods and technologies of leisure procure—if in fact they do—romantic pleasures. Contrary to my expectations, these pleasures did not have the unruly Dionysian character postulated for postmodern experiences. Instead, they displayed the highly ordered Apollonian aspect of religious rituals. Thus the romantic disorder presumably brought about by the postmodern sphere of consumption is paradoxically mediated by socially binding and ordered rituals.

The third feature characteristic of postmodern regimes of representation concerns the *blurring of the boundary between the real and its representation*. The perception that this boundary was becoming increasingly vague is already discernible in cultural commentaries of the early twentieth century, which suspected that the romance was becoming a mere fabrication by Hollywood and that romantic fiction had replaced the real thing. Chapter 5 examines the validity of the belief, still held by postmodern sociologists as well as by laypeople, that romantic love is nothing but a simulation of cinematic fiction. The analysis of respondents' interpretations of three different love stories and of their own "most memorable love stories" suggests that individual histories are crisscrossed by narratives from the mass media that conflict with narratives grounded in everyday life. The analysis of this contradiction between glamorous and mundane stories of love leads to the third part of the book, which examines how the discourses of the sphere of production give meaning to the experience of love in everyday life.

On the basis of middle-class women's magazines, chapter 6 shows that their discussions of love draw on the utilitarian language and values of the work sphere. To be precise, in advising women on how to improve romantic relationships, articles in these magazines employ two conflicting sets of metaphors: one uses the hedonist motives of the sphere of consumption (e.g., to create or rejuvenate spontaneity, adventure, fun, authenticity); the other—dominant—one employs the economic vocabulary of the sphere of production (e.g., "investing" in a relationship, the relationship as a "transaction" in which the partners are "coworkers"), which contradicts the expressive and irrational values of the hedonist discourse.

Pursuing this contradiction, chapter 7 shifts back to my interviewees and shows that the rationalized language of homo economicus structures the categories of thought and feeling through which romantic sentiments develop and marital unions are formed. Such languages not only pervade their romantic feelings but orient practically people's choices of a mate. I argue that the influence of such rational languages helps explain how people can at one and the same time love irrationally and yet end up making choices congruent with their strategies of social mobility.

Chapter 8 brings the inquiry on class and love to a conclusion by examining how different categories of the subjective experience of love relate to such resources as money, leisure time, and education. The argument that working-class people are "symbolically dominated," that is, at once "dominated" and "deprived," can be made only in the framework of marriage, not in the framework of dating. This in turn suggests the broader idea that the class distribution of the romantic utopia entails deprivation only in certain situations, but not in others.

ON METHODOLOGY

The heterogeneity of theoretical traditions from which this work draws goes hand in hand with an equally heterogeneous set of material for analysis, spanning a wide variety of advertising images, movies, novels, autobiographical narratives, self-help books, magazine advice columns, and interviews. Such a methodological strategy is resolutely that of Lévi-Strauss's "bricoleur," a "handyman who could fix things, make things, out of whatever bits and scraps of material happened to be around."[40] This does not mean, however, that my choice of material was haphazard, but rather that, in trying to make sense of the variety and complexity of the cultural practice of love, I deliberately assembled it as a puzzle made of assorted pieces.[41] This strategy is motivated by a simple observation, namely, that cultural representations and subjects' cultural knowledge lack the coherence, the homogeneity, or the self-reflexive character of theoretical thought and that they are instead heterogeneous, fragmented, inconsistent, and many-faceted. Culture makes available a number of discourses, many contradicting one another, from which people draw at different times and in different circumstances to make sense of different aspects of their romantic experience. Because cultural practices are context-dependent, they might be more fruitfully viewed as a kind of quilt, a crisscross of cultural repertoires of different shapes, sizes, and content.

My *parti pris* for bricolage, as well as the heterogeneous character of my material for analysis, raises two important questions: First, does the simultaneous use of texts in the narrow sense, that is, print or images produced by identifiable cultural agencies, and individual interviews mean that both categories are equivalent (as "texts" in a more general sense) and can be used interchangeably? Or are they different in ways that affect analysis? The perennial predicament of interpretive analysis gives rise to the second question, namely, what are the criteria on which my interpretation of cultural phenomena relies? By what standards should the interpretations I offer be evaluated and therefore criticized?

Although this book addresses postmodernism at length, it does so only as much as it is a prominent feature of contemporary social and cultural theory. My own brand of analysis is guided by the project of rationality, that is, by the idea that there are criteria by which knowledge can be criticized and which are the foundation of an open-ended debate that is vital to the sociological enterprise. Thus it will come as no surprise that I do not view social life as a juxtaposition of "texts" and interpretations. Instead, I insist on distinguishing between the texts manufactured by the mass media and the spontaneous texts produced by my interviewees.

A multitude of studies of the way the mass media are "received" by their audiences have tried, if obliquely, to find correspondences (or deviations) between the meanings of media texts and the meanings used by people in the context of their daily life. Although the concerns of this book are far from those of reception theory, it subscribes to the broad view that there is a hiatus between media texts and individuals' interpretation of these texts and that this hiatus needs to be bridged by an analysis of the role of culture in the class system of contemporary American society. Mass media texts condense and codify meanings, languages, and outlooks otherwise existing in a diluted, diffuse, and scrambled form among lay actors. Unlike the "texts" of everyday life, media texts are purged of all irrelevant meanings and thus tap directly into the pool of cultural symbols. They correspond closely to what Kenneth Burke dubs the "ideal-typical" symbol.[42] Thus, the movies, magazines articles, and advertising images used in this book make up an abbreviated lexicon of the main concerns, anxieties, and dreams of our culture. On the other hand, although they are always reconstructed textual accounts rather than transparent representations of people's actions, interviews provide a better access to the variety of self-understandings that are determined by and in turn determine people's positions and interests in the social structure.

The question remains, then: How are we to grasp the relationship between media texts and the frames of meaning provided by people in interviews? Media texts draw from the meanings of everyday life, while everyday life uses and appropriates symbols codified in mass media organizations. To put it a different way, culture is sometimes only a context in which people relate to each other, but sometimes culture has a power of its own to shape and transform social relationships.[43] The methodological problem then is to devise strategies that can grasp the dense entanglement of everyday life with media texts and to understand when culture operates as background and when it has an efficacy of its own. (Chapters 3, 4, and 5 illustrate such strategies.)

The accent of my cultural analysis is primarily on the activity of making and using symbols. But my interpretation does not, I hope, succumb to the temptation of subjectivism, either my own or that of social actors. Although it is now fairly well established that the separation between fact and meaning, explanation and interpretation, is problematic, I maintain this distinction by making my analysis emerge from the *tension* between these two terms. I do this by using a two-tiered analysis throughout, one that pays attention to the subjective meanings people ascribe to romantic love but disengages the subjectivity of these experiences by mapping out the public *forms* to which they point us. The size of my samples in this book and the methods used to establish and analyze them will make the statistically minded doubtful that I am well enough equipped to achieve this task. But culture cannot be understood in terms of probabilities. To understand culture is to understand, in Michael Schudson's words, the social significance of the statistically insignificant, as well as the seamless web of meanings people draw on to make sense of social situations.[44] This book, then, is an attempt to reconstruct the various cultural repertoires that shape people's understandings of their romantic feelings, a task to which the otherwise useful methods of statistics do not have much to contribute.[45]

To unearth the building blocks of these repertoires, the main methodological criteria I have used is that of *consistency* across samples and that of *coherence* of my analysis between different levels of generalization. The criterion of consistency is apparent in my systematic attempt to play off various samples of media texts against each other and against respondents' interviews. Such a strategy sheds considerable light on the patterns that structure the private and public meanings of love. This concern with consistency is coupled with a concern for coherence not only across various corpora but also between data and theory, for theory enables data to be embedded in a higher order of coherence.[46] "External coherence," the fit between data and theory, is vital to the sociological enterprise, as it makes possible an open-ended dialogue with conflicting views and provides the ground from which this work can be evaluated and criticized.

THE SAMPLE OF INTERVIEWEES

The fifty men and women who shared with me the content of their romantic experiences were found in a number of ways: many of the working-class respondents were found by "snowballing" from the initial lead, met through an acquaintance living in a working-class neighborhood of a major East Coast city. Other working-class respondents were found at local stores or through chance encounters in the street but, more frequently, were maintenance personnel in the various official buildings in which I worked during this research. Access to middle- and upper-middle-class respondents was much easier, both because my own social location facilitated snowballing and because members of these classes proved much more willing to respond to questions about their opinions, tastes, and activities than working-class people, especially men.

Compared to random sampling, snowballing has the insurmountable disadvantage of making any sample more homogeneous, a critique undoubtedly relevant to the sample of interviewees whose experiences and life stories are analyzed here. I hope, however, that this limitation is skirted by the fact that this homogeneity is a significant one: these respondents offered what I believe are some of the most important meanings assigned to romantic love by working-class and upper-middle-class groups. Because of the limited number of interviewees (fifty) and the variety of variables already present in my study (gender, class, age, marital status), I interviewed only native Caucasian Americans. Thus, the people discussed in this book are not "abstract" or "universal" Americans, but rather urban, white, upper-middle-class, middle-class, and working-class people.

The main axis along which I compare respondents' answers is class, a dimension of social interactions often neglected by cultural studies.[47] Although chapter 6 briefly discusses love in the context of the feminist movement, at no point does feminist theory per se appear in this book. This omission is explained partly because the link between gender and romance has already been given a fair amount of attention and partly because, having been trained in the tradition of French sociology, I am convinced that class, no less than patriarchy, structures the social organization of love.[48] By analyzing how love relates to class, I hope not only to contribute to a sociology of emotion but also to make class a more central issue in a cultural study of love.

Many argue that in terms of lifestyle, the main social division is between the upper-middle class and the combined working and lower-middle classes.[49] I concur with this view and compare respondents along this basic dividing line. But my sample does not claim to represent the majority of the romantic experiences to be found even in these urban groups. Respondents with working-class occupations tended to belong to the upper rather than to the lower strata of the working classes. Most of them owned their homes, and approximately half had an average or slightly above-average income. The members of the middle- and upper-middle class tended to belong to the category of "professionals" (lawyers, doctors, accountants) and cultural specialists (moviemakers, painters, musicians, university professors) rather than to the financial elites or corporate owners and managers. My middle- and upper-middle class sample is thus undoubtedly biased toward people whose profession deals with the manipulation of knowledge and information rather than with the control of economic and human resources; but this serves my purposes, since one of the main arguments of the book is that the "postmodern romantic condition" has been promoted by an urban, highly educated group of cultural specialists working in cultural institutions and the mass media. This also helps me substantiate my claim that cultural capital—high culture and the forms of knowledge acquired through formal education—is the invisible but powerful thread linking romantic love to late capitalism.[50]

A questionnaire has obvious limitations: it cannot account powerfully for peoples' actual cultural behavior, and rather than giving us insight into meaning in context and in action, it gives us insight, as Robert Wuthnow points out, into discourse about meanings. I have tried to partially alleviate this problem by putting the interviewees in the situation of interpreting and interacting with cultural artifacts (stories, images, greeting cards, and so on). However, in spite of this attempt to recreate interactions with culture artificially, this study can grasp "not what people [are] doing but what they believe or claim should be done" and, one may add, what they believe they have done.[51] Being fully aware of these limitations, I follow Wuthnow's argument that we have to "admit our lack of knowledge about hidden states and examine the discourse itself, because that is all we have, to determine why it was meaningful for some things to be said and others not to be said."[52]

INTERPRETIVE AUTHORITY

A last word needs to be said about the much-debated question of interpretive authority. Especially on a matter in which everyone has at least some degree of expertise, how much more can and should the sociologist claim to know than the actors she tries to understand? Behind this question are two further ones. First, what do actors know about their own romantic practices and representations, or inversely, what do they ignore or misread in them? Second, is the sociologist's aim to ratify people's accounts of their emotions and actions or to "unveil" their hidden underpinnings? In short, does the sociologist have a privileged point of view? My answer is unfashionably positive, for I believe the task of sociology is to lay bare the forces that determine us. Magritte's painting *Lovers,* showing a man and a woman offering each other amorous yet veiled faces, offers a powerful metaphor for the task of sociology this book sets itself. For the sociologist, like the psychoanalyst, is in a position of pointing to the veils that hide our faces from others and from ourselves.

However, like the psychoanalyst, the sociologist can bring such knowledge to the actors only on the basis of the self-understandings, inner struggles, anxieties, dreams, and hopes the actors provides about themselves.[53] I am less interested in tearing down the veil than in pointing to its presence. Thus the interpretive authority of the sociologist is a fragile and paradoxical one, in that it evolves from attentive listening to actors with the ultimate purpose of making them aware of the forces determining them, in the hope that sharing such knowledge will ultimately grant them a greater autonomy. The sociologist exercises her interpretive authority in order to increase or restore the authority of the actors in interpreting themselves. I hope to have accomplished this task by having carefully listened to the inflections of the voices interspersed in this book.

This book, then, is set to argue that the *promesse de bonheur* of the romantic utopia has been ambiguously incorporated into the culture of consumer capitalism. While the romantic ideal echoes and helps maintain the democratic ideals of consumer capitalism, the inequalities constitutive of the market have been transferred to the romantic bond itself. Far from being a "haven" from the marketplace, modern romantic love is a practice intimately complicit with the political economy of late capitalism.

PART I

When Romance Met the Market

CHAPTER I

Constructing the Romantic Utopia

To the historian, inquiring into the relationship between romantic love and capitalism may seem banal; the link between the two has already been extensively investigated in what have become classic studies of the ideologies accompanying the rise of capitalism.[1] But while we understand better how romantic love has helped reinforce such aspects of the ideology of industrial capitalism as individualism, privacy, the nuclear family, and the separation of spheres by gender, we still come up empty-handed in understanding the mechanism through which romantic love and the market actually intersected, that is, how the experience of romantic love was translated into economic practices and how, in turn, economic practices were translated into a structure of feeling. More specifically, any approach that views love as a byproduct of bourgeois ideology is ill-equipped to explicate how romance intersected with the capitalist market in the later stages of its expansion, when the market became oriented toward the manufacture of goods on a mass scale. What role did the cultural motive of romance play in the construction of mass markets of consumption and, vice versa, how did romantic practices incorporate economic practices of the market?

Studies of divorce and of dating at the turn of the century have paved the way to understanding this relationship by identifying the pressures that new definitions of leisure and consumption exerted on marriage or its prospects. Bailey's pathbreaking analysis of the emergence of "dating" and May's pivotal study of the crisis marriage underwent during the early twentieth century have pointed to the many ways in which consumption mixed and interfered with new definitions of romance and intimacy.[2] However, where May and Bailey have concentrated on the relationship between gender, consumption, and marriage or dating, especially on women's altered status and self-definitions, I focus on how the new standards of romance were cast within *class struggles* over the meanings of consumption, intimacy, and technologies of leisure. More specifically, I pay close attention to the ways in which the meaning of romance became enmeshed with that of consumption, commodities, and technologies of leisure. Thus this chapter and the next try to frame the intersection between romance and the market in terms of class relationships; they should be used as a map highlighting the intricate crossroads where an emotion—love—meets the cultural and economic sphere of consumption.

This intersection is produced by two processes: the romanticization of commodities and the commodification of romance (analyzed in chapters 1 and 2 respectively). The "romanticization of commodities" refers to the way in which commodities acquired a romantic aura in early twentieth-century movies and advertising imagery. The "commodification of romance," on the other hand, concerns the ways in which romantic practices increasingly interlocked with and became defined as the consumption of leisure goods and leisure technologies offered by the nascent mass market.[3] These two processes took place during deep upheavals of the cultural, economic, and social spheres.

Between 1870 and 1900 the population of the United States grew enormously, enlarging markets for manufacturers and increasing the gross national product from $15.8 billion to $70.3 billion between 1897 and 1921. Indeed, the period between the Civil War and the stock market crash of 1929 has been characterized as the "golden age of capitalism." Stimulated by the impetus that railroads gave to economic exchange, a massive influx of private investment occurred, which remained unabated until 1929. By 1930, urban centers had swollen to the point that 80 percent of the labor force worked at nonfarming jobs. Working-class as well as white-collar occupations expanded. The period also saw the emergence of large-scale national corporations, which increasingly came to dominate the U.S. economy. According to economic historian Alfred Chandler the 1920s saw the maturing of the mass market, in that by this time manufacturing industries were fully equipped to respond to the new demand for mass and luxury products.[4]

The enormous expansion of economic production and exchange went hand in hand with a shift in patterns and intensity of consumption.

Middle-class household consumption and the consumption of nonessential ("superfluous" or "luxury") goods had already increased by the middle of the nineteenth century.[5] As per-capita income grew, spending on leisure increased even further, accelerated as the work week decreased. By the 1920s, the eight-hour workday had gone into wide effect, and by 1935, the average American was spending 8 percent of total income on recreation.[6] These new leisure activities took place within the newly expanded cities. In small towns amusements continued to be traditional and informal, but big cities witnessed a spectacular development of commercial amusements. This trend was accentuated by the emergence of a national advertising system that became a major force pushing the American economy toward a mass market of consumption.[7] This new advertising system fed and was fed by a strong demand for luxury products.

Romantic love became prominent in America as early as the eighteenth century. Americans, more so than citizens of other Western, industrializing societies, tended to base their marital choices on emotional considerations rather than social calculations, a tendency that accelerated toward the end of the nineteenth century.[8] The choice of a mate was left to the individuals involved because love was deemed to be of paramount importance for conjugal bliss. The autonomy of the couple grew with college attendance for young men and women in the 1920s, further relaxing family and community control.[9] The emergence of a separate social sphere of youth culture progressively legitimized intimacy with the other sex as an intrinsic feature of socialization into adulthood. As Fass puts it, "On the coeducational campuses of the 1920s (matrimonial bureaus, as they were sometimes called) sex was a perpetual peer concern."[10] This meant a relaxation of Victorian sexual mores among the middle classes; dating and petting now appeared as accepted forms of sexual exploration prior to marriage.[11]

The increasing level of women's education and their entry into the workforce explain, at least partially, the weakened adherence to the Victorian ideology of separate spheres. The change in sexual mores and the increasing push toward the equalization of men's and women's status in the public sphere in turn affected the ways in which they spent their leisure time: they began to engage in the same leisure pursuits and became full and equal members of what historian Kathy Peiss has called a "heterosocial world."[12] These new heterosocial leisure pursuits were encouraged by the increasing commercialization of leisure. During the decade from 1880 to 1890, the number of dance halls, amusement parks, and movie theaters grew dramatically.[13] It was only after 1910, however, that the leisure industries consolidated their economic power as some of them (for example, the film industry) began to engage in monopolistic practices. Finally, new technologies restructured the cultural landscape of early twentieth-century America as inventions such as the telephone, typewriter, high-speed printing press, phonograph, radio, photography, and motion pictures expanded the general public's access to mass culture through newspapers, magazines, popular songs, and film.

These cultural, social, and economic changes helped transform the meanings of love, as it became progressively incorporated within the emerging mass-market and mass-media culture. While my analysis builds on previous studies of love, it differs from them in focusing on the interplay of different meanings of love in various media, such as advertising, magazines, and movies. In this respect, my main argument is that practices of consumption assumed a multiplicity of meanings, which an examination of the mass media can help uncover and untangle. The transformations undergone by the meaning of love are characterized by

the extrication of love from religion, that is, the secularization of the discourse of love;

the increasing prominence of the theme of love in mass culture, especially in film and advertising;

the glorification of the theme of love as a supreme value and the equation of love with happiness;

the association of love and consumption, more specifically, the romanticization of commodities;

the inclusion of "intensity" and "fun" in the new definitions of romance, marriage, and domesticity.

These different cultural developments articulated a new utopia of romance that would become all-pervasive and lend new meaning to many acts of consumption.

THE SECULARIZATION OF LOVE, OR LOVE AS A NEW RELIGION

Victorians virtually worshipped heterosexual love, making it a deity to which they willingly devoted their existence.[14] The pinnacle occupied by love in the private lives of middle-class Victorian men and women can still be seen in early twentieth-century magazine articles:[15]

> Consider that no crown on earth is so resplendent with grandeur as that crowning glory of the human life: the mutually reciprocated love of a good man and a good woman.[16]

> The greatest love, the love of man and woman, is necessarily, as I take it, the highest type of love that our girlhood can attain. It should be the ultimate bloom and blossom, the normal unfolding of all our young years. All other loving is but a mere preparation for this.[17]

Love was central to Victorians' sense of self because through it they learned to know not only their partners but themselves. Love was a template for the authentic, albeit restrained, expression of their inner self, but it was also a means to attain spiritual perfection, as was made clear by the consistent association of the romantic discourse with the values and metaphors of religion.[18] This interweaving of the religious and amorous discourses was also still felt during the first two decades of the twentieth century, as the following two excerpt from well-known magazines of the time will illustrate:

> There is no such thing as true love without reward; for even if one is denied what we call "love returned," there are all the other beautiful rewards that come with loving: the *nobler views and higher ideals that love gives one,* the *joy of serving,* the wider sympathy and better understanding, the richer and more complete living.[19]

> Sacred love may be and ought to be a flame. "Our God is a consuming fire." And our God is love. And the human love, the pure passion, with which God has endowed us, may be and ought to be a consuming flame which burns away our wantonness and our animalism and consecrates our dearest human joys.[20]

In middle-class magazines of the period, the romantic sentiment was a religious feeling capable of sublimating base instincts and elevating the soul, through the ongoing dedication to one's loved one. Furthermore, this ideal was expressed within the Victorian gender division into "separate spheres," presenting love in terms of nurturing, elevating, and spiritual "female" tasks and holding out to women an ideal of sexual and spiritual purity.

But as the centrality of religion declined during the closing decades of the nineteenth century and the beginning of the twentieth, romantic love was inevitably carried along by the new wave of secularization.[21] The themes of selflessness, sacrifice, and idealism were more and more brushed aside. Romantic love ceased being presented in the terms of religious discourse, at the very time it started playing a central role in the culture at large. In fact, in the view of some historians, romance replaced religion as the focus of daily life. Lystra suggests that this process started in the nineteenth century and was an important factor in bringing about the secularization of the male-female bond. She suggests that, "Especially during courtship, it can be shown that romantic love contributed to the displacement of God by the lover as the central symbol of ultimate significance. . . . [Lovers] were making deities of each other in the new theology of romantic love."[22] Albert Ellis goes even further by suggesting that, "fighting the restrictions imposed by a mighty religion, [romantic love] eventually became almost a religion in its own right."[23] Once religious discourse and the ideology of separate spheres were no longer its primary ideological frameworks, romantic love became a value in and of itself. Mass culture turned it into one of the most pervasive mythologies of contemporary American life.[24]

One source of this mythology's power was a new equation of love—and marriage—with personal happiness. The feelings of one 1931 magazine reader may stand for those of many: "To me, there can be no question but that *happy marriage is the best way to attain true happiness.* The mere fact I have had ten years with my husband outweighs everything else."[25] The systematic association between love, marriage, and bliss was different from nineteenth-century representations, in which love was more often a tragic rather than a happy feeling. For example, in Susanna Haswell Rowson's *Charlotte Temple,* one of the most popular novels throughout the nineteenth century, a virtuous young girl is seduced by an officer and then abandoned to her fate of disgrace and misery. This story showed and taught that, uncontrolled by virtue and reason, love was a dangerous emotion leading to utmost wretchedness.

For the Victorians, then, love was contained within morality; it was a means to the ends of self-knowledge and spiritual edification. As the twentieth century approached, however, romantic themes underwent an important transformation: love began to be represented not only as a value in itself but as an important motive in the pursuit of happiness, now defined increasingly in individualistic and private terms. In contradistinction to the earlier moralistic and melodramatic representation of love, the early twentieth-century representations of love in movies and magazines, carrying forward a development first seen in the nineteenth-century theater, equated it with personal happiness and the affirmation of self.

The growing preeminence of love in mass culture during the first three decades of the twentieth century can be mapped by the *Guide to Periodical Literature,* which shows a constant increase of articles under the entries "romance," "marriage," and "courtship." In 1900, the guide contained less than ten references to articles dealing with love, but by the 1930s this figure had increased dramatically. In addition, surveys conducted in 1932 on the content of movies show that the theme of love was more prominent than either sex or violence, a particularly significant finding, since movies were then the most popular form of entertainment.[26] There was also a steady increase in romantic plot lines in stage productions from the early nineteenth-century on. With regard to novels, historical romances (as well as Westerns) were the most popular forms with women between 1880 and 1920, their popularity increasing along with the commercialization of novels.[27]

Love as an ideal was far from new; it was already held by Victorians as a supreme value.[28] What was new was not sentiments per se but the increasing *visibility* of romantic *behaviors* such as petting and kissing in the public settings, often opulent and glamorous, represented everywhere through the collective and ubiquitous mass media, and the merging of these behaviors with values opposed to the sexual and moral reserve of Victorians. Mass culture did not create the ideal of romance, nor did it inspire it in the actors of the period. What it did do, however, was transform the old romantic ideal into a "visual utopia" that combined elements of the "American dream" (of affluence and self-reliance) with romantic fantasy.

Thus, while the theme of romance was not born with the movies, the movies provided a never-ending supply of films about romance. As Rhea Dulles puts it, once the motion pictures discovered love, they "clung to it."[29] The theme of love in the movies was such an important one that a 1928 article in *Photoplay* magazine, which was presumed to be a guide to box-office hits, half-facetiously advised filmmakers that if a movie had the words "love," "romance," or "passion" in its title, it should take place in a city with a romantic connotation, such as Vienna or Paris. Moreover, all box office titles should hint a sex situation. "The word 'love' in a title is guaranteed to make men, women and children part with their quarters. Next in importance to the word 'love' are such luscious words as passion, heart, kisses, woman, scandal, devil, marriage, flesh and sin. . . . If an hour of the day must be picked by all means pick midnight. Thus a 'midnight kiss' . . . is far hotter than an 'afternoon kiss.'"[30] This view of movies as the scene for torrid passions is supported by a survey taken in 1935, when the film industry was at its peak, showing that love was the most important theme represented in movies, and further confirmed by a later study of Hollywood movies of the 1930s, which found that ninety-five out of a representative sample of a hundred movies had romance as one of their plot lines. Hollywood's use of what

Bordwell and his associates label "the romantic formula," which reached
its peak during this decade, utilized old as well as new romantic themes.[31]
The old themes, drawn from such traditions as chivalric and bourgeois
romance and American melodrama, intertwined love with marriage and
offered the ideal of conjugal bliss as true happiness and the "happy ending" as married life.

Besides this recycling of traditional themes, romance—and sex—took
on new values and behaviors, associated with the emerging ethic of consumerism. To create the audience that the increasingly powerful movie
industry needed, "some movies opted for images from the consumer
marketplace."[32] As early as the 1910s, films were working out a self-
conscious formula of middle-class romantic and sexual morality that
drew upon the main characteristics of contemporary American culture:
individualism, consumption, leisure, dating outside parental control,
and exploration of the new sexual morality.[33] The Hollywood system established in the interwar period codified and publicized this formula.[34]
Many works of most popular filmmaker of this period, Cecil B. DeMille,
for example, focused on the "do's and don'ts of a successful marriage":
as Lary May suggests, the message conveyed by his movies was that men
expected women to be beautiful and make themselves as attractive as
possible and that women not only expected marriage to be entertaining
but waited for their husbands to provide the entertainment.[35]

Such messages were reinforced by the emergence of the star system, an
apparatus through which the lives and personalities of movie stars were
transformed into cultural icons and commodities. For, in addition to widely
publicizing the actors' personal lives, the emerging celebrity journalism
echoed and underscored the themes of the movie romances in which they
appeared. Thus, once the film industry saw the extraordinary box-office
success of *The Sheik* (1921), starring Rudolph Valentino, its moguls did
everything possible to capitalize on his popularity by making him appear
as great a lover off-screen as on. Further, Hollywood directors manipulated the casting of their films so that screen lovers corresponded to real
life couples. "We know that screen romance is often real for it has often
led to the wedding of the hero and heroine after the picture fades out."[36]
Such tactics tended to blur the increasingly tenuous line between the cinematic and real life of actors, thus creating an effect of verisimilitude which
gave "the impression that the stars were merely playing themselves"[37].

When "real life" movie stars lived the same glamorous lives they portrayed on the screen, their personal lives not only illustrated romance
per se, but were used to reconcile the seemingly contradictory ideas of

marriage as a fragile enterprise, as confirmed by the growing divorce rate, and marriage based on everlasting romantic love, as illustrated by the allegedly idyllic married lives of the stars. An article in *Photoplay* illustrated this duality in claiming of Mary Pickford and Douglas Fairbanks, "They are living a great love poem in the practical, difficult, much discussed relation of modern marriage."[38] These movie stars helped legitimize the new link between romance and consumption. And few couples in the history of America embodied the "ideal romance" as did Pickford and Fairbanks. What made them such an ideal couple was precisely the fact that they merged the desirable yet contradictory requirements of consumer culture: lifelong conjugal bliss and consumption. Pickfair, their exotic and luxurious Hollywood home, was the ideal place for such an ideal marriage.

Fairbanks and Pickford were not the only Hollywood couple through whom the association between romance, marriage, and consumption was elaborated. This association served as a paradigmatic model for every ideal couple, as exemplified by the case of actors Vilma Banky and Rod LaRocque: "Aside from their love and their profession, money is the most important question between them. 'We want to be very rich,' Vilma announced frankly."[39] The star system reinforced the connection of romance with the new ideal of beauty promoted by advertising, through commercial endorsements in which stars "lent" their faces and/or bodies to the promotion of beauty products. Here too, many of the stars coupled in advertising images were known to the public as couples in both real life and on the screen (for example, Claudette Colbert and Herbert Marshall). Because they combined beauty, youth, glamour, wealth, conspicuous consumption, and relentless excitement, these stars embodied the ideal of the perfect couple as constructed by the culture of consumption.

The nascent movie industry, then, exploited the themes of love, marriage, and happiness in terms of consumption, leisure, and fun, and it collaborated with the burgeoning advertising industry to make these ideas widely available to a public eager to learn and adopt new standards of romantic and sexual behavior.

LOVE ON SALE

The emerging national advertising system associated romance not merely with consumption, leisure, and physical attractiveness, but also with a host of attendant values. These values can be identified by the image of the couple in the already powerful cultural industry of advertising in the decades before World War II.[40] During the 1920s, the advertising agency changed from brokering space in newspapers to serving the interests of the giant corporations, and this shift helped raise the agencies to the status of economic and cultural tastemakers. While it is not easy to establish the direct contribution of advertising to economic output, it is hardly debatable that it helped transform the marketplace into a national (and later international) system for the circulation of shared images and meanings. As Robert Darnton notes, "[one] could learn a great deal about attitudes . . . by studying the . . . strategy of the appeal, the values invoked by the phrasing" employed in ads.[41]

An analysis of ads portraying couples illustrates how the values surrounding love have changed over time. Advertising images reveal that the image of the couple was connected, first, with domestic products associated with the comfort of the home and, second, with "ego-expressive" products associated with the expression and enhancement of the self. Middle-class magazines such as the *Saturday Evening Post (SEP)*, *Ladies Home Journal (LHJ)* and *Good Housekeeping (GH)* usually linked the image of the couple with middle-class household products and appliances like cereals, bread, silverware, refrigerators, washing machines, and furniture; ego-expressive products appeared less frequently in these magazines, at least until the 1920s. In contrast, working-class magazines such as *Photoplay* contained fewer ads for domestic products but focused almost exclusively on such fashion and beauty products as soap, shampoo, deodorants, mouthwash, and skin creams. *Photoplay* advertising images from the early twentieth century exhibit a marked link between romance and the "flamboyant style" Kathy Peiss found to characterize working-class women.[42] Almost invariably, and regardless of whether the product advertised is shampoo, soap, face creams, perfume, or clothes, these ads feature a couple in close embrace, the man wearing a tuxedo, the woman an evening gown and pearls, clothing that then as now represented luxury and glamour. In the very few cases in which the couple is not in evening dress, the man and the woman are still shown wearing elegant apparel. Opulence and soft eroticism were part of the new model of "hot" romance exploited by advertisers in their efforts to promote mass-produced consumer goods.

Until the 1930s, domestic and ego-expressive products represented two competing value systems: Victorian middle-class morality and a new morality influenced by working-class values and the consumer society promoted by mass media persuasions. While the Victorians vehemently disapproved of the new ethos, its advocates celebrated sexuality and consumption, calling into question the ideology of separate spheres that consecrated home, family, hard work, and gender division. In fact, the visual and thematic opposition between domestic and ego-expressive products articulated a broader (and somewhat surprising) opposition: between romantic love and marriage.

In ads for domestic products the couple is obviously married, while the marital status of the couple in ads for ego-expressive products is often left equivocal. In the advertisements for food, appliances, and furniture analyzed for this study, the couple typically act out domestic scenes: the woman is serving her man food; the couple is seated comfortably in an attractive living room or shown contemplating a newly purchased modern refrigerator. In all these scenes, the significant spatial separation between the man and the woman both dampens any suggestion of sex and perhaps symbolizes the separate gender spheres (the woman serving the man, who is about to leave for or is returning from work). The images in ads for ego-expressive products, however, portray the couple as physically close, thus expressing, one presumes, emotional intimacy. Not only is there no spatial separation between man and woman, but especially in working-class magazines such as *Photoplay,* the couple is shown in close embrace, hugging and kissing. This visual permissiveness reflects editors' and advertisers' awareness of the more relaxed standards of sexual intimacy held by working-class men and women. Couples in domestic product ads are more distant and are presented in settings that convey a Victorian ideal of family tranquility and stability. Ego-expressive ads, by contrast, detach the couple from the institutions of marriage, home, and family and suggest that a hedonist consumerist ethos (as opposed to the productive ideal of family) was used to motivate the purchase of these products.

Ego-expressive products and their ads offered the means to the realization of new conceptions of the self. The rise of consumerism coincided with the period between the two world wars when the self became both locus and focus of culture, the domain in and through which one enacted one's social identity.[43] In the new ethos, individuals were encouraged to express themselves "creatively" and "authentically."[44] Romance and physical beauty were seen less as means to the attainment of marriage and family than as advantages in the ongoing process of what Erving Goffman has called "the presentation of self." The new ads encouraged their readers—mostly women—to use "ego-expressive" products as weapons of "seduction," of self-assertion. Consider the following ad copy: "Magnetic, mysterious, the subtle fragrance wove its irresistible spell" (1930 ad in *Photoplay*); "More enthralling than mere beauty" (1930 perfume ad in *Photoplay*); "Beauty is Romance" (1930 ad for beauty cream in *Photoplay*); "Can a woman change a man's idea of her personality? A subtle, delicious fragrance worked this magic for me" (1930 ad for perfume in *Photoplay*). The beauty-romance link was extended to cover the desire for self-expression, and the new nexus of beauty, self-expression, and romance was in turn fostered by the culture of consumption. Love was thus made to reinforce a definition of selfhood centered around the commodities that provided youth, beauty, charm, glamour, and seductive power.

These advertisement images systematically associated romance not only with the motifs of youth and beauty, creativity and spontaneity, but also with the themes of thrill, adventure, exoticism and intense experience for its own sake—themes that are all aligned along the same symbolic axis, which may be categorized as "anti-institutional,"[45] "hedonistic,"[46] or (following Lears) "antimodernist."[47] The following ad for a 1926 film illustrates this new connection: "What is the struggle of life worth if it does not win you something of romance adventure while you can enjoy it? Win a fortune and you are still a failure if you have not loved!" The intertwining of love and romance with hedonist and antimodernist themes marked the shift from a Victorian morality to a consumption-oriented or "hedonistic" one in which pleasure was encouraged actively rather than dealt with ambivalently. Until the middle of the 1920s middle-class magazines tended to espouse a conservative, Victorian consumer ethos congruent with family oriented ideals and values. As these magazines came to adopt the flamboyant style of the working-class magazines, which resonated with the ethos of consumption, the number of ads they ran for ego-expressive products and the romantic manner in which they portrayed couples dramatically increased. Consider the explicit hedonism in the following ad from a 1931 issue of the *Saturday Evening Post*:

> Go to a motion picture . . . and let yourself go. Before you know it, you are living the story—laughing, loving, bating [*sic*], struggling, winning! All the adventure, all the romance, all the excitement you lack in your daily life are in—Pictures. They take you completely out of yourself into a wonderful new world. . . . Out of the cage of everyday existence! If only for an afternoon or an evening—escape!

The theme of romance is casually added to this enthusiastic invitation to join in the new morality of fun. Far from promoting the sober and practical comforts of domesticity, the new advertising advanced an "antimodern" morality of "fun living," which associated the new leisure goods being offered by the market with thrill, exoticism, the search for intense authentic experiences, and, one may add, the quest for romance. By the 1930s, this association was fully incorporated in romantic practices. The sociologist Willard Waller, examining the courtship patterns of the time, concluded that they differed significantly from previous periods in that they were a "thrill-seeking behavior."[48]

To sum up, then: During the first quarter of the twentieth century, the theme of romance became increasingly associated with consumption. At the same time, although at a slower pace, the romance-consumption link became an integral part of the middle-class lifestyle. During the same period, ads for ego-expressive products promoting new models of romance not only disentangled that emotion from domesticity, the ideology of the separate spheres, and religion, but were actually opposed to marriage. By contrasting the "dullness of marriage" to the "thrill of romance," these ads presented a negative image of the married state.

Thus the theme of romance was used for the promotion of a wide array of products, a process I called the "romanticization of commodities." In these images, the "aura" of romance impregnates two levels of consumption. The first is the consumption of the product being advertised, what I call *candid consumption*. But romance is also associated with another type of consumption, never explicitly referred to: the activity in which the couple is engaged, which often consists in the consumption of leisure. I term this last category of consumption—equated with romance but never made explicit—*oblique consumption*.

In all these images, the couples shown are made-up, well dressed, and expensively bejewelled. And they are engaged in leisure activities that are presented as equivalent to intimacy and romance. These activities include dancing, which was extremely popular during this period, especially in dance halls; eating dinner at an obviously elegant restaurant or having a drink at a sophisticated bar or cocktail lounge; riding in a car; picnicking outdoors; traveling and taking vacations; going to the movies. These background activities lend support to the explicit promotion of products as diverse as shampoo, beauty creams, cars, motor oil, and cereals and *are* acts of consumption, albeit presented obliquely. That is, the objects of oblique consumption are never referred to directly as objects of consumption but are insinuated into a scene as part of what makes it "naturally" romantic. For example, the ad for "Mobiloil" showing a couple sitting in a movie theater encourages readers to consume this rather unromantic product by implying that by so doing they will intensify the romance in their lives (the couple was able to get to the movie theater by car in winter; hence Mobiloil helps maintain the romance provided by going to the movies). Movie-going is thus referenced as a romantic moment. Mobiloil helps maintain romance not because it helps intimacy per se, but because it facilitates leisure, which here means the purchase of leisure and which is referenced as "naturally" romantic. Furthermore, the couple turns out to be movie stars Herbert Marshall and Claudette Colbert, a romantic team in real life as well as on film; they are shown in a close embrace in a dark movie theater, where they are watching a movie in which a couple is also shown kissing. This second couple is none other than Marshall and Colbert sitting in the movie theater (presumably watching themselves hugging and kissing each other). The boundary between "real life" and the glamorous life of Hollywood fantasy disappears into a hall of mirrors.

Oblique consumption is important to notice because it illustrates how leisure activities were deeply fetishized by the romantic aura cast over so many other commodities: through romance, consumption acts are invisibly multiplied and redundantly affirmed. That is, romance is the departure point for multiple acts of consumption, candid and oblique, which are mutually enhancing: Mobiloil, for example, borrows the taken-for-granted desirability of leisure, romance, and Hollywood stardom, while the use of these to sell Mobiloil reinforces their value. In the second place, since the economic underpinnings of oblique consumption are never presented as such, this form of consumption is mystified as "experiences" or "interactions" between people. Thus, for example, the movie theater or the dance stands for intimacy, and the car ride for romantic adventure and excitement, rather than for economic transactions. The way in which unglamorous, everyday products were turned into the take-off points for oblique consumption can be seen in a 1930 *Photoplay* magazine ad for a clothes-washing powder: "Why is it that so many girls think romance must wait for just the right moment? That moonlight, music, atmosphere are essential? *Romance is everywhere*—afternoons at the beach, hiking in the country—simple picnics—*all* have their opportunities. But you must always look your charming best!" The oblique presentation of romance is based on the unconscious equation between consumption of leisure and romance: the beach, hiking in the country, and the "simple" picnic all demanded a car, disposable income, and disposable time. The essentials of romance remain understandable in only vague and essentially undefinable terms, associated with what Leiss, Kline, and Jhally call "bundles of attributes" grouped around such themes as luxury, pastoral simplicity, and thrill.[49] In the language of Marxist sociologists, acts of oblique consumption fetishize romance, denying its economic underpinnings and the social relations that have produced it. Thus, it is not only the products directly promoted that are subsumed under "bundles of attributes," but also the multiple acts of consumption defining and implicitly equated with romance.

Three main sets of attributes are used as background to "naturalize" the romantic activities presented for oblique consumption: (1) glamour and elegance accompany the oblique presentation of luxurious commodities (clothes and jewels especially); (2) "intensity and excitement" are usually associated with nature in the form of a travel commodity (the couple often being shown on a boat or in the countryside); (3) "intimacy" and "romance" are associated with movie-going, dancing, or with candle-lit dinners. These leisure commodities and the bundle of attributes under which they are subsumed feed into the new cultural theme of antimodernism, as characterized by images of nature, simplicity, exoticism, speed, adventure, fun, and intensity.

These changing representations of romance give us some clues as to the changes in conceptions of love and matrimony. During the period under discussion, love was presented as a natural and necessary ingredient of marriage at the same time that it was constructed as something outside it.

ROMANCE VS. MARRIAGE

One tradition in American popular culture has opposed marriage and romance. The opposition between marriage and romance was present in popular lower-class melodrama of the nineteenth century, wherein married couples were shown engaged in knock-down-drag-out domestic battles. But in the context of advertising, this old saw acquired a new edge. Although advertising served up a positive image of marriage (after all, families represent a larger consumer group than singles), it also portrayed marriage as a potential threat to the "thrill of passion." And what, these ads cautioned, could lead to passion being dissipated? They sought to convince their audience that passion would flee if either partner (particularly the wife) became careless about his or her physical appearance and seductive behavior. Thus an ad for a deodorant, featuring a bride and groom, asks, "Will they be as proud of each other 5 years from now? Love cools when husband or wife grows careless about B.O." While such blunt applications of cause and effect are common in today's advertising, the link between products and passion was first forged in the early twentieth century. For example, a 1924 soap ad called attention to its product's ability to sustain romance with the slogan "Still the thrill of courtship." And the detailed text accompanying the image of an embracing couple advises, "The supreme test of a wife's charm, a famous novelist recently was quoted, comes after two years of marriage." Another soap ad, also featuring an embracing couple, declares: "You would never guess they are married. It is only of a clever wife that this is ever said," clearly implying that being recognized as married renders a woman less glamorous and seductive. As Rothman's study of Victorian courtship suggests, "[couples courting after about 1900] no longer identified home with the transcendent power of marriage. Now it was sexuality, rather than domesticity, that united and uplifted a couple."[50]

Although advertising was the most ubiquitous purveyor of the view that the demands and behaviors of the outside world must be introduced into the private world of family life if romance is to be sustained, these ideas were not confined to advertising. The opposition between romance and marriage, and how this opposition could be reconciled, were hot topics for magazines. A 1930 article entitled "Should We Leave Romance Out of Marriage?" summed up succinctly the association between romance, a flamboyant style, and sexuality in asking plaintively, "In the ideal household of romance one would have thrills, beauty, glamour— but would one ever feel at home?"[51]

Some ads went so far as to suggest that romance could be maintained eternally within marriage if one used the appropriate commodities. This argument was carried to such an extent that even mundane products were associated with romance and beauty. For example, a 1929 ad for a bran cereal links its product with romance in a rather convoluted reasoning:

> Romance never left their home. Through the years her husband adored her. But such devotion was easy to explain. She had those possessions which women know are priceless. Sparkling eyes. A lovely skin. A radiant manner. Charms that health alone can give. Isn't it a pity that countless women who strive for such health and beauty do not realize why they are so unsuccessful? Body toxins are often the reason—insidious poisons which are the result of constipation. Many have constipation and do not know it. They are only aware of what are often the effects. Sallow skin. Dull eyes. Fatigue. But constipation can be safely relieved and prevented. Thousands of women—men too, have freed themselves from body toxins. They have learned that their systems need roughage regularly. And they have found this necessary roughage in Kellogg's All Bran.[52]

Similar strategies were used for cleaning products. In 1930 countless ads appeared in magazines praising cleaning products for their ability to make marriage more romantic. Efficient cleaning products, the arguments ran, would make the wife happier and therefore more available to experiencing romance with her husband.

Products that would today be promoted on the basis of health or efficiency were then hawked for their ability to create or maintain romance in marriage. This associative strategy—making commodities "romantic"—worked because it played on the new anxieties about the future and stability of marriage that had emerged in the first few decades of the twentieth century and that were widely discussed in both academic journals and popular magazines: that marriage was a fragile enterprise and divorce a likely outcome. To calm these new fears, the advertising industry recommended the consumption of intense romantic experiences and of seduction-enhancing products aimed at maintaining the initial thrill of romance. In other words, ads began to present marriage as a naturally dull state unless one took appropriate measures to maintain the thrill of youth and seduction. As one ad put it: "Yes, falling in love was pretty easy. But our diamond says we are going to make it last." The home was no longer perceived as the altar to love and as the refuge from a "harsh" world. Instead, it was threatened by boredom and as such was now open to the incursion of ego-expressive and leisure goods.

But why make marriage outlast romance? Why did these ads so actively promote a model of intense passion based on the romance of early courtship instead of focusing on romance as a sustained bond that continues throughout marriage? However mechanistic, a functionalist economic explanation is tempting. By extending the intensity of early romance by connecting it with seduction and making excitement and seduction intrinsic components of successful marriages, advertisers prolonged the couple's need to engage in practices of consumption.[53] And by suggesting that a successful marriage can eternally maintain the initial thrill of romance and seduction, these ads clearly imply that these practices must be continued during marriage.

To summarize, between 1900 and 1940, advertising and movies, the emerging and increasingly powerful cultural industries of the period, developed and advanced a vision of love as a utopia wherein marriage should be eternally exciting and romantic and could be if the couple participated in the realm of leisure.[54] The new culture industries provided the symbolic framework within which new ideals of intense passion were associated with and merged within new practices of consumption. The association of romance and leisure enforced the idea that intensity and longevity were not mutually exclusive, and that intensity could be maintained as long as one purchased the appropriate means. As we will see, this ideal, the fusion of hedonist intensity with marital stability, would become one of the privileged sites to observe the entanglement of love with the cultural contradictions of capitalism.

How new or different from earlier periods were these themes and images? Although they resonated with already-existing and powerful traditions of individualism and the exaltation of love, these cultural motives pointed to an important shift in the romantic imagination of Americans. Not only were leisure commodities increasingly infusing the cultural definitions of romance, but the very *categories of thought* as well as the *perception of time* involved in the romantic sentiment were significantly altered. The dominant mode of representation of love shifted from print to images; and the elongated process of courtship was diluting in a newly present-oriented and pleasure-saturated cultural atmosphere.

A ROMANTIC TALE SPECTACLE

If during the premodern era love was expressed through poetry, drama, or myth, in the twentieth century it has become an essentially narrative and visual affair. After the middle of the nineteenth century, the urban landscape started to change dramatically, displaying colorful windows and multicolored department stores, the dazzling spectacle of electricity, and a flow of images which altered categories of perception and the scale in which collective dreams were cast.[55] "The importance of the shift to visual representation in general cannot be underestimated."[56] It is notoriously difficult to assess the extent to which new media change culture and social relationships. Images had been influential during medieval Christendom and continued to play an important role in premodern print culture. But the novelty of visual mass media such as advertising and cinema productions was to give images of happiness, love, and consumption both the allure of fantasy and the sharp focus of realism. Advertising and movies came to occupy a central position in shared American daydreams. Recalling Rosalind Williams's expression about electricity, one may say that the constant depiction of romance in the movies and advertising put at the center stage of American culture a "romantic tale spectacle."[57]

An analysis of the transformation of the visual style of the advertising images hints at four new elements characterizing this increasing visualization of romantic love.

1.   As we move toward the 1930s, photographs, as opposed to drawings, were increasingly used by advertisers. As many scholars have suggested, photography is characterized by its power to appear to represent reality transparently "as it is," thus immersing romantic love within the intense realism of mass culture.[58]

2.   Within the use of photography, one can also observe a more extensive use of close-ups during this period. Close-ups magnify dramatize the human face and are likely to increase identification with the subject represented by reducing the distance between actors and spectators.[59]

3.   Movie stars, often in couples, were increasingly used to advertise products. As movie stars were becoming cultural heroes, such representations further glorified and glamorized the image of the romantic couple.

4.   Finally, the images spread by the national advertising system often were limited to a small core of what Marchand has called "icons," images at once well codified and held in holy respect. The pervasiveness of these icons might have provided ready-made stereotypes that permeated and saturated people's cognitions, a hypothesis explored in chapter 3 in the context of contemporary culture.

The convergence of these four elements—photographic and cinematic realism, abundant use of close-ups, stars as symbols of romantic perfection, and (stereo)typification of romantic vignettes—probably intensified mechanisms of identification with romantic heroes.[60] Many songs of the period, for example, took as their explicit theme identification with love stories and movie stars.[61] A 1915 song illustrates the point:

She would say to her beau, wedded life is so slow
For this is the way that I feel:
I want to be loved like the girls on the film
I want to have heroes galore
I want to be queen like you see on the screen
With Princes and Knights by the score.
I want to be saved from a watery grave
I want to dare death all the time,
I want to be loved like the girls on the film
It's the life in the movies for mine.

Elaborating on the division between the "dullness" of marriage and the "excitement" of cinematic love, this song suggests that women strove to have their "real" life love story resemble that of the movies. But as other songs of the same period made plainly clear, such identification was dangerous. The following song about Theda Bara (the popular actress who played "femme fatale" characters) cites some problems caused by confusing reality with the movies:

> Every night Sarah Cohn would go
> To a moving picture show
> And there she saw up on the screen
> Miss Theda Bara, The Vampire Queen
> She saw men fall for her devilish,
> They loved her,
> But she fooled them all the while,
> Then Sarah said "It's an easy game
> I think I can do just the same."

> CHORUS
>
> Since Sarah saw Theda Bara, she became a holy terror
> Oi, how she rolls her eyes, oh, she can hypnotize,
> With a wink she'll fascinate and she wiggles like a snake
> She'll take you and try to break you
> Then like a Vampire she'll vamp a way,
> The fellers all fall at her feet,
> And her smile is as false as all her teeth,
> Since Sarah saw Theda,
> She's a werrawerra dangerous girl.

These songs put in simple language a more complex psychological phenomenon. Because they combine two modes of representation likely to increase identification—visualization and narrative realism—movies began going beyond just triggering daydreams; they started providing the plots as well.[62]

Autobiographical accounts from the period confirm this hypothesis. In 1933, the Chicago sociologist Herbert Blumer, participating in an enormous research project known as the Payne Fund Studies, examined the effects of movies on adolescents. He asked hundreds of adolescents to describe what they learned from the movies, if anything. The autobiographical reports indicate that visualization played a very important role in their romantic imagination. Examples abound:

> While I sat in school I used to dream about the hero of the picture, visualizing that some day I would play the part in real life by rescuing one of the pretty little girls in my class on whom I had a "crush." I used to continually love to scrap, picturing myself as one of the fighters in a picture I had seen.

> Movies have definitely formed part of my day-dreams. Every girl, I think, must have the mental image of a man to idealize and build dreams about. Before she finds an actual person, she draws an imaginary figure. In any event that was what occurred in my case. And my imaginary man was made up of movie stars. At one time it was even the height of my ambition to marry Dick Barthelmess. I spent much Latin-grammar time thinking up ways of becoming acquainted with my various heroes. Sometimes, though not often, I identified myself with the heroine of a picture I had seen. . . . These day-dreams took up pretty much time, especially during my second year at high school, when I was in a strange environment. . . . [63]

The pervasive visualization not only intensified daydreaming but also provided cognitive maps of romantic behavior (e.g., kissing) that helped adolescents orient themselves in the changing mores of the first decades of the twentieth century. Indeed, the Blumer's findings showed that a very high percentage of adolescents learned romantic behaviors, mannerisms, and skills from the movies. A few typical answers illustrate this:

> The technique of making love to a girl received a considerable amount of my attention, and it was directly through the movies that I learned to kiss a girl on her ears, and cheeks, as well as on the mouth.

> When I saw "The Pagan" I fell harder than ever for Ramon Navarro. All my girl friends talk about is these wonderful love stories. When I see a picture like that it makes me like my steady boy friend all the more . . . it happens that through the movies I have learned to close my eyes, and I use that "Deep Bend" pose.

> From watching love scenes in the movies I have noticed that when a girl is kissed she closes her eyes; this I found that I also unconsciously do. . . . When [boys] go to make love, to kiss or hug, I put them off at first, but it always ends in them having their way. I guess I imitated this from the movies because I see it in almost every show I go to.[64]

A number of "social learning" theories in social psychology show that a behavior is likely to be imitated if it meets three conditions: if the source of the behavior is prestigious, if the behavior is associated with a social reward, and if there are no alternative sources of learning.[65] Cinematic representations of romantic love fulfilled these three prerequisites: it was performed by the most admired heroes of the time, movie stars; it was associated with the highest reward of all, true happiness; finally, being related to the private domain of sexuality, it was not overtly taught by family or even peers. It was not surprising that adolescents would use movies to gain knowledge about "appropriate" romantic behavior. The use of visualization by these teenagers in drawing their "maps" of romance echoes the increasingly important role of visualization in the representation and mental construction of romance in general, a development that, as we will see in chapter 3, would have important ramifications in postmodern culture.

CONCLUSION

The new romantic ideal exalted by the media industry can be usefully contrasted with the eighteenth-century ideal of marriage. At that time, according to Lawrence Stone, "almost everyone agreed . . . that both physical desire and romantic love were unsafe bases for an enduring marriage, since both were violent mental disturbances which would inevitably be of only short duration."[66] Even in the 1910s we can see a similar conception of marriage still in place:

"Friendship is a spiritual thing, instead of a sentimental exuberance, or a passionnel ebullition [sic]. It is a community of interest in the realities of character. Attachments which rest on this foundation [of marriage as friendship] are apt to be enduring. . . . Marriage, at its best, is a sacrament of friendship. . . . Deeper than passion, deeper than sentiment, is that more intellectual and more ethical bond which we rightly call friendship."[67] As this quote illustrates, the traditional ideal of marriage attempted to expel the ardent but unstable feelings of passion. The view of marriage as friendship is less noteworthy than the exclusion of precisely all those feelings that, after the 1910s, were to become necessary ingredients of a successful marriage. The idea that through the purchase of leisure the initial intensity of romance should and could be maintained was relentlessly affirmed through advertisements that expressed the new expectations and attitudes of married people.[68] By the 1930s, ads and movies were suggesting that marriage should fulfill not only its traditional requirement of providing a framework for the reproduction of the species but also those of intense passion, fun, and excitement.

These changes affected not only definitions of matrimony per se but also very process through which the couple came to know and love each other. In Victorian courtship, even if a suitor declared his love and commitment early on, the courtship was envisaged as a long and careful process, punctuated by a series of tests inflicted by the woman on a suitor to demonstrate the depth and durability of his feelings. The new emphasis on intensity and on the pursuit of leisure not only made the system of "testing" irrelevant but also altered the perception of time involved in the romantic encounter. A more "present-oriented" approach was substituted for the longer, slower, gradual process of courtship.

Furthermore, because Victorian courtship contained built-in obstacles, pain was considered, almost by definition, to be intrinsic to the process of coming to know and love each another. Indeed, men and women of the nineteenth-century often recognized that pain was "essential and even unavoidable in romantic love."[69] And pain was precisely what was slowly but surely eradicated from the hedonist idiom of love. As pleasure and excitement became paramount features of the romantic experience, the pain, the obstacles, and the difficulty that had long been seen as necessary and unavoidable features of love became not only unacceptable but, more importantly, unintelligible. The "heaviness" of loving was starting to melt into the air of consumption, leisure, and pleasure.

Finally, unlike Victorian narratives of love, the hedonist romantic experiences did not contain a program of self-knowledge. The view that love invited introspection, a gradual disclosure of intimacy, and the careful effort of knowing another person changed to an "outward" view of romance, oriented toward an ideal of shared participation in the public sphere of leisure. Where previously introspection and the revelations of intimacy had been interwoven in the dense fabric of love, now knowledge of self and other were increasingly directed by guidelines dispensed by the new discourses of psychology and the social sciences. As will become clear, this had the effect of splintering the experience of love within the self and making it intelligible in terms derived from either the market or psychology. This did not necessarily herald a decay of the sentiment of love, but it did usher in love in its postmodern form. In part 2, we will see how these various elements—visualization, hedonist consumption, and the compression of linear time within a present of intensity (analyzed in chapters 3, 4, and 5, respectively)—were paving the way for what would become a postmodern romantic condition.

CHAPTER 2

Trouble in Utopia

the dream — *the means*

love for all ———— *consumer market leisure*

simultaneous democratization of love + consumption

UTOPIA

need for the ideal to be supported by social structural relations

The previous chapter showed that at the beginning of the twentieth century in America, romantic love moved to the center stage of culture and became the focus of a collective utopia. A utopia is a realm of the imagination within which social conflicts are symbolically resolved or erased through the promise and the vision of ultimate harmony, in both political and interpersonal relationships. A utopia utilizes powerful emotional symbols, metaphors, and stories that infuse both the group and the individual imagination; it has binding power in that it orients individual and collective action. But for utopian symbols to have binding power, they must rest on a configuration of social relations that makes them relevant to the social order. In our case, this configuration was the "encounter" between the swelling consumer markets of leisure and evolving definitions of family, intimacy, and sexuality. This utopia offered to all classes the vision of an organic bond that exploited and celebrated the sphere of consumption to its full and yet at the same time promised to transcend it. Mixing the idea of "love for everyone" with the idea of "consumption for all," this utopia resonated with the democratic ethos so deeply embedded in American culture. But at its very inception, many cracks were already fissuring this utopia of love, wealth, and equality.

The new images and models of romance articulated a shift in the definition of marital and premarital relationships, and this shift in turn expressed changes occurring in several cultural arenas: the increasing importance of leisure, the commercialization of recreation, the relaxation of sexual prohibitions, the consolidation of a self-conscious middle-class ideology, new definitions of selfhood centered on the pursuit of intense experience, and increasing equality in the status of men and women. These cultural changes took place at different times and at different paces but coalesced in the 1920s under the pressure of the fantastic economic forces unleashed by consumer capitalism.[1] The convergence of these different processes is apparent in new definitions of matrimony and, especially, in new dating practices.

THE PRICE OF LOVE

Public discussions of love during the first decades of the twentieth century were dominated by the perception that the institution of marriage was undergoing a major crisis. Contemporary historians and sociologists confirm the era's own perception that marriage faced a severe challenge, as evinced by the highest divorce rate recorded in American history. Among the contributing factors they cite were the growing autonomy of women, the unreal and hedonistic expectations of romance within matrimony, and disagreements over household expenditures.[2] The same causes were often cited by magazine columnists of the time. In fact, the worries voiced in the older print media about the crisis of marriage were attempts to make sense of the increasing penetration of romantic relationships by the market and by new media technologies.

One author, blaming women for the growing number of divorces, stated that "If today every woman could be given a hundred pounds a year, I believe that scores of thousands of divorce actions would be instituted by them. Their impulse is toward freedom, and nothing will arrest them."[3] This columnist was articulating what has since been recognized as a major change: women of that period were increasingly rejecting the constraining definitions of marriage and womanhood. They were asserting themselves in the realm of work.[4] More fundamentally, they were rejecting the institution of marriage as the only safeguard of their economic standing. Becoming less dependent financially, women were expecting from marriage emotional fulfillment rather than economic security. Thus, by offering them the means to attain financial autonomy, the expansion of the labor market contributed to the dislocation of the traditional institution of marriage as an economic unit and made it possible for working women to follow the emotional rather than economic definitions of marriage. And the price for this newfound autonomy, the magazine columnists lamented, was the increased rate of divorce.

The search for enjoyment promoted by the new leisure and entertainment industries was also blamed by magazine pundits for the dissolution of marital relationships: "And out of Puritanism, Romanticism,
and Feminism, as well as from prevailing economic conditions, have
grown false standards of happiness. . . . Modern civilization says: 'Do
not think of marriage until after you have had a chance to enjoy your-
selves in a life of independence; until you have sufficient means, a fine
house, an automobile or two, a mate with whom to continue your good
time; certainly do not have more than one or two. And do not stay married for a moment if anything disagreeable occurs to mar your happiness.'"[5] Articles criticized romance on the ground that its focus on pleasure and its basis in fantasy and unreal expectations were destructive of
marriage, and they cited the new ideals of passion and thrill as causes of
the increasing rate of divorce. For example, "In the romantic stage that
precedes marriage both the man and the woman are far too excited and
upset emotionally to realize fully what they are doing. . . . The stern,
hard . . . facts of reality are camouflaged by love until even over-
looked."[6] Attributing the new definitions of romance to the enthralling
power of the new media of film and advertising to shape fantasies, these
articles argued that the new romance was the figment of an overexcited
imagination. Their authors made sense of the changes around them in
terms of an old discourse opposing "hot passion" to a realistic view of
marriage. As one writer put it in 1928, the problem was the "struggle
between realism and romance."

Then, as now, magazine columnists held the emerging mass culture
responsible for instilling the new ideal of romance and rejected it on the
grounds that it was a Hollywood invention, criticizing it with the same
vocabulary they used to criticize the mass media. The perception of romance as a purely fictional or cinematic entity, indirectly supported by
studies claiming that movie images were increasingly shaping people's
cognition and behavior, tapped into the old idea that novels and other
popular forms of romantic representation cultivated false and unrealistic ideas.[7] For example, a 1930 cultural commentator, writing in the middle-class *Forum* magazine, expressed a widespread suspicion of new
forms of romance: "The objection to the romantic creed is not that it is
a fiction, but that it happens to be a pernicious fiction."[8]

The new expectations of pleasure exacerbated another source of marital tension, the spending of discretionary household income. Sociologist
Viviana Zelizer notes that domestic money had become "a controversial
currency at the turn of the century." She suggests that the controversy

arose as a result of "a rise in real income and the increasing monetization of the American economy [which] forced a reevaluation of family finances," but we can see other pressures at work as well.[9] In her analysis of divorce suits filed in Los Angeles at the turn of the century, Elaine May confirms that new expectations placed burdens on marriage that contributed to the steady increase in the divorce rate.[10] These expectations led women to demand that their husbands provide them with a "good time" and at the same time led husbands to demand that their wives make themselves attractive. In the arguments over the management of domestic money, women typically wanted to spend it for entertainment, while men wished to bank it. Disagreement over this issue was cited by a divorce lawyer in 1924 as the most common cause of divorce. The lawyer concluded that a successful marriage was one where the woman was frugal and the man generous, and he advised that "girls ought to have much more training in the value and use of money": "The first 'don'ts' advice to women is: don't be extravagant. Every man wants to be financially independent, and a husband loses interest in providing when money he earns is spent foolishly." His first "don't" for husbands, on the other hand, was: "Don't be stingy. A woman has the right to expect liberal support."[11] These tensions, May argues, can be related to the transformation and consolidation of commercial amusements which were becoming so important in the economic and cultural arena.

In short, marriage was perceived to be under the assault of women's increased autonomy and of Hollywood fantasies, which led to unrealistic expectations of marriage as an arena of hedonistic satisfaction and consequently to disputes over money. The new concept of romance, linked to leisure and fun, was thought to undermine common sense, pragmatism, and realism; the threats it posed to the traditional family were translated into an old moral discourse opposing "fiction" to "reality."

The more traditional media played an important role in making sense of, analyzing, and attempting to resolve the "current crisis of marriage." Their solution was a hybrid ideal of marriage that took the new expectations into account but tried to hold on to the old values of security and stability. In tandem with their rejection of romance, many magazine authors began prescribing new ways to sustain a stable, "healthy" marriage. The "experts" who were mobilized in these efforts—lawyers, psychologists, and sociologists—invoked alternative models of the good marriage: marriage as friendship, marriage as a partnership or companionship, marriage as a contract, marriage as a skillful art, and marriage as requiring effort. Although they differed in their emphases and drew on different cultural traditions, all the new experts agreed that the marriage relationship should be controlled by the dispassionate logic of friendship and restrained feelings. The rhetoric of "fire" and "ebullience" previously extolled by the mass media was replaced in these sober commentaries by a new lexicon of adjectives like "painstaking," "long-term," "daily," "commonsensical," "enduring," "stable," "real," "practical," "useful," "old-fashioned," and "realistic." The "uncontrolled" drives of passion and romance were exchanged for the "controlled management" of one's emotions. "There is an alternative conception of marriage which is not less beautiful than the romantic view. . . . Let us believe that [marriage] is subject to willful guidance and control, not ruled by the capricious destiny of the selection of a mate."[12] Another writer cautioned, "Companionship, however tender, is not love. Love, let us repeat it, is not enough. Skill is required to convert companionship into true love."[13]

Many articles, however, revealed an ambivalence about the new, rationalized ideal of marriage, suggesting that the crux of the issue was finding a more reliable basis for love than romantic passion without losing love itself in the process. According to these authors, the very virtues of pragmatism, realism, and hard work promoted to save marriage were in fact destroying it. "More love is bored to death than is killed in any other way, and more women are driven to seek affinities because they are married to men who never have an idea except about the stock market or the grocery trade or the baseball score."[14] The idea that boredom can kill love was gaining credence among the public, another indication that Americans were convinced that marriage could and should be sustained through fun and enjoyment. Indeed, a 1932 article advised a woman to ascertain whether her future husband "would make a gay and entertaining life companion, or [if] he would make her yawn her head off."[15] Women, too, were warned that they must shape up: "The old idea used to be that the way for a woman to help her husband was by being thrifty and industrious . . . but a domestic drudge is not a help to her husband, she is a hindrance. . . . The woman who cultivates a circle of worthwhile people, who belongs to clubs, who makes herself interesting and agreeable . . . is a help to her husband."[16] Clearly, expectations regarding marriage were changing: the ability in both men and women to be amusing and entertaining was becoming more important than the husband's role as a provider and the wife's as a helpmate.

Articles promoting one or another new model for marriage all intertwined "fun" and "work" in an effort to accommodate the modern, hybrid romantic ethos. On the one hand, these new models translated the Victorian idea of marriage as companionship into the idea that couples should share common tastes and recreational activities. The idea that the partners in a marriage should be "compatible" and share companionship rather than the thrill of love was not a new one.[17] However, the new notion of companionship was based on a hedonistic view of the couple, whose life together must be cyclically punctuated by leisure pursuits. On the other hand, the new marriage attempted to integrate an emerging therapeutic discourse that borrowed social scientific and medical models to explain and ease troubled marriages through the deliberate guidance of reason and the skilled and temperate management of emotions. In this view, making a marriage last, even keeping its passion alive, required "hard work." The new ideal thus attempted to combine attitudes and activities not otherwise easily reconciled. To be successful, a couple now had to combine spontaneity and calculation, the ability to negotiate with a taste for "hot romance." The hedonistic-therapeutic model that emerged was characterized by such phrases as "having a good time together," "sharing common interests," "talking," "getting to know each other," "understanding the other person's needs," and "compromising."

This new hybrid ethos, which mixed "work" and "self-control" with the pleasures of the spheres of leisure and consumption, was thus a cultural "resolution" of the contradiction between the rational demands of long-term marriage and the new hedonist definitions of love. It attempted to combine in marriage the contradictory requirements of stability and intensity: "A great lover wants a woman as . . . thrilling, as endlessly satisfying as her own ideas of romance. He wants a woman who can make a mother and a mistress all rolled into one."[18] On the one hand, then, ads and movies were saying that marriage and love should be intense and that this intensity was realizable through consumption. On the other hand, magazine articles and the rising pop psychology oscillated between rejecting this model and accepting it in a form reconciled with the idea that intensity and longevity could be harmoniously intertwined if one "worked" at it.[19]

These magazine articles suggested that the crisis in marriage, if not caused by, was at least exacerbated by the contemporary association of the marital relationship with the values of "fun" and pleasure. These values made the commodification of romance, its dependence on money, commodities, and consumption, meaningful and desirable. But if this new model of marriage did not override other models based on cooperation and traditional family values, there was one form of romantic

interaction where the new hedonist and consumerist standards were becoming the triumphant norm, namely, the emerging practice of dating.

ALONE IN PUBLIC

Although historians usually explain the emergence of dating in the late
nineteenth century as the result of changing sexual mores, it might be
more fruitful to view the phenomenon as one of the ways in which people endeavored to negotiate the complex interaction between new definitions of privacy and sexual intimacy and the culture and economy of
leisure. Dating appeared alongside the rise in real income of the early
twentieth century and was defined within the practical and symbolic
boundaries of an emerging mass market of goods.[20] These developments
moved the romantic encounter from the familiar confines of the home
to new locales that were both public and anonymous. At the same time,
these circumstances made consumption an inherent element of any romantic encounter. The "commodification of romance" designates the
process by which evolving conceptions of intimacy and sexuality came
to be defined by the new business of leisure and new technologies of
leisure (e.g., the automobile, the movie theater). More precisely, romantic encounters were enclosed within temporal, spatial, and artifactual
boundaries defined by the technologies and forms of leisure offered by
increasingly powerful industries.

To understand the relative novelty of dating, it will help to contrast
it with leisure practices in nineteenth-century America. In rural America
people spent their free time in informal get-togethers like picnics and
other food-oriented meetings, or combined it with such practical activities as quilting bees, barn raisings, or religious functions such as revivals
or camp meetings. Going to church, fairs, or dances were other popular
forms of entertainment (because of religious influence, dancing was more
often conducted in groups than in couples). In rural areas, in short,
leisure was essentially communal.

In middle-class, urban America of the period, leisure was closely associated with "calling" on one another at home, a practice that had its
source in the upper classes of England, whom the American middle class
was eager to imitate. Thus, formal teas and dinner parties became important avenues for socializing in the home. Public amusements were
eschewed by middle-class Puritan morality, which claimed that they
were responsible for lowering moral standards. In fact, throughout most
of the nineteenth century, leisure was the arena for class struggles in

which the middle classes attempted to discipline the "dangerous classes" and instill in them the habits of rationalized labor and restrained sexuality. These class struggles are particularly visible in the shift from calling to dating.

"Calling" was considered to be the most genteel way of courting a woman. A 1890 etiquette book, *Webster's Ready-Made Love Letters*, instructed suitors, "In whatever way the attachment may have originated, whether resulting from old association or from recent acquaintanceship between the lovers, we will assume that the courtship is so far in a favorable train that the lady's admirer has succeeded in obtaining an introduction to her family, and that he is about to be received in their domestic circle on the footing of a welcome visitor, if not yet in the light of a probationary suitor."[21] This manual demonstrates that in the middle (and upper) class, courtship was expected to take place within the protected boundaries of home and family, even when the family was not present to chaperone the courting couple.[22] The family and the home were the invisible yet always present context of courtship. But by the turn of the century, the practice of calling was fading away and being replaced by "dating."[23] By 1920, *Webster's Ready-Made Love Letters* seemed obsolete.

Historians and sociologists have observed that, by the third decade of the century, "going-out" among both adolescents and adults had spread to the Protestant middle classes, who had previously been opposed to courting in public.[24] As cultural historian D. R. Braden notes, "Both the custom of extended visiting (derived from rural traditions), and calling (derived from aristocratic and urban conventions), declined after World War I."[25] Della Lutes's 1923 *Gracious Hostess* instructed its readers that "formality in the use of visiting cards, as . . . in sending invitations, has lessened with the growing intimacy and democracy of our lives. Much of this is due to the outdoor life that we are now living. . . . Formal visits and 'duty calls' savor of dullness, and we refuse to be dull."[26] The injunction "not to be dull" resonated with the new rush "out" to the pleasures offered by commercial leisure (what Lutes meant by "the outdoor life"). Going-out replaced not only the formal urban practice of calling but also the more informal rural get-togethers of small-town and village youths. In their study of Middletown in the 1930s, Robert and Helen Lynd noticed a "growing tendency to engage in leisure-time pursuits by couples rather than in crowds, the unattached man and woman being more 'out of it' in the highly paired social life of [the twenties] than a generation ago when informal 'dropping in' was the rule."[27] Moreover, the Lynds found that college dates consisted of "motoring, a new film, or a dance at the nearby town," thus confirming that the new commercial entertainment was encroaching upon rural life. In 1937, sociologist Willard Waller concluded from his own studies that the 1930s had witnessed the definitive substitution of courtship by dating. By the 1940s, going out on a date had become completely incorporated into both urban and rural romantic practices in the United States.

Dating differed both from the communal and informal encounters that characterized rural forms of socializing and from traditional courtship, which was concerned only with the selection of a lifelong mate.[28] Incorporating the emerging forms of commercial entertainment, elements of the emerging and increasingly powerful youth culture, and new forms of sexual freedom, dating made romantic encounters more sporadic and casual than middle-class Victorian courtship could have allowed.

Taken at face value, such withdrawal from the watchful eyes of community and family seems to confirm the diagnosis of the many cultural critics who argue that modern identity has become saturated with a private "self" severed from membership in the public realm of social and political concerns. Richard Sennett and Christopher Lasch have argued forcefully that withdrawal from public life has made social and public identity collapse and relocate itself in the overheated sphere of private personal relationships.[29] Such analyses are correct insofar as they describe how we moderns have come to focus and concentrate on inner psychic life and on private and interpersonal, rather than formal and public, relationships. But as the example of dating illustrates, there is no simple equation between the "privatization of the self" and "privacy." Romantic interactions became a public form of experience, taking place in an anonymous and public sphere of consumption at the same time that they presupposed a temporary withdrawal from group and family membership. "Dating moved courtship into the public world, relocating it from family parlors and community events to restaurants, theaters, and dance halls."[30] Modern definitions of love rendered it a public interaction at the same time that they suffused its inner experience with privateness. By relocating the couple to the public realm of consumption, the new dating system restructured the boundaries between private and public spaces by creating "islands of privacy" in the midst of the public realm. And these islands were consolidated by new technologies of leisure.

Perhaps nothing in the new technology had more of an impact on the couple's ability to be alone in public than the new-found popularity of the automobile, especially Henry Ford's two-seater Model T made available in 1914. Before this, cars had been limited for the most part to the upper-middle and higher classes; they now became increasingly common-place. There were eight million car owners after World War I, and the number had tripled by 1930.[31] By facilitating the search for privacy, it replaced the "parlor" as the scene of courting for the upper middle class especially, thus enabling beginning couples to "get much further away from front porch swings, parlor sofas, hovering mothers, and pesky siblings than ever before"—increasing the opportunities to act out the increasing sexual freedom of the post-Victorian era.[32] "As soon as manufacturers began to put a roof over motorists' heads, with the innocent idea of shielding them more effectively from the weather, it was another story. The motorcar (like the hansom cab) became an intimate and exciting little box, and it is basic if little-advertised human law that men and women cannot be tucked side by side into cosy little boxes without getting ideas in their heads."[33]

Many of the songs of the period from 1900 to 1930 testify to this. For example, one written in 1905 celebrates being

> Out in an automobile, in with the girl that you love.
> Riding at ease on the wings of the breeze, like birds in the blue sky above.
> Teach her to steer the machine, get both her hands on the wheel.
> You kiss and you squeeze just as much as you please.
> Out in an automobile.

This song and others like it illustrate what would become a cliché of cinema iconography and a reality of American life: cars, like the dance hall, the movie theater, and coed campuses, rendered possible the growing emancipation of sexuality. By 1912, the privacy the car afforded was being viewed as a mixed blessing, as evinced in the Irving Berlin song "Keep Away from the Fellow Who Owns an Automobile":

> Keep away from the fellow who owns an automobile.
> He'll take you far in his motor car; too darn far from your pa and ma.
> If his forty horse power goes sixty miles an hour say
> Good bye forever, good bye forever.
> There's no chance to talk, squawk or balk.
> You must kiss him or get out and walk.
> Keep away from the fellow who owns an automobile.

The automobile was soon seen as a threat to traditional forms of control by parents, making possible a more uninhibited sexual interaction than previous settings had allowed. Although the automobile could be seen a motorized version of the "Sunday afternoon carriage ride" of the nineteenth century—one of the few unchaperoned forms of romantic

interaction of the period and hence a very popular one—the design of
the Model T rendered it significantly more impermeable to outside eyes
than the carriage, providing even more privacy for sexual exploration.
Among the other qualities that set cars apart from carriages were speed,
adventure, and excitement. Indeed, the association between automobiles
and romance fed into the same hedonistic romantic ethos that promised
eternal excitement through intense experiences. For example, a 1912
song by C. J. Fitz-Gerald proclaimed:

> Oh listen here, my honey dear, an auto ride we'll take.
> My touring car will speed afar, don't stop to hesitate.
> Why, baby dear, I'd never fear when I am by your side,
> For I can see as plain as can be, a Kissel-Kar you drive.
>
> Goodness, my hon, we're going some ninety miles an hour.
> Rounding a curve, never a swerve,
> Feels like a hundred horse power.
> Now on two wheels, lawdy it feels just like a bi-plane ride.
> You can pass them all and never stall,
> Honk, honk, on a Kissel-Kar ride.

With the popularity of automobiles came increased tourism, a basic
element of the social construction of romance. With the new improve-
ments made in roads in the 1920s and the growth of motels in the 1930s,
tourism to New England towns or to the Florida seashore increased.[34]
The car enabled couples and families to travel overnight to places where
no one knew them. By the 1930s, visiting national parks and small towns
and camping along the roadside had become widely popular forms of
recreation for couples and families. Even during the Depression, people
of more modest means—the working class and the lower middle class—
could go to resorts on the outskirts of urban centers (for example,
Philadelphians went to Atlantic City).[35] The national prosperity after
World War I, the shortened work week, and the growth of trade unions
during the Roosevelt era contributed to democratize vacation.[36]

Romance and speed formed part of the new equation between tourism
and excitement, intensity, and adventurousness. These themes are apparent in a 1937 song evocatively titled "Gasoline Gypsies":

> I always envied the delights of the knights of the road;
> Happy-go-lucky tramps, living in tourist camps
> In a little cottage that it is streamlined, a dreamlined abode.
> Darling, if you'll just agree, this is what I think we should be
> Just a couple of gasoline gypsies, and the happy-go-lucky at kind
> Hummin' a love song and joggin' along, waggin' our trailer behind

Just a couple of gasoline gypsies in a regular palace on wheels. . . .
We can go to Mexico or any place you suggest;
Thanks to Mr. Texaco we'll have the whole darn West for a little love nest.

The themes used in this song—nature, "gypsying," the exploration of the wild West, the quest for exoticism—were probably inherited from bicycling, a very popular sport at the end of the nineteenth century, and are now associated with the new technology of motoring.

From the end of World War II to the 1960s, the romance-car nexus took on particular significance in the drive-in culture. By the 1950s, four thousand drive-in movie screens were available across the country, providing romancing adolescents with easy and inexpensive ways to escape their daily routines and the watchful eyes of their parents. Drive-in restaurants could often be found at the border of towns and served inexpensive foods which made them particularly appealing for young people with little money to pursue their courtship rituals.

While automobiles were inaccessible to the lower classes at the beginning of the century, movie theaters were within the reach of all.[37] In fact, since the upper classes still regarded the movies as morally inappropriate, if not repugnant, the working class and immigrants then constituted the bulk of the movie audience.[38] Social historian Francis Couvares even views movie-going as a form of resistance against and release from increasing attempts to control the workplace.[39]

Certain segments of working-class society were freer sexually than the middle class and as a result flocked to flirtation in movie theaters, where romance and permissiveness were promised. These theaters provided working-class people with what their crowded apartments could not: privacy and intimacy. As Braden suggests, "The anonymity offered by the darkened theater proved a great boon to romance."[40] Many songs of the period evoke the dark theater and the kissing or "spooning" it facilitated. A 1914 song, "The Picture Show Spoon," elaborated:

Oh, oh, that picture show spoon
That's what puts kissing on the boom,
Just grab your girlie but don't squeeze her tight,
For she may holler with all her might
Oh you seven come leven,
Kiss me hon for I'm in heaven
When you start that don't you know what?
When you start that picture show spoon.

And a 1919 song was even more explicit. Titled "Take Your Girlie to the Movies (If You Can't Make Love at Home)," the lyrics celebrated

> Beatrice Fairfax gives advice to anyone in love
> That's why Johnny Gray wrote to her one day
> When I call to love my girl, her folks are always there
> That's why I'm blue, what shall I do?
> And Beatrice said: "Never despair.
> Take your girl to the movies if you can't make love at home.
> There is no little brother there who always squeals
> You can say an awful lot in several reels
> Take your lessons at the movies and have love scenes of your own
> When the picture is over and it's time to leave
> Don't forget to brush the powder off your sleeve.
> . . . .
> Pick a cozy corner where it's nice and dark
> Don't catch influenza, kissing in the park."

As these two songs indicate, the movie theater was used by working-class people to explore new forms of sexual freedom in their romantic encounters.

Unlike the working classes, the middle and upper classes did not at first adopt the movie theater as a form of entertainment, considering it a threat to morality. The watchdogs of middle-class morality even tried to control films, for example, by imposing regulations on the theaters. By 1922, however, Emily Post, the famous arbiter of good taste and etiquette, was commenting that "[although] she may not lunch with him in a restaurant, she is sometimes (not always) allowed to go to a moving picture matinee with him! Why sitting in the dark in a moving picture theater is allowed, and the restaurant is tabu is very mysterious."[41] Apparently, socializing in movie theaters was sanctioned in practice if not in principle. However, such approval was reserved for matinees, not movies at night.

Middle-class resistance to movies was not overcome until filmmakers and theater owners, wanting to increase the size of their audiences, made enormous efforts to attract the "respectable" segment of the population. Cultural entrepreneurs equipped their theaters and dance "palaces" with the accoutrements of middle-class taste and began to institute rules of behavior aimed at eliminating some of the more outrageous forms of intimacy practiced there.[42] These efforts succeeded, and by the end of World War I, moving pictures had become the single most popular form of public entertainment in the United States. Once the movie theater became a legitimate place of entertainment for the middle class, it also became a legitimate arena for middle-class romance—albeit romance exhibited modestly.

The history of dancing as a romantic activity is similar to that of the movies. At the end of the nineteenth century, under the influence of black minstrel traditions and ragtime music, dancing became a popular form of leisure for the working class.[43] Because the new dances "emphasized the importance of the individual dancing couple rather than that of the entire social group," middle-class spokesmen and spokeswomen attacked them as "blatant eroticism."[44] Although dances such as the "lovers' two-step," "turkey trot," or "bunny hug" defied the restrained public reserve of Victorians, dance halls spread very rapidly across American cities. The reformers' denunciations did little to prevent a dramatic increase in the number of new dances or to slow down the construction of new halls. By 1910 there were at least five hundred dances halls and one hundred dance academies, which provided classes to eager youth. These dance palaces offered the working class opportunities not only to hone their dancing skills but also to socialize and experiment with flirtation. In exchange for small sexual favors, working-class women expected to be "treated" by working-class men, whose salaries were higher.[45]

But as dance-hall owners made the changes necessary to render them more amenable to the middle class, this form of leisure grew in popularity and became legitimized, although it was often segregated by class. In fact, by the 1930s, dance halls had become one of the most widespread places for young people to meet and engage in flirtatious behavior.[46]

Although they became a key part of acceptable middle-class culture, working-class romantic and leisure practices presupposed a sexual permissiveness and a release of emotions that were, until then, incompatible with that culture.[47] In fact, as mentioned earlier, going out, the basic dating activity now practiced by all segments of American society, originated with the working classes, whose cramped homes lacked the space and privacy necessary for "calling." As Beth Bailey puts it, the only place where a working-class couple could socialize was "out."[48] The increase in commercial leisure activities facilitated the spread of dating by giving the young couples places to go. Ironically enough, it was the efforts of the capitalist entrepreneurs that finally breached middle-class "reformer" morality. In orienting their corporations toward a national mass market of leisure, entrepreneurs built thriving commercial "coalitions" with the "genteel" middle classes to develop amusements that were ultimately incompatible with middle-class morality.[49] Many such forms of entertainment were an explicit mockery of middle-class genteel values. For example, the famous amusement park at Coney Island marked entry into a world that was "[against] the values of thrift, sobriety, industry, and ambition." Instead "it encouraged extravagance, gaiety, abandon, revelry. Coney Island signaled the rise of a new mass culture no longer deferential to genteel tastes and values, which demanded a democratic resort of its own."[50] This new popular hedonism paralleled an onslaught against traditional values from the cultural elite, although the two embodied differing worldviews. Among the upper classes, a new climate of sexual freedom and general permissiveness, embodied in the Bohemian artistic circles of Greenwich Village in the 1920s, dealt a blow, ultimately fatal, to middle- and upper-middle-class Victorian respectability. Thus, the romantic practices progressively adopted as standards of middle-class behavior contained "carnivalesque" elements of working-class culture as well as the hedonistic values of the artistic bohemia of the 1920s.

Because class struggles are addressed, albeit obliquely, in cultural creations, we find support for these observations from two very popular movies, starring one of the most romantic actors of all times, Rudolph Valentino. They are a good starting point for understanding how the struggles around the constitution of a middle-class formula of romance were made sense of and—to use Clifford Geertz's metaphor of culture— "interpreted out loud" by actors of the period.

The Sheik was an instant and unprecedented hit in 1921. Its story line was simple: a young British woman, daughter of a deceased poet, shows her spirit of independence and her defiance of middle-class respectability by deciding to undertake alone a trip into the Arabian desert. The night before her departure, disguised as an Arab woman, she intrudes upon a slave auction of Arab women. She is discovered by the Sheik (Rudolph Valentino), who mocks her and her project. When she starts her trip into the desert, the Sheik kidnaps her and tries to marry her by force. She resists him but is slowly defeated, at first by his despotic rule and powerful will and subsequently by her realization that he is a "good" person. Her change of heart is helped by the active intervention of a visiting friend of the Sheik, a distinguished and refined European. When she finally yields to the realization that she loves him, she discovers that he is not an Arab but is in fact the son of an English father and a Spanish mother who had died in the desert when he was still a small child.

The exoticism and adventurousness acted out in the movie are congruent with the antimodernist ethos that was undermining the Victorian heritage of American culture in the 1920s. The movie was an attempt to come to grips with the question of the nature of manhood and womanhood and of the bond that ought to unite them. Although the movie explicitly rejects the objectification of women and the view of marriage as a sales contract—the buying and selling of women is explicitly denounced as a "barbaric" custom—it cannot come to terms with the overbearing personality of the Sheik nor with the woman's defiance of the norms attached to her sexual identity. The intensely "virile" masculinity of the Sheik and the "untamed" femininity of the dashing young British woman are acted out as a threat not only to the possibility of love but also to middle-class containment of male and female sexuality. Only when the Sheik abandons his cruel demeanor and reveals a more humane aspect and only when the woman relinquishes all claims to independence can they unite. The masculinity displayed by Rudolph Valentino resonated with the sexual style of immigrants and the working class and is explicitly opposed to the more refined but more repressed style of his European captive and his European friend. Although the movie embraces the tempestuous romantic style of the Sheik and signals the decline of a Victorian sexual morality, it ultimately reconciles itself with the older values by the final revelation that the "savage" was in fact a true European and by the characters' abandonment of their unruly sexual style.

The 1926 sequel, *The Son of the Sheik,* made the class-based undertones of the story more explicit and gave to the confrontation between middle-class and working-class sexual styles a different cultural resolution. In this story, the daughter of the leader of a band of desert thieves is seen dancing in the street for money by a richly dressed man, who is none other than the Sheik's son. Upon meeting her, he gives her an expensive ring as a token of his desire to see her again. The poor and beautiful dancer and the mysterious, handsome, rich man meet in the moonlight and declare their love for each other. Their bliss is terminated one night when the thieves kidnap him in the hope of obtaining a ransom. The head of the gang, the dancer's father, tells the Sheik's son falsely that his daughter lured him for money. After the son is rescued by his friends, the rest of the movie is spent on the conflict between his wish to get revenge for her betrayal and her unsuccessful attempts to prove her innocence. The main story line intersects with two parallel subplots that increase the obstacles between the lovers: the Sheik wants to see his son marry his wife's genteel European cousin, while the dancer's father tries to force her into marriage with an old rich man. The Sheik's son captures the dancer and tries to make her acknowledge her betrayal. Their animosity intensifies, but the son finally releases her, giving her some money. The dancer throws this money away, revealing to the son her lack of mercenary motives and giving the lie to her father. The Sheik's son kills her father, and the two lovers ride happily toward a radiant future.

Because in *The Sheik* the parents of both protagonists were deceased, the story did not act out as clearly as in the *Son of the Sheik* the conflict between romance and parental control. In place of the traditional exchange of women between men, we have here expressed the aggressive and uncompromising affirmation of the couple's autonomy, even at the cost of the killing of the woman's father and breaking away from the Sheik's rule. Furthermore, while the dashing and daring young woman of *The Sheik* fully belonged to the genteel aristocratic world she only appeared to defy, in *The Son of the Sheik,* the heroine belongs indisputably to the underworld and is far from having a respectable exterior, as is made clear by her heavy jewelry, her dress and the large amounts of flesh it exposes, and her daily routine of dancing in the streets for money. The movie clothed the liberated style and soft exoticism of working-class behavior under the veil of "exoticism," thereby making it more palatable and legitimate to middle-class audiences. The class undertone of the character of the dancer is confirmed by the opposition the movie constructs between her and the beautiful, refined, and aristocratic European woman the Sheik has promised his son to. His son's preference for the alluring and flamboyant style of the street dancer makes more explicit the message that was ambiguous in *The Sheik,* namely, that middle-class gentility was defeated by the freedom of style and dress of the "underworld."

Another class-related issue that figures in this movie concerns the "venality" of women. In a system that both glorified female beauty and integrated it into the market yet still denied women full access to the work sphere and economic resources, and in an ideology that trumpeted the supremacy of love and disavowed economic considerations in mating, the issue of the "venality" of women was an increasingly pressing one.[51] Were women interested only in men's money? The dancer's alleged venality and her attempts to prove her innocence are at the very heart of the movie's plot. It is only when she throws away his money and proves her genuine disinterestedness that their love story can resume and the movie end.

These two widely popular movies of the 1920s illustrate how the cultural struggles around the constitution of a middle-class romantic formula were publicly discussed, albeit euphemized as exoticism, and how working-class romantic practices had made a breach in traditional middle-class gentility. Furthermore, the second movie resonated with cultural anxieties about women's "interestedness." The second movie brought the question to a happy resolution by making the Sheik's son wealthy and the woman supply convincing evidence of her indifference to his money.

The "legitimation" of working-class or immigrant forms of romance and their appropriation into commercialized leisure practices appealing to all strata demonstrate the ability of the new entertainment industry to impose itself triumphantly on the cultural habits of the middle classes. The new institution of "going out on a date" resulted not only from the desire of people of all classes to participate in this new realm of leisure but from other, equally profound cultural changes such as looser parental control and looser sexual mores. Within a relatively short time, forms of entertainment and of romantic encounter previously decried became acceptable and standard for the middle classes. Attendance at such entertainment venues as movies, dance halls, and amusement parks satisfied the need and desire for privacy and intimacy sought by post-Victorian Americans, a need in turn greatly stimulated by the efforts of advertisers and entrepreneurs to expand their markets. Thus, the images and the goods offered by the leisure markets and the interests of cultural entrepreneurs met and interlocked with the consumers' desire for romance and "soft" forms of eroticism.

This incorporation of romance into the marketplace was achieved through a process of commodification. As participation in the leisure markets became increasingly associated with romance, the experience of romance became increasingly associated with consumption. This process, which was consolidated into a middle-class formula of romance that gelled between 1900 and 1930, operated simultaneously on two seemingly contradictory levels. Whereas the formula implied that the romantic encounter take place on the margins of the family and society, thus giving it the appearance of being less controlled by society, that same formula reintegrated the couple into society through the "back door," so to speak, in that it brought them into the anonymous and abstract sphere of commodity exchange. The new technologies of leisure and the cultural meanings associated with them constructed romance in isolation not only from the family but from society at large. Paradoxically, though, this experience of withdrawal from the social world was achieved not through a separation of the lovers from their environment

but through their full participation in the commodified and public realm
of leisure.

DATING AND THE SPIRIT OF CONSUMERISM

As romance was liberated from certain social controls, money tied it to
the market through multiple and often invisible acts of consumption.
Money played an important role in redefining the romantic interaction,
thus inaugurating a "political economy of romance." On a general level,
political economy can be defined as the study of the ways in which the
unequal distribution of power in social relationships is shaped, maintained, and reinforced by the organization of the economy.[52] I call here
the "political economy of romance" the class relationships that made
possible and sustained the incorporation of romance within the economic practices of the sphere of consumption. Did this new cultural and
economic matrix reinforce or alleviate social differences? Did it exclude
working-class men and women from what the middle classes deemed
"legitimate" forms of dating, as in the case of "calling," or did it facilitate their integration into the new middle-class order? Since the answer
to these questions is by no means straightforward, I shall offer only tentative hypotheses and preliminary directions of inquiry.

As we have seen, consumption became part of romance with the dif-
fusion through mass culture of the notion that "seduction" was to be
achieved and maintained through the consumption of products for self-
enhancement. The marketing of such products relentlessly employed the
theme of love as its ultimate justification. Romance became increasingly
identified with participation in the cultural realms of entertainment and
leisure. By their very nature these two objects of consumption, beauty
products and leisure, imply that money is a central component of romantic encounters, both prior to and during the date.

In its ideal-typical representations, dating presupposed access to
leisure and wealth, requiring not only disposable income but what Veblen identified as a central value commodity, leisure time. As Elaine May
succinctly puts it, the "cultivation of romance was not cheap."[53] These
requirements did not go unnoticed by those involved. The contrast between "old" and "new" style romance was the theme of many articles,
many of which, all written by men, pointed out that the main difference
between romantic practices "then" and "now" had to do with cost.
"Then" one did not need money to court. Men complained about the
new rules of the romantic game, lamenting that now a woman would

not go out with a man if he could not afford to take her someplace exciting. A 1930 *Photoplay* article complained that "[today] the fun starts at 60 miles an hour . . . the first cloud looms over the romance when he begins to wonder if he'll have enough money after paying the couvert charge, to buy a marriage license."[54] One young man called his his parents' courtship "a story of poverty and young love, of long years of waiting." His parents, he wrote, courted by "go[ing] on hay rides and barn dances, to sugar off during the spring when sap starts flowing from sugar maples, go[ing] on school picnics on Sundays, skat[ing] on the beagles pond, roast[ing] corn, go[ing] to Halloween parties, and . . . call[ing] at her house (ibid)."[55] Indeed, this article accurately detected that the informal and communal forms of romantic encounters that had prevailed were vanishing, steadily replaced by money-based and individualistic forms of pleasure-seeking.

The descriptions of contemporary dates provided by these men follow a set pattern. The 1930 article "Who Says the Woman Pays?" makes it clear how dates were conducted and what their perceived cost was: "We would have dinner at the Ritz, go to the opening of 'Artists and Models' and then drop in at the Central Park Casino for dancing. It sounded fairly modest, innocent that I am. Well, if $75.30 is a modest New York date, I'm Santa-Claus."[56] Another writer recounted that "I saw Edna for four months. We went to expensive restaurants, bought expensive theater tickets, roses, high priced chocolates, taxi-rides, went to Coney Island see the new film."[57] Songs echoed the same anxieties:

> Johnny took Geraldine out one night to show her a wonderful time
> When they sat down in a cabaret, he bought two cigars for a dime,
>
> "Bring us a couple of sodas," Johnny cried when the waiter drew near
> After an hour Miss Geraldine whispered in Johnny's ear
> "If that's your idea of a wonderful time, take me home."
> Johnny looked foolish and said, "My dear the evening has only begun.
> I'll take you down to a picture show, we'll have a barrel of fun.
> I know the fellow who owns the place, I'll ask him to pass us inside."
> Geraldine looked into Johnny's face, shaking her head, she cried:
> "If that's your idea of a wonderful time, take me home." (1914)

Among the working classes, men's anxieties about being able to afford the price of a date were probably a response to the customary practice of "treating" a woman. Among some segments of the working class women would exchange men's treats to various forms of amusement (theater tickets, drinks, amusement parks, etc.) for small sexual favors (kissing, petting, and sometimes intercourse). While women competed for attractiveness and sexual allure, men competed in their ability to provide for the price of entertainment.[58]

The standard middle-class romantic formula, as codified by popular and middle-brow culture, required the consumption of the luxury goods associated with the affluent lifestyle (theater tickets, restaurants, taxis) as well as mass-produced "cheap" goods (films, amusement parks, etc.). However, a "prestigious" date was always an expensive one, requiring a considerable outlay. One author complained about the "too-high cost" of dating: "Like most men between the ages of eighteen and thirty, I have invested my surplus income in the variety of things which girls nowadays seem to require. . . . My purchases have averaged one thousand dollars a year, or twenty dollars a week."[59] Such problems were faced by many men who had left small towns for the big city and sought relationships with women by offering the expected amusements. In the end, however, single men of modest means found themselves unable to keep up with the level of expenditure required by frequent dating.

The "moral" of the story was that men who failed to provide for the cost of dating faced the risk of being turned down by women. Although the practice of "treating" was especially widespread among the working class, these articles suggest that middle-class men were facing the same expectation to entertain, only at greater expense and with a less certain promise of the woman's return of favors. Many contemporary articles suggested that men, especially those struggling to attain a comfortable income, felt both used and disadvantaged by the new economy of love, which rendered leisure commodities central to the seduction process. Two 1924 songs show the role of such status commodities as automobiles in helping men get dates:

> If you have a little sweetie and you don't know how to win
> Just tell her you have a real auto for that will be no sin
> . . . .
> They don't care what you look like—it's the car you drive today
> They don't care how you get it, but they want it anyway
> The sweeties, the sweeties today. (1924)

> Ray was just an ordinary fellow;
> Couldn't get a girlie though he tried and tried
> He never did get far
> Because he didn't own a car
> And all the girls he knew loved to ride
> He saved up every penny of his pay
> And bought himself a little Chevrolet. (1924)

Automobiles were by this time fairly commonplace, but their cost still placed them out of the reach of many. Although the middle-class formula for dating incorporated inexpensive forms of entertainment, such entertainments were not acceptable if they were dissociated from status commodities. The high cost of dating, and the fact that its goal had changed from marriage to temporary intimacy, which rendered it an act of consumption that could be and was repeated with a number of partners, meant that many of low and middle-income people were, at least partially, excluded from the new romantic utopia. The working classes, as well as the lower fractions of the middle classes, were excluded from the glamorous ideal-typical definitions of dating.

To see whether some of these trends became increasingly apparent over time, let us look at the situation after World War II. Examples taken from the advice literature of the 1960s shows that the problems of the 1920s continued to plague the average-income couple. For example, the 1963 *Complete Guide to Dating* portrays the disappointment of a woman who has not been asked out on a date: "There goes the phone and the call's for you: 'Mind if I drop over for the evening?' asks the current man in your life. And what do you say? For a moment you may feel angry: why didn't he ask to take you to a movie, or at least for a soda at the Malt shop? Well, simmer down for a moment before you give him a cold brush off."[60] Obviously, this author took for granted that a "good" date meant going out and engaging in some form of leisure consumption, even if minimal. By the end of the 1960s, the equation between a date's expense and its quality had become commonplace.[61] Thus the 1967 *Art of Dating,* directed to high school and college students, specified a clear division of expenditure between young men and young women: men should pay for transportation, entertainment, and food, while their dates needed money to give parties; both needed to pay for clothes and grooming. This clearly implies that both before-the-date (grooming, clothes) and during-the-date (entertainment, food, transportation) acts of consumption were perceived as "natural," intrinsic elements of the dating system. Moreover, the fact that this book targeted such a young audience indicates the changing demographics of dating and suggests that the age—and presumably the class and ethnic affiliations—of participants in the commercialized formula of romance had not stopped expanding since the beginning of the century. This implies in turn that the money-related anxieties voiced by adult males in 1920 were being "transferred" in the 1960s to young adolescents, whose problems in fulfilling the requirements of a date related to their not yet being full members of the market. "Both boys and girls have many date expenses. To some young adults it's a real problem; to others it's a real challenge, how they can make their dates both interesting and inexpensive. . . . If your money is limited, there are ways to earn more money or to cut down dating expenses. . . . Money is necessary. You need it for school and grooming expenses, for gifts and even for clothes. But you do not need a lot of money to have a good time on a date."[62] The author's attitude toward money is ambiguous: despite the last, comforting reassurance that a good date can be inexpensive, the messages that come across are that "money is necessary" in the dating system, that dating cheaply can be a difficult task, and that an expensive date is the norm. This advice book tries to help young people cope with this fact.

The conclusion that middle-class affluence was a prerequisite for achieving the standard requirements of dating holds valid not only for the amount of money required but also for the manners considered appropriate to rituals of consumption. Legitimate romance required not only a certain affluence but familiarity with "proper" manners as well. To return to the early decades of the century, a 1923 advertisement for an etiquette book described a romantic dinner that turned increasingly sour as the couple noticed small faults in each other's demeanor: "He had invited her to dinner. She had accepted. Now sitting opposite each other at the table, they begin to see things they never saw before. They begin to see each other for the first time as they really are. . . . She sees with a little pang of disappointment that *he is not the cultivated man she thought him.* . . . Why does she stumble *so awkwardly with her fork?* Why does he seem so self-conscious, so ill at ease? Her evident embarrassment makes him feel uncomfortable, and suddenly he finds himself wishing he had never invited her." Taking for granted that dining out was part of dating, this ad mixes the motif of date nervousness with a rhetoric of class by suggesting that a good date demanded the ease, comfort, and manners appropriate to middle-class "gentility" as well as familiarity with high-status forms of consumption. Embedded within the formal system of calling was the ability to erect barriers against "class intruders," suitors who were socially inappropriate. Dating threatened this well-protected order, for at the same time that it made vulnerable those who had no access to genteel manners and etiquette, it also offered greater possibilities for class mingling. And the etiquette books that had been widely available since the middle of the nineteenth century were linked to the rise of middle classes in avid search of guidelines for social mobility and gentility.[63] The rules provided by these advice books fed on middle-class insecurities and strategies of social mobility. The romantic formula therefore drew on the genteel manners that the middle class associated with the consumption of leisure.[64] The underlying idea that, for a date to be successful, appropriate middle-class manners are essential indicates that the romantic formula was associated with the emergence of what have been called institutions of "legitimate culture."[65] Indeed, as Paul Dimaggio and Lawrence Lavine have documented, during this period elites were particularly concerned with establishing new cultural boundaries to counter the trends of cultural democratization that were threatening the legitimacy of their leadership.[66]

Guides to etiquette published in the 1960s, such as the 1963 *Complete Guide to Dating,* extended the realm of familiarity with legitimate culture by giving precise instructions on how to behave at elegant restaurants, "concert dates," or "museum dates." To facilitate the restaurant date, the book provides translations of the French names for dishes offered on the menus of the elegant restaurants that are presumably the venue of such dates. Dining at expensive foreign restaurants was the expected norm, and when on a date, men and women were strongly advised to display the linguistic skills, the tastes, and cultural competence necessary to show ease in such settings. The 1963 advice about concert dates also sounds similar to the ad for the 1920s etiquette book: "You are nervous . . . because going to a concert isn't like going to the movies—everybody does that. . . . [Unless] you know the music awfully well, don't try to lead the applause. You may find yourself clapping alone."[67] This book, an aid to the socialization of young people into romantic and dating behavior, simultaneously provided socialization to middle-class gentility and cultural capital. As I argue more fully in chapters 7 and 8, in the course of the twentieth century, love became increasingly intertwined with new forms of social "distinction": surplus income and time to invest in leisure pursuits and the knowledge and practice of the right upper-middle-class manners for each type of leisure consumed (Bourdieu's "cultural capital"). Romantic love thus became closely associated not only with the consumption of leisure goods but also with forms of "positional" consumption, aimed at displaying status in a competitive system of social stratification.

Taken at face value, these elements seem to indicate that the middle-class dating system required a lifestyle, an income, and a level of education that discriminated against the lower classes. Dating not only presuppose surplus time and money to invest in "disinterested" pursuits but also requires the manners of middle- and even upper-middle-class "gentility."

However, several factors in the cultural history of leisure mitigate this conclusion. As argued earlier, certain middle-class forms of leisure originated with working-class practices. Furthermore, when leisure became commodified, it was also democratized. The cultural association of romance with leisure resulted from the legitimation of lower-class cultural practices as well as the democratization of luxury goods. If mass leisure did not make uniform the heterogeneous class practices of the upper and lower segments of society, it nevertheless drew them within the common arena of the market.

Analyzing the market of early twentieth-century America, historian Charles McGovern suggests that "the democracy of consumption also meant a universalizing of luxuries previously reserved for the rich. In this light consumption was a leveling force in the social structure and the heir to traditional republican hostility to privilege."[68] The leisure and market-based formula of romance can be seen as contributing to this democratization. This is borne out by the history of automobile ownership, restaurants, and tourism. Beginning as the exclusive property of the wealthiest strata of society, they were increasingly purchased by poorer and younger people as they became less expensive. The practice of dining out has upper-middle-class and aristocratic origins, but by the mid-1920s it had become democratized and spread throughout society.[69] If we believe that advertising images reflect cultural practices, the sample of images analyzed earlier suggests that in the years between 1900 and 1930 restaurants became closely associated with romance; by the 1930s, certainly, they had become fully naturalized in the advertising representation of romance. And while what might be called "educational" tourism had long been practiced by aristocratic classes, it was only during the opening decades of the twentieth century, with the increasing success of workers' struggles for leisure time and the efforts of local and national commercial promoters, that tourism became a popular pursuit, albeit still largely exhibiting class differences.

This "trickle-down" process was accompanied, as we have seen, by a contrary, upward movement, the adoption and legitimation of certain working-class behaviors and values by the middle classes. Middle-class and working-class romantic styles and leisure practices initially confronted each other but ultimately merged, through the appropriation and legitimation of working-class style by the middle classes and through the democratization of luxury goods in the consumer markets.

The mixed class underpinnings of romance and dating are well illustrated by a reader's letter to *Photoplay:* "My husband cannot afford an automobile and as a result we are denied much of the enjoyment that ownership of a car affords. With financial worries and lack of outdoor life, we have discovered that 'Jack can become a dull husband and Jill a bored wife.' To preserve romance in our lives and to escape from dull evenings at home, we find adventure in the darkness of the movie theater. . . . And we walk home with renewed love and courage anticipating the next of the best pictures of the month."[70] As we saw earlier in this chapter, a successful marriage must be "entertaining." Her husband fears being dull, and the reader herself fears being bored. She assumes that having a car would relieve these anxieties, but their income is not sufficient to allow them to enjoy the pleasure of motoring.

The conclusion of this letter, however, invites us to resist a reductionist view of the working class as simply being "deprived" compared to the middle class, by strongly suggesting that the inexpensive movies, with their exciting and romantic content, provided an easy outlet for this woman's thirst for romance in her life. The reader's fulfillment suggests that by legitimating inexpensive forms of leisure, the new twentieth-century middle-class formula of romance enabled members of the working classes to enjoy their own practices within the boundaries of middle-class forms of consumption.[71] This situation contrasts sharply with the exclusion of the working class by nineteenth-century middle-class romantic practices. But because romance and leisure originated partly in working-class courtship practices, their social location was ambiguous.

On the one hand, the new system discriminated against those who could not afford the trappings of what would later become the "affluent society." On the other, the incorporation of inexpensive dating practices into the romantic utopia and the democratization of luxury goods may have allowed those with fewer resources to compete in the dating scene. In its new guise the dating system included those who had not been able to partake of the system of "calling" but who could afford to "go out" to movies, dance halls, and amusement parks; it excluded them, however, because they still lacked the means to attain the expensive luxury goods deemed necessary for ideal-typical romance. It therefore becomes clear that the formula for middle-class romantic behavior was not middle-class per se but a compromise between "upper" and "lower" cultural forces. The mass market of leisure incorporated romantic practices from both the bottom and the top of society. The impulse common to both movements was the expansion of the market, whose main agents were the commercial entrepreneurs who rejected traditional middle-class standards of gentility even as they tried to cater to middle-class tastes. The emergence of this middle-class formula of romance seems, then, to have been part of the elaboration of the "middle-brow" that gelled during the twenties.[72] Although this process had started during the nineteenth century, the emerging, rapidly spreading technologies of culture and leisure readily lent themselves to the simultaneous claim that high culture ought to be "democratized" and that popular cultural practices ought to be gentrified.

Two objections to the idea of a "political economy of romance" can be raised. The first is that the commodification of romance could be more fruitfully viewed in terms of gender politics than in terms of political economy. For example, in her excellent study of dating, Bailey argues that the expectation that men would pay for women weakened the power women had traditionally held in the courtship process and conferred it on the men, thus shifting from a system that regulated class relationships to one that regulated gender relationships.[73] Because they were expected to pay, men were now entitled to initiate or terminate a romantic encounter. While it is undeniable that men's money became key to the dating process, it is, to say the least, very arguable that the new dating system downplayed the class relationships that had hitherto presided and that it instead inaugurated unprecedented forms of male control. Men were expected to pay for the date, and women had to spend money for "grooming." The market constructed and reinforced definitions of masculinity and femininity that made *both* men and women depend on different practices of consumption, practices that were ultimately congruent with the interests of capitalist entrepreneurs, whether they sold beauty products, gasoline, or movie tickets. Because women espoused rather than resisted the distribution of roles within the dating system, this system favored men with the requisite surplus income and tended to discriminate against men with much fewer resources.

Furthermore, while it is true that the market reinforced a definition of womanhood based on "seduction" and "physical beauty," the combination of the hedonist ethos of consumption and the ideal of romance paradoxically provided women with an empowering narrative of personal liberation that sustained broader ideals of women's self-realization, autonomy, and claims to equality.[74] This narrative was already contained in the idea of romantic love as the rationale for choosing a partner, for romantic love by definition contains the idea that the choice of a partner is made freely rather than coerced and that partners' feelings must be equal and reciprocated. This vision of an autonomous amorous subject was underscored by the values of liberation and self-expression cultivated by the culture of consumption in general and by advertising in particular. What is more, by shifting the encounter from the confines of the home to the public and anonymous sphere of amusements, dating widened the pool of partners available to women and increased their sense of autonomy and empowerment. Finally, the rhetoric of consumption that presided over the inception of the dating system undermines its own tendency to polarize gender identities and tends to draw male and female identities within a genderless rhetoric (see the next chapter).

The second possible objection to the claim that consumer capitalism is responsible for the role that commodities play in the pairing-up of couples could come from the ranks of anthropologists of the family. It is well known that in most societies marriage is marked by the open and explicit exchange of goods.[75] This is clearly the case in preindustrial and to a certain extent modern non-Western societies. Why shouldn't the exchange of commodities in the romantic bonding in market economies be another instance of this widespread cultural practice?

The two kinds of exchange differ in several important respects. To begin with, the modern ideology of romantic love is based on the idea that the bride and groom "price" is extraneous to the romantic sentiment. In modern romantic love, money and social status are not supposed to interfere with sentiment, and choosing a partner solely on these grounds is usually considered improper. This "disinterested" ideal stands in sharp contrast to the openly acknowledged view of marriage as an economic and even profitable transaction that predated the rise of the modern romantic ideal. It is indeed the rejection of "interested" or calculated action that is at the crux of the modern romantic ideal (and ideology). Thus, in contrast to the openly "interested" nature of traditional marriage, modern romance is equated with "disinterestedness."

Moreover, while the premodern marriage involved an exchange between two people or two families, the romantic consumption of leisure is not strictly speaking an act of exchange, but the mutual participation of two people in the consumption (that is, the purchase) of goods provided by the market. In other words, the market and not the romantic partner receives compensation for the commodity. In traditional marriage, the goods exchanged were usually durable and of instrumental value, satisfying physical needs and increasing property; the goods consumed in modern romance are transient and experiential, purchased to provide pleasure and thus having the character of "hedonist" commodities. Finally, the substantial value of goods traditionally exchanged is meant to seal the bond between the partners (and their families or clans), but the exchange does not constitute the event of marriage itself. In modern dating, however, the consumption of commodities becomes an end in itself, the attainment of an intimacy that is only temporary. Indeed, since the cultural novelty of "dating" lies precisely in its *not* implying marriage, the dating period is often one of intense consumerist activity whereby two people interact with the surrounding public culture and come to know each other within this framework.[76] In the modern romantic ideal it is the very act of consumption that constitutes and creates the romantic moment.

The modern formula for romance has imbued the commodities—and the technologies of communication they rely on—with a symbolic and emotional life distinct from their economic value as such. What is truly novel about the role of commodities in romance is that they structure its experiential boundaries and are endlessly repeatable, "recyclable." The hedonist, transient, and highly symbolic aspect of these commodities point us to a "postmodern cultural economy of romance," explored in the next section of the book.

CONCLUSION

Cultural analysts typically assume that the content of culture is not divorced from the social and economic conditions under which it is produced, although the extent and the nature of this "dependence" are highly controversial topics. While the market occupies a central place in this framework, in my own analysis I do not offer a causal model that would explain the commercialized formula of romance in terms of the "functional needs" of all-encompassing and ineluctable market forces. As I have argued throughout, market-based practices of consumption were encouraged by evolving cultural definitions of love and marriage, which lent new meaning to the purchase of leisure, beauty products, and a wide gamut of other mundane goods. Although the expansion of the leisure market was certainly a necessary condition for the commercialization of romance, this commercialization was articulated within a system of cultural meanings and class and gender relationships that inscribed the new, market-based formula of romance deeply within people's everyday lives, aspirations, and anxieties. The commodification of romance cannot be separated from growing cultural appetites for such "goods" as abundant leisure and eternal excitement, appetites that rendered meaningful and desirable the new leisure goods offered by cultural entrepreneurs.

As we have seen, in the early years of this century courtship and marriage, romance and love became increasingly tied to new markets for leisure and personal commodities. As it came to be increasingly associated with signs of affluence, the meaning of "romantic" changed, referring more and more to an *atmosphere* and a type of *setting* conducive to certain feelings. The possibility of romance came to depend on the correct, external mise-en-scene: theaters, dance halls, restaurants, settings seen in movies and advertising images. This dependence was extended by the intrusion of the pressure to consume into the intimacy of marriage. Paradoxically, at the same time that the distinction between intense but ephemeral romantic experiences and long-term, effortful relationships was being sharpened, the terms of this distinction were becoming less intelligible, because the new ideal of marriage and love prescribed that fleeting and intense pleasures should and could be mixed with domestic models of love based on compatibility and rational self-control. As we will see in chapters 5, 6, and 7, the blurring of the boundary between "romance" and "long-lasting love," or rather the attempt to merge them into a single model, has rendered problematic the ability to choose between two incongruent cultural and emotional repertoires.

This new, self-contradictory formula of romance was the outcome of social and symbolic struggles between different worldviews. The early resistance to the introduction of hedonist values into marriage expressed a broader conflict, between the traditional, "Protestant" work ethic of the sphere of production, whose sobriety and self-control were seen as central to family life as well, and the hedonist ethic of the sphere of consumption, exemplified in the new "hot" romance. The hedonist and the entrepreneurial economic ethics paralleled respectively a romantic ethos based on the pursuit of fleeting pleasure and one oriented toward long-lasting bonds based on reason and control. Following Daniel Bell's famous thesis, I propose that already in the early twentieth century there was a disjunction between a vision of love based on the themes and images of the sphere of consumption and one based on the values and discourse of the sphere of production.[77] Contrary to Bell, however, I view the contradiction between these two ethics as subsumed by a higher order of rationality, that of capital in the largest possible sense, cultural as well as economic. By incorporating middle-class culture of respectability and "genteelity," the new romantic formula introduced forms of "cultural capital." According to Pierre Bourdieu, cultural capital is expressed in one's familiarity with legitimate culture that in turn positions one in a system of social classification and differences. At the same time that the traditional, "legitimate" middle-class culture of solid economic achievement and respectability in romantic-sexual behavior continued to exert its claims, men and women came to expect each other to display a familiarity with the rules of dating. Men and women were supposed to consume leisure, but they were supposed to consume it by displaying their familiarity with middle-class legitimate culture. The new formula presupposed not only a relative degree of affluence but also a familiarity with manners that marked partners as "respectable" and "educated." Thus the new definitions of romance were not the ineluctable expression of broad market forces, but rather *a cultural form articulating economic forces within class relationships*.

My refusal to yield to a "final" causal model of cultural change is due to the very character of the transformations discussed. This new "romantic political economy" was neither based on autonomous economic forces unleashed by consumer capitalism nor was it the straightforward outcome of emerging cultural trends.[78] Rather, it foreshadowed the reconfigured relations of the cultural and economic that characterize post–World War II "postmodern culture." As many authors now recognize, postmodern culture is characterized by the fantastic outgrowth of the cultural sphere vis-à-vis the economic one—not because the former has overridden the latter, but because the zone of control exerted by capitalism moved from production to the sphere of culture via the threefold articulation of consumption, leisure, and mass media. Postmodern romance is thus firmly located in the discourses and institutions that have been designed by the cultural entrepreneurs of capitalism. It is within this framework that I turn to examine contemporary practices of romance.

PART 2

All That Is Romantic Melts into Air

Love as a Postmodern Condition

CHAPTER 3

From the Romantic Utopia to the American Dream

I would like to remind us . . . that numerous so-called
utopian dreams . . . have been fulfilled. However, insofar as
these dreams have been realized, they all operate as though
the best thing about them had been forgotten—one is not
happy about them.

> *Theodor Adorno, "Something's Missing: A*
> *Discussion between Ernst Bloch and*
> *Theodor W. Adorno on the Contradictions of*
> *Utopian Longing"*

From the 1920s on, as advertising shifted its concerns from providing information about products to linking products with such intangibles as happiness and warm human relationships as well as fashion, beauty, celebrity, and glamorous lifestyles, advertising started to have the ethereal quality of dreams, made all the more persuasive by being represented in the realistic media of photography and film. "By the 1920s in the United States, advertising had become a prolific producer of visual images with normative overtones, a contributor to the society's shared daydreams."[1] Persons and things linked in dreamlike fantasies, offering glimpses of a realm where abundance and love flowed freely, tapped into consumers' desires for love, freedom, and equality as well as for youth, beauty, status, and wealth. Advertising thus made available a rich lexicon and a powerful syntax to formulate visions of harmony, intimacy, and success. As the iconography . . . of abundance,"[2] advertising has linked market forces and consumers' desires through meanings. The central meaning of advertising, as Raymond Williams has so aptly suggested, is to have elevated material goods to a spiritual level, and in this sense, it has promoted consumption through a multiplicity of desires. At the center of advertising is the metaphor that relationships between people and individuals themselves are mediated by things.

In this chapter we turn from an historical account of how romance met the market and begin to map the contemporary "reincarnation" of the romantic utopia in postmodern culture. Advertising is a privileged site to study utopias because it is itself primarily an aesthetic of utopia, drawing on a well-established pool of symbols, images, and *topoi* that, even when fallen to the level of clichés and double-speak, can stir up and express deep desires for freedom, pleasure, abundance, intimacy, power, happiness. It offers not only a coherent universe of idealized objects, landscapes, and social relationships but also an aesthetic combining the art of rhetoric with the evocative power of dreams. The power of advertising lies not in regimenting consciousness but rather in articulating meanings that bind consumers' desires to market forces. Romance was one of the most powerful "channels of desire" used by advertisers to make their imagery at once lifelike and dreamlike.[3] By presenting commodities as attributes of erotic attraction or achieved intimacy, advertisers used romance to fetishize consumption, that is, to transpose erotic desire onto goods, which in turn became themselves the very objects of desire. In this way, the inert realm of commodities was insufflated life through the "spirits" of love. Thus, as Raymond Williams noted, advertising does not make culture "materialistic" but rather elevates material goods to a quasi-spiritual level and in this way becomes the "official art of capitalism."[4]

In this respect, advertising is an abbreviated lexicon of contemporary American dreams and can provide a map to orient ourselves in the intricate meanings and ideals that haunt the romantic imagination of contemporary culture. Thus, if we cannot always comprehend the nature of social relationships from the content of advertising, we can at least get a glimpse of the dreams dreamed "out loud" by postmodern culture. Deciphering such dreams can be instructive, for they point us to structure of meaning, feeling, and personal identity within which *some* of the contemporary cultural standards of romance are formulated. Postmodern romance is characterized by the fusion of culture with commodity, the construction of desire within the idioms of consumption. As I show in this chapter, if the union of romance and commodities is such an obsessive theme of American capitalist culture in general and of advertising in particular, it is because it intertwines and puts at the center stage of our collective imagination two powerful motives, a euphoric vision of harmonious human relationships and the American dream that consumption affirms both democratic access to affluence and the originality of the individual self.

"YOU COULD BE HERE, NOW"

I collected and analyzed eighty advertising photographs from diverse American magazines directed toward a heterogeneous middle- to upper-middle-class audience (*Time, Newsweek, Harper's, The Atlantic Monthly, The New York Times Magazine*).[5] All the images appeared between 1989 and 1991. Although I expected romance to be associated with a wide variety of products, as was the case during the 1920s, I found that it is in fact associated with a relatively narrow range, primarily perfumes, makeup and clothing, liquor, cigarettes, hotels, travel destinations, and diamonds. Unsurprisingly, these products were targeted to relatively affluent consumers, for whom leisure and the cultivation of "good taste" are central to lifestyle and identity. These images therefore provide us with a convenient access to the *ideal-typical definitions* of what advertisers, relying on marketing research and the cues provided by the surrounding culture, consider "middle-class" desirable standards of romance and affluence.[6]

By and large, the three product categories in this sample most often associated with romance were those contributing to image-building (e.g., perfume, dress, and makeup), leisure (e.g., hotel, travel, and drinking), and gift-giving (e.g., diamonds). During the 1920s and 1930s these products were explicitly summoned either to help one find a mate by increasing one's attractiveness or to consolidate an existing but fragile bond, but the ads for those products never amounted to what has become, in contemporary sensibility, a crude solicitation to consumption. A woman was not explicitly advised to use a perfume to increase her chances of finding a mate or of preserving her marriage. Instead, the product typically appears as one element among others (or may even, as in the hotel advertisement that follows, be virtually invisible) of a spectacle in which the act of consumption is merged with the vision of a reciprocated intimacy. A 1990 advertisement for Continental Hotels shows a man and a woman having lunch in elegant surroundings. Part of the text below the image reads: "'*I'm sorry,*' she apologized, '*I've got the giggles.*' '*I didn't know they were on the menu,*' he said." This image and text do not try to convince or to sell in the traditional sense. Instead, the goal is to allow the viewer-consumer to penetrate the private intimacy of a romantic moment in which consumption is taken for granted as natural. In contemporary advertisements, the viewer-consumer is not targeted for a rhetoric of persuasion—"buy me because I will get you love"—but rather is made a vóyeur to a spectacle of intimacy and *inconspicuous* consumption. The absence of a mediating sales pitch reveals more clearly the metaphysics of advertising, in which the distance between subject and object of consumption, between the product and the relationship that it helped realize has vanished. Products not only point to but *are* shared intimate moments of celebration (e.g., champagne), sensual pleasure (e.g., cognac), or, to quote an ad for Parliament cigarettes, a "perfect recess," the recessed filter of the cigarette suggesting a recess for two (or three, if one includes the cigarette), a withdrawal into a lovers' grotto created by the act of sharing a smoke.

Another, even more radical way of breaking down the boundary between consumption and feeling, object and subject, consists in making the product itself the end of the erotic and romantic desire. For example, an advertisement for Hennessy cognac shows a close-up of a man and a woman, passionately embracing and kissing. The ad reads, "If you have ever been kissed *you* already know the feeling of Cognac Hennessy." The message of the advertising supported by the pictorial amalgam of the kiss and the bottle is that consumption provides an equivalent, even a substitute, for erotic intimacy. Furthermore, in their embrace the couple form the shape of the cognac bottle. Not only does this visual pun drive home the inseparability of romance and consumption, but the product itself evaporates, leaving the feelings it has evoked as a pure, distilled essence.

A widespread advertising image of the 1930s showed a woman successfully captivating and enthralling an otherwise reluctant partner. The implicit problem addressed by the product was seduction, how to attain or rejuvenate an intimate relationship. The majority of contemporary images, however, offer the spectacle of fully realized, repeated intimacy. The sharing of moments, objects, words, and gestures known or accessible only to the couple is at center stage. Couples display their ostensible closeness by hugging, kissing, dancing, holding hands, looking at each other insistently, closely embracing each other—poses of physical intimacy in which the relationship of bodies and faces approaches physical and emotional fusion. The intimacy shown in such images always transpires during an act of consumption, but the consumption is subsumed under or merged with the realm of emotion and sensation. The concrete, specific materiality of the products has vanished into the impalpable realm of feeling. Romance—as well as the products that signify it and are signified by it—takes place in an idealized, timeless utopia of intimacy and consumption. The imbibing of alcohol condenses all the feelings of celebration; smoking cigarettes signifies relaxation and withdrawal into a private world; in diamonds love goes on forever.

Although these couples seem to be well-established and happily married, these ads rarely refer explicitly in text to marriage, and certainly never refer to marriage on the brink of disaster, as ads did during the 1920s and 1930s. Instead, they summon the understated vision of a stable and intimate conjugality (usually manifested by a conspicuous wedding ring, primarily through the use of models older than young adults: many couples seem to be in their twenties, but a larger number seem to belong to the category of "thirty-something," people who have attained the marital stability and middle-class or upper-middle-class professional status often associated with "maturity." The target audience reflected by these models is not a surprising choice: married couples represent a larger share of the market and are more likely to have greater financial resources than single-headed households or dating couples.

Nevertheless, although marriage is subsumed under the cultural category of "romance" (in contrast to the ads of the 1930s, which presented the two as potentially incompatible), this model of couplehood is non-domestic. It is significant that children never appear in these images of married couples and that the setting almost never appears to be "home." Excluding a vision of reproductive and institutionalized family life, they offer vignettes of couples oriented to the pursuit of private pleasure and the cultivation of personal sentiments. In the rare cases where the couple is shown at home, the domestic vignette is highly aestheticized. For example, in an ad for diamonds, a man and a woman dressed in casual clothes are shown playing their piano, while passionately kissing each other. An ad for a coffee brand pictures a couple lying on the floor in front of an intense fire in a rustic and beautifully sculpted fireplace. Another ad for china shows the man dressed in a tuxedo and the woman in an elegant evening gown, laughing while preparing their meal together in their kitchen. In its refusal of the mundane and everyday, this vision of ideal romance, as we shall see, enacts an anti-institutional self within the confines of economically successful and institutionalized couplehood.

Congruent with the utopian vision, the physical intimacy depicted in ads offers a vision of equality and not one of domination or submission. Occasionally, the pictures do show men in protective postures and women in admiring ones, but in the majority the poses do not indicate that the man dominates the woman. To the contrary, the physical and, we can infer, the emotional closeness manifested in these images point to an egalitarian bond in which the two selves strive to merge. The frequent use of extreme close-ups (of kissing lips, enraptured faces, etc.) precludes identification of what sociologist Erving Goffman called "hyperritualized signs of gender," by which gender is emphatically underscored by clothing, makeup, and body postures. Although these signs occasionally appear in vignettes of seduction or first encounters, they are conspicuously understated when the couple shares an intimate moment. For example, the soft focus—typically used to signify gentleness, emotion, and intimacy—has connotations of "femininity" and tends to blur, at least visually, the gender differences normally apparent in clothing, makeup, and demeanor by associating men with "feminine" attributes. The intimacy of a couple partaking of leisure hence offers the image of an eroticized equality, which defuses the male's traditional protectiveness and the female's submissiveness.[7]

The equality of most of these couples can be explained in part by the fact that many of the products advertised (cigarettes, liquor, travel) are geared to both men and women. And because in the world of advertising the subject of consumption is always "free" to consume, such freedom implicitly conveys that consumers are equal. The rhetoric of seduction is no less geared to men than it is to women in the encouragement of image building and physical attractiveness and in the promise to both of an eternal, leisure-filled romance.[8] But the "gender-free" tonality of these images is not a postmodern androgyny. Instead, it is a blurring of the distinction between male and female attributes within the traditional female sphere of emotions and intimacy.

The genderless face of romance is also that of consumption at large. As historian Lawrence Birken argues, the nineteenth-century gender division has been erased by "an egalitarian ideology of consumers united under the single function of desire."[9] According to Birken, the long-term trend of Western culture toward the dissolution of hierarchy found a powerful catalyst in the encounter of psychoanalysis, which underwrote assertions of humans' initially androgynous nature with claims to be a science, with the democratizing culture of consumption. Although mass industrial capitalism, Birken's argument goes, continued to insist on gender stereotypes and division of roles (in nonromantic advertising or in the department store, for example), it enabled children and women to gain emancipation as consumers. Psychoanalysis played an important role in shifting the view from the productive subject to the desiring one and in disentangling sexuality from the realm of reproduction and relocating it in the realm of desire. The genderless double desire for goods and romance has increasingly permeated what is usually thought to be a bastion of gender stereotypes, advertising images featuring men and women in romantic poses.

This intimate equality is emphatically marked by the almost total seclusion of the couple from the rest of the world. Among the eighty advertisements I reviewed, seventy-three present the couple as completely isolated: no one but the couple appears in the picture. The other seven contain people other than the couple, but in three of these, these characters are so blurry and distant that their presence is negligible. In the four remaining pictures, the supplementary characters are present only to serve the couple (e.g., a waiter, a pianist playing only for the couple, or a bystander benevolently looking at the romantic couple). The only image where the surrounding characters are not expressly directed toward the couple involves a sailor passionately kissing his "girl" in the midst of an indifferent crowd. But even here, as in Robert Doisneau's famed photograph "Le Baiser de l'hotel de ville," the circle formed by the embraced bodies in the midst of the crowd underscores the intimacy and spontaneity of the kiss.

The vignette of the secluded couple is the visual embodiment of what cultural historian Karen Lystra has dubbed the "romantic self." In her study of nineteenth-century love, Lystra shows that the ideal of the romantic self was a crucial component of individual self-realization and personal happiness.[10] Undoubtedly, the romantic icons of contemporary advertisements resonate with the nineteenth-century cultural ideal of the romantic self, but the mundane passion of material success has been replaced by the spectacle of leisurely consumption. In contradistinction to the nineteenth-century vision, the contemporary vision of secluded couplehood does not mean a retreat from the public sphere and an entry into the warmth of familial privacy. Rather, it signifies a complete withdrawal from the proceedings, rules, and constraints of the urban industrial world and an entry into the euphoric realm of leisure. Whereas during the nineteenth century the middle-class romantic self gave access to family stability, gender roles, and the elevated world of introspection, in contemporary culture the cultivation of the romantic self can release Dionysiac energies, geared toward living the present moment to its fullest. Numerous ads present romance as a realm of pure feeling, sensuality, and instantaneous pleasure, free of the friction and power struggles of real relationships and attained more by magic than by work.

Examples abound: "If you believe in one great love as many people do . . . then you should wear Jontue," or "If you've ever been kissed you already know the feeling of Cognac Hennessy." A tourism ad for Jamaica reads, "The realm of the Seven Senses, where all pleasures begin." An ad for champagne uses the theme of magic: "Find a moment. Make it magic. Uncork the Magic of Korbel." An ad for a man's cologne gives the simple but intense motto "Pure Attraction." An ad for Martell cognac invites us to "Pour two glasses of Martell Cognac: one for you and one for someone you love. Then proceed to kiss in whatever manner pleases you." An ad for Quebec mixes gastronomic hedonism with the excitement of falling in love: "Somewhere between the *salade d'endives* and the last spoonful of *mousse au chocolat,* we fell in love all over again." A clear picture of the ideal romance emerges from these slogans: romance offers the experience of intense feeling, uninhibited sensuality, instant gratification, spontaneous pleasure, fun, in highly aestheticized settings removed from everyday life. Romance has little place for values of self-control, effort, and compromise, which, according to advice literature and conventional wisdom, are necessary for a successful relationship as well. The pursuit of the romantic self no longer bases personal identity, male or female, on the effortful model of relationship or on the values of productive work in general.

According to the structuralist theory of culture, a cultural category finds its meaning in the relationships of difference it entertains with other cultural categories. In the realm of advertising, romance is opposed to the routine of everyday life and, more specifically, to work. This opposition transcends appeals to either gender and provides the key to understanding the category of romance in postmodern culture. It can be seen at work in numerous examples. In an ad for men's diamonds, a woman is shown kissing the man after she has given him a diamond ring. Both are dressed in business clothes, but the man's tie is untied, indicating either that they have finished their workday or that romantic passion undoes the constraints of the workplace. Further, the ad appeals equally to men and women in its reversal of stereotypical gender behavior (here, the women is active, the man the passive recipient).

The icon through which the opposition of romance and work is most effectively expressed, however, is that of travel. One ad, which can stand for many, shows a man and a woman smiling at each other with radiant faces as they sit on the terrace of a cafe behind which stands the famed Eiffel Tower. As Roland Barthes succinctly put it, the Eiffel Tower "belongs to the universal language of travel."[11] This symbol makes clear the couple's removal from their everyday life back in the United States and confers on their experience the beauty, prestige, and romance conventionally associated with the city of Paris. In an ad for Hyatt Hotels, which bills them as escape sites for romantic partners, a couple walks on a rope bridge, in the midst of luxuriant exotic vegetation. The caption on the bottom of the advertisement reads "Here's to long commutes, bad meetings, worse weather, and being as far away as possible from all of them." Because it is not clear whose voice, man's or woman's, is speaking, the ad in effect addresses men's and women's common desire to be away from the anonymous "them" of work. Another Hyatt ad, showing a couple dressed in elegant silk robes sipping from glasses of champagne, relaxing near a basket of orchids, reads, "Tomorrow Sunday brunch and then what? Whatever we feel like!" This ad, also geared equally to men and women, tries to sell "the Hyatt touch," a vague concept arousing vague feelings, the appeal of which comes from opposition to the workday world of constraints, control, and frustrations. Similarly, a number of advertising images show a couple dressed in elegant clothes, walking barefoot on the seashore or dipping their feet in a swimming pool. This cliché mixes the value of luxury with freedom from protocol, going barefoot adding a pinch of nonconformism and spontaneity. In another ad, *Money* magazine sells itself as an instrument for financial success by showing a stereotypical vignette of vacation: a man and a woman dressed in casual summer clothes are on a beach watching the sunset, a boat in the distance. The text of the advertisement reads, "Travel magazines tell people about places like this. We actually help them get there." Here again the ad is gender-neutral and—surprisingly for a magazine targeted primarily to the business world—includes both men and women in its promise for "life after work," a package deal encompassing romance, leisure, and travel.

With the "traveling couple" image, the search for different and intense experiences that has become such an intimate part of contemporary definitions of romance translates into visions of natural landscapes and exotic locales. The title of this section, "You Could Be Here, Now," exemplifies advertising's persistent invitation to bring the world of travel and exoticism to the here and now. The motto appears in an ad for Citibank showing a man and woman dressed in summer clothes walking under the bright light of the sun near a swimming pool. Gone are a bank's usual appeals to the cautious mentality of saving and future-oriented rationality to ensure domestic security. Instead, by enjoining people to be full consumers of leisure, travel, and romance, this ad suggests that we abandon the linear temporality of work and dip into an intense present of pleasure and leisure. An ad for Mexico (a rare case where the man and the woman are not involved in close physical contact) shows the naked torso of a man standing on the balcony of a hotel room furnished in rural Spanish style. Beyond the balcony appears a white stucco church, also in the Spanish style. A woman is sitting on the bed, in a nightgown, after what we presume was an intense scene of lovemaking. The text of the ad reads "Mérida, evening. At the window, as evening nears, you hear a faint guitar, a song of love floating in the breeze. And though you don't speak the language, on this night you know every word." By mixing travelogue style, romantic rhetoric, and the direct address characteristic of advertising propaganda, this text interweaves the foreign and the exotic with romantic clichés of love songs and the sensual languor of tropical countries, thus creating a highly aestheticized vignette in which the longing for exoticism and perfect leisure mixes with the sensuality of lovemaking. An ad for the British gin Beefeater shows a couple in bathing suits, the man sitting on the branch of a palm tree, the woman lying in a hammock attached to the same branch, both just above the sea. The ad reads, "There are 15 private islands for sale in the Caribbean. But there's only one Beefeater." Playing on a dream thought to be familiar to most American middle-class men and women, that of owning a private island, the ad mixes the fantasy of everlasting romance obtained through liberation from the constraints of productive work with fantasies of absolute private property (an island gives the illusion of complete sovereignty) and consummate individualism (Robinson Crusoe transformed into an eternal vacationer).

The double theme of travel and romance is so ubiquitous that it can be abstracted, reduced to a few key symbols, and still be understood. For example, a series of advertisements for Parliament cigarettes shows a couple standing amid monumental, blank, white geometrical forms that, despite representing no recognizable referent such as the Eiffel Tower or the Mérida cathedral, nonetheless successfully evoke exotic locales: vertical white columns for "Greece," a white pyramid for "Egypt," a low white cylinder for "Mediterranean" houses, just as the bare background of intense blue suggests generic Southern skies. These are highly stylized and quasi-abstract symbols of nonindustrialized, nonurban countries stereotypically associated with romance. The reduction of realistic scenery to minimalist geometrical forms, caricatures of exotic locales, suggests that advertising's clichés have become so well established that they, rather than the actual locales, can function as referents and objects of desire. (The sliding of meaning can be seen in another visual cliché, couples photographed in a magnified close-up with their shoulders naked. Because this image most often is used to sell sunglasses or has a beach in the background, naked shoulders become a sign of summer vacation rather than, as one might expect, of eroticism.)

These abstract symbols point to an essential aspect of these icons of romance: they are meant not to refer to specific times, places, or monuments but rather to evoke a generic space of travel and leisure. Analyzing the aesthetics of advertising, Michael Schudson argues that "abstraction is essential to the aesthetic and intention of contemporary national consumer-goods advertising. It does not represent reality nor does it build a fully fictive world. It exists, instead, on its own plane of reality, a plane I will call capitalist realism. By this term, I mean to label a set of aesthetic conventions, but I mean also to link them to the political economy whose values they celebrate and promote."[12] I would add to Schudson's statement that if abstraction is central to capitalist realism and, more specifically, to the advertising icons of romantic travel, that is because it transmutes complex symbols into collectively shared *utopias*.

More than any other romantic icon, the vacation image has a utopian significance, for as Ernst Bloch has argued, utopia describes an alternative, more desirable set of relationships in a different time and place.[13] Although produced by and for specific classes, vacations aim to transcend class boundaries. As in ritual holiday celebrations, during vacations social boundaries collapse as participants share relaxation and pleasure. Leisure time in general and vacation time especially (the epitome of leisure) contain dreams not only of freedom and affluence but also of authentic, uncoerced social bonds. Such a dream opens up a vision of sacred time, in which boundaries of past, present, and future are also suspended. As historian of leisure Gary Cross suggested, vacation is the "transcendence of modern industrial people for whom an afterlife [has] become less tangible."[14] As we shall now see, the alternative space and time of the romantic utopia are most completely expressed in the image of the natural landscape.

SUCH A NATURAL LOVE

At the heart of contemporary Western culture is the division between the "staged" self, enacting itself in the public sphere, and the "true" self, whose home is the private sphere of family, love, and emotions.[15] However, departing somewhat from this dichotomy, contemporary advertising suggests that the genuine and authentic romantic self is best revealed not in the private confines of the domestic sphere or in the crowded spaces of commercial entertainment but rather in the intermediary, liminal zone formed by leisure, travel, and nature.[16] Nature is the romantic decor par excellence because it is the only symbolic site that, by minimizing or eliminating references to social, family, or gender roles, enables the full expression of "pure" feelings and thereby releases the authentic self.

Natural landscapes constitute by far the most widespread visual syntagm in advertising images of romance. Thirty-one images out of the eighty in my sample are situated in natural settings, with twenty-two by a sea or lake and the rest in the woods or the countryside. The ideal-typical romantic moment occurs in a remote place, on an exotic island, near the sea, a dense forest, a serene lake—in short, in a space symbolically cut off from the industrial and urban world of work, offices, and business. The nature of advertising is not the nature of farmers or farm workers, however. Rather, its is signified through the conventions and iconography established by nineteenth-century landscape painting. The French iconographic tradition—which was so influential in modern iconography—encapsulated nature within codified "scenes" and tableaux and incorporated it into emerging forms of urban consumption. Nicholas Green, cultural historian of French nineteenth-century painting, observes that the nineteenth-century landscape painting is essentially a "private and domestic affair," an apt remark in relation to advertising. In this packaged nature, divided into recognizable vignettes, the viewer-buyer could contemplate the spectacle of a Nature at his own scale, readily available for gaze. In advertising imagery, the natural landscape is replete with residues of this nineteenth-century bourgeois ideology. Nature's seemingly untamed wilderness evokes Crusoe-like fantasies of sovereignty and mastery, yet also reflects the couple's feelings and allows the expression of their authentic selves. In this symbolic space, which negates the world of consumption and cities, the couple finds the "confirmation of self alongside the immersion of individuality into something larger."[17] This "something larger" opens up the possibility of a utopian vision of the romantic self in which nature functions not only as an alternative geographical space but also as a vehicle that transports the couple into utopian time, through two different modes of representation, the nostalgic and the sublime.

The aesthetic of nostalgia transports the viewer-consumer to the past through established codes that both signify the past and erase our distance from it. The nostalgic, as Frederic Jameson observed, approaches the present "by way of the pastiche of the stereotypical past, endows present reality and the openness of present history with the spell and distance of a glossy image."[18] Advertising's images are literally "glossy," and the stereotyped past they most often invoke is an imagined time before modernity. The "premodern" is realistically signified through clothes, a natural decor from which most or all references to technology have been erased, and a softness in the grain of the photography stereotypically associated with the "genteel" world of the nineteenth century. Drawing on the ideal of nature articulated by American artists, writers, poets, and philosophers of the nineteenth century, the pastoral utopia in advertising imagery, and in mainstream American culture in general, embodies values and ideals opposed to the decay brought about by technology, large urban centers, and the competitiveness of the workplace.[19] Roland Marchand has found this antimodern bias already present in advertising images of the 1920s, in what he called the "great parable of civilization redeemed," the idea that civilization is bad and that nature can save us from it.[20] Nature—and with it romantic love—is thus connected to what has been called an "anti-institutional self," which arose during the nineteenth century. As Lystra has suggested, "Though variously expressed, nineteenth-century lovers utilized an 'anti-role' concept of the self to stress that the truest portion of their personal identity was concealed by social conventions. This sense of a hidden, but purer individual essence is the basis of the 'romantic self.'"[21] This cultural theme, mixing authenticity and isolation, emerged in the second half of the nineteenth century. As Ellen Rothman and Elizabeth McKinsey have documented, around 1870 newlywed couples began to shun the traditional honeymoon visits to family and community and were increasingly isolating themselves in grandiose natural settings like Niagara Falls.[22] "The nineteenth century American middle-class concept of intimacy was an ideal of the fullest, most natural self-expression. . . . This most often involved an attempt by both parties to unmask, to abandon all outward forms of propriety, and to shed all normative social roles except the romantic self."[23] Formerly, this bourgeois notion of romantic love was tied to the domestic sphere of the home. The contemporary vision of romance, however, strips its participants of any clearly defined social role and setting by placing them in the liminal zone of nature. It does not stress female and male identities and their respective gender roles but blurs and fuses them in a common, genderless sphere of leisure in which pure attraction and emotion reign.

The evocation of a lost world of nature and love is meant to redeem the self from its fall not only into modern artificiality but into a kind of weightlessness, restoring to the gestures and intimacy between men and women the seriousness and consequence they seemed to have in the Victorian era, whose social distance and reserve lent romance an exciting aura of transgression. By metonymy, moreover, the nostalgic mode elevates consumption as well, into something denser and more profound. Nostalgia reverts to the past and to the precious scarcity of goods to imbue objects with a value and a uniqueness that have disappeared but that, as the ad images imply, can be resuscitated, phoenixlike, by consuming it in the circumstances displayed. In these images, nature functions less as a spatial than as a temporal signifier, through which the (mythical) uniqueness and density of premodern consumption are regained and projected onto the present. Thus, the nostalgic mode telescopes past and present or, more exactly, evokes the past as a means of breaching and transfiguring the present.

The nostalgic image of nature is used by advertisers to promote a vision of consumption that euphemistically denies the very nature of the world that makes consumption possible. Through advertising, this ideal of nature was sanctified by the very corporate order that actually destroyed it. Where productive work demands the systematic control or destruction of nature and the increasing regimentation and conformity of the self, the image of nature in contemporary advertising claims that consumption is a means to regain access to lost treasures, authentic self, genuine relationships, and a benevolent, majestically beautiful nature. Antimodernism and the nostalgia for a lost paradise of nature and truth are indeed leading themes of the culture of capitalism and are amplified by their obsessive association with the theme of romance and leisure.[24]

The other aesthetic mode of representation transporting romance and nature into a utopian time is that of the sublime. The sublime, according to Burke and Kant, expressed the overpowering, even terrifying face of nature, evoking a feeling of awe and wonder that brought representation itself to its limit.[25] The romantic movement, which dominated American landscape painting in the nineteenth century, advocated an intellectual and aesthetic sensibility sympathetic to the sublime in nature.[26] Artists found in the sublime the basis for a cult of nature that could mix their nostalgic reaction against modernity (whose scientific rationality, technological progress, and industrial capitalism were destroying nature) with the new desire to represent nature as a maelstrom of powerful emotions.

In the nineteenth century, the sublime was found primarily in mountainous landscapes, and thus it survives today primarily in tourist ads showing such wonders as the Alps or the Andes, or Hawaiian waterfalls. However, other landscapes, more conducive to leisure and romance, have been endowed with a quality of the sublime, namely, an association with the ineffable and pure intensity of feeling. The beach, by far the most widely pervasive natural setting for romance, can serve as the paradigmatic example. At the heart of the notion of the sublime, Fredric Jameson has said, is the idea of the unspeakable, a natural power and a corresponding emotional response that transcend attempts to communicate them.[27] On the beach of romantic ads, solitude and silence, the removal of the couple from the noise and distraction of other people, convey this idea. While the beach is primarily a construct of the tourist industry, in advertising it is detached from the crowded and highly commercialized vacation resorts. In fact, in advertisements beaches are invariably deserted. The couples in such ads are absorbed in an intense gaze of nature as well as in each other, and the feelings their image evokes have a corresponding, ineffable weight and profundity.

The time to which these utopian visions of romance and nature appeal does not open up on the linear future of messianic utopias; rather, it is a mixture of three temporal categories: the past of our lost authenticity, the eternal present of intensity (and consumption), and the atemporality of the sacred. The abstract, generic spaces and symbols of nature and travel settings interweave categories of the past that are transfigured through the nostalgic, the eternal present of the sublime, and the sacred atemporality of leisure. According to Jean-François Lyotard, this blend of heterogeneous times defines the postmodern, characterized by one commentator as a "perpetual present tense within which human beings have always lived at all times and in all places, pinioned forever between a disintegrating, irrecoverable, half-remembered past and an always uncertain future."[28] Unlike "classical" utopias, the romantic utopia of advertising does not offer a narrative of progress, but instead implodes different temporalities within the category of "romantic intensities."[29]

ROMANCE AS INVISIBLE AFFLUENCE

The postmodern is not only an aesthetic category but also a way of representing and making sense of social relations. What then are these social relations? What is the social meaning of such images?

If one compares cursorily the 1900–1930 sample of advertising images to the sample from 1989–1991, two main differences appear. First,
the ostentatious display of luxury that had characterized the earlier period has considerably decreased and been replaced by the visual themes
of leisure and nature. Second, whereas during the first decades of the
century it was very easy to distinguish married couples from courting
ones, in the contemporary sample only discreet clues like wedding rings
signal the couple's marital status. In other words, the visual representation of marriage has become euphemized (usually avoiding the depiction
of daily life), and the attributes of marriage have increasingly been subsumed under those of flirtation and relaxation.

Even when romance is associated with the visual display of luxury, it
is often presented under casual circumstances of informality, spontaneity, and intimacy that defuse one customary function of luxury, namely,
the affirmation of social power. For example, an advertisement for an
expensive china shows a married couple, with suggestively naked shoulders, lying in bed under their blankets, about to eat a copious breakfast
on their china. The formality of elegance is subsumed by intimacy and
what we presume to be the leisurely pace of a breakfast in bed. Given
the seductive, effective association of romance with opulence in the history of advertising, the question arises, why has the theme of luxury
become underplayed while the theme of nature has become so overwhelmingly dominant? Why is the image of the isolated beach so prominent in contemporary advertising images of romance?

I submit that, unlike the theme of luxury, the themes of nature, isolation, simplicity, exoticism, and romantic intimacy are class-free and
gender-free.[30] Since the 1930s, romance has moved from an association
with the glamorous image of elegance and wealth to an association with
a classless image of nature. Already by the nineteenth century, the image of nature was becoming hegemonic because it encompassed diverse
social groups and transcended social divisions and distinctions.[31] Nature, like romance, leisure, and isolation, blurs and transcends social
boundaries because it resuscitates the buried authenticity of a primitive
self and addresses what is presumably our universal common denomi-
nator of humanity.

Nature, and the cluster of symbolic meanings attached to it (simplicity, authenticity, and freedom), harmonizes two utopian visions, one offering relationships free of social and gender inequalities and the other
an easy abundance of time and affluence. The first is a utopia of pastoral
simplicity, authenticity, and intimacy, which addresses the "truest" part

of ourselves and thus transcends consumption and society itself. The second is a utopia of leisure in which man and woman merge their identities and experience a sensuous pleasure and freedom that takes them out of the discipline and hierarchies of the workplace. The theme of nature can symbolically mediate and merge these two motifs, however, because nature signifies not only an ideal space and time beyond consumption but also the very real privileges of those with the resources of money and leisure time necessary to enjoy its landscapes. Congruent with the populist, inclusive aesthetic of postmodernism, the image of leisure and the syntagm of romance and nature that underlies it promote consumption as a universal and all-inclusive idiom that embraces and blurs differences, and yet consumption is the motor of the economic and class system from which these differences arise.[32] This simultaneous denial and affirmation of consumption is at the heart of the utopian dimension of romance in postmodern culture, as is most apparent in the images of travel and tourism that abound in the world of advertising.

Tourism is the most intensely commodified realm of leisure. On the consumers' side, it usually demands significant amounts of disposable income and time. On the producers' side, it presupposes an intensive exploitation of the landscape and its transformation into a commercial zone that can serve tourists' needs and desires. Tourism demands that natural landscapes, ethnic groups, or cities be organized—geographically and symbolically—to fit commercial exploitation (the "travel package"). The landscape is classified and parceled out into units ready to be integrated into the commercial network of tour operators and travel agencies. The economic exploitation of nature and local cultures is achieved when they are transformed into objects for the "gaze," into an iconography saturated with meanings that can be sold by the tourist industry: the deserted beach for the couple's intimate seclusion, the exotic locale for adventure and intensity, the playful dip into the luxury swimming pool for romantic relaxation.[33] In tourism and in romance alike, the boundary between the sign, the commodity, and the referent becomes tenuous or disappears altogether. These images are simulacra, stereotyped copies that have no originals. Presumably, tourists who purchase these packages don't want real adventure, with its attendant risks and discomforts (if they did, they wouldn't purchase packages); they want to experience themselves within a safe, prefabricated image that the tourist industry has implicitly labeled "adventure." The sign—the image—becomes the commodity it is intended to sell.

Almost by definition, leisure has overtones of classlessness and afflu-ence. The "right to leisure" started as one of the most important social demands made by workers during the 1920s.[34] As a result of the strug-gles of workers, their wages expanded considerably, and leisure time was generalized to all segments of society. Leisure has since then come to sym-bolize a classless utopia, both in the sense that it speaks to and includes all social classes and in the sense that it promises the abolition of social divisions.[35] However, since World War II and especially since the 1960s, leisure has expanded to such an extent that it has come to be one of the defining characteristics of late capitalism. The spectacular expansion of domestic and international tourism, popular culture, and the mass media—all selling leisure products—displays one of the most dramatic transformations of our economy and culture: the move of the capitalist system from the exploitation and management of natural resources to a "service economy" of intangible products and multinational corpora-tions. To this extent, the inscription of romance into leisure naturalizes these changes and offers the icon par excellence of the economy and cul-ture of late capitalism.

Leisure is distinctly postmodern in yet another respect. It has be-come the distinctive attribute of the new service class (also called "new petty bourgeoisie," "new cultural intermediaries," or more popularly, "yuppies"). According to British sociologist Scott Lash,[36] these fast-growing "new middle classes" are the outcome of the growth of the service sector of the economy. They are located in communications ser-vices (media, advertising), information technologies (computer pro-gramming), and international finance. These new classes are the pro-ducers and the primary audiences of postmodern culture, which in turn legitimates and promotes their interests. Although they have substan-tial amounts of educational and economic capital, these new classes cultivate a rhetoric of opposition, subversion, and difference. This helps explain why contemporary advertising images presuppose afflu-ence and yet betray a longing for a classless pastoral frugality and a pure expression of intense feelings.

As Bourdieu argues, this group, which he calls "new cultural inter-mediaries," mixes contradictory exigencies: its members lack cultural capital and are socially insecure, yet aspire to cultural legitimacy.[37] They are relatively well placed in mainstream firms and institutions yet culti-vate self-expression, adventure, and spontaneity incompatible with the hierarchical order and ethos of middle-class workplaces. They are inte-grated into the work force, yet search for new and intense experiences and are obsessed with appearance, identity, and self. Leisure has become an important sphere for expressing and reconciling these contradictory tendencies: in leisure, the new petty bourgeoisie can aspire to cultural capital through the consumption of tourism (in historical sites, in exotic cultures) and express their consumer identity (e.g., hotels, restaurants, night-clubs, car rentals) yet cultivate the appearance of individualism, self-identity, pastorality, and spontaneity. This contradictory ethos is all the more exploited by advertisers in that it helps them euphemize, yet promote, consumption.

The prevalence of images of nature and, more specifically, of deserted beaches can be explained in terms of the ethos of this new class. The deserted beach is a liminal space that inverts the values of work and celebrates the wholesomeness of a fully recovered individualism, yet it presupposes the rental-car agencies, shopping areas, cafes, and restaurants that are now appendages of most beach resorts. The deserted beach is a consummate rhetorical inversion of the world of service employees. The beach and the sun are visual and sensory inversions of the world of offices, which demand tight bodily control, clothing and manners governed by etiquette, delicate and controlled management of one's and others' feelings, bodily inactivity, and seclusion from the open air and the sun. On the other hand, on the beach clothing is close to nakedness, yet concerns about appearance and beauty are paramount, for the semi-naked body is supposed to show the signs of good care, good health, and good shape that are part of the "fitness" ethos of the new bourgeoisie. In this equation of leisure, romance plays the role of making the public expression of the self more informal at the same time that it binds the self to the private sphere and puts feelings and self-disclosure at the center of this paradise regained.

But the beach is also an ideal type of what political economist Fred Hirsh calls a "positional good," the value of which derives from its scarcity and thereby depends on the number of people who want to consume it.[38] That is, the enjoyment one gets from the good depends on the monopoly one has over it. A natural landscape falls under the condition Hirsh calls "objective scarcity": the greater the number of people who consume the landscape, the less one particular individual will be able to enjoy it. If scarcity entails economic value, then the ability to secure a private, secluded portion of the natural landscape carries cultural as well as economic payoffs: the elitist affirmation of individuality, accentuated by the prestige derived from the possession or use of a scarce commodity. Thus, capitalism has appropriated and destroyed not only the

natural landscape but precisely the ability to enjoy a landscape uncontaminated by the visible hand of capital, the intensive exploitation characteristic of tourist resorts. Advertising images of romance hence paradoxically affirm the very economic values that have been made scarce
and thereby costly by capitalism at the same time that they deny the presence of money and commodities. The most romantic landscape is inci-
dentally also the most expensive, at least in terms of its travel costs: it is
primarily "wild," that is, far away from the industrial world, and isolated, that is, uncontaminated by capital and the presence of
working-class or middle-class vacationers.

But why is this vision of wildness primarily carried out by couples?
Part of the explanation has to do with contemporary economic stratification. Despite the upsurge in single-headed households for the past two
decades, the best way for most people to reach a relatively affluent
lifestyle is to establish a dual-income family.[39] It should therefore come
as no surprise that advertising privileges the representation of the
couple, since in late capitalist social structure marriage is a key element
of social mobility and the main unit of consumption.

The power of the romantic utopia resides in its Janus-like ability to
affirm the values of late capitalism and at the same time to invert them
into symbols of primitive simplicity and pure emotionality. The postmodern romantic utopia contains the classless dream of leisure and
authenticity at the same time that it affirms new class divisions and
class identities. According to Ernst Bloch, false consciousness alone
cannot explain the pervasiveness and persistence of certain cultural
themes. There remains a "surplus," which is the "hope" contained in
utopias.[40] Utopia erases contradictions and presents the spectacle of
fulfilled humanity, not by the transcendence but by the denial of current social relationships. The romantic utopia draws on symbols of
the good life, at one and the same time embodying and denying the
values of capitalism. This double-sided aspect of the romantic utopia
can be understood in terms of the sociological properties of postmodern culture at large.

Scott Lash proposes a useful dichotomy between two forms of postmodernism, one mainstream and the other oppositional.[41] The first does
not pose any challenge to bourgeois identity and in fact recenters the
subject on consumption, fixed identity, and cultural hierarchies. The second tries to break down boundaries and to question traditional anchor
points of representation and identity. The romantic utopia incorporates
and fuses the rhetoric of the oppositional and all-inclusive form of post-

modernism, while legitimating the bourgeois consumer ethos and the identity of the new middle classes.

CODES ARE GETTING TIRED

To claim that these postmodern themes are utopian may sound incongruous; postmodernism is notoriously anti-utopian.[42] Utopia presupposes the projection of self and community in a rational narrative of liberation and progress, whereas the utopia of advertising plays on semiconscious, individualist daytime reveries of love and power and bears the fragmentary character of night dreams. The romantic utopia abolishes the classical distance between commodities and aesthetics, signs and reality, sentiments and spectacle. As Jean Baudrillard has argued, signs, and only signs, are now at the center stage of capitalist production and consumption.[43] Furthermore, the romantic utopia has bid farewell to the coherent, goal-oriented, and rational subjectivity that once dominated industrial capitalism as well as the collective utopias that opposed it. Evading the traditional unity of narrative discourse, the romantic utopia offers a collage of disjointed images whose sole unity is the triumphant expression of desires. The question then arises whether advertising images of love articulate a utopia in which identity can be coherently articulated, or do they point to the fragmentation and implosion of postmodern identity. What does the relentless visual obsession of our culture with love, leisure, and nature do to the constitution of a romantic utopian imagination? The remainder of this chapter and the following two chapters address these questions empirically.

In his sweeping analysis of early twentieth-century advertising, Roland Marchand suggests that advertising plays an important role in shaping the content of the imagination. "To the extent that individual daydreams are shaped by an available vocabulary of familiar images, the clichés of popular art of an era, particularly if they are dramatically and repeatedly paraded before the public eye, may induce individuals to recapitulate in their own fantasies some aspects of the daydream of the society. By the 1920s in the United States, advertising had become a prolific producer of visual images with normative overtones, a contributor to the society's shared daydreams."[44]

In moving from an analysis of images to an analysis of respondents' visual imaginations, I do not intend to explore how their interpretations fit or deviate from the meanings advertisers intended their ads to convey. Individuals do not merely interpret cultural texts but organize their experience around them. As Leiss cogently put it, "it is by means of the iconic representations that marketing seeks to provide the points of coherence around which consumers can organize social experience into meaningful patterns."[45] The question is whether these images provide such points of coherence and reference for my respondents.

Respondents were presented a series of photographs and advertising pictures of various couples. Three sets of photographs were used: the first set contrasts a well-known photograph by Walker Evans of a family during the Depression (figure 6; not reproduced) with a photograph of a richly dressed couple, who are smiling and ostensibly happy (see figure 5 in appendix 3). The second set consists of four pictures featuring couples in different settings and romantic poses (see figures 1, 2, 3, and 4 in appendix 3; three of these pictures were advertisements; one was an illustration for an article published in a women's magazine). The third set consists of three black-and-white photographs of couples, of different ages, involved in various poses of physical intimacy (figures 7, 8, and 9; see the note to appendix 2 for descriptions).

The respondents were asked to choose the most romantic picture among several and to justify their choices. In trying to understand why respondents interpreted a picture as romantic, I established a number of categories on which they may have based their interpretations: geographical (i.e., the setting: urban versus natural; street versus home etc.); proxemic (in close embrace versus distant); atmospheric (fun versus solemn, peaceful versus "noisy," etc.,); consumerist (rich objects versus frugal); sexual (provocative versus modest); facial (happy versus solemn or gloomy); pictorial (soft focus versus hard focus; close-up versus long shot, etc.); and activity (cooking, eating, rowing, etc.).

Respondents used *all* of these categories to identify and classify romantic pictures. Some categories, however, seemed to be more salient than others. The most relevant categories were (in their order of importance) the geographical, the atmospheric, and the facial. That the sexual and gestural codes proved less relevant to these evaluations of pictures as romantic was, to say the least, surprising.

When asked to compare figure 5 and and the Walker Evans photo, most respondents chose the picture with the rich, happy, and glamorous couple. But when asked to choose the more loving couple, many respondents switched their choices to the picture of the poor and gloomy family (see next chapter for more on this). Similarly, when respondents were shown the third set of images, many of them chose the young couple kissing in the street (Doisneau's photograph) as the most romantic, and figure 8 (couple sitting in the cafe) as the most expressive of love. A majority of my respondents clearly held two separate visual constructs for these two feelings. Romance was more often inferred from atmospheric signs created by the youth, elegance, and external signs of happiness and relaxation. Visual signs of romance were typically associated with such feelings as spontaneity, ease, excitement, and happiness. The visual signs of love, however, were associated with endurance, solidarity, and stability. The meaning of "romantic" did not always coincide with that of love, for, on the one hand, the former was associated with atmospheric signs of wealth, youth, happiness, and glamour. Love on the other hand was constructed as an enduring and intimate bond transcending the highly aestheticized cultural category of the romantic.

Among the four advertising pictures, figure 3 (row-boat on the lake) emerged by far as the most romantic picture, followed by figure 1 (restaurant) and figure 4 (dinner at home). Figure 2 (man kneeling in the street) was not chosen as romantic by any of the respondents. Significantly, this picture is the only one of the four that is *not* an advertising picture. In fact, the respondents' unanimity that figure 2 is not romantic was so blatant that it shed light on the cultural significance of what is romantic. In contrast to the other pictures, the meaning of figure 2 was often viewed as unclear. Many respondents were baffled by the couple's pose, wondered whether the man dominates the woman or the other way around, why the woman is dressed in a leopard-skin dress, and why they are in the street.

What about 2? Why is it less romantic than 4?

2 is more, uh, it does not strike me that the two of them are in love. It looks more like going out, she is dressed very sensually and I don't really understand what she is doing there (laugh), he is kneeling, there is a police car, it is kind of a strange picture. (Female lawyer, interview 23)

That's just perverse. A person kneeling on the street and the guy has the coat on the street and who knows what the woman is up to. And the police car in the back, God knows what they are doing. (Male Ph.D. student, interview 24)

Why is 2 less romantic?

It's out, it's out in the street. There is nothing romantic about that. It's noise and everything. (Female security officer, interview 37)

Figure 2 is not romantic primarily because it does not offer ready-to-be-interpreted *atmospheric* signs of romance. For my respondents, the sensuality of the dress, the provocative pose of the man kneeling in the middle of the street, the "noise," and the police car in the background convey meanings of rawness and crudity discrepant with the gentle intimacy and tranquility conventionally associated with images of romance.

The division between the unromantic and the romantic revolves around a broad division between "male" and "female" spheres. The adjectives used most frequently by my respondents to describe the images they chose as romantic were stereotypically feminine: "nice," "intimate," "quiet," "peaceful," "comfortable," "spontaneous," "serene," "sweet," "gentle." These lexical choices confirm Francesca Cancian's claim that romantic love has become "feminized."[46] In opposition to the chivalric ideal of courtship, which aimed at perfecting a male spirit of valor and ascetic heroism, respondents drew on a cultural ideal in which the distinction between masculine and feminine spheres is blurred and traditional male attributes are subordinated to the feminine sphere. To be romantic, men are required to (temporarily) give up their emotional control and assertive authority and switch to qualities of "openness," "gentleness," and "care." Women are simply required to remain what they "naturally" are. Thus, as suggested earlier, the image of romance neutralizes gender differences by drawing men and women into the female sphere of sentiments.

In sharp contrast with figure 2, figure 3 was chosen as "most romantic" by many respondents and was recognized as "romantic" and even "typically romantic" by all respondents. (Figures 1 and 4 were also frequently identified as romantic but were almost never called *typically* romantic.) The single most often-stated reason for choosing figure 3 as romantic was the seclusion of the lovers:

Why did you choose picture 3?

Well, because there's a solitude, the two people sharing time and thoughts together and in one secluded spot away from the rest of the world, when I love someone I want these times where I can be away. . . .

But why, for example, is 4 less romantic to you?

I mean it's fun, they're getting together and enjoying . . . having some laughs, and share an evening, but there is just something about the whole appeal of the scene that makes 3 more, uh, like I said the solitude of 3 really strikes me in the heart.

What about 2, now, why is it less romantic than 1?

I don't think I am that kind of person in public. (Male doorman, interview 11)

Many respondents further justified their choices in terms of the setting and invoked the fact that figure 3 is "in nature." The soft focus and pastel colors of the picture induced respondents to view it as "quiet," "peaceful," and "serene." For example, in explaining why she preferred it, one respondent commented:

> . . . and I guess maybe because it's simpler, and I tend to like things simpler than 4, 1, and 2, which are very extravagant, because people are all dressed up and in fancy, 1 is in a fancy restaurant and I think 3 goes more with my personality where I like the country, I like simple things, things like a fancy dinner don't impress me, it's very easy to take somebody to a fancy dinner, but to think of something like this, to go for a rowboat ride, to me is much more unique and much more special. So I guess that's why it's more romantic. (Female university professor, interview 19)

This woman drew on the cultural repertoire of the pastoral utopia and evoked simplicity and authenticity as the core meanings of romanticism. It is noteworthy that when contrasted with nature, luxury was not perceived by respondents as a pertinent or salient feature of romance. Quite the contrary; luxury items were often perceived as "fake" and deliberate manipulations of their feelings by advertisers. On the other hand, when explicitly contrasted to poverty, luxury did function as a sign of romance. Because romance presupposes and demands "distance from necessity," it is closer to images of luxury than to images of poverty. But it demands that this distance be euphemized by the ethereal goods of the postmodern market: nature, silence, solitude, leisure, and travel are the "spiritual" assets demanded by the typical practice of romance.

Furthermore, these meanings helped some of the respondents recapitulate their experiences and romantic dreams. Two examples illustrate this.

Can you tell me a very romantic moment you have experienced recently?

Let's see. I would say the first that comes to my mind, walking along the beach, we happen to be in Mexico, in a foreign country, on vacation. Just the two of us taking a walk and talking, just feeling close and enjoying the time we had together.

What was romantic about that moment?

Just like being a thousand miles away from home in our little, almost kind of fantasy world. Real world seemed so far away, so we were just in our paradise almost. And there was a certain intimacy about being there and being in that type of setting. (Male corporate banker, interview 20)

What was the most romantic moment you have had?

I had dinner with a girlfriend when I was living in Paris. My girlfriend came over to Paris and we had dinner at the top of the Eiffel Tower. I gave her a ring.

What was romantic about that moment?

The setting was overlooking Paris, and the Eiffel Tower. I was about to travel around the world so I had another six or seven months to go, I wasn't going to be seeing her for a while so this was our last evening together, because we broke up but that's separate. I think it was, uh, conceived of to be romantic and it was, it was conceived of "this would be a wonderful thing to do." (Male actor, interview 29)

These two respondents recapitulated their experiences using the same highly aestheticized vignettes that advertising imagery has codified. That the trip to Mexico is even referred to as a "fantasy world" indicates that the respondent perceived this experience in the mode of "unreality" precisely because it reenacted the codified aestheticized properties of the romantic utopia. This fantasy world recaptures the vision of romance continuously paraded in advertising: it is secluded, located in a foreign and exotic country; the couple are walking along the beach and reenacting a feeling of paradise regained. The second example is similarly filled with the visual props of the Parisian vignette of romance. In fact, the respondent himself suggested that he experienced the moment as romantic because "it was conceived of to be romantic and it was." These moments are experienced and remembered as intense because they crystallize "romance" in a few key symbols and images, which in turn condense the fantasies and scenarios of consumer culture. Meanings of romance are experienced intensely because they are intensely recognized.

Paradoxically, it is precisely because these vignettes have so widely infiltrated our imaginations that their time-honored capacity to constitute identity has become uncertain. At the same time that figure 3 has the uncontested status of the "typical" or "true" image of romance, it also appears, at least to some of the respondents, as its most fake and meaningless representation. Here an interesting class difference appeared: Although it was identified by almost all respondents as "the typically romantic" picture, upper-middle-class respondents more often chose figures 1 or 4 as romantic and rejected figure 3, precisely on the ground that it was too obviously romantic. On the other hand, working-class people unreservedly viewed figure 3 as the "true romantic picture," and were the most likely to subscribe, uncritically, to its utopian meanings. The postmodern romantic utopia, which mixes a rhetoric of classlessness and the ethos of the new postindustrial bourgeoisie, is more readily espoused by working-class respondents than by their more educated and more affluent counterparts. As I show in chapter 8 this difference is explained by the fact the most educated respondents cultivate an ironic, deconstructive distance from the signs and codes of mass culture.[47] For example, evaluating figure 3, one respondent said:

> The rowboat is very Hallmark card, it could be on a Hallmark card of two people hugging, you could put yourself in the situation but I mean I just think it's just an overused image of two people in a rowboat, you know, the guy rowing all the time and the girl kind of thing, you know it's hard to relate to it as something real, as a cliché. (Female artist, interview 13)

Another female respondent, also highly endowed with cultural capital, voiced similar reservations about the picture:

> That's very romantic too. That's very stereotypically, for example, if you read like [inaudible], you see people out in the rowboat, that's very stereotypical, I mean I bet if you asked somebody "what do you think would be a romantic thing to do?" they would say "go out on a lake in a rowboat" and I agree with that but I also think there is something nice about just being able to be where you are, without nothing special around you and be very close to somebody. (Female lawyer, interview 12)

The difficulty in assigning "real" referents to these images, and the tendency to view them as empty signs fabricated for the sake of profit, corroborate Baudrillard's diagnosis that in the postmodern age people are aware of the "simulations" of mass media and have become nihilistic because signs have become meaningless. According to postmodern sociologists, the cacophony of signs created by media technologies offers flat, depthless meanings that convey pure "noise without referent and meaning."[48] Echoing this nihilistic view of meaning, some of the middle- and upper-middle-class respondents in my study often suspected that media images of romance were simulations rather than representations of their experiences.

Where do you think your ideas of love come from?

Multiple sources, obviously movies and books. From personal experience, from friends' experiences, and from a little bit of reading. (Male physician, interview 14)

Do you think that a pornographic movie or picture is romantic?

No, because in my mind romance is this kind of fantasy-like concept, of the boy in boat with the girl, it's a fantasy of dinner with candlelight in an expensive French restaurant.

Where do you think your ideas of love come from?

Probably more from my parents than anything else, I just think that for most people that's the first example you sort of incorporate, your fears about what it will be like or your hopes for something different, or something like that. And a large part I guess from media and from myths about love.

Which myths?

Oh, the myth about happily ever after and the myth of being swept off your feet, the myth you know, I think the most dangerous myth for women finding a man or being attached to a man somehow is, is so terribly important in order to make your life all right or something, I think those are very powerful for most people whether they think about it or even know it. I think those are probably the most powerful things, and I'm sure for me too even though I have thought about it a lot. Some of my ideas are from not wanting what my parents what my parents had and I guess mostly just from those *images that you see in the media and that you see your friends all trying to live up to, probably the most influential things.* (Female editor, interview 48; emphasis added)

This woman, like many of her educated counterparts in my sample, expressed the feeling that her experience is derealized, a simulacrum of empty and media-fabricated images. For example, the thirty-year-old male doctor quoted above preferred to go hiking rather than go to a restaurant because, he said,

The interactions are going to be more genuine, like "do you watch your cholesterol?" I mean the kind of topics that would come up over dinner . . . or "what a wonderful movie! Didn't you like the way Fellini directed?" and that sort of artistic bullshit, it's not very. (Male doctor, interview 8)

The choice of words such as "more genuine" and "artistic bullshit" points to the fact that this man feels as unreal precisely what he also feels are the "artistic" (in my terminology, "aestheticized") elements of the romantic interaction. Although my respondents' experiences were structured by the same codes used by advertisers to construct their images, the same respondents also perceived these codes as unreal and fabricated, extrinsic to the fabric of their lives. These reactions potently illustrate the postmodern perception that reality and its representations have been substituted for one another, and this postmodern sensibility is seen most clearly in the experience of those groups most concerned with the manipulation of signs, linguistic or visual, namely, the new service class. Members of this class are both the most vocal critics of these images and the people most likely to use the same images to re-capitulate their romantic experiences. People who declare themselves the most aware of and immune to the false and unreal icons of media imagery are also most likely to use these icons as the poles of meaning around which their own experiences are organized and condensed (see chapter 8).

However, romance retains some aspects of the process of meaning-making and identity-making of "modernity" and to this extent qualifies for the status of utopia. My work casts doubt on the postmodern claim that media images implode the traditional anchors of identity formation and cor-roborates Douglas Kellner's conclusion: "Against the postmodern notion of culture disintegrating into pure image without referent or content or ef-fects—becoming at its limit pure noise—I would argue that television and other forms of mass-mediated culture play key roles in the structuring of contemporary identity."[49] This, I argue, is especially true for the working-class respondents but also, to a certain, albeit more ambiguous, extent for the educated respondents as well. Here, for example, is a professional man struggling between the meaning and the meaninglessness of figure 3:

> You look at this picture and you say, "Isn't that what romance is about?" Yet I would never experience that kind of romance, so therefore I feel it's phony.
>
> *Even though you wouldn't experience it, you were still able to say that this is a romantic picture?*
>
> Yes. All the pictures are somewhat romantic, the serene beauty in the, the big beautiful lake, sunset and all the like. . . .
>   It is almost as if there is romance and that I should be experiencing it but I am not. And that there is this true version of that boy and girl [in the boat, in figure 3] and there is this warmth and intimacy in romance and all of that I don't experience.
>
> *Would you like to?*
>
> Yes, I think I'd like to. Because it looks like so much fun. (Male doctor, interview 8)

Later in the interview, this man related the images to his own experiences of romance:

> The picture of the boy and girl in the cafe, giggling, that I have experienced, like laughing, and that can be happy and fun and romantic but the serene beauty, in the, uh, the uh, beautiful lake, sunset and all the like. What I usually do is go out on a boat canoeing, go rowing in Central Park but it's, uh, we would go canoeing in the Delaware, it's fun if you do it with somebody you really like, it could be romantic. To me that picture [figure 3] is a little too, uh, for me.

This man's response warrants special attention because it illustrates the uncertainty whether these images connect in some way with elements constitutive of his romantic identity. He moved uncomfortably between acknowledging that these images exerted a certain power of fascination over him—that "canoeing on the Delaware could be romantic"—and emptying the images of their romantic meaning and interpreting them as hollow clichés, signifiers without any referents. Like many other educated respondents, this man viewed the stereotypical image of romance as an empty signifier. Paradoxically, he also acknowledged that it exerted a binding power over his imagination that he wished would fill the content of his experience.

CONCLUSION

The analysis of advertising ought not to make the images of the type analyzed here deliver more than they can. In and of themselves, these images cannot inform us of the extent to which the romantic utopia is a sheer fabrication by advertisers or a residue of already existing cultural symbols and traditions. Nor can it inform us of processes of meaning-making in people's experiences. Undoubtedly, *some* of the meanings prominent in these images are reincarnations of meanings embedded in older cultural and pictorial traditions, for example, the image of nature and its pastoral associations. By the same token, other meanings, such as a soft eroticism allied with hedonism or a visual association of love with glamour, have been, if not created ex nihilo, at least codified, used, and relentlessly paraded by advertisers.

But these images can tell us something about the way romance is represented in postmodern culture. Because the vocation of advertising is to transmute commodity into meaning and to ferry the world of objects into our inner self, it is a privileged site to understand how postmodern romance gives voice to a new language of commodities. This language both euphemizes and denies the world of objects, presenting them through visual themes of leisure, nature, exoticism, adventure, vacation, travel, and the refusal of the urban world of production and exchange. In the romantic utopia, the material world of commodities and luxuries has vanished. Instead, it is replaced by a discreet and ethereal affluence that subtly addresses "universal" and classless desires for authenticity, freedom, and pure emotion. Love, like consumption, is destined to all and in this sense purports to offer a radically classless and genderless face. In this promise of an ecumenical project to overcome the divisions of social structure, the market-based romantic utopia articulates what Lash and Urry and many others deem to be central to postmodern culture, namely, "something importantly classless."[50] Advertising's utopia of leisure telescopes different layers of historical time into highly aesthetic images of romance. Opposing the values of work discipline, it affirms the expression of the body and of sexual energy and consecrates the playful and organic fusion of personal bonds. But at the same time that these images offer a rhetoric free of class and gender antagonisms, under the cover of pastoral simplicity, a Crusoe-like individualism, and the cult of pure emotions, they promote a postmodern ethos of affluence and social distinctions. As I show in the next chapter, these contradictory meanings articulate another important cultural idiom of the postmodern sphere of leisure, that of liminality.

CHAPTER 4

An All-Consuming Love

Florists turn feelings into flowers.
Advertisement for flowers

The founding fathers of sociology assumed that if human relationships are to retain their meaning, they must be kept separate from the sphere of economic exchange. It has since become one of the clichés of sociological thought that the triumph of capitalism has led to the collapse of religion and that consequently industrial societies are plagued by a chronic crisis of meaning. If we follow this thinking, the preceding analysis apparently leads to diagnosing the modern experience of love as undermined by money and commodities.

Postmodern social theorists have also argued that coherent and homogeneous meanings have fled the texture of everyday life; but in contrast with classical social theorists, they view the collapse of old overarching systems as salutary, for it has unleashed the desires of a pleasure-seeking subject. Postmodern theorists thus rehabilitate all that in classical social theory was deemed to "pollute" culture and social relationships: commodities, mass culture, the unbridled search of pleasure, fragmentation, a dispersed subjectivity.

This chapter participates in this debate by asking the following questions: Has the sphere of consumption robbed romance of a meaning hitherto preserved by precapitalist culture? Has it undermined the capacity of people to engage in an authentic experience of romance? Does the transient, fragmentary nature of postmodern romantic experience render romance meaningless, or does postmodern culture offer other ways of making romantic meaning?

Instead of engaging in a normative critique of the role and effect of commodities on the romantic bond (for example, from the standpoint of a utopian project of emancipation), I turn to how my respondents construct, enact, and live the consumption of commodities within their romantic relationships. I analyze the meaning of this consumption from "within," that is, as it is subjectively experienced or dreamed about by respondents. This approach eventually leads me to dispute a blanket condemnation of consumption and to argue that commodities and participation in the leisure market provide the romantic bond with meanings and pleasures congruent with rather than inimical to the phenomenology of the romantic bond.

REENCHANTING THE WORLD

Courtship is commonly referred to as a ritual. The metaphor may have roots in premodern courtship, which followed a highly codified sequence of actions analogous to formal rituals, but because twentieth-century manners have swept away the rigidity of courtship etiquette, the metaphor of ritual would seem obsolete, no longer capturing the symbolic meaning of romance. However, a cultural analysis of modern romantic practices, as reported by my respondents, reveals that the meaning of romance does indeed draw from religious rituals, even more literally than is usually implied by the word "ritual."

For Durkheim, ritual is the category of religious behavior that delineates and demarcates sacred time, space, and feelings from nonsacred, that is, profane. The marking of such boundaries must follow a formal set of rules to make it a collective and binding behavior. Participants in a ritual, says Durkheim, "are so far removed from their ordinary conditions of life, and they are so thoroughly conscious of it, that they must set themselves outside of and above the ordinary morals."[1] Sociologists since have expanded the definition of ritual, suggesting that the secular realm of daily life is also susceptible to formalized rules of conduct similar to those of religious rituals.[2] Any symbolic meaning, when it is intensified, can be ritualized within (rather than outside) daily life.[3] Although romance is a secular behavior, it is experienced to its fullest when infused with ritual meaning. More specifically, an interaction becomes "romantic" when four kinds of symbolic boundaries are set: temporal, emotional, spatial, and artifactual. These boundaries carve a symbolic space within which romance is lived in the mode of ritual.

TEMPORAL BOUNDARIES

According to Eviatar Zerubavel, sacred time has boundaries, that is, points at which it starts and ends.[4] A person experiences a romantic moment as taking place during a different time from "regular," profane time. Most readers will recognize these words of a woman film-maker: "You have to set aside time, to set aside time to make things romantic" (interview 2). Such "setting aside" of time is a very conscious and purposeful action, as the following answer given by a working-class woman demonstrates:

How does one work on [a relationship]?

You have to make the time, or find the time to do special things that are romantic moments with each other. It's much easier after a long-term relationship to just follow [*sic*] into a pattern, you do what you have to do and stay home in front of television and watch it and sometimes that's easier than putting yourself out, like getting yourself dressed up a little bit, like finding a place where to go, making an arrangement for your children to be taken care for. (Working-class woman, no profession, interview 16)

"Romantic time" is constructed to mark out "special things," and as such it is explicitly opposed to the "ordinary" time of everyday life. "It [a romantic moment] would be either early in the morning or late at night, when no one else is around" (working-class man, interview 36). Why do these two slices of time, before or after the regular workday, seem equally romantic? Preceding or following work or domestic chores, they are thus located on the margins of the productive and reproductive time of society.

Could you say what was romantic about [a particular moment]?

Night, I think, is more romantic than the day. And the forest and the natural environment, that I found to be very romantic. (Male lawyer, interview 5)

Here, temporal boundaries are associated with geographical ones; both mark the seclusion of the lovers. The night is more romantic than the day because it facilitates the lovers' symbolic and physical isolation from their ordinary daytime identities. Night is both a typical marker of romantic time and also the private time par excellence, and this suggests that the boundaries of romantic time are often structured by the boundaries dividing private and public life.

Romantic time is often compared to or called "celebration time." This is often seen in women's magazines: "Your intimate relationship is the most precious gift in your life. It deserves to be celebrated every day."[5] This metaphor was also commonly used in the interviewees' responses.

For example, this interviewee explained her choice of figure 4 (see appendix 3 for the figures) as most romantic as follows:

> *When you say they drink champagne, they are dressed up, do you mean to say that therefore it is romantic?*
>
> It is just that they are going to do something together, they plan something together, they are going out, celebrate or something. (Female lawyer, interview 23)

Romantic time feels like holiday time: it is perceived as different and special and is therefore experienced in the mode of celebration. The life of the couple is susceptible to cyclical celebration, similar to the cycles of religious life. For example, the wedding anniversary demarcates the event of marriage and celebrates it regularly. It commemorates periodically the marriage ceremony and reaffirms the bond through the exchange of gifts and a semipublic celebration. Similarly, Valentine's Day is a collective cele-bration of private feelings of love. Even unmarried couples, feeling the need to celebrate cyclically the romantic bond, often ritually observe the "first day they met" as a substitute for a wedding anniversary.[6] Romantic moments are lived and remembered both as literally "festive" time and analogously to the experience of religious time.

SPATIAL BOUNDARIES

Related to this reconstruction of time as festive or consecrated is the rearrangement of the space of everyday life. The setting of new spatial boundaries marks the experience of romance, as evidenced by people's frequent need to move away from their regular domestic space. Even when lovers find themselves in the midst of a crowd of people (as, for example, on the street or in a restaurant), they symbolically construct their space as private and isolated from the surrounding people.[7] For example, "When I am at home, it's not special. I have had also romantic evenings at home but if I had to pick my most romantic moments, it seems more special, maybe I am more relaxed then, when I go out" (female university professor, interview 19).

Although isolation and privacy are intrinsic elements of romance, that home is frequently viewed as unromantic suggests that romance is equated with the couple's ability to construct a new private space around them, even in a public place. When the couple reaches such a sense of isolation from the surrounding environment, they can switch to a space properly distinct from that of daily or ordinary life.

> *What was romantic about this moment [in Mexico]?*
>
> Just like being thousands miles away from home in our own little . . . almost kind of fantasy world. Real world seemed so far away, so we were just in our little paradise almost. And there was a certain intimacy about being there and being in that type of setting. (Male corporate banker, interview 20)

In this quote, the geographical distance not only marks but also induces the feeling of romance. Because being in a foreign country is a culturally and linguistically isolating experience, it sharpens the construction of romance as an "island of privacy" in the public world.

ARTIFACTUAL BOUNDARIES

A common way of signaling a romantic moment is to include objects different from those used for daily purposes, ritual objects being more precious or beautiful than ordinary ones. Gifts are one obvious example, but elegant clothes and expensive meals are also associated with romance.

> *If you wanted to have a romantic moment with someone, what would you do?*
>
> I'd say I had a pretty romantic evening one night recently. I went to a formal dance, so you get dressed up really nice and you go to a pretty place, you do some dancing, and then I think we came back here for the dessert.
>
> *What was romantic about that evening?*
>
> Getting dressed up is romantic, and going out and doing nice things, and then also spending some private time, and also doing things that are slightly different from sort of the usual. This results from formal dancing, you know waltz and swing, things like that, so that makes it romantic. You are also served champagne after, which is a little bit different from the usual, though I have it pretty often. (Male university professor, interview 1)

This man invoked two elements frequently found in religious rituals: special vestments and beverages. Aesthetic or expensive objects distinguish the romantic interaction from others by making it at once more intense and more formal. Certain objects, like champagne, roses, or candlelight, have fixed attributes of quasi-sacredness that under the appropriate circumstances can generate romantic feelings. Others acquire sacredness by virtue of their association with intense romantic feelings; for example, a scarf or a napkin used on a romantic occasion can become impregnated with sacredness, able to transport the lover back to the "sacred" moment of the first meeting.

EMOTIONAL BOUNDARIES

More than other sentiments, the romantic feeling is expected to be different, unique, for if a romantic emotion cannot be unambiguously distinguished from other feelings, the very ability to feel "love" can be jeopardized. The necessity to make romantic love intrinsically different comes from the norm of monogamy, but it also stems from the fact that if boundaries between romantic feelings and other feelings are blurred, as can be the case for example in "amorous friendships," the perceived uniqueness of romantic feelings is put into question.[8] When asked if there is a difference between friendship and love, everyone says with no hesitation that the two are different and *have to* be different, even if they claim at the same time that friendship is a subcomponent of love.[9] In contrast to love, the sentiment of friendship is not jeopardized by having more than one person as its object. Thus, romantic feelings are commonly described as "special," since they are directly related to a person made separate from the rest of the world.

One of my respondents characterized being in love as "a sense that the other person is so wonderful that you don't understand how it can exist, that you look at the person and the rest of the world disappears" (male art gallery owner, interview 43). The same man described his encounter with a woman whom he fell in love with:

> I met someone and I was so attracted by her that I was frozen, I went out with her, I socialized with her, and it was obvious that we were incredibly attracted to each other. There was electricity. It was a tremendous satisfaction that I had these very strong feelings I haven't felt before. There is a sense of connection that happens, for a time, an intermingling of the soul, that you become the same person. There seems to be for me, an absence of sexuality, that you become sort of a spirit, more than a male or female, you become a pure essence.

Although this man gave no religious affiliation, his terminology is obviously religious, and his statement evokes motifs familiar to the phenomenology of religion: a strong sense of bonding and deep connection with the God-lover, the replacement of a sense of personal identity by a feeling of merged identities.[10] There is a similarity between the awe and the intensity felt in the religious experience and the romantic sentiment. Both overwhelm the religious person or the lover, and in both the object of worship or love is perceived as unique and overpowering. The feelings evoked in romantic love are reminiscent of what Rudolf Otto described as the "numinous," which is characterized by such terms as awe, ravishment, and majesty, and by the feeling that the subject is overwhelmed by God (or the lover).[11]

Although they did not use the traditional religious rhetoric of awe and fascination, other respondents also indicated that in love emotional states are intensely altered. "A romantic moment for me is a time of crisis, in which the adrenaline and the nerves are at a certain pitch" (female editor, interview 3). Or, "Romance makes a relationship more exciting, more invigorating" (female police officer, interview 21). Words such as "crisis," "emotional pitch," "invigoration," and "excitement" clearly suggest that one's emotional energy is heightened and intensified. The heightening of emotions, as Durkheim noted, is central to the experience of the sacred. In fact, his descriptions of the feeling of the sacred could easily be applied to the feeling of romantic love: "Vital energies are over-excited, passions more active, sensations stronger. . . . A man does not recognize himself."[12] The romantic feeling is reminiscent of the exhilaration often felt by the religious person during moments of religious celebration and communion.

In the terminology of phenomenological sociology, a romantic moment stands outside the taken-for-grantedness of the everyday world. This idea was explicitly stated by the respondents who held that romance is and should be different from daily life, for example, in their frequent use of the word "special" to signal the unique character of the relationship. When explaining why romance was so important to his view of marriage, a respondent invoked this idea: "I would like to have that extraspecial, something out of the ordinary" (male lawyer, interview 5). The feeling of "that extraspecial" is so important that when it is not felt, people call into question their romantic attachments. Romance is described as that which prevents one from taking the other "for granted," even when one shares ones' daily life with that significant other. It is "that little extra" one adds to a relationship, a small but crucial difference commonly conveyed in such metaphors as a "spice," a "flavor," a "zest." And this difference is more likely to appear when the moment stands outside the realm of day-to-day life.

Examples of this difference are numerous in my interviews:

Do you think that it is important to be romantic to keep love going between two people?

Yeah (pause) because it reminds you not to take that person for granted, I guess, break out of everyday routines and (pause) see the other person at their best, not when they're in their bad moods, in the middle of everyday problems [laughs]. (Female editor, interview 48)

Romance can last if you keep it alive . . .

How do you keep it alive?

By making sure to plan out sort of romantic evenings as opposed to just going out in the usual way, making sure you get dressed up even though sort of not courting anymore, make sure you do things out of the ordinary once in a while. (Male university professor, interview 1)

speazhess shifts to consumption over time

To have a romantic moment, do you usually prefer to stay home or go out?

Go out.

Why?

Because it is unfamiliar. (Female avant-garde filmmaker, interview 2)

I don't think of [romance] as something that naturally goes along with cooking breakfast or washing clothes and stuff. (Female collagist, interview 45)

These examples illustrate the same points: romance is opposed to dailiness, routine, and taken-for-grantedness. Romance represents an excursion into another realm of experience in which settings, feelings, and interactions are heightened and out of the ordinary.

One interviewee even construed the contrast between romantic and unromantic as an opposition between what we might call the "too real" and the "surreal."

Have you already been in a situation that you thought was totally unromantic?

Yes.

What was it like?

Things like losing your luggage at an airport, I guess things where reality intrudes itself, getting stuck on the subway.

These things happened to you?

If you have had a long wonderful weekend trip somewhere, or you have gone some place romantic, Hawaii or something, and you come back and your luggage was lost, I find that very unromantic.

Can you say what you find unromantic?

The fact that the spell that you have cast in your trip to Hawaii is now shattered by the fact that you have to deal with officials and paperwork

and trouble. The relaxation that I spoke of before as being important in romantic situations is gone, anything stressful, something that has to be dealt
with, your car breaks down.

What about the subway? You mentioned earlier that was unromantic.

It depends if you need to be some place, if you are to the airport or being
on the subway dressed in your party clothes or not dressed in your party
clothes and holding hands with someone, and suddenly a bagman comes
along and wants a dollar, again, it is an intrusion into your romantic haze
or glow or haze or whatever. (Male actor, interview 29)

This respondent captured the essence of the opposition between the
romantic and unromantic. Romantic is exotic (Hawaii), fun (the trip,
the party), affluent (a plane ticket, dressy clothes), magic (the "spell"),
and relaxed. The romantic stands above and outside the stream of
everyday life conceived of as effortful, practical, routine, and unplay-
ful. The unromantic, by contrast, is practical and requires that one
deal with the daily problems of everyday life (lost luggage) and institutions (airport clerks). Moreover, the image of the bagman as a symbol of the unromantic suggests that the figure of poverty, with its suggestions of neediness, distress, and social problems, is antithetical to
the glamour with which romance is usually associated.

Furthermore, the experience of romance exhibits attributes of religious rituals: by isolating the objects of their emotions from all others,
dressing in a specific way, eating special foods, rearranging the space,
or moving to another space and setting a special time of celebration,
people are able to experience a time that has the subjective "texture" of
holiday celebrations, in a space physically or symbolically removed from
that of everyday life. They reach a domain where their feelings are
heightened, their vital energies are regenerated, the bond to their immediate partner is reaffirmed. Romance is lived on the symbolic mode
of ritual, but it also displays the properties of the staged dramas of everyday life. The use of artifacts (clothes, music, light, and food), the use of
self-contained units of space and time, the exchange of ritual words of
love make romance a "staged reality," an act within which public meanings are exchanged and dramatized to intensify the bond.

A CONSUMING ROMANCE

During the interviews respondents were asked to compare figures 5 and
6 (the Walkers Evans photograph of the Depression-era family; not re-

produced) and choose the "picture that most expresses romance" and the one that "most expresses love." For some respondents, the two choices coincided; in this case, the picture of the affluent couple was seen to signify both romance and love. For other respondents, the two meanings did not converge in one picture: they chose the picture with the affluent couple as the most romantic but viewed the picture of poverty as signifying love. Some of these respondents contrasted romance with love, perceiving the latter as a depth of feelings beyond the trappings of conspicuous consumption. For them, the cultural category of romance was associated with an affluent lifestyle, while "love" was more readily associated with a family unity transcending the pleasures of wealth. The first group explicitly claimed that love cannot survive in conditions of dire poverty, and for this reason they chose the picture of the smiling and affluent couple as embodying both love and romance. Thus even though respondents disagreed as to whether love belongs to the category of affluence (some choosing figure 5 and others figure 6), *none* of them ever chose the picture of poverty as representing the cultural category of romance. Romance was *always* associated with affluence, while love sometimes associated with it and sometimes viewed as extraneous to it.

The fact that some respondents merged romance and love within a single cultural matrix ("romantic love") while others viewed the two as separate underscores some of the concluding remarks of chapter 2: the cultural categories of romance and love are somewhat intermixed. Although respondents could differentiate between romance and long-lasting love, when they were faced with actual representations, the distinction was not always intelligible to them. The emotion of love was intertwined with romance, defined in terms of the props and settings that induce a "special atmosphere." The most significant implication of this amalgam of meanings is that the boundary between romance as an ambience and intimacy as mutual knowledge and trust is fuzzy, even for those who insist that it should remain distinct.

Asked to report how they "usually spend" or "would like to spend" a romantic moment, fifty respondents gave a wide range of answers: having dinner in a restaurant, having dinner at home, drinking champagne by the fireplace, walking in Central Park, canoeing, going to Mexico, walking along the beach, making love, talking, and so forth. (The variety of these answers is outlined in table 1.)

Three main categories of activities are apparent: *gastronomic* (e.g., preparing or purchasing food at home or in a restaurant); *cultural* (e.g., going to the movies, the opera, or a sports event), and *touristic*

TABLE I. RESPONDENTS' ROMANTIC ACTIVITIES

Activities	Direct consumption	Indirect consumption	No consumption
Gastronomic	Restaurant Drink	Dinner at home	—
Cultural	Movies Theater Dancing: formal/ discotheque Opera Museum	Reading a book or newspaper Crossword puzzle Watching TV Listening to music Painting together Looking at photographs	Talking (sharing secrets; talking about art and politics)
Touristic	Cruise Skiing Travel Abroad Weekend at seashore Waterskiing Canoeing	Fishing Gardening Picnicking	Walking (river or woods; city streets or park)

(e.g., going to a vacation spot or a foreign country). The last category includes exploration of the natural landscape, whether in the city in which the respondent lived (e.g., walk in Central Park, walk near the river) or in a foreign country. Tourism in ethnic or cultural centers and travels into nature are lumped together because both imply geographical or symbolic removal from the daily urban landscape. "Making love" is the only romantic activity not included in the table because it stands as a category on its own: it is neither cultural, commercial, nor touristic.

Romantic encounters can be further divided into three categories according to their relation to consumption: The first is *direct,* where the romantic moment is predicated on the purchase of a commodity, either transient or durable (e.g., eating at a restaurant, buying a cruise to the Caribbean, or giving a diamond ring). An example of a direct consumerist gastronomic activity is eating at a French restaurant, while a more indirect consumption of food is having drinks or dinner at home. Directly consumerist cultural activities are going to a movie, a concert, a play, theater, a baseball game, or dancing. A typical "direct consumption-touristic-natural" activity is a weekend trip to New York or to Cape May at the seashore or, even more dramatic, a worldwide cruise. Here are some actual examples of romantic moments with direct consumption:

What did you use to do together?

It was the time where discotheques just started; there was this place, Studio 54. So we used to come to New York City and go dancing and sometimes too, we did that a lot. We went and visited places. (Female artist, interview 13)

Did you use to do things together?

All kinds of things, travel together, be with each other at all kinds of different situations, see things in New York. (Female lawyer, interview 7)

The second type of consumption is *indirect,* where the romantic moment depends on consumption but is not the direct outcome of the act of purchasing a good. For example, watching television or listening to records presupposes the purchase of the television set or a stereo system, but the purchase of these products does not circumscribe the romantic moment itself.

Finally, the third type of romantic activity along this dimension takes place *without mediation* of consumption. For example, talking and making love do not in and of themselves imply or presuppose consumption, although in practice they often do (e.g., having a good conversation in a restaurant setting or making love at a hotel on vacation). A nonconsumerist touristic activity consists in walking within an urban or natural landscape (park, street, near a river). But defining this category solely by the absence of purchasing is problematic because many activities that do not demand money are modeled on consumerist ones (e.g., going to a museum with free admission or to a lecture on art) and because these activities often presuppose substantial cultural capital. Hence, I do not include in this category any activity predicated on cultural products funded by outside agencies. A nonconsumerist romantic moment excludes the intervention or mediation of cultural products and artifacts in the romantic interchange, whether the lovers or someone else paid for them, and whether they are purchased during or before the romantic moment. By and large this means that three categories of romantic activities qualify as nonconsumerist: walks (in nature or in the city), domestic interactions (e.g., talking), and making love at home. In my sample, the following examples are *closest* to non-consumption:

> *Can you give me an example of an actual romantic moment you have had with somebody?*
>
> What I would really consider romantic isn't like I say not so much a dinner out in front of all kinds of people, and dancing, but more an intimate type moment, just laying around the house real comfortable, not, just wearing comfortable clothes, watching TV, snuggling up together under the blanket, watching TV. (Male boxer, interview 15)

A woman, recalling a recent romantic afternoon with her husband, ended her recounting by saying, "and we watched a video and we just stayed home together" (female lawyer, interview 23). These two accounts insist on the domestic intimacy of these moments. In both of them "just" staying home together or lying around the house was romantic because these activities were informal, comfortable, and therefore intimate. But it is instructive to notice that even in such moments, respondents used modern technologies (video, television) as a focal point of their interaction. Even domestic romantic moments that were removed from the public sphere of consumption were somewhat organized around an external activity (e.g., cooking or watching a movie) or object ("making love" being the most noticeable exception to this rule).[13] In fact, as I show more amply in chapter 8, the *only* respondents who sustained romantic interactions without the mediation of a technology or a commodity (through talk mostly) were the ones with the highest cultural competence. And even then, consumption sometimes plays an invisible, though powerful, role:

> *Can you remember a romantic moment you have had with somebody?*
>
> Like I said . . . I met this man on a train and we talked for two nights and two days without getting any sleep. (Female editor, interview 3)

Although the act of talking seems here to be thoroughly divorced from consumption, the fact remains that the romantic character of this moment was related to the couple's presence on a train, consuming a trip.

A few conclusions can be drawn from this short review of the variety of romantic activities. Consumerist practices *coexist* with nonconsumerist or moderately consumerist ones and do not completely override them. Although people often mention that "staying home," "talking," and "making love" are romantic, it remains that the range of consumerist activities is much wider and varied than that of the nonconsumerist ones. Finally, technologies and/or commodities are frequently present in romantic moments because through their mediation partners communicate with each other. We can now take this a step further and show that consumerist romantic moments are culturally *more prevalent* than nonconsumerist ones. Although coexisting, consumerist and nonconsumerist romantic practices do not lie on a continuum, nor are they simply opposed to each other; rather, consumerist romantic moments serve as the *standard against which nonconsumerist moments are constructed*. This accounts for the primacy and preeminence of the former. The following analysis of gastronomic and touristic-natural romantic activities will help clarify this.[14]

DINING IN, DINING OUT

Of all romantic activities taking place within the framework of daily life, the sharing of food is the most frequently cited in my interviews. Undoubtedly, one reason for this is that in most societies, partnership and social bonds are usually marked by the sharing of food. But this observation leaves one of my findings unexplained: dinners at restaurants were viewed as more "typically" romantic than dinners at home. Even if dinners at home and dinners in the restaurants had been cited equally as romantic, the choice of the restaurant differs from that of home in that it corresponds to the "purest" ideal type of romance. Research by Bachen and Illouz clarifies this difference.[15]

The research was based on a sample of 180 American children, ranging in age from eight to sixteen, who were interviewed in a major city on the East Coast. Among other questions, they were asked to describe a "romantic dinner." Almost all the children referred to a restaurant dinner and, more specifically, to dinner in an elegant restaurant, as the following example from the study illustrates:

> They went to a French restaurant or something and had French food, I guess, but I don't know any French food.
>
> *What kind of lights?*
>
> It is a really fancy restaurant with real fancy chairs, and it is popular and I guess with chandeliers. (Girl, white, ten years old)

They are sitting there and eating this dinner and—

What would they have had for dinner?

Well, like maybe a French dinner or something really fancy.

How would you imagine the restaurant looked?

Well, really fancy, and nice tablecloths and tables. (Girl, white, nine years old)

Overall, these interviews indicated that, although these eight- to six-teen-year-olds had never experienced romance in such settings, they were able to summon the mental picture of a restaurant in highly precise and concrete detail. The authors argue that, in terms of romance, the visual representation of the restaurant dinner precedes and super-sedes, cognitively, the representation of the dinner at home. That is, the association of romance with consumption *is acquired earlier and is mentally more salient than the representation of nonconsumerist romantic moments.*

This claim can also be applied to adults, as evidenced by my respondents. One seventeen-year-old interviewee acknowledged that she had no romantic experience, but when asked to describe a romantic moment, she answered, "I would probably go to a restaurant, have wine, just the common thing to do." This young, inexperienced adolescent immediately conjured up the image of a restaurant and commented on it as a standard romantic activity. So too, my adult respondents, who had firsthand experience of romance, frequently referred to the restaurant as "standard" or "cliché" or "routine." A few examples illustrate this:

Do you consider yourself a romantic person?

Yeah, I am probably not the most romantic person in the sense of doing typically romantic things or—

What is doing typically romantic things?

Buying a woman flowers or taking her, you know, getting dressed up to go out to a very formal restaurant or all sorts of clichéd things. It's just not my style. (Male executive, interview 20)

What would you do if you wanted to have a romantic moment with someone?

Umm, I don't think there has to be any type of romantic setting, candlelight or anything like that for it to be romance. It can just be a certain way to look at someone or certain vibes that you feel. I don't think there has to be any kind of scenario to set up any type of feeling or romantic encounter. (Female legal secretary, interview 18)

If you wanted to have a romantic moment with someone, what would you do?

Ummm (pause), I guess I like very private places, ummmm, very private cozy places rather than, you know, really glitzy places, a big party or a really fancy restaurant or something. It does not appeal to me as much as the cabin in the woods, something like that. (Female editor, interview 3)

In a more subtle way, a young man answered the same question as follows: "Somewhere alone, dinner, I'm likely to say dinner and a show and *all that*." A little later in the interview, asked to provide an example of a romantic moment he had had, the same man responded, "What I would really consider romantic isn't, like I say, not so much a dinner out in front of all kinds of people, and dancing, but more an intimate type of moment, just laying around the house real comfortable, not just. . . . " (male boxer, interview 15).

These quotes share the image of the restaurant, characterized by candlelight, luxurious and elegant appointments, and so forth.[16] Even if respondents preferred "informal" and "nonfancy" restaurants, they found the "standard" image of a romantic dinner in a luxurious and expensive restaurant ("formal," "glitzy"), rather than at home. Foremost in respondents' minds, the restaurant dinner is the romantic cliché; dinner at home (the private, cozy place) is seen as a deviation from this standard. (The expression "all that" of the last respondent implies that he was drawing on a pool of knowledge that he assumed was known to the interviewer.) The choice of the dinner at home was a choice *against* the dinner in the restaurant.

Although dinner at home is often viewed as romantic, why is the restaurant dinner the standard definition of a romantic dinner, both in the imaginations of ordinary people and in the imagery of the media? This question suggests more general ones. Why are these images pervasive and not others? From where do they get their symbolic power, their ability to impose themselves on one's consciousness and to function as collective representations? Even if we establish that the market is the main purveyor of these images of restaurants, this fact in itself does not explain why people prefer restaurant dinners on dates and why they conceive of restaurants as more stereotypically romantic than dinners at home or picnics. Unless we assume that people's representations and experiences are produced mechanically by symbols and goods provided by the market, we cannot deduce subjective experiences from the market. If dining at a restaurant stands as a standard romantic activity (albeit a scorned one, at least by some of my respondents), it is because this activity accomplishes "things" that are useful and meaningful to people. The problem, then, is to identify what these "things" are.

Taking up a previous strand of my argument, I claim that romantic activities involving consumption carry more powerful and resonant symbols than those that do not involve consumption because the former facilitate the ritualization of romance.

ROMANTIC CONSUMPTION AS RITUAL

Restaurants are romantic because they enable people to step out of their
daily lives into a setting saturated with ritual meaning. The design of
the restaurant reinforces and transcends the temporal, spatial, artifactual, and emotional boundaries discussed earlier. Time in a restaurant
is self-contained: entering and leaving set the temporal and spatial
boundaries, and furthermore, the self-contained time of the meal is not
susceptible to the schedules and constraints of the outside, "profane"
world. For example, one respondent mentioned that a restaurant dinner is romantic because it takes place at a much slower pace than dinner at home. If, in the course of everyday life, people are time-conscious
and end their meals quickly, or at least under the pressure of outside
constraints, then the "slowness" of the restaurant meal is perceived as
romantic by contrast, because its slowness implies that the relationship
is the center and the goal of the interaction.

The restaurant is usually an alternative space to the home or workplace. For teenagers living with their parents or for people with children, the restaurant provides temporary isolation from the constraints
of the family. Within the restaurant, the tables are arranged so as to
isolate each group of diners. The typical romantic restaurant is
arranged with "niches" and isolated dark corners, in contrast, for
example, to the unromantic Irish bar in which many people crowd
together. The sense of a spatial boundary was also evoked by respondents, who referred to the feeling of "being separate amidst a crowd":
"I guess my idea of romance is an idea of isolation, in a nice setting,
in a nice restaurant, being away from everyone else, or in a nice bar,
away from everyone else, maybe being able to watch everybody else
but being able to be very much in our own world" (female avant-garde
filmmaker, interview 2).

The restaurant displays an array of artifactual boundaries that sets it
apart from the stream of everyday life. In restaurants, the food is often
"different," more "special" or "exotic" than daily foods.

If you wanted to have a romantic moment with someone, what would you do?

I think maybe I would go out to dinner (pause). I think it is nice because you are sharing something sort of physical or sensual and food is, I like food almost as much as romance or sex, or whatever.

You said before that you would go to dinner.

Yeah.

What kind of restaurant would it be?

Nothing glitzy or shiny or fancy. Something sort of quiet and peaceful, you know. Someplace like I went last night, Chez Mamoona, the servers are friendly and helpful and the food is good and interesting. That means unusual.

Do you like to go with your dates to restaurants that serve unusual foods?

Yeah, I like unusual foods. (Male movie distributor, interview 34)

As the interview went on, this man elaborated on the role of food on dates and emphasized that he liked to explore new and exotic dishes. Another interviewee responded in a similar manner:

On dates, what do you like to do?

Well, if the woman is into it, I like baseball games or that sort of thing, not all women enjoy doing that. But I also enjoy just going out to dinner.

Where do you go?

My preference is like ethnic restaurants, Mexican or different types, Indian, Thai, Ethiopian, whatever. (Male banking executive, interview 20)

These two men stressed the unusual or exotic character of the food served in restaurants, so different from "daily" foods. Other interviewees mentioned different artifactual characteristics as important for the romantic atmosphere: music, candlelight and other forms of soft lighting, white tablecloths.

The emotional invigoration of the romantic bond that usually accompanies the consumption of food in a restaurant can be traced to the formal, ritualized nature of interactions there and the conventionalized significance of the various articles involved. The clothing, the usually elegant tablecloth and silverware, the service of a waiter, the presentation of the meal, and the meal itself all make the restaurant a more formal experience than dinner at home. As Finkelstein has observed, "dining out is a highly mannered event."[17] People usually dress up to go to restaurants and interact in a more constrained way than usual, and the presentation and reading of the menu delay the immediate satisfaction of hunger. More importantly, the presentation of a written list of food items—a list that often uses unusual or poetic names—brings, at least temporarily, the signifiers of the food to the fore of the diner's consciousness, if not to the fore of couple's conversation. The menu is a formal cultural device that defuses the taken-for-grantedness of daily consumption of foods and ritualizes the act of eating, turning it into a symbolic event. In a restaurant, food is not only food. It is part of an ordered set of symbols and signifiers that "mark" the restaurant dinner as "romantic," codifying its meaning and making it more cognitively salient than dinner at home. In structuring the interaction between the participants in this way, the restaurant meal intensifies their interaction. (It is noteworthy that when respondents described a romantic dinner, "wine" was often mentioned. In virtue of its association with religious sacraments and celebrations, wine has a more loaded meaning than, say, beer or liquor.)

At the same time that the restaurant heightens the private bond between the couple, it takes that bond to the public sphere.[18] In that respect, the restaurant dinner carries contradictory sociological properties: it affirms the "regressive" intimacy of the couple and at the same time makes the meal a public experience. That is, the couple retreat to their "island of privacy" through highly codified and standardized meanings.[19]

Compared to the restaurant script, dinner at home appears on the informal end of a continuum ranging from formality to informality. Domestic nonconsumerist activities in general (staying home, cooking together, gardening together, talking after dinner, etc.) stress comfort, informality, and intimacy, while the restaurant dinner, a more formal and public experience, tends to mobilize higher levels of energy and intensity.

If you wanted to have a romantic evening with someone, what kind of things would you do with that person?

Well, I am thinking of different things I have done with Bob, because that's the most recent romance that I have had. I was thinking of one night when we made dinner here, he was supposed to make me dinner but, you know, I was making part of it, he always says that I can't cook, but he is wrong. We were just, uh, he was just doing something for me that a lot of men don't do or can't do. In this case, I can't, well, he says I can't, we were doing something together, doing something very informal, and we both felt very comfortable where we were. And then we sat and we ate it, and that does not sound very romantic but it was. And there was another time when we went out dancing, and that was very romantic too. (Female lawyer, interview 12)

This respondent was aware, even self-conscious, of the simplicity and informality of these moments, indicated by her apologetic "just" and "it does not sound romantic but it was."

Dinners at home and dinners in the restaurant, however, are not always diametrically opposed. The dinner at home can imitate the restaurant dinner, as illustrated by the following:

> *If you wanted to have a romantic moment with someone, what would you like to do?*
>
> It would be at home. If I had my ultimate place. A very nice long dinner. Discussing things at candlelight. I am very attracted by candlelight and very beautiful music, uh, talking about issues that interest us, uh, starting somewhat formally but then breaking down (inaudible).
>
> *What do you mean, "formally"?*
>
> A kind of a lot of ritual. Very nice dinner, nicely dressed, nice music, whatever. Very comfortable but yet, not vulgar, very tasteful.
>
> *What kind of food?*
>
> Umm, something either really nice, Italian or French, really nice wine.
>
> *How would you be dressed?*
>
> If I was in my home, I wouldn't be dressed in suit and tie, although I would dress very nicely, very nice shirt, very nice sweater. She would be nicely dressed but not formally. If we went out, I would wear a tie and suit. (Male orchestra conductor, interview 33)

The romantic dinner at home uses many of the elements of restaurant rituals: food and dress "nicer" than usual, soft lighting, background music. These elements make the dinner at home a ritual experience analogous to the consumerist version of dinner in the restaurant. This respondent even referred to the moment as a "ritual," thus suggesting that he was aware of the formal character of romance and intentionally constructed it as such. The symbolic meaning of restaurants can be skillfully reconstructed by respondents within their homes through their manipulation of the boundaries implied in ritual. This in turn suggests that the sphere of consumption and the rituals it affords are not straightforwardly opposed to the domestic sphere.

Conversely, going to a restaurant can be often associated with such "at-home" meanings as informality and simplicity. The social groups that Bourdieu viewed as having much cultural capital but little economic capital (e.g., the cultural specialists) prefer informal, simple, unpretentious, "homey" restaurants, in contrast to groups with more money but less cultural capital (the "bourgeoisie"), who are more likely to prefer the classical elegance of a French restaurant.[20] However, the *expensive dinner* is still the cultural standard against which other tastes are articulated.

THE LUXURY OF ROMANCE

The link between luxury and love is not new in the sociological literature and originates in Werner Sombart's analysis of capitalism.[21] Sombart argued that nineteenth-century French upper-middle-class men chose "expensive" mistresses as a way to display their social status. Their wives, in an attempt to compete with the mistresses, imitated them and spread the use of luxury in romantic and conjugal relationships. Although Sombart's analysis is hardly relevant to Victorian or even post-Victorian sexual mores and to the economic asceticism of nineteenth-century Protestant America, it is still useful in that it points to the connection between social power, love, and luxury. Unlike Sombart, however, I pay close attention to the ritual meaning of luxury.

Luxury items figured conspicuously in my respondents' construction of the romantic. Women who chose figure 4, an advertisement for expensive china, cited the china itself as well as the champagne as making the scene romantic. "We had a really romantic afternoon yesterday," another woman recalled, "we went to see a movie, *New York Stories,* we came back in a cab, we came home, and I made champagne cocktails, and we had the champagne and we made love and we had dinner and we watched a video and we just stayed home together" (female lawyer, interview 23). This vignette weaves together informality and intimacy with consumption of both luxury (that is, nonnecessary) items such as a movie, a taxi ride, champagne, a rented video. Such details are meaningful because luxury is part of the larger cultural scenario of romance. Although not all respondents mentioned luxury items, champagne was stereotypically constructed as more romantic than beer, salmon or caviar more than hamburgers, formal dress more than jogging clothes, a French restaurant more than McDonald's or a diner.

Why are details such as the cab ride and champagne as relevant to a script of romance as the informal intimacy of a domestic moment? The responses of two of my interviewees help to answer this question. The first example is from a movie distributor, the second is from a cameraman. Both had high cultural competence but incomes below $30,000 at the time of the interview.

> These things [going to a restaurant] are less important, you know. Actually, it's interesting, because I went out with somebody once, and we went to an Italian restaurant which happened to be a restaurant that I wanted to go to, and I thought it would be a nice place to invite her, and it was a very sort of, like, you know, low-key lighting, you know, candles on the table, all that thing. I had absolutely no sort of intentions. I mean, I wasn't even sure what kind of a date or what this was going to be, in terms of whether this was going to be a real date, like, are we going to be romantic partners or whatever? Um, and ah, when I remember, having dinner and her remarking "Oh, this is so romantic," and sort of swooning and I was like—
>
> *Swooning?*
>
> You know.
>
> *Oh yeah, yeah.*
>
> And ah, I just thought, all right, I guess it is. I mean, I wasn't like setting the stage, but it happened anyway. I mean, she was sort of susceptible to that. See, I was more, sort of, I think, in that particular case, I was going out with her because I sort of wanted to get to know to know her better and figure out how I felt about her. As it turns out, it was a funny sort of date. I mean I wasn't sure and she wasn't sure what we were looking for there, so, we ended up going out after that and sort of becoming romantically involved for a very short period of time, but, um, that was what I would call "romantic setting." I mean, in its really very clichéd form and it all had everything to do with the props and the lighting and I suppose that it could be a very effective means of seduction, but I've never really thought, not that I've thought about seduction, but I've never been all that, perhaps, um, ha, disin—, well, I was going to say "disingenuous."
>
> *Why did you say it may be "effective"?*
>
> Well, I mean, clearly, that in this situation, with this young woman, if I had been bent on seducing her, then that would have really sort of helped set the stage, you know. That wasn't my intention. I was more sort of saying, "Let's see what happens." (Male film distributor, interview 34)
>
> *What kind of restaurants do you go to? [The respondent had just mentioned that he would take a woman to a restaurant if he wanted to have a romantic moment with her.]*
>
> Generally not chic, unchic restaurants because I find the food isn't so good and the prices are too high [at chic restaurants] and also just geographically, there are so many restaurants in New York. [Pause] I have tried to go to

expensive restaurants with special dates and it works! It does work! But I don't know that it necessarily is worth it.

What do you mean, "it works"?

Every time I have taken a woman to a French restaurant in Soho and spent $120, I can be pretty sure that the evening will end agreeably but it seems, it seems, a little like a set up.

How do you explain that it works?

I think that anybody who is, I think that if a woman took me to a very expensive meal which was very good, and the wine was great, that was obviously a really good restaurant, that would turn me favorably in their direction.

Can you explain why?

I think when you go to a really nice restaurant it just sets up a nice tone to your conversation and to just being with the other person. (Male camera-man, interview 25)

The answers of both men begin by denying that restaurants are important to their experience of romance. Yet their examples suggest that luxury goods have two crucial functions in romantic interactions: they are "seduction aids" (they helped both men reach sexual goals), and they make the romantic moment an intense ritual experience in which the couple's feelings are intertwined with the ostentatious act of spending. While the first argument pertains to what we might call the sociology of seduction, the second pertains to the symbolic anthropology of goods.

Luxury goods may be viewed as instrumental in seducing because they point to the social status of their users. Veblen, for example, suggested that the consumption of luxury commodities is an index of prestige and power and therefore more seductive than ordinary commodities.[22] Since expensive French restaurants are associated with an upper-middle-class lifestyle, taking a woman to such a restaurant is a display of social and cultural power. Because women, the reasoning goes, tend to marry men above their class (hypergamy), the display of luxury commodities is seductive as it conveys implicit messages about the man's social status. The second perspective, from symbolic anthropology, views luxury commodities as symbols whose use and efficacy lie in the meanings they make the couple experience and enact.

Despite the fact that both men declared their distaste for "chic" restaurants and for what they referred to as a "stage" or "set up," they proceeded to explain that nice restaurants are effective in seducing a woman. Both accounts clearly presuppose that the expensive restaurant has a symbolic efficacy that lies beyond a man's conscious and willful control. The first example is particularly illuminating as the respondent explicitly suggested that the feeling of romance followed rather than preceded the dinner, confirming the hypothesis that luxury (the "nice Italian restaurant," the "expensive" meal, the "great" wine, the "obviously good" restaurant) intensifies the romantic interaction ("turns you favorably," "sets a nice tone to the conversation," etc.).

Luxury goods gain their symbolic potency by marking a couple's entry into a realm defined as nonutilitarian, even anti-utilitarian, in which social bonds are forged in the mode of celebration. Indeed, luxury reinforces two crucial dimensions of rituals, formality and embellishment. As we have seen, fancy restaurants are always very formal. The elegance of the restaurant (as manifested, for example, in antique or designer furniture or sophisticated interior architecture) and its explicit attempt to provide an aesthetic decor obviously embellish the setting of the romantic interaction and make it a theatrical event, that is, a staged interaction that heightens emotions and dramatizes relationships through a conventional use of symbols.

According to Robert Wuthnow, embellishment and formality give rituals dramatic as opposed to purely instrumental qualities and make their communicative functions more intense: "The dramatic, formalistic character of much that is known as ritualistic behavior aids communication."[23] If so, then luxurious commodities undoubtedly enhance the communicative functions of romantic rituals (and in fact, respondents indicated that the expensive restaurant "sets a nice tone to the conversation"). Luxury commodities generate a romantic atmosphere because, in Jeffrey Alexander's terminology, they are highly "energized symbols" and therefore useful in establishing or reinforcing a bond with another person.[24] Luxury can help crystallize and heighten an already existing but diffuse romantic attraction, or, when the relationship is already established, it can help set the romantic moment apart from the routine of shared everyday life.

Luxury commodities have the important symbolic function of drawing more firmly the boundaries between ordinary and extraordinary moments in a relationship. If we assume that luxury items are not consumed routinely by members of the middle classes, then in all likelihood their use reinforces the perception of romantic moments as taking place in "special" places, with "special" people, and at "special" times. Luxury commodities generate emotional intensity because they carry their user into a category of experience that is aesthetic, formal, and ritual. Hence they take people, symbolically, far away from their daily lives.

But the centrality of luxury for the ideal-type definitions of romance points to perhaps its most interesting meaning, that of expenditure. The notion of "expenditure" was first developed by Georges Bataille.[25] According to him, "expenditure" accounts for all that a society produces in "excess," that is, all that evades the useful and utilitarian order and that consumes rather than preserves energy, wealth, equilibrium. Art, rituals, carnivals, feasts, luxury, laughter, sexual perversions—all such phenomena, according to Bataille, participate in an order that opposes the productive and reproductive functions of society. From an economic standpoint, the consumption of luxury for romance corresponds to such acts of expenditure, for it ostentatiously sacrifices wealth and evades the law of accumulation and utility. To the extent that these experiences of romance use intangible and ephemeral goods that can neither be recuperated nor recycled for further accumulation, "waste" is intrinsic to them. In this approach, luxury goods are appreciated not for their status-displaying function but rather as signifiers that enable people to step into a realm of experience alternative to the utilitarian, accumulative, and profit-oriented order of their daily lives. Thus, romantic love has been and continues to be at the cornerstone of utopias because it reenacts, symbolically, rituals that affirm the supremacy of the individual and the display of sacrificial waste.

The use of luxury in romance points to a fundamental ambivalence in the role of consumption in the romantic utopia: through the use of luxury goods, people temporarily "declassify" themselves, in the sense that they momentarily step out of their social class and the entire system of classification and experience through romance a symbolic waste of wealth, a "loss" all the more intense and pleasurable in binding the couple in the mutually shared pleasure of erotic and emotional fusion. However, in contemporary society, such consummation cannot be divorced from the fact that it is most conspicuously enjoyed by the "rich and famous," and in this respect it is imbued with the status-signaling function of "mundane" consumption.[26]

William Leiss suggests that absolute levels of consumption are less significant than its actual use and meaning in the various social contexts of interpersonal relationships. For him, consumption and its icons are increasingly the "point of contact between these two realms of goods and needs, mediating between objects and the broader world of culture."[27] This view usefully suggests that luxury commodities mediate between the realm where individuals compete with one another to secure socially desirable partners and a realm of ritual where people strive toward fusion, equality, and waste. We reach here what seems to be a paradox: while luxury goods tie people to the realm of status competition, their symbolic meanings enhance the ritualistic, non-utilitarian, and emotionally intense character of romance, thereby defusing the perception that one is involved in an act of consumption. The deeper the objective hold of the market on the romantic experience, the more ritualized and therefore subjectively remote from the market this experience becomes. Thus the notion of ritual accounts not only for the cultural meaning and experience of romance but also for the very *mechanism* through which the market structures the subjective experience of romance. Ritual is the cultural form through which the public meanings of the sphere of consumption are translated into a subjectively lived practice of romance.

The question remains: how does the category of ritual apply to those romantic moments that were the most invigorating to my respondents, namely, encounters involving travel?

TRAVEL, NATURE, AND ROMANCE

When asked to recall the moments that were most romantic to them, almost everyone mentioned a moment that took place far away from his or her home and from the city, either symbolically or geographically. Typical answers included "it was in the Poconos Mountains," "when we were at the beach eating potatoes cooked on fire," "walking on cliffs in an Irish island," "in South America touring," "in Mexico walking on the beach," or "when we went to the country."

> It was wonderful. [This respondent is recalling a trip to England with his girlfriend and another friend.]
>
> *What was wonderful about it?*
>
> It was very spontaneous, we went very spontaneously. There was, it was just happy, easy relating, lots of laughter, it was exhilarating and nothing to do but have fun and eat. (Male actor, interview 29)

The theme of romance is here intertwined with the theme of travel as intense, exciting, and fun, which has pervaded American mass culture since the end of nineteenth century.[28]

Can you remember a romantic moment?

Probably when I was traveling with someone through Italy and we were at the Spanish steps in Rome, the moon was out, we bought some wine, and we sat on the steps. We were a little older, everybody around was students, and I started to sing. I was an opera singer, and a whole group came and surrounded me, was applauding me. When they left, it was just the two of us. It was a very special moment, a very special feeling. (Male investment banker, interview 4)

This last example contains some of the most basic components of the visual clichés of romance analyzed in chapter 3: a foreign country, a European city steeped in history, moonlight, wine, an event that breaks the routine as the lover sings an aria, and the final isolation of the two lovers. All these elements constitute a highly aestheticized vignette of romance.

Another respondent illuminated the strength of the connection between romance and travel:

What was a romantic moment for you?

I don't know, uh, I think the most, uh, the one I remember, when I was in [inaudible] in the mountains.

What?

Paradise Stream in the mountains, it was very, uh, that's all it was, just couples, that was very nice, the setting was very nice, the whole week was, uh, [inaudible].

How long ago was this?

It was a very nice week, the setting, everything there was nice, really nice, nice views, nice music, that whole week was a very romantic week, as far as I am concerned, uh—

How long ago was this?

Uhmm, that was, uh, twelve years ago. I have had some [laughs] but that stands out. I guess it was the setting, in the house you have the same setting all the time, unless you go out for dinner, you know [inaudible]. (Male janitor, interview 40)

This answer is remarkable because, although twelve years old, this memory is nevertheless the first one mentioned. The respondent himself rejects the possibility that this was the only romantic moment of his life and suggests that, for reasons he does not understand, this moment among all oth-

ers "stands out." The occurrence of his experience during travel to a relatively remote place had a long-lasting impact on the memory of this man
who, because of limited income, has traveled very little in his life.

A fourth example underscores the emotional invigoration of travel.
At different places and times I interviewed two respondents who at the
time of the interviews were going out together. When asked about a romantic moment they had experienced in any of their relationships, each
recalled separately the same episode: walking on a beach, at sunset, in
Mexico—a moment that corresponds to one of the most codified vignettes of romance.

Theoretically, travel can be divided into two subcategories: in "wild nature" and in luxurious or comfortable settings. Both are removed from the
daily urban world, symbolically and geographically. Although the two can
sometimes be mixed (e.g., staying at a luxury hotel in the midst of a wild,
exotic landscape), they are analytically distinct. When recalling and recounting their romantic moments, however, even the wealthy respondents
did not mention luxury as a feature relevant to the romanticism of their
travel memories, though luxury was evoked in the case of restaurant
memories. Quite predictably, it was the romantic pastoral utopia that
exerted the most powerful influence over respondents' experiences and
their accounts of romance. These accounts drew from various cultural
traditions of depicting nature, as illustrated in the following example:

Do you like going out [for a romantic moment]?

I like outdoors, like hiking or playing ball in the park, like walking
through Central Park, or roller skating, canoeing on the Delaware, camping, those kinds of things. It's real, you're out there with nature, with
beauty, with God, and you are there with someone you care for. (Male
physician, interview 8)

For the romantic sensibility, nature is the direct manifestation of and offers the possibility of communion with God.[29] This answer embodies
three other themes that also have their source in nineteenth-century romanticism: nature, personal authenticity, and the emotional fusion of
two people.

Examples of the sublime, analyzed in the previous chapter, can be
found in the following respondent's report:

Well, once, I was seventeen, I was in Ireland, and we were staying on an island and I met a man who was very charismatic and I really kind of admired

him. And we went for a walk one day and we walked and walked for miles and miles and miles and miles and, as we walked, it was like, we got to a certain point, well, we came, at the end of the walk, at the very end, when we decided to turn around, we'd come to some cliffs and, looking down, it seemed like just this incredible transformation at that time, from the beginning of our walk to where we got to the cliffs and, talking about all kinds of things, it seemed kind of spiritual at that moment. It just felt like there was a deep connection between this person and I and, you know, this country where my ancestors came from and the walk back was pretty compacted and it felt also sexual to me. (Female artist, interview 35)

Except for the concluding reference to sexuality, this description has all the characteristics of nineteenth-century romanticism. Spiritual themes, reference to ancestors, and intensity of bonds seem interwoven with a Freudian "oceanic" feeling of undifferentiated fusion with the environment.

A very different invocation of nature can be found in the following response of a young woman who also recalled a memorable romantic moment that had taken place a few years before the interview.

Can you give me an example of a romantic moment you have had, recently or not?

One romantic moment was in Wisconsin, in the lake district of Wisconsin. I was with somebody on a lake with nobody around, we were there for four, five days and didn't see anyone else and it was so empty that you could jump with no clothes into the water, take your bath into the water. Later we sat down and had some caviar and vodka.

What was romantic about it?

Being with somebody and feeling completely away from the rest of the world. (Female filmmaker, interview 2)

Here, clearly combined, are the simple innocence, the authenticity of nature, the isolation from the outside, urban world, and the Edenic abundance of luxury euphemized as nature. The description evokes a mythical vision of a paradise where people rediscover the original and primal purity of their bodies.[30] The caviar and vodka, which are luxury items (consumed by people who have a taste in foreign foods and thus a certain amount of cultural capital), do not disrupt this pastoral vision but, on the contrary, accentuate the aesthetic and Edenic themes of this vignette of romance.

How can we account for the extraordinary power that their travels seem to exert over people's memories? Why is a romantic moment experienced in a natural or exotic setting more powerful than one spent in a luxurious restaurant or hotel? The answer is multifold and is at the heart of the fascination with romance in contemporary American culture.

Traditional theories of memory predict that people are most likely to remember events that correspond to an already existing schematic structure.[31] As we saw in chapter 3, the theme of travel is the most widespread and codified visual vignette of romance. Because it is so well established, we can speculate that people have well-defined schematic structures to process, organize, and retrieve their romantic travels. However, since luxurious romance is also abundantly represented in our media imagery, this explanation alone will not do.

A second explanation, which does not exclude the previous one, derives from the social psychology of emotion. When people find themselves in new and unfamiliar situations, their level of physiological arousal is higher.[32] If the sensations of this arousal, such as fear and excitement, are associated with a person to whom they might feel attracted, their feelings toward this other will be heightened. With male subjects, for example, Dutton and Aron have shown that, when associated with the sight of a pretty woman, feelings of fear significantly increased subjects' perceived attraction to the woman.[33] It is easy to see how travel could bring this psychological mechanism to bear. Travel is likely to induce feelings of uncertainty (the universe is unknown) and excitement (the universe is new). When the physiological arousal provoked by such circumstances is associated with the presence of a lover, it is likely to increase the intensity of the bond.

A third explanation encompasses the previous two but integrates them in a more comprehensive cultural framework. As we have seen, the association of romance with travel often evokes images of nature, purity, and authenticity in which the self is regenerated. Such mental images tap into and recapitulate the romantic utopia, for both romantic love and nature are presumed to represent the most authentic parts of our selves, as opposed to the inauthenticity of urban life (the usual setting in which romance is associated with luxury). These symbols are particularly powerful because they are institutionalized in the media and are supported by a powerful tourist industry. But, most of all, they resonate with the emotional intensity of ritual and the gratuity of expenditure. The rituals lived during travel are especially potent because they enable people to withdraw thoroughly from daily routine, work, and social obligations. They represent not only a separation from but also a dramatized suspension of ordinary constraints and a shift to a purely gratuitous, noninstrumental mode of relationship. Travels take people to the frontier of liminality and are the most pristine expression of expenditure, and in this respect they embody our ideal-typical definition of romance.

ROMANCE AS LIMINALITY

In Turner's famous definition of liminal ritual, the individual separates from the environment through symbolic behavior and is detached from an "an earlier fixed point in the social structure or from an established set of cultural conditions." Liminal rituals propose "inverted" or "subverted" social arrangements. "In this interim 'liminality,' the possibility exists of standing aside not only from one's own social position but from all positions and of formulating a potentially unlimited series of alternative social arrangements."[34] The concept of liminal ritual applies only to religious rituals. Later, Turner forged the concept of "liminoid" rituals for analogous but secular phenomena.[35] Liminoid rituals are defined by the three respects in which they differ from liminal ones: (1) The liminoid ritual takes place in secular industrial societies. In modern societies, liminality has been transferred from religious rituals, which transgress and invert regular symbols, to the areas of leisure, art, and popular culture, which assume the function of engaging the actor in the ludic activity of liminality. (2) Liminal rituals are produced and consumed collectively and anonymously, whereas liminoid rituals are produced or embodied by identifiable personalities such as actors and pop stars. (3) While liminal rituals are wholly related to the social system in which they take place, liminoid rituals occur on the economic and political margins of modern societies.

We have seen how, during travel, people remove themselves, geographically and symbolically, from the normal conduct of their lives. "Getting out into nature" can increase romantic feelings not only by reinforcing the sense of isolation that is an intrinsic part of the cultural definition of romance but by intensifying experience in general. As Jakle and MacCannell have shown, tourism emerged as a way to experience intense feelings as well as escape daily routine.[36] Institutionalized as vacation, travel takes on the ritual character of cyclical events in which people detach themselves from their daily urban lives and gain access another order of reality.[37] Romantic travel enacts the three stages that characterize liminality: separation, marginalization, and reaggregation. As MacCannell argues, the cultural experience of tourism stresses the claims of the "natural," authentic self against those of society.

The mode of sociality promoted by romance is organic and anti-institutional rather than contractual or formal. My respondents made clear that they share this anti-institutional experience of the romantic self by insisting that in romantic moments they feel more "relaxed," that they let "their guard down," that the "interactions are more genuine," and that they can reveal their "true selves." The form of emotionality involved here is that of *communitas,* which Turner defines as a state of intense emotional fusion among members of the same group.[38]

These cultural meanings are also those lived in liminal—or rather, liminoid—rituals of romance during which energies are released and the rules presiding over social interactions inverted. As an interviewee said about his trip to England: "It was wonderful. It was very spontaneous, we went very spontaneously, there was, it was just happy, easy relating, lots of laughter. It was exhilarating and nothing to do but have fun and eat" (male actor, interview 29). Another interviewee expressed the liminal character of romance very well: "Romance goes more naturally with a life free of responsibility or life that is, or perhaps an [inaudible] period like a vacation where you can put them aside for some reason" (male art dealer, interview 43). These responses concur in suggesting that, on travels, romance brings about spontaneity and a sense of freedom lacking in the regular conduct of life.

As cultural critic Frederic Jameson aptly observed: "Romance is a wish fulfillment or Utopian fantasy which aims at the transfiguration of everyday life in such a way as to restore the conditions of some lost Eden."[39] In capitalism, this Eden is one in which relations of production seem to be miraculously erased. The fantasy of romance matches the utopian fantasy of capitalism: a society of perpetual leisure. Liminal rituals are particularly potent because they erase all that which characterizes the sphere of production: work, effort, profit, self-interest, and money. (Sexual relationships during vacation symbolically negate not only work but even childrearing, the productive, reproductive meaning of love.) In this respect, travel is a more consummate case of expenditure in Bataille's sense than more urban romantic activities like dining out or even luxury goods. Not only do vacations require larger amounts of time and money, they also have weaker instrumental functions of displaying status, since they are usually undertaken after one's partner has been chosen.

However, although romantic travel, in its spontaneity and freedom, seems opposed to the formality of luxury goods, such travel is still complicit with consumer capitalism. Corresponding to what sociologists of consumption call an "experience good," travel is inscribed within the high-profit industry of leisure and a structured market of local and international tourism: as already discussed in chapter 3, it usually requires travel expenses, accommodation expenses, and participation in the local tourist trade. Furthermore, as cultural historians such as Roland Marchand and Jackson Lears have convincingly shown, antimodernist motifs such as the quest for the authentic self and the saving power of nature have been elaborated by and within consumer culture. Far from being divorced from consumer culture, the nexus travel-romance is fully merged with it and may even be considered *its epitome*.

The consumption of travel for romantic purposes represents a perfect example of a "postmodern" commodity. The lived experience of such a commodity is interlocked with the attributes or meanings of the object consumed as well as with the act of consumption itself. In other terms, in a postmodern commodity the sign suffuses and subsumes the material constituents of the commodity itself. As Michael Featherstone puts it, in consumer culture "commodities masquerade as experiences and experiences are turned into commodities."[40] Furthermore, the experiences promised by postmodern commodities are themselves peculiarly "postmodern": such commodities purport to offer a threshold to symbolic practices of transgression, inversion, and "carnivalesque pleasures." According to Featherstone and Fiske the profusion of images and styles, the unbridled expression of multiple identities, the practice of transgression, the celebration of disorder, and the release of libidinal pleasures are intrinsic to postmodern culture.[41] It is easy to see how such phenomena also express Bataille's notion of expenditure and Turner's concept of liminality.

The liminality of the romance-travel nexus, however, is not achieved through the depthless meanings and fragmented subjectivity that accompany and characterize postmodern experience. Quite the contrary: liminality is here attained through a limited and highly codified range of symbolic meanings and mental images revolving around the signifieds nature and exoticism, authenticity, and isolation. Furthermore, these experiences, far from fragmenting the identity of respondents, seem to bring them back to a craved-for unity through the emotionally compact experience of ritual.

That there is a spillover from the religious to the secular sphere of meaning is far from new to Durkheimian sociology. Jeffrey Alexander argues that secular symbols and commodities can be the departure point for the experience of sacred meanings insofar as they can undergo a process of decommodification and be incorporated within personal meanings that confer sacredness.[42] However, the sacredness of commercial rituals of romance is not the result of a process of "decommodification": they are not withdrawn from the sphere of consumption and their meanings are not personalized.[43] Because the sacred meanings of travel, going out, luxury goods, and all the other components of romance are largely established and (to borrow Douglas and Isherwood's characterization of rituals) "immobilized" through the public channels of mass media, they are collective. They interlock with the private experience of romance by retaining their collective and public meanings.

According to Durkheim, the experience of ritual has the function of renewing the individual's connection to the social whole. Although here the other to whom one feels intensely connected is a single individual, consumption-based rituals of romance do renew the couple's relationship to the social body by drawing boundaries that seal them off from the profane world and by immersing them in the pseudo-symbolic and public community of media images.[44] Having said this, it is important not to overdraw the analogy between religious rituals proper and romantic rituals based in commercial leisure. The question is precisely to know the extent to which Durkheim was correct in implying a symmetry between religion proper and the secular meanings forged in modern society. I address this question obliquely by inquiring about the utopian content of the commercial rituals of leisure.

THE COMMERCE OF LOVE: IDEOLOGY OR UTOPIA?

Paul Ricoeur differentiates ideology from utopia on the ground that, while the latter articulates the rational fantasy of alternative social relationships, ideology reproduces power and interests.[45] Whence the question, is modern romantic love a utopia, that is, a category of the imagination that articulates values alternative to the market and commodity exchange, or is it an ideological system serving and furthering the interests of capitalism? To put the question more broadly, how is the meaning of love affected by its incorporation within the culture of capitalism?

Marx's analysis of the impact of commodities on human relationships remains the place to begin answering these questions. His critique makes at least four analytically distinct claims: commodities have thoroughly pervaded the fabric of human relationships, they mystify consciousness, they debase the nature of human needs, and they are obstacles to any project of self-liberation. Critical theory has extended this critique to the phenomenon of global mass consumption, arguing that capitalism has invaded the innermost elements of subjectivity, debased our freedom and autonomy, and neutralized our creativity.[46]

My own analysis confirms the Marxian claim concerning the all-pervasiveness of commodification: capitalism has implacably invaded the most private corners of our interpersonal and emotional lives. Although the market does not control the entire spectrum of romantic relationships, most romantic practices depend on consumption, directly or indirectly, and consumerist activities have thoroughly permeated our romantic imagination. But can we conclude from this that the quality of the romantic bond has been debased? How are we to shift from this observation to a normative evaluation of romantic practices as either debased or enriched?

A standard charge brought against the commodification of romance is that it has lowered the quality and intimacy of the romantic bond by making objects mediate between people and by focusing on the impersonal public space of consumption. Such a claim is problematic, however, because, historically, the move of courtship from the parlor to the impersonal realm of consumption was perceived by the actors of the period—especially women—as a gain in freedom and not as a confinement. Stephen Kern, for example, has illuminated the ways in which, during the Victorian era, a variety of "others" exerted stifling pressures on the couple, on women especially.[47] The evaluation of the role of goods in the romantic bond must therefore wrestle with the question of whether direct constraints exerted by some individuals (families most notably) over other individuals (women most notably) are in some sense "preferable" to the fuzzier constraints exerted by the invisible yet all-powerful market forces embodied in consumer goods.

Undoubtedly, as Marx and Weber observed, it is far more difficult to identify and therefore resist the abstract and diffuse power exerted by capitalism than that of an individual or a community. But just how commodities and consumption curtail personal freedom is far from clear. For one thing, consumption was accompanied and sustained by a modernist project of freedom and emancipation that was actively promoted by advertisers.[48] Equating choices between brands of commodities with freedom would probably be derided by communitarians or neo-Marxists as the false freedom allotted by the alliance between media and capital, but I would argue that such rhetoric of freedom—however morally impoverished—provides a powerful cultural idiom articulating freedom to choose, enter, or leave one's relationships. Such freedom is inherent in the liberating and individualizing effects of romantic love and for that reason has been avidly capitalized by the market. Furthermore, commodities lend themselves far more easily to cultural resistance than direct relations of power exercised between individuals. That is, goods can be and often are used to oppose or bypass the same market forces that produced them. Although it is indisputable that these forms of resistance do not threaten the structure of capital, it remains that we cannot simply equate goods with an unrestricted subservience to the market; we must examine how moral meanings interlock with economic forces. Finally, far from lowering the standards of intimacy, the move of romance into the public sphere of consumption has been accompanied by a staunch celebration of emotional intimacy.

Having said this, however, I would like to argue that even if consumerist romantic rituals are important sources of meaning, these meanings are a far cry from the awe-provoking meanings of religion and premodern romantic love. The reason for this is plain enough: the increase in the objective freedom to choose whom one loves or does not love and the conception of love as a field for personal experiments have dealt a fatal blow to the absolute character of the Romantic or even Victorian rhetoric of love by making love subject to the moral and emotional relativism that has pervaded secular culture at large.

With respect to the mystification of consciousness, the Marxian concepts of fetishism and reification all assume that consciousness ignores the real nature of social practices and mistakes appearance for essence. The commodification of all spheres of life is achieved by making commodities seem divorced from the social relationships that produced them, the result of abstract economic forces rather than of concrete relations of production. Lukács, pursuing Marx's analysis, argued that reification comes to function as a "universal structuring principle" penetrating all spheres of social experience.[49]

When people recount moments they found romantic, they perceive them as entirely divorced from acts of consumption that made them possible. Consumption is always, in one of Bourdieu's favorite expressions, misrecognized, especially when the moment recalled has liminal meanings.[50] In remembering romantic moments, respondents stepped into the emotional experience of romance and evaded ("forgot") its consumerist character. It is within the suspension of suspicion (required by the experience of ritual) and their absorption in the emotions of the romantic bond that people lose sight of the consumerist character of their own practices and (unconsciously) reproduce the consumerist order. Romantic encounters displays characteristics of what we might call, reversing Marx, "person fetishism": that is, it is not the commodity that seems to be divorced from the persons who produced it, as in commodity fetishism, but rather the people who seem divorced from the commodities that produced their experience. Relationships between people and objects take on the appearance of relationships between people.

However, when respondents are asked to express an opinion on romance or to react to a cultural artifact representing romance—that is, when they are removed from the emotional intensity of their own memories—they switch to a critical mode and show clearly that they are aware of the economic and ideological underpinnings of romantic practices. Far from being "duped" by and unaware of the origins of their cultural models, some respondents can readily identify the commercial character of romance.

> [Romance is] just like selling cars, selling computers, selling cosmetics, selling women's lib, it's a journalistic hype and it really has nothing to do with the way I feel. (Female editor, interview 3)

> In my mind romance is sort of a fantasy-like concept, of the boy, in the boat with the girl, it's a fantasy of dinner with candlelight in an expensive French restaurant, it's a phoniness kind of thing. Romance is this bullshit Park Avenue restaurant, wine and roses and flowers type of concept. (Male physician, interview 8)

> I think romance is an overworked expression that is a general rubric for things more specific to a particular person.

> *What do you mean by "overworked"?*

> Well, romance is one of these pop words, in my mind, that is everything from these flashy magazine photographs, to the relationship between your psychiatrist and his patient. I mean, it just doesn't mean anything, it is just an overcommercialization of an emotion which is far more complex than the term relates. (Male cameraman, interview 26)

In Marxist terminology, these answers are attempts to defetishize the commodified construction of romance. It is important to mention, however, that in my sample, the respondents most likely to manifest such critical distance are middle- or, more frequently, upper-middle-class who score relatively high on educational capital and are involved in the creation or distribution of culture.[51] Such "defetishization" of commodities is often accompanied by a self-conscious irony and is characteristic of postmodern culture and of the social groups that are the its chief producers and consumers. Additional research should determine the extent to which these iconoclastic practices are expressions of an upper-middle-class ethos or whether such social critique and defetishization are commonly found among lay actors in general.[52]

The third Marxian claim pertains to the nature of needs. Marx argued that consumption creates compulsive needs because ultimately it can never satisfy them. This frustration of needs makes us engage in repeated attempts to fulfill them.[53] Consequently, capitalism reifies subjectivity by reducing us to what Herbert Marcuse called "unidimensionality," the stunted development of one side of our being at the expense of others. This is related to the fourth Marxian claim, that consumption is inimical to any project of emancipation. Theorists criticized the culture of consumption on the grounds that it transformed people into passive consumers, denying our utopian potential to be creative users.[54]

Contrary to the Marxian critique of consumption, however, numerous examples from my interviews suggest that people feel especially in control of their lives precisely when they devise romantic moments based on consumption.

Do you prefer to go out or stay home?

It's kind of hard to say right now because [of their new baby]. Before, I guess, I would prefer to stay home, just because we're both working in the city. So on Friday it would be nice just to stay home, really just to have wine and stay home.

And now?

Now, it's a treat to go out! We have been out only once to dinner since the baby was born. That was nice, that was nice to just get away, see something different than 127 Crestview. (Female, homemaker, interview 27)

If you really love somebody, you're going to work on your relationship and try to do different things to make it not boring. That's the way I feel.

What kind of things does one do not to make it boring?

Like I say, go on different trips, just go places. It could be anywhere. Walk, go to the mall or something. Just be together. (Female security officer, interview 37)

Do you think that romance is important to keep love going?

Yeah, I do. I think it's always important, it's part of life as far as I am concerned, it's one of the better parts. And what else do you do, besides work and eat and drink. Yeah, I think it's very important. (Male janitor, interview 40)

All these examples illustrate similar important points. The experience of "going out" or "doing things together" gives people a sense of pleasure and empowerment. Both working-class and upper-middle class respondents—if for different reasons—felt empowered, creative, and active when they experienced romance, consumerist and nonconsumerist.

Thus, one can find no traces in people's *subjective accounts* of critical theory's diagnosis of consumerism as a cultural pathology. Commodities function as expressive symbolic tools that increase the dramatistic and communicative qualities of the romantic interchange. Far from inhibiting and repressing the self, commodities in fact serve as useful aids for its dramatization.

It is important, however, not to fall into the naive view that people are always aware and in control of all the conditions of their practices and that their discourse is the yardstick by which we should evaluate the effect of commodities. Rather, the challenge is to explain market-based romance through mechanisms that *take into account, rather than exclude, people's own understandings of their practices.* Any explanation of the commodification of romance must *also* "involve individuals—their properties, their goals, their beliefs and their actions."[55] Although in Durkheimian sociology the notion of ritual discounts the purposive character of human conduct, here it enables us to explain the intentional, pleasurable, and active character of people's participation in the leisure-based formula of romance. The notion of ritual is the link between mass-marketed goods, mass-marketed symbols, and the subjective feelings of pleasure, creativity, freedom, and withdrawal from commodity exchange. This in turn implies that there is no simple dichotomy between the realm of intersubjective relationships and the sphere of consumption, for the meanings that maintain the "life-world" of romance are constructed within, rather than outside, the capitalist system.

CONCLUSION

The findings of this chapter undoubtedly support the postmodern idea that our cultural experience and social relationships have become thoroughly enmeshed with the goods and meanings of the sphere of consumption. Although romance often occurs outside consumption, romantic moments proper nevertheless are based on the consumption of luxury goods and cultural products. The most conspicuous commodities in respondents' accounts were restaurant meals and, especially, travel experiences. Even the moments experienced by respondents as domestic, intimate, and quiet involved the presence of a technology of communication or the indirect presence of another type of commodity, or both. This, in turn, confirms that the commodification of romance analyzed in the previous historical section has deepened: it is not confined anymore to the public sphere of consumption but has extended its hold to the home.

The consumption of leisure goods offers more than mere "depthless meanings," however. Such periodic, deliberate participation in the sphere of consumption knits together goods and meanings of public culture into a cyclical regeneration of the romantic bond through the experience of stable, ordered, and codified meanings of ritual (seclusion from the outside environment, temporary withdrawal from the meanings of everyday life, and disclosure of an authentic self.)

This romance-ritual-consumption nexus occupies two opposed symbolic axes, with opposing visions of utopia: the first stresses formal and luxurious expressions of romance, through which people temporarily access the glamour and aestheticized lives of celebrities. While tapping into a utopia of love, this experience of ritual accepts social distinction and the unequal distribution of affluence. The second symbolic axis, on the contrary, invokes anti-institutional definitions of the self and the cultural experience of liminality. In conjuring the transgression of social constraints, the release of an authentic self, and the lovers' fusion in an organic bond, the experience of liminality provides a temporary access to the egalitarian utopia most often associated with pastoral and wilderness.

My results indicate that the romantic bond has indeed been colonized by the market, but I argue that capitalism has neither debased a more meaningful (Victorian) love nor "domesticated" a more subversive love.[56] Consumerist love invokes values and principles that have had an emancipatory potential throughout Western history: individualism, self-realization, affirmation of the individual's personal qualities, and equality between the sexes in the mutual experience of pleasure. However, as becomes apparent in the next chapters, there is a price to pay for this: the meaning of our relationships is now under the assault of discourses and regimes of representations that make our quest for relationship ever more elusive.[57]

CHAPTER 5

Real Fictions and Fictional Realities

For if theater is a double of life, life is a double of true theater.
Artaud, The Theater and Its Doubles

Life does not imitate art; it only imitates bad television.
from Woody Allen's Husbands and Wives

When we invoke Romeo and Juliet as mythical figures of love, we conveniently forget that before he loved Juliet, Romeo went through the turmoils of an equally intense and impossible passion for Rosaline. Still sick of love for Rosaline, Romeo accidentally sees Juliet and, instantly transferring his flame, falls in love with her. Upon confessing his new-found love to Friar Lawrence, the latter ironically comments on Romeo's sudden change of heart:

> Is Rosaline, that thou didst love so dear,
> So soon forsaken? Young men's love then lies
> Not truly in their hearts, but in their eyes.

Later in the dialogue, Friar Lawrence ventures to explain that Rosaline did not return Romeo's love because "she knew well [Romeo's] love did read by rote, that could not spell."[1]

Friar Lawrence's remark, hinting at the fact that Romeo has mimicked a culturally prescribed language of love, raises a question that, some five hundred years later, haunts the postmodern sensibility: is authenticity possible when using culturally prescribed languages? Friar Lawrence's gentle rebuke is acutely relevant to the contemporary condition, for at no time as in ours has romantic love seemed so irreversibly captive to the scripts of culture, yet at no time as in ours has the individual been so encouraged to express creatively and spontaneously his or her romantic passions. It is in this consciousness, split between the disenchanted knowledge that our lives are the pale shadows of powerful, machine-produced dreams and the utopia of the individual's creative self-fulfillment, that romantic love situates itself in contemporary culture. The present chapter attempts to understand how this split consciousness permeates contemporary romantic relationships and how the contradictions in which it is inevitably caught have been shaped by the values of late capitalism.

It is a commonplace that the media shape our notions of love. Love stories have penetrated the fabric of our everyday life so deeply that we suspect they have altered, even transformed, our experience of love. Already in the nineteenth century, Flaubert powerfully illustrated this theme in the character of Madame Bovary, struggling to accommodate her mundane married life to an imagination saturated with the romantic fiction she so eagerly read.[2] Tragically confusing the representations of love with love itself, Emma Bovary was able to experience love only as a category of romantic fiction. That romantic fiction is responsible for "disorders of the heart" has frequently been argued in moral discourse for the past three centuries, but as we saw in chapter 2, this claim has been made with particular insistence since the emergence of mass culture.[3] Film and television have replaced novels in our culture, and their power to affect our fantasies and daydreams with their obsessive representation of romance partly explain the pervasive belief that fiction overpowers our romantic experience.[4] *Madame Bovary* prefigures our postmodern condition as perpetual audience, dramatically illustrating the collapse of the boundary between "reality" and its fictional representation, the "copy" ultimately prevailing over its referent.[5] Romance, then, offers a potent case through which to examine the postmodern claim that the boundary between fiction and reality has collapsed, and that "models take precedence over things."[6]

The postmodern question of romance continues an old tradition of moral inquiry into the power of romantic fiction to shape "real" emotions. La Rochefoucauld expressed this in his well-known maxim that many people would never have fallen in love had they not heard of it. This moral discourse contrasted an idealist and a realist approach to love, usually endorsing the latter over the former. The idealist approach affirms the absolutist claims of love and passion and has strong affinities with the capacity to construct fantasies. The realist approach, by contrast, dismisses these "imaginary" constructions of the mind, which it sees as the result of overexcitable imaginations or, worse, a mere fabrication of poets and novelists. It asserts that love ought to be motivated

by the practical needs and conditions of people and that one should accommodate oneself to a less-than-perfect other in order to maintain the
durable bond of marriage.[7]

Because romantic fiction seems to have had a problematic relationship with the "real" experience of love long before the so-called postmodern age, it provides an opportunity to "differentiate between what
is specific to the postmodern and what may be an accumulation and intensification of tendencies long present within the modern, and even premodern."[8] How is the classic distinction between "romantic fiction" and
"reality" that articulates itself on the opposition between idealist and realist love translated into the particular idiom of postmodern culture? In
what follows, I address this question by examining the forms and meanings that romantic autobiography assumes in postmodern culture. More
specifically, I try to establish terms within which to examine the claim
that romantic experience "simulates" the love stories that are the staple
of Hollywood and television.

In the last decade, psychologists, anthropologists, and historians have
devoted new attention to the conventions and symbolic structures of
autobiographical discourse. There is now a broad consensus that the
"life story" constructed and communicated by autobiography is articulated in culturally prescribed narrative structures.[9] The philosopher Alas-
dair MacIntyre has further suggested that "we dream in narrative,
day-dream in narrative, remember, anticipate, hope, despair, believe,
doubt, plan, revise, criticize, construct, gossip, learn, hate and love by
narrative." Emotions are embedded within narrative structures of
various scope, shapes, and sizes. Romantic love is frequently embedded
in a higher-order narrative, or "life story," in which past, present, and
future are linked in a coherent and overarching vision of the self.[10]

Although postmodernism has endorsed the idea that our identity is
based on narratives, it categorically rejects the idea that the self leans on
key "master" narratives—whether of love or anything else—that unify
the self by providing it with continuity and direction. For postmodernism, autobiography has no "center" of action or decision. It is com-
posed instead of intersecting layers of texts, which forever fragment the
"narrative unity of the human quest" and, for that matter, the unity of
the romantic quest.[11]

Interestingly enough, the question of "autobiography" has not played
any significant role in the study of the influence of media on culture.
Scholars have more readily studied the power of media in terms of
"worldviews," "perceptions," or "reception" but have neglected the

fuzzier and more elusive points of contact between mass media stories and autobiographical discourse. Even less examined are the tangled relationships between autobiography, media stories, and consumer culture—an entanglement at the heart of the postmodern condition.

The remainder of this chapter tries to disentangle some of these relationships in the context of postmodern debates on representation. Here also I follow Featherstone's injunction that it is high time to move the study of postmodernism from theory to the analysis of everyday practices.[12] To this end, I asked my respondents to tell me their "most memorable" love stories, ones either taking place at the time of the interview or already ended. During another part of the interview, I asked respondents to interpret three short love stories designed for the purposes of the interview. Such a strategy was based on the conjecture that the structure of one's autobiography uses or overlaps with the same structures that are used to interpret stories. My overall goal was to determine whether there was a relationship between the respondents' life narratives of love and their interpretations of the fictional love stories I provided them with during the interview, and, if such a relationship was found, to understand the intersections between the cultural models used to interpret the three short stories and the respondents' own life stories. (See the appendixes for further methodological details.)

STORY 1

On Monday of June 19 . . . Floyd Johnson and Ellen Skinner, total strangers, boarded a train at San Francisco and sat down across the aisle from each other. Floyd crossed the aisle on Wednesday and sat in front of Ellen. Ellen looked at him and thought: "I would say yes if he asked me to marry him." As Floyd would say later, "They did all the talking with their eyes." Thursday, the couple got off the train in Nebraska with plans to be married. Because they would have needed the consent of the bride's parents to get married there, they crossed the river to Council Bluffs, Iowa, where they were married on Friday.[13]

STORY 2

When Robert turned thirty, he felt he was ready to start a family. He told this to his parents, who were happy to hear that their son was ready to settle down. Robert's parents knew their friends' daughter, Theresa, who, they thought, was a promising match because of the many good qualities she and her family had. They decided to talk to Robert and Theresa to make the match. Both agreed and met late one afternoon. The first meeting was a bit awkward but they liked each other and decided to meet again. With time, the awkwardness disappeared as they came to know, understand, and appreciate each other. Both families were happy. After a few months, Robert and Theresa started thinking about marriage. Robert told Theresa: "I want you for my wife." Theresa and Robert discussed the issue for a while and both came to the conclusion that their relationship was good and healthy enough to make a good marriage. They got married the first day of spring. It was a joyous and solemn celebration.

STORY 3

Amy was successful in her professional life and had many good and reliable friends. But she was starting to feel she wanted a greater sense of security and stability in her life. One of her friends introduced her to Tom whom she found lively and intelligent. Tom also liked her calm strength and warmth. They dated each other for a few months, and except for occasional fights, they seemed to get along well. One night, Tom held Amy in his arms and told her how good he felt with her. Amy agreed with a kiss. Two years passed. Amy and Tom had known each other well enough to decide that marriage was the right decision. They waited eight more months to get married in order to get the professional promotion that would grant them a secure future. They married the following October and knew they were ready now to have the family they had wanted.

LOVE AT FIRST SIGHT

While the interpretations of stories 2 and 3 varied to a certain extent, story 1 evoked overwhelmingly similar responses: all respondents interpreted it as an immediate and intense attraction which led to an irrational decision to get married. On the other hand, story 2 was viewed alternatively as a "fix-up," an "arranged marriage," a "relationship that begins without love but which might end up with love," or as "a mature marriage of love." Similarly, story 3 was viewed as a "Yuppie story of people who do not love each other," or as "a nice combination of passion and reason," or as a "modern love story." Thus, while story 1 was almost invariably interpreted as a marriage undertaken on the basis of impulsive passion, the interpretations of stories 2 and 3 varied between "a mature love" and "a cold-hearted and calculated enterprise." This result suggests that the meaning of slow-paced love stories is not as well codified as that of fast-paced ones.

It is not difficult to account for the high degree of agreement in the interpretation of story 1. Confirming that this romantic model has thoroughly pervaded popular culture, respondents viewed it as "the most stereotypical" and "closest to novels or movies," the "typical storybook," or a "Hollywood fantasy." These responses go hand in hand with my own conjecture that story 1 corresponds to the romantic code of love unrelentingly depicted and disseminated by novels and cinema fiction, in both elite and popular culture.

Where respondents disagreed with regard to story 1 was on the nature of the irrational emotion felt by its protagonists. While they agreed on the structure of the story (its pace, order, and progression), they disagreed on the frame within which to interpret that structure. A small minority saw it as "love at first sight," whereas almost all others viewed it as an infatuation, or—a twist performed independently and enjoyably by many respondents—as "lust as first sight." The first interpretation is explicitly opposed to the second because "often people think that it's love at the beginning of a relation when that's just infatuation, or a sexual need, but not necessarily love, they can be easily mixed up" (working-class female, homemaker, interview 9). This careful separation between different emotions boils down to an attempt to demystify the "love at first sight myth" and was voiced by many respondents, of all socioeconomic strata and of both genders. For example:

> When I read the first story I had the sense of it taking place a long time ago and maybe because it's trains. I have a feeling of it being a time where the only way you could sleep with somebody is to marry them. So here is two people who were just very hot for each other so they decide to get married so that they can do it. (Female filmmaker, interview 2)

In answering an explicit question on the issue, most respondents do not believe in or subscribe to the idea of love at first sight.[14] Instead of interpreting story 1 as the beginning of a possibly lifelong love story, as could have been the case in the Romantic tradition, respondents viewed it as merely the beginning ("infatuation") of a story with dubious chances of lasting the lifetime of its protagonists. In its frequent resort to "lust at first sight" or "[sexual] chemistry at first sight," this interpretation shifts the lifelong projected narrative of "love at first sight" to a beginning sequence or fragment of a story with a rather different emotional tonality, that of sexual desire or infatuation.

Whenever sexuality was mentioned as a necessary element of romantic love, it was always differentiated from love; that is, love can encompass sexuality as long as it supersedes and "elevates" it. Some respondents even viewed sexuality for its own sake as "very unromantic."[15] Although romantic love has become sexualized, it is still viewed as a "higher" value, both symbolically and morally, than sex per se. Thus, even if sex has been assimilated into the romantic bond, a normative hierarchy between romantic love and sex persists.[16] This hierarchy appears clearly in the meaning of the word "infatuation," which respondents often used to interpret the feelings of the protagonists of story 1.

It was not until the end of the eighteenth century that "infatuation" began to acquire its modern sense of "being foolishly in love." Prior to that, it meant "being fatuous and foolish" in an unspecified way (*Oxford English Dictionary*). The concept of "infatuation" dismisses the sentiment of "love at first sight" by viewing it as an illusion, a mistaken identification of love with the fleeting feeling of sexual arousal. And this carries a double ideological message: intense and immediate emotions are deceptive and unreliable, and sexual attraction is an insufficient and even dangerous reason to choose a mate.[17]

If, as is reasonable to surmise, the cultural ideal of romantic love, and more specifically of "love at first sight," is anchored in the bodily experience of sexual arousal, these findings are somewhat surprising. The twentieth-century integration of sexuality into romantic love might lead us to expect more hospitality to a sexually based "love at first sight." But the acceptance of sexuality as part of love has come with an acceptance of the value of sexuality for its own sake. As sociologist Steven Seidman argues, concurrently with the increasing legitimacy of sexuality as a medium for the expression of love, political and medical discourses have disentangled it from the emotions it was supposed to express and reinforce.[18] I submit that this legitimation of sex for its own sake has demystified the cultural narrative of "love at first sight," precisely on the ground that it is "just" sexual attraction. Whereas in the Romantic tradition sexual arousal was sublimated—and therefore made legitimate—into the scenario of "love at first sight," today love at first sight is suspected of being a pretense for what can now be openly acknowledged, namely, sexual desire. Because sex is now an acceptable and necessary component of intimacy, even a form of self-expression, its sublimated expression in the cultural ideal of love at first sight is paradoxically jeopardized. This in turn implies that love and sex can now form the bases for *separate and parallel life narratives*.[19]

To the fast and intense narrative of story 1, respondents usually prefer a slower one where two people should spend time together, "know each other," and "become friends" before they become lovers. These respondents therefore viewed story 1 as "foolish," "risky," "adventuresome," "a sort of a fairy tale," "cute as a story, but silly in real life," "a silly story," "teenage infatuation," "unrealistic," "unreal," or "surreal." Almost everyone considered the marriage of the protagonists as too hasty and "most likely to have problems." The view that to be successful a relationship should rest on the secure ground of mutual knowledge and familiarity was almost unanimous.

There is a long tradition, grounded in the various discourses of religion, philosophy, psychotherapy, and folk wisdom, condemning the use of intense and immediate emotions as a way to gain self-knowledge.[20] The suspicion of intense emotions seems to be especially marked in American culture, as evinced by my respondents' repeated claims that one can never trust such immediate and irrational feelings. Although they did not employ the vocabulary of moralists, in dismissing story 1 they indicated a belief that intense and hasty emotional attachments are unreliable indicators of future feelings and should therefore be controlled and appropriately managed rather than simply yielded to. This, it should be noted, differs from the sensibility of European Romanticism, which asserts that spontaneous and turbulent feelings can and must be sustained and developed into a larger narrative because they originate in and affirm the lover's total being.

As expected, the code of love represented by story 1 was the most commonly understood by respondents, but only in the negative: it was also the most delegitimized by the "commonsense" idea that infatuation is a volatile and unreliable emotion. This implies that the most widely established and thoroughly codified model of love is not the model considered most likely to be successful. How do my respondents perceive and manage such an incongruity?

REALIST LOVE

On the surface, respondents deal with this question by substituting for the model of intense and irrational love more modest and "realistic" views. Using metaphors such as "partnership," "hard work," "foundations," "building," "growth," "working at love," respondents expressed the idea that if a romantic relationship is to be "successful," true love has to evolve with time and increasing mutual knowledge. Despite their differences in content and structure, stories 2 and 3 were often lumped together into the same narrative frame when contrasted with story 1. Both the other stories were considered slow, "plausible," "comfortable," "more about friendship than passion and sex," "nice and healthy," "practical," "wonderful" and "realistic," a "nice combination of love and practicality" or of "comfort and passion." The positive responses to these stories revolve around such notions as, the characters "didn't jump," they "feel very real," "[the relationship] provides a secure future," "stability."[21] The facts that both stories unfold and develop over a longer time span (a few months and a few years, respectively) and that the protagonists seem to ground their choice of partner on personality traits cue the reader into a "realist" narrative of love. Realist models of love are systematically opposed to "fantasy-based" ("Hollywood," "story-like") models. They enact the phenomenological categories of everyday life experience, as set forth by Alfred Schutz, the central proponent of the "sociology of everyday life."[22] These categories include:

Common Sense: a type of knowledge invoked in the course of everyday life.[23] The realist model is viewed by respondents themselves as the most "commonsensical" one, as seen in the following example:

What do you think of [story 1]?

. . . it's sort of a fairy tale, I guess. It's something that I would never do; and it's like, common sense tells me that you don't do something like that. You hear those things and you think, well, that's stupid, that's dumb. (Female editor, interview 3)

The perception that the first model is a fairy tale, while the second appeals to common sense is also articulated by other respondents:

Do you think that romance is important to keep love going between two people?

No, I really don't. I think it can even get in the way.

How so?

Because, especially if you're seeing a person every day or frequently, you have to accept at some point that you are dealing with a real person which has concerns which are very down-to-earth. And I think you can escape into an unreal world, and it basically means that you are neglecting these concerns. (Male Ph.D. student, interview 24)

The first model is perceived as unreal because it occurs outside the experience of everyday life. In contrast, the second exemplifies attributes of "realism" such as "practical," "down-to-earth," "real," "commonsensical."

Time: A realistic story is one that unfolds within the phenomenological experience of the time of everyday life. The condensed, "packed" time of the narrative model of love at first sight and its attendant dramatized and ritualized character are perceived as "unrealistic" and not characteristic of the "looser," longer, and less dramatic plots of everyday life.

Comfortable Relationships: The different temporality of everyday narratives of love points to a particular category of attachment. Instead of viewing love as resulting from an immediate, intense, and organic bond, respondents preferred to view love as evolving from "friendship" and being "comfortable," a relationship with the informal, casual, and unceremonious character of everyday interactions.

> [If] I ever get married—I am twenty-five years old now—it's not going to be a [inaudible] encounter on the train. It is going to be with somebody who I have grown with as a friend and a confidant and a lover and grown to love as someone I want to spend the rest of my life with. This [story 1] is strictly the story book. (Male doorman, interview 11)

In the same context, many other respondents noted that feelings of love for their partner evolved from doing "casual" and "informal" things together ("cooking together," "hanging out," "waking up together").

Taken-for-Grantedness: The expectation that everyday life should "flow" in a continuum of taken-for-granted settings and actions on which there is reliable and tacit agreement underwrites the notion of "compatibility," central to the realist conception of love. In such a union, partners should see their lives in a similar way so that disagreements can be kept to a minimum. Explaining why story 1 is not likely to have a successful outcome in the long run, one respondent said:

> I think they [protagonists of story 1] were wrong in getting married so
> spontaneously. I think they were dealing with infatuation and not real love,
> and I don't agree. I think they were not spontaneous but, uh, when you do
> something on a whim without thinking . . . love is not enough [of a reason]
> to get married.

> *What more is required?*

> You need to be able to get along with each other. You need to be compat-
> ible. You need to, there is a lot more than just loving someone. That's why
> I didn't marry Paula after the first week or so. I was feeling madly in love,
> but with time I found out the problems of personality we had. We would

have been irresponsible to get married after the first week. I do believe in love, perhaps infatuation at first sight, in terms of planning on the basis of that I think. (Male physician, interview 30)

In a similar vein, another respondent reached the conclusion that

I think marriage is a pretty heavy thing and I think, well, how could you know for sure, for sure, that this is the right person. You could know that you were tremendously attracted to them and that you had everything in the world in common with them, but maybe a good marriage has got to, um, have a few more. Maybe they just didn't describe what else they had in common, 'cause I think that it just seemed like there might be, that they fell in love, but, I just don't think it's that believable. 'Cause I think that, to get married, you have to, uh, I don't know, more than romantic love.

More than romantic love. What, for example?

Ah, well, I guess I'm more practical. I think you have to, um, know what kind of lifestyle you want and if you have that in common and if you're both night people or morning people or if you both like to eat the same things or, uh, if you want lots of children or no children, that kind of thing. (Female artist, interview 35)

Everyday Life as Work: For the idea that love results from an immediate, effortless, and organic bond, respondents substituted the commonsensical notion that "love is work." For example:

[If] you're in a good love relationship, it means that it is alive, that it is changing. You put energy into it, you put effort into it, you give something to the other person, and they give something to you. It is always work. I don't think that relationships ever sit idle. Well, if you are people for whom romantic things occur, it's gonna occur. I don't think you can seek it out. I don't think it makes sense. (Female artist, interview 33)

The idea of "love as work" generalizes the experience that everyday life is managed through delayed gratification rather than through play and instant pleasure. Furthermore, the metaphor reflects the pragmatic orientation of everyday life, geared toward "making things work" and "getting things done" rather than toward contemplation or aesthetic experience.

Long-term relationships, lived and shared daily, embody all five characteristics of everyday life, and these characteristics are the context for such phrases as "realistic" and "down-to-earth" used by respondents. In everyday life, as set forth by Schutz, there is no place for intense, extreme emotions. Thus, stories 2 and 3 were seen as "realistic" because they were grounded in the everyday, while story 1 was seen as unrealistic. The realm opposed to everyday life was associated with fantasy and mass media representations.

The answers I received when I turned from questions such as "What do you think of this story" to "Which story do you like best, and why?" require the findings presented above to be seriously qualified. Thus, although most respondents initially rejected story 1, when they were asked to compare it with the other stories, they viewed it as the most "interesting," "original," and "fascinating" of the three. Even though they had earlier viewed it as a "typical story-book romance," respondents acknowledged that it stimulated their imagination more than the other two. The same respondents who evaluated story 1 as "stereotypical" and "unreal" also viewed it as the "true romantic [story]," "the most passionate" and "fun," "the most interesting" and "unconventional," "[having] spice and adventure," "a wonderful romance," and "spontaneous." The characters were viewed as "enchanted," "enthralled," and "totally spontaneous." In the words of one respondent, the story is "magical" and "pure fantasy." All these evaluations underscore the same idea: that the story embodies intense, spontaneous, and exceptional feelings, typical of the genuine romantic sentiment. Because this story does not specify the nature and quality of the protagonists' feelings for each other, respondents must infer romance only from the suddenness or intensity or seeming irrationality of those feelings. Thus, even though almost all respondents disapprove of the haste with which this marriage occurs, they still consider it an example par excellence of romanticism in its affirmation of pure passion.

This evaluation of story 1 was expressed by the *same* respondents who had earlier dismissed it. Respondents thus rejected and praised the same story, depending on the question asked and the context. Story 2, which was often interpreted positively at the beginning of the interview, was later rejected as "an arranged marriage," a "business-like deal," "cold, dry and clinical," "conformist," a "calculated decision," and "unromantic." That is, when evaluated in the semantic context of romance, story 2 was viewed as unappealing and old-fashioned. Similarly, story 3 was deemed to be too "rational," "cold" and "calculating," "the dullest possible relationship," "structured," "mapped out," "mechanical," "typically yuppie," "carefully planned," having "no warmth," "too slow-moving," and "unromantic." The protagonists of story 3 were viewed as looking for stability and security at the price, as one respondent put it, of "sacrificing something important: enchantment." Thus, while these two stories satisfy criteria of realism and compatibility, they lack the romantic qualities found in story 1.

The simultaneous affirmation of both models can be seen clearly with the following respondent, a working-class man, fifty-five-years old, without a high-school education. Earlier in the interview, this man had dismissed story 1 as a simple infatuation and had called the other two stories more "real." Later in the interview, however:

Which one of the three stories is the closest to your ideal of romantic love?

I don't know. If you talk love, I guess the first one, because they never really thought about something else, they didn't have time to think about anything else, it's just . . . I guess they just fell in love and they got married.

Which story is the furthest from your ideal?

[Long pause.] I don't want to contradict myself now.

You can say whatever you want.

But I think I want to contradict myself.

That means you want to say story 1?

You see, it's hard. I don't really know whether this was love or not. To me this strikes me as if it was just—they were just attracted to each other, right away. I don't know, I guess story 2 would be probably the furthest. That's my opinion. (Male cleaning man, interview 40)

When asked to choose the story closest to his ideal, he was faced with the contradiction inherent in simultaneously professing two incompatible narratives of love. This man's hesitations and self-conscious remarks point to his awareness of and discomfort with his inconsistency.

Hence, in their evaluation of the three stories, respondents alternately embraced both narrative frames, the idealist and the realist, at different points of the interview. The narrative frame elicited by story 1 served as the normative ground against which the other two stories were compared and contrasted, and vice-versa, as we see in the following examples.

One female interviewee read story 1 and immediately responded "That's ridiculous. This story is unreal." She also responded immediately to story 2 by saying: "It's a nice story . . . I wish it would happen to me." Later in the interview, when asked which story she liked best, this respondent answered without hesitation "story 1," declaring that "story 2 made her mad" because it reminded her of her mother trying to fix her up with men she did not want to date. After reading story 1, a male respondent said, "It [is] not romantic because it is too impulsive"

and represents "simple sexual desire." Later in the interview, when asked
which was his favorite story and the one that came closest to his ideal
of love, he chose story 1 on the grounds that it was the most romantic
and spontaneous. Another man responded that, although the relationships in stories 2 or 3 are more likely to last, he preferred story 1 because
one should "take a shot, take a risk, be spontaneous." The same interviewee further suggested that even though the relationships in stories 2
and 3 were the most likely to last, they were also the most boring.

Both the romantic and the realist narrative frames were held as ideal
by the same people, who invoke them for different reasons at different
points of the interview to evaluate either the stories' romanticism or the
couples' chance of marital success.

REALITY AS FICTION

How do these narrative frames and their interpretations translate into
respondents' autobiographical accounts of their own love stories? According to which model do people "author" their own love stories? Despite respondents' insistence that the realist model is the most likely to
be successful, their most "memorable" love stories are structured according to narratives of love at first sight.

When asked to remember their own "most memorable love stories,"
respondents *always* narrated real-life stories that corresponded to the
first narrative model. The fantasy-based model of love is cognitively and
emotionally more salient than the realist one.[24] Consider the following
example of a man who declared earlier in the interview that he found
story 1 the least appealing. When he recounted his encounter with the
woman he was involved with at the time of the interview, he responded
as follows:

> The most romantic moment that I can remember quite well was the first time
> that I met my former to present girlfriend, January 31st of last year, and I
> had been invited to a Super Bowl party and she had been invited to the same
> party by mutual friends. And it was the kind of thing that we looked at each
> other and we first saw each other, it's like in the movies, you know, where
> the whole rest of the world, everybody else, fades into oblivion and it's just
> you and her. That's how it was like. We just knew right away that we were
> struck by this whirlwind of emotion, and we went to the fire escape away
> from the party. We talked and hugged, we left the party early. We went out
> to a place to eat, and we found ourselves hugging each other in the restau-
> rant, because of this newfound attraction, chemistry, love which had whirl-

wind. And she asked me to drop her off, and it wasn't even a question of "Am I going to take your number," because we knew that there was this tremendous love that we had for each other. And that to me is the most romantic experience I can remember. It wasn't planned or anything, there was this tremendous tremendous love at first sight which subsequently was problematic. (Male physician, interview 8)

The stereotypical character of this account is so marked that the respondent himself self-consciously admits it was "just like in the movies" and invokes such clichés of love at first sight as the world fading into oblivion. Moreover, although the relationship subsequently turned "sour," the story recounted is cut off from the present and is narratively self-contained. That is, it does not offer a diachronic continuity between the first meeting and its disillusioning development but rehearses only the synchronic vividness and intensity of the initial encounter.

Another response, from a married woman, further illustrates how the model of love at first sight suffuses respondents' memories. She tells two most memorable stories. In the first, she fell in love with a man who was sitting near her on a plane. Here is her second story:

At the concert [in a city she had just moved to] I sat near a man who—I just liked his energy and every time I looked at him, he kind of made me feel excited, and he would look at me and smile and I would smile back and—I remember, I was having a particularly good time. I got up and danced with my friend Nancy and I kept thinking, Should I go over and talk to him? I didn't. As we were leaving, he gave me his card and said, you know, I can't even remember if he said anything. And I called him up a few days later and we talked. I went over to his apartment and I was tremendously attracted to him.

Did you have a relationship?

Yeah, all summer long. . . . It was a wonderful romance . . . it was very exciting. It was in a place that I never lived in before. I didn't know anyone, that kind of thing. So it was a real adventure and I was kind of thrilled by the whole thing, and I was very excited. (Female artist, interview 35)

Although this woman is married, she did not choose her encounter with her husband as her most memorable love story. Like the previous respondent's, this story bears the characteristics of the adventurous model of love at first sight. It occurred in an unfamiliar environment under the "extraordinary circumstances" of a long summer vacation. The attraction was immediate, and the relationship began in excitement and wordless communication, through looks and smiles. Conversely, when she described her relationship with her husband—which she did not cite even as her second most memorable story—she described a slow and progressive relationship that was neither intense nor engrossing.

Similarly, a male orchestra conductor gave as his most memorable story a one-evening encounter with a woman he did not even have sex with.

> *Do you feel that you have had a love story that has corresponded to your ideal of love?*
>
> The woman I spent that one evening with after the concert. The evening, except for the fact we hadn't had sex, that evening was pretty much what I always dreamt. (Male musician, interview 33)

For this respondent, this episode was more romantic than anything in three long-lasting relationships he had had, which had been serious enough for him to live with the women involved. Here again, the story shares its structure with the idealist model of love at first sight. It is contained within a neatly self-contained temporal unit, a single evening, and fulfilled all his "dreams," and this despite the fact that the woman's departure was the obstacle that prevented them from consummating the relationship.

Finally, here are the stories of a twenty-eight-year-old female avant-garde filmmaker and a married cleaning man, respectively:

> The most memorable [story] is when I was 18 I met a man who was 35 and who was incredibly. . . . I met this guy who was a musician. I was selling fruits and nuts on the street at that time. He came by the car a couple of times and asked me out on a date and I had never . . . the idea that somebody like him could find me attractive made me feel very sophisticated and. . . . I had this very intense affair with him for a couple of weeks, and then I ended it."

Again, a relationship that lasted "a couple of weeks" made a more memorable story than that of her five-year relationship with another man.

> I could tell you [the story], but I don't know if I could tell you or not.
>
> *It's totally up to you.*
>
> It does not involve my wife. This happened years ago. You say no one will see this?
>
> *If someone does, it will be without mention of your name or even of the place where I interviewed you.*

> I tended bar years ago, and a nice French girl, I spent, uh, I don't know how to describe, uh, it was a passionate woman, it's all I could say, it was a very nice experience because it was a very romantic winter and we really did a lot of fun things together, I don't know how to put it into words, but it was a very very nice thing.

Like the previous stories, these two accounts contain the emotional intensity and swift pace of the idealist narrative and take place in what is recalled as "extraordinary" or "unusual" circumstances (adultery in the latter case; sexual initiation by a much older man in the former).

As we see from these accounts, the romantic self "authors" its most memorable romantic experiences by mimicking the intensely ritualized temporal structure of mass media love stories. The self-contained and tightly knit structure of these adventures is more *aesthetic*, in Georg Simmel's sense of the word, than the shapeless, unstylized, and open-ended flow of romantic relationships in everyday life.[25] All the experiences of my respondents had a clear beginning and a tight dramatic structure. Events happen quickly and have a strong emotional effect on the protagonists. All stories have obstacles which prevent the protagonists from carrying on the love story into marriage or a long-lasting bond. Finally, they differ from the ongoing and fuzzier plots of everyday life in coming to a sharply marked end: almost all these memorable love stories have a strong narrative closure.[26] Only three out of the fifty interviewees cited a relationship that was under way at the time of the interview as their most memorably romantic; all the others had been brought to a clear closure.

These aestheticized autobiographical accounts seem to be pure signs, the imitations of fictional codes without underlying referents, and it is tempting to see them as quintessentially postmodern. For, as a regime of representation, postmodernism is characterized by its claim that life is a text, a code with no real referent. Such a conclusion would not be justified, however. Moralists and scholars of all persuasions were claiming long before the postmodern era that the codes of love prevail over their "real referent." Even as circumspect a historian as Lawrence Stone expresses the opinion that romantic love "is a product . . . of learned cultural expectations, which became fashionable in the late eighteenth century thanks largely to the spread of novel-reading. . . . [The romantic novel] of the late eighteenth and early nineteenth centuries has much to answer for in the way of disastrous love affairs and of imprudent and unhappy marriages."[27] The system theorist Niklas Luhmann, who has argued at length that romantic love is less a sentiment than a "symbolic code, has remarked of the eighteenth century that "English women who try to emulate characters in pre-Victorian novels have to wait for visible signs of nuptial love before allowing themselves to discover consciously what love is."[28] While these scholars share the postmodern assumption that romantic love is a cultural form with no independent referent, they also believe that the romantic code has been responsible for romantic emotions for quite some time.

But ultimately this new view of history, finding postmodern love in "modern" or premodern moral discourse, does not resolve the question of whether romantic fiction has or has not replaced our actual "experience." These autobiographical stories cannot be simply reduced to a copy or simulacrum of their fictional "code." The influence is mutual; as psychologist Jerome Bruner aptly puts it, "narrative imitates life, life imitates narrative."[29] This intrinsically blurred and fuzzy boundary between life and texts must be addressed and recast by a postmodern theory of love.

FICTION AS REALITY

To clarify how life and narrative imitate each other, let us further clarify categories of experience, to understand which category is more likely to lend itself to fictional representation. In their seminal work in phenomenological anthropology, Lyman and Scott distinguish two types of experience that parallel the realist and idealist romantic narrative frames: the "ordinary" and the "extraordinary." "Adventure" is a particular type of experience that is isolated from the flow of daily events precisely because of its highly dramatic and tightly knit narrative structure. "Adventures start and end with stacatto notes. In contrast, routine life moves from episode to episode as in a symphony, each one marked by the ending of one melodious strain and the beginning of another. Routine life falls into a context of continuities; adventures are cut off from the entanglements of and connections to everyday life."[30] Interestingly enough, these authors use "romantic affairs" as the paramount example of the social experience of "adventure." As they explain, "[Sex] is always potentially adventurous because it uniquely combines physiological stimulation with social risks and psychological thrills."[31] A compact and self-contained narrative structure such as that of story 1 can more easily make sense of sexual attraction because sex is physiologically climactic and stands outside the stream of ordinary life. Love affairs, potential or actualized, are physiologically, emotionally, and cognitively salient. By contrast, long-term relationships are less salient because the "dramas [of everyday life] reside precisely in their dullness. They do not stimulate the imagination."[32]

From another theoretical tradition, economist Tibor Scitovsky distinguishes categories that also parallel realistic and idealist frameworks, what he calls the drive to comfort and the drive to excitation. The latter is elicited when one experiences something new; comfort is attained when an initial level of arousal is reduced, for example, by stretching excitation over a "longue" or "moyenne durée."[33] Thus, the narrative models of stories 2 and 3 would reflect the drive toward comfort; story 1 the drive to excitation. In fact, "comfort" is the word used most frequently in positive evaluations of stories 2 and 3, and "exciting" and "adventure" are cited in descriptions of story 1.

Thus the dichotomy between the idealist-fictional and realist-everyday narrative frames of love cannot be adequately reduced to simple oppositions between "texts" and "reality" or "representation" and "referent." There is thus a kind of "fit" between the narrative frameworks and *different categories of physical and phenomenological experience*: the "idealist" story is propelled by the drive to excitation and enacts the highly aestheticized properties of "adventure," while the "realist" narrative is driven toward comfort and the shapeless but reliable flow of everyday life. These two narrative romantic codes are embedded in the distinction between the uneventful, routine character of everyday life and the upsurges of emotion that periodically erupt in the realm of the everyday and make for "drama."

My respondents' highly aestheticized autobiographical accounts of romantic passion are thus anchored in bodily experiences of excitation and in a universal distinction between routine and drama. This gives a new twist to our understanding of the postmodern condition of romance, one that includes the paramount reality of bodily experiences. As Featherstone suggests, certain forms of experience embedded in the body are "progressively submitted to the codification of cultural producers."[34] *These codes in turn feed back into everyday life and provide stylized narratives within which one makes sense of his or her experience.*

Now, if the romantic experience is organized around two poles that are phenomenological and physiological as well as narrative, what difference does it make that one type rather than the other is endlessly represented and codified in the highly visual and realistic narrative codes of media culture and enters the realm of everyday life via the consumption of mass media forms? Following Simmel, Featherstone contends that highly stylized narratives (such as my respondents' autobiographical accounts) can provide a way to overcome the heterogeneity of everyday life by supplying it with an art-like unity and coherence.[35] However, I would argue that these aestheticized narratives of love do not unify the romantic self with a "heroic" telos but rather split it into incompatible narratives, making it the site of the very contradictions of late capitalism that Featherstone thinks these codes overcome. Moreover, far from being viewed as a desirable or "heroic" life narrative, the romantic ideal was treated by my respondents with suspicion, derision, and ironic distance.

A POSTMODERN ROMANTIC CONDITION

In an analysis of consumer dissatisfaction, Scitovsky suggests that too high a level of arousal leads to discomfort, but too low a level results in boredom. "Pleasure" is the experience of a change from either too much or too little arousal back to a level of optimal comfort.[36] Extending Scitovsky's argument, Albert O. Hirschman suggests that there is "a contradiction between pleasure and comfort: for pleasure to be experienced, comfort must be sacrificed temporarily."[37] In our context, this means that to be pleasurable, that is, "exciting," relationships must sacrifice comfort—at least periodically. But it implies also that exciting relationships are "doomed" to end in comfort and, if we are to believe Scitovsky, eventually in boredom. Accordingly, the stories presented to my interviewees tap into different and ultimately incompatible psychological drives. The most salient memories are those associated with high levels of arousal, and it is these that the romantic self recalls as "exciting." But in evaluating the chances of success of a relationship, the romantic self opts for pragmatic narratives of longevity and stability, in short, for "comfort." The splitting of the romantic self into conflicting narrative structures entails the experience of a psychological contradiction.[38] I would like now to argue that this psychological contradiction feeds into and is sustained by a broader cultural contradiction characteristic of consumer culture.

Most traditional societies privilege comfort and carefully attempt to control (or suppress) the expression of the drive to excitation exemplified in sexual attraction.[39] The cultural ideal of romantic love has given a greater legitimacy to the intensity of passion and sexual attraction. It restricts the possible number of partners by emphasizing the uniqueness of the beloved and subsuming the romantic biography under a single, lifelong narrative ("le grand amour"). But this narrative of love almost never becomes a narrative of comfort. Since it must affirm the supremacy of passion, it is usually doomed to end with the parting or death of the lovers.[40] Postmodern culture has seen the collapse of overarching, life-long romantic narratives, which it has compressed into the briefer and repeatable form of the affair.

The cultural prominence of the romantic affair is related to the transformations undergone by sexuality after World War II. During this period, sex for its own sake has been progressively legitimized and even promoted by the political discourses of feminist and gay liberation, a process that was aided by the powerful cultural idioms of the sphere of consumption.[41] In its intrinsic transience and affirmation of pleasure, novelty, and excitement, the affair is a quintessential postmodern experience and contains a "structure of feeling" with affinities (in Max Weber's sense of the word) to the emotions and cultural values fostered by the sphere of consumption.[42]

As Scitovsky argues, consumption rests on the drive toward excitation because the purchase and experience of new commodities are a source of pleasure, and the affair, with all the excitement of a new lover, feeds this drive as well. "Novelty is a major source of satisfaction, to judge by the large quantity we avidly consume every day and the high value we place on it. First love, first taste of some special food, or a naked body, together with many firsts, are among our most cherished memories."[43] Moreover, the affair is undergirt by a consumerist definition of identity as a series of lifestyle choices. During the Victorian era, people chose from a very narrow pool of available partners and often felt compelled to marry their first suitor. The contemporary affair, by contrast, presupposes variety and freedom to choose. This "shop-and-choose" outlook is the effect not only of a much wider pool of available partners but also of the pervasion of romantic practices by a consumerist mentality: the belief that one should commit oneself only after a long process of information gathering.[44] The consumerist motive of "freedom of choice" among transient but renewable pleasures has radically altered the premodern romantic narrative structure.

The traditional Romantic narrative of "le grand amour" was a double narrative, not only of revelation (a sudden, unforeseen conviction of the unique desirability of another person) but of a kind of secular salvation: from "love at first sight," lovers projected themselves whole into a future that could redeem their entire existence, even though they might die of it. Thus Emma Bovary clings to the idea that her relationship with Rodolphe is no mere "affair" but rather the prelude to the "great" narrative she strives for and waits for. In this respect, Emma stands on the threshold between the (modern) Romantic sensibility in which lives are spent waiting for—or consuming themselves in—a life-long "master" narrative of love and the postmodern one in which several affairs—self-contained and "local" narratives of love—occur serially in the course of a life. The affair can be viewed as a postmodern expression of what Fredric Jameson calls *intensities*. In contrast to the premodern era, romantic intensities have eliminated the experience of "waiting," which was so central in Victorian women's lives, and are characterized by a total absence of the tragic. Tragedy is the inscription within a narrative structure of cosmic, ineluctable forces that rule over and ruin individuals lives. By their involvement, however, these forces raise those lives beyond the level of the merely individual, the subjective, the haphazard, giving human lives the weight of "destiny." In the equanimity with which they recount falling in and out of love, the respondents' autobiographical accounts bear a decisively untragic "lightness." Nowhere could I find the poignancy and existential gravity of the Romantic idea of the "great love," because respondents—both men and women—do not project their selves into an all-encompassing narrative of love initiated by the revelation of a unique and eternal love. Their stories start in a mode of "excitation" rather than "revelation." They have a sharply marked beginning and end—which is why they deserve the name of "story"—but little intermediate narrative development, the frequent presence of an obstacle that might have driven such development (e.g., being already married, living in different places). Affairs, then, are self-contained narrative episodes disconnected from one another in the flow of experience, resulting in a fragmenting of the experience of love into separate emotional units (the transitory settings of so many of these stories exhibit a corresponding spatial fragmentation). Romantic intensities similarly fragment time into what Jameson calls "charges of affect" and thus contribute to the "flat" present deemed characteristic of the postmodern contraction of time: temporality loses the unifying continuity of a life characterized by either a stable, enduring relationship or a grand (or grandiose) passion.[45]

While human beings have doubtless always had sex before or outside marriage, the "affairs" we have been looking at are peculiarly postmodern in a number of respects. First, they share with the romantic travel analyzed in the last chapter a central feature of postmodernism, namely, the institutionalization of liminality inside the market.[46] This form of liminality provides postmodernity a defining rhetorical figure—the inversion of normative hierarchies—and symbolic form—the reversal of identities and blurring of boundaries, social, aesthetic, and cultural. Almost all the affairs recounted above took place on geographic, institutional, and temporal margins, away from the routine space of home and work, outside the framework of family, marriage, job, in the exceptional time marked by romantic intensities and the merging of selves.

Second, the sexual flavor of "liberation" since the 1960s makes the postmodern "affair" significantly different from the indiscriminate and power-ridden search for sexual pleasure embodied by the archetypical characters of Don Juan or Casanova. Contemporary affairs are more likely to be lived as sexual pleasure by *both* sexes. Third, they do not contain any element of transgression and do not oppose any normative or moral imperative. Instead, they affirm the diffuse equalitarian eroticism and primal liberation of the instincts that, according to Daniel Bell, has marked the postmodern onslaught on middle-class values.[47] Finally, underlying the postmodern affair is a definition of identity based on lifestyle choices and consumer rationality. Although as yet there is little empirical data on this matter, I submit that the "affair" characterizes the romantic experience of those professionals and new cultural intermediaries, located in large urban centers, who are most proficient at switching between sexual pleasure and forms of economic rationality. One might even venture to suggest that the "commitment phobia" so remarked on in this population is a by-product of an identity largely based on the affirmation of autonomy through lifestyle choices, resulting in a reluctance to give up the freedom to choose and the prospect of "finding a better mate."

Postmodern mass culture privileges the consumption of leisure as a ritual of liminality and expenditure, a withdrawal from everyday life with the purpose of regenerating one's connection to society through the liberation of energy and the reversal of customary constraints in an intense, euphoric, and transient experience of novelty. As we have seen, "extraordinary" experiences are, by their nature, more susceptible to ritualization than the experiences of everyday life. The meanings of everyday life are less formalized, paler and fuzzier, and therefore emotionally less intense than the meanings contained not only in "adventures" and "affairs" but in leisure in general.

The narrative within which memories are organized and the one within which the romantic self projects its chances for success do not match each other and may even contradict each other, thus thwarting the possibility of a continuous temporal structure containing a homogeneous self. The contemporary romantic self is marked by its persistent, sysiphian attempt to conjure up the local and fleeting intensity of the love affair within long-term global narratives of love (such as marriage), to reconcile an overarching narrative of enduring love with the fragmentary intensity of affairs. This splitting of the romantic self into incompatible narrative structures, the patching of self-contained, discontinous affairs into narratives of lifelong love, breaks the coherent, "heroic" self of modernity into a "collage" of conflicting narrative selves.[48] We now turn to the crisis of representation that accompanies this unhappy postmodern romantic self.

Approached as fiction, stories 2 and 3 are readily interpreted as expressions of "realistic" love and used as a narrative frame within which respondents project a desirable, lifelong love story. In respondents' own autobiographies, however, similar stories are interpreted according to a standard set by the affair and are consequently suspected of not referring to the actual feeling of love. In other words, when experienced, the realist narrative frame seems to empty itself of its signified, or at least to struggle to find one. By contrast, when the first narrative frame is presented as a fictional story, it is viewed as "fabricated" and "unreal," but when experienced it is no longer viewed as an empty signifier but rather as the "real referent" lived to its fullest meaning. For example, when asked to choose the most romantic story, one man chose (the realist) story 2, but when he recalled and explained what had gone wrong in his own most recent relationship, he said:

> The last [relationship], we understood each other and we got along so well, but there was almost a spark missing.
>
> *What do you mean?*
>
> We were very compatible. We loved being together on a day-to-day basis. We got along very well. But the more romantic, ideal side really never, uh, so I missed that.
>
> *What do you mean when you say that the romantic side was missing?*
>
> I felt almost as if I was going to bed with my best friend instead of with a lover. (Male orchestra conductor, interview 33)

Clearly, this story has the "fuzzy" character of the plots of everyday life and refers to the notion that compatibility is necessary if a relationship is to succeed. However, although this narrative model is normatively viewed as an ideal one, it is *experienced* as problematic in its lack of intensity and passion. This in turn prevents it from being incorporated into the romantic self as readily as the first model of love. In a similar vein:

In which of the marriages is it likely that there will be problems?

Number one.

Why?

'Cause that's me and that's why we had all the problems.

What were the problems?

The problem was, the romance ended.

So, what remained?

What remained? Another friend.

Why did the romance end?

Because we did not follow stories 2 and 3. (Male private investigator, interview 22)

This response exemplifies the crisis of representation contained within the contradictions observed above: this man had chosen story 1 as his favorite story, but its story structure became problematic in real life because it "did not follow" the careful path laid out in stories 2 and 3. Conversely, when this respondent's actual love stories did fit stories 2 and 3, he ceased to identify them as "romantic." As he said, his relationship stopped because the "romance ended." Not only does the model of love considered most likely to succeed diverge from the one experienced as most "striking," "interesting," or "memorable," but the realist model of success is evaluated against the background of the love-at-first-sight model, which renders it even more lacking in intensity and romance.

While the first narrative frame of intensity signifies "romance" without including the signified love, the second narrative frame, by contrast, offers this signified without the romantic signifier. This disjunction between the signifier of romance and the signified of love is one of the characteristic features of the "postmodern condition." In this disjunction appears a split autobiographical narrative structure: while the narrative signifier that best organizes respondents' most memorable stories embodies Jameson's "romantic intensities," this signifier is disconnected from the less-memorable but longer-lasting narrative that, respondents presume, captures the signified, love.

Even more interesting is the way in which respondents accounted for this discrepancy. Far from being viewed as an existential dilemma or a tragedy of human existence, these semiotic quandaries were analyzed and explained as *the by-product of mass-media culture.* For example:

Where do you think your ideas about love come from?

I think a lot of them come from the movies and they are, I think, I think the movies have fucked us up a great deal in terms of our images about love.

Fucked us up?

Yeah, I think that like the first story would be more like in the movies. They meet in the train and fall in love instantly, and they ran off and they get married, and we are supposed to believe that that's possible. And I don't think that it happens that way very often. So in that sense I think a lot of us spend our lives on trains hoping to fall in love. Sitting across the subway maybe I will meet my wife. It doesn't work that way. But there is still this expectation from the movies. (Male actor, interview 29)

Or:

Where do you think your ideas about love come from?

A large part, I guess, from media and from myths about love.

Which myths?

Oh, the myth about happily ever after and the myth of being swept off your feet, the myth, you know, I think the most dangerous myth for women, finding a man or being attached to a man somehow is, is so terribly important in order to make your life all right or something. I think those are very powerful for most people whether they think about it or even know it. I think those are probably the most powerful things, and I'm sure for me too even though I have thought about it a lot. Some of my ideas are from not wanting what my parents had and I guess mostly just from those images that you see in the media and that you see your friends all trying to live up to, probably the most influential things. (Female editor, interview 48).

Respondents self-consciously used stereotypical expressions ("love conquers all," "the princess being rescued," "a man for every woman") to describe early expectations that they suspect were formed by media stories and images. Like postmodern artists and sociologists, the respondents maintain the ironic stance that their representations and experiences are "simulacra," imitations of manufactured signs devoid of referents. The romantic self perceives itself ironically, like a pre-scripted actor who repeats the words and gestures of other pre-scripted actors, simply repeating repetitions.

We have now come full circle: the same narrative structure that respondents view as "Hollywoodian," "unreal," and "fabricated" is also the same one that respondents unproblematically use to name their romantic love stories. On the other hand, the narrative viewed as authentically reflecting the real feelings of love is also the one respondents have more difficulties seeing as unproblematically referring to love.

If, as Reinhart Koselleck argues, modernity is characterized by the increasing distance between reality and aspiration, postmodernity is best typified by the self-conscious creed that this distance results from imaginations overexposed to the overcodified culture of the mass media.[49] It is not pure chance that Umberto Eco chose love to define the postmodern: "I think of the post-modern attitude as that of a man who loves a very cultivated woman and knows he cannot say to her, `I love you madly,' because he knows that she knows (and she knows that he knows) that these words have already been written by Barbara Cartland. [He] loves her in an age of a lost innocence."[50] In other words, the postmodern romantic condition is characterized by the ironic perception that one can only repeat what has already been said and that one can only act as an actor in an anonymous and stereotypical play. Even Hollywood can no longer dispense unself-conscious formulas for romantic plots and is self-reflexively aware of the clichés of the genre.[51]

A final romantic memory provides an apt recapitulation of these themes.

What do you think of [story 2]?

It's also romantic.

Romantic.

I suppose it's not romantic in the classical sense. It's nice. It feels good. I mean it's nice. What we discussed earlier vis-á-vis whether it's better to start off quickly or, the first one is obviously love at first sight kind of, whereas the second is more developing, two people who are comfortable and share certain qualities or interests or desires and love develops.

Do you think that Robert and Theresa marry for love?

I think the long-term possibility, prospect of having a long-term, loving, strong relationship, if they are not in love yet.

Would you have liked to have met the partner of your life in the same way?

[Long silence.] I guess it wouldn't be my first choice, but it would certainly be a reasonable [one].

Why not your first choice?

Well, it lacks the excitement or the strong attraction that is most desirable thing to have, the sort of excited attraction and the strong feelings, and it does give, the story does give a sense that everyone is just kind of as if you choose a car.

So is it nice or not nice? You started by saying the story was nice.

Well, if it had more of a sense, the story is a little vague in terms of whether in fact they do develop any kind—

What is you impression? The story is vague on purpose so that I can see how you interpret it.

It wouldn't be my first choice . . . maybe it's what I think I should want and maybe it would be more practical . . . The truth of the matter is that one of the reasons I didn't get married some years ago when I was engaged was it was more of story 2 kind of situation and without real passion and excitement attached to it and I ultimately decided to break it. And in some way I did wrong.

In what way was it wrong?

Because I think in the long-term it would have been a healthy and viable and loving relationship. Maybe there was a little less excitement than one is promised by reading novels and watching what happens between Cary Grant and Gina Lollobrigida, sometimes have to sit in the living room and, ten years later, just read a book. It's part of life. (Male physician, interview 38)

This respondent was aware that he held conflicting representations. He also illustrates how the same narrative frame is interpreted differently when used as a memory structure and as a projective structure. When it structures his memory, story 2 is clearly not very exciting, but when projected into the future it is a desirable goal ("in the long run it would have been a healthy story"). Moreover, this man also held media (specifically cinematic) representations responsible for instilling in him what he perceived to be "unrealistic," "fabricated," and incompatible models. The romantic self is the site of deep contradictions that are not easily overcome even after one has committed to living one narrative.

The difficulty in choosing one narrative is accentuated by the perception that the romantic self is the result of textual determinations, "fabricated." The romantic self perceives itself in the halo of an ironic semiotic suspicion. As Jean Baudrillard has argued, in the postmodern era, the "masses" (as he mysteriously calls them) know their own lives are "simulations," repetitions of authorless signs empty of any real referent.[52] Thus postmodern love brings a crucial twist to La Rochefoucauld's saying that "few people would fall in love had they not heard about it." In the postmodern condition, many people doubt they are in love precisely because they have heard too much about it.[53]

CONCLUSION

The blurring of romantic reality and romantic fiction is not a characteristic confined to postmodern sensibility. The realist models of love codify the cultural experience of everyday life, while the romantic code derives from the bodily experience of sexual arousal and is embodied in the cultural scenario of the "adventure," an intense sexual interaction on the margins of social control, which displays marked dramatistic features and high emotional pitches. I have argued that the romantic code becomes a postmodern emotion only when it articulates other postmodern cultural idioms: the fragmentation of an overarching love narrative into a series of intense and usually short-lived experiences in which the first encounter is demystified; the replacement of a tragic structure of feeling by an ironic view of one's own romantic ideals; the cult of sexuality and self-realization in place of the religious devotion to another; and finally, the belief that texts and media shape one's romantic identity.

A review of the various findings of chapters 3, 4, and 5 reveals that the experience of liminality is a key feature of this new postmodern romantic sensibility. It is manifest in multiple cultural forms that echo and reinforce one another: through a pastoral utopia of romance in which the lovers isolate themselves in nature and invert the ordinary rules of conduct (chapter 3); through the consumption of leisure goods, especially travel, during which lovers release emotions and energies and abandon their everyday conduct (chapter 4); and finally through the experience of love affairs, or stories, in which the foregrounding of the present prevails over a linear projection into the future (chapter 5).

Liminality is the emotional mode through which romantic partners access the romantic utopia proper: in this utopian mode, the painstaking difficulties of relationships are erased within an organic bond; gender divisions, social identities, and class inequalities are negated by the mutual access to leisure, the suspension of responsibilities, and the fusion of selves within nature. The seclusion of the lovers is replete with cultural meaning, for it suspends and reverses not only everyday rules and norms but the spheres of production and reproduction as well. The intense, self-contained "vertical" temporality of liminality annuls the everyday "horizontal" time of effort, work, and routine. To the extent that the love affair exhibits together a liminality grounded in the sphere

of consumption, an intense fusion of selves, a transgression of normative conduct, a flat temporality, and a blurring of gender hierarchies, it
is a postmodern experience par excellence. Attempts to recover "romance" in long-term relationships usually come down to restaging the
liminal conditions of the affair. The couple thus initiates or rejuvenates
its bond through the temporal and cyclical withdrawal into conditions
of liminality: not only withdrawal from formal public selves, release of
emotional control, and so on, but also full participation in the realm of
commodified leisure. Encoded in commodities as well as images and stories, liminality is thus the means by which the sphere of consumption in-
heres in the phenomenolgy of romance.

Liminality is essential to the definition of the romantic utopia, and as
chapters 3, 4, and 5 show, it exerts a powerful fascination over respondents. Asked to remember their most romantic moment, respondents
cited one that took place in an exotic or natural setting, removed from
their home, symbolically and geographically. Asked to recount their most
memorable love story, even married respondents remembered ones that
preceded or were marginal to the institutional framework of marriage
and daily life. These stories were usually brief, intense, and suffused with
feelings of "enchantment" or "euphoria." These liminal experiences are
highly aestheticized and are the domain proper where media-like
lifestyles are experienced.

As Chapters 3, 4, and 5 highlighted in different ways, when reflecting on an image of romance or when thinking about the sources of their
representation of romance, respondents claimed that these images and
representations are fabricated by the "media" or created by and for
"commercial" interests. But when respondents attended to and retrieved
the salient, emotional meanings of their experiences, they become oblivious to what they otherwise readily "deconstruct" as mere media fabri-
cations. Undoubtedly, as Pierre Bourdieu incisively put it, the logic of
practice is different from the logic of logicians; people act according to
the shifting definitions of situations rather than according to the coherent script of the sociologist. While there is much truth to this, I would
argue that, in this case, my respondents' shifting frames of meaning also
reveal a postmodern crisis of representation, of which romance is a consummate example.

Laypeople sometimes act as sociologists and often engage in a critique
of the sources of their cultural representations. In the self-reflexive posture of the interview, respondents perceive the commercial underpinnings of the most aesthetic representations of romance, for example, in

natural or luxurious settings. However, the same signs that they readily deconstruct as "stereotypical" or "commercial" provide them with the most pristine and "clearly" defined experiences of romance. When enacted, these meanings are the "paramount romantic reality," upon which no "semiotic doubt" is cast. Liminality has a semiotic transparency in which the sign impeccably fits the "romantic referent."

By contrast, the "realistic" romantic signs, viewed by respondents as the only "real" ones, when they structure respondent's own experience, are more likely to provoke an anxious "semiotic query" as to whether the experience corresponds to the code of love. When actually used to construct one's romantic experience, the realistic model of romantic love provokes a semiotic breakdown, such a dissociation between the sign and its referent that the subject may wonder if it has an emotional referent at all. Intense and liminal romantic experiences are semiotically the most sturdy, even if, when reflected upon, they are readily viewed as "unreal," that is, as signs with no "real" referent.

Here we reach a paradox: although the liminal experience of love is perceived as the most potent semiotic frame and provides the most readily understood, remembered, and retrieved meanings—in short, imposes itself as the most powerful and "real" meaning—it is also suspected of being the most "unreal." The sign really appears to be more real than the paler reality, not because it has replaced it, but because the enactment of highly energized, monosemic, ritualized, and collective symbolic scenarios is semiotically and experientially more binding than the fuzzier, attenuated meanings of everyday life. In this sense can we say that in postmodern culture the relationship between the "signs" of romantic love and their referent has become problematic. The cultural categories through which romance is understood and lived as an intense and total emotion are the most likely to make its experience an immediate and direct one, but they are also the most likely to generate irony and self-consciousness. Because the less ritualized, more informal meanings of everyday life are more reluctant to point to "love" and are implicitly compared to the ritual meanings of romance, elaborate conceptual work is needed to bring "love" back in. In contemporary culture, such conceptual work is provided by various forms of therapeutic discourse, which stress that the true meaning and experience of love are beyond its ready-made images. In both cases, what the postmodern romantic lover is left with is either the ironic self-suspicion that one imitates Hollywood glamour or the therapeutic suspicion that one does not "work hard enough" to reveal the true essence of love beyond its dull appearances.

The result, I would argue, is that the quasi-universal contradiction between two equally powerful forms of love is not experienced as such. Instead, this contradiction is understood as the by-product either of one's vulnerability to mass media or of one's lack of self-knowledge.

If, as Fredric Jameson suggests, utopia is based on a temporal structure that links past to future and on the ability to restore the full clarity of one's freedom and desire, postmodern romantic love has an ambiguous utopian value.[54] Because it espouses an ironic self-consciousness and a "cool" emotional mode, it has flattened the forceful clarity and drama of emotions. Furthermore, its privileging of fragmentation and of a present-oriented intensity hinders a deepening of the meaning of love. However, utopian meanings are not entirely absent from the contemporary romantic condition, for postmodern love affirms a pleasure-oriented sexuality and even an androgynous equality between the genders.

PART 3

The Business of Love

CHAPTER 6

Reason within Passion

If romance is a potent idiom through which the culture of consumption addresses our desires, it does not necessarily mean that all of our romantic practices have been colonized by the market. In current research, there is a tendency to play media messages and consumer goods against "everyday life," viewed as a zone of "resistance" to the hegemony or cultural domination of the former. Indeed, as the preceding chapter has shown, narratives of everyday life are opposed to "media-made" fantasies and by this token possess an aura of authenticity. Taken at face value, this could mean that relationships based in the realm of everyday life have remained out of the reach of late capitalist culture and thus offer a genuine alternative to market-based relationships. In the following three chapters, I show that this is not the case; everyday life is neither an alternative nor an antidote nor even a zone of resistance to the market. Rather, everyday life is a cultural extension of discourses that emanate from or at least have a close affinity with those of the *sphere of production*. If, in the utopian sphere associated with consumption, romance negates social reality in a fantasy of free-flowing abundance, equality, and leisurely pleasure, in everyday life romance uses the language and values of the sphere of production, entailing a rational maximization of effort and profit.

Such a proposition is reminiscent of Daniel Bell's well-known thesis on the "disjuncture" between the realms of consumption and production, which has entailed an insurmountable contradiction within the culture of capitalism. For Bell, the work ethic that has presided over and made possible the enormous growth of the capitalist mode of production is now contradicted by the hedonism that characterizes the realm of consumption.[1] Extending Bell's thesis, I argue that the contradictions he describes divide a single cultural practice, romantic love. Whereas part 2 showed that the subjective structure of the romantic experience displays the temporal and emotional properties of postmodernity, part 3 shows that romantic love is *also* bound by the language of the work ethic; that it is rational, self-interested, strategic, and profit-maximizing; and that romantic relationships are conceived and managed in the categories of the utilitarian and instrumental ethos that lies at the heart of the capitalist economic system. This discourse conflicts with the hedonistic utopia of love based in the sphere of consumption, but it echoes the entrepreneurial semantics of work, control, and purposive rationality characteristic of the sphere of production. Thus, romance has become interwoven not only with the pleasures, images, and dreams of the sphere of consumption but also with the economic rationality of entrepreneurial capitalism. To clarify this other link I shall analyze the discourses of women's magazines because they provide an established forum within which romantic relationships are discussed, prescribed, and formalized.

Max Weber has most compellingly described the relationship between entrepreneurial capitalism and the personality structures that made it possible. Like Marx, Weber was concerned with the transformation of human values brought about by capitalism and commodity exchange, but he accounted for this change with a different historical narrative, that of "rationalization." The cultural logic running through capitalism, Weber suggested, is the increasing rationalization of the legal, cultural, and economic spheres. This is a twofold process, cognitive and practical. The cognitive aspect encompasses the attempt to comprehend reality through "increasingly precise and abstract concepts," whereas in the practical sphere, which Weber termed *Zweckrationalität*, or "purposive rationality," "the individual rationally assesses the probable results of a given act in terms of the calculation of means to an end."[2] Cognitive rationalization is seen most clearly in science and technology, while practical rationalization finds its historical expression in capitalist market relationships. The purpose of practical rationality in economy is to maximize profit, while cognitive rationality helps us understand and master nature through abstract and formal thought.[3] For Weber and his heirs, "rationalization"—the cultural logic of capitalism—orients not only organizational but personality structures toward calculation, control, and predictability.

On the surface, these characterizations of capitalism seem irrelevant, if not incongruous, to the modern romantic sentiment. Weber himself viewed love or erotic life in general as a private respite from public processes of rationalization in economics, law, and politics and even held that only the "erotic sphere" could save modern human beings from the negative consequences of excessive rationalization.[4] Summarizing Weber's thought on this matter, Randall Collins suggests that "we need a respite from the impersonal realm of politics, economics . . . the impersonality of science, and the irresolvable disputes of these different rationalized spheres against each other. Love is that respite. Precisely because it is irrational, it provides the personal element that the modern individual needs, to give some meaning to a world of conflicting institutions that have become too rational."[5] However, against Weber and despite historical changes that, on their face, would contradict this hypothesis, I argue that love *has* become rationalized.

The most noteworthy of these changes is the increasing dominance of irrational models of love within the rational institution of marriage (as discussed in chapters 1 and 2). Although American marriage has always emphasized romantic love more than its European counterpart, the romantic-realist division still had currency during the nineteenth century, for marriage was still explicitly motivated by the rational evaluation of a partner's current or prospective social standing. As the "realist" justification of marriage became replaced by a purely romantic view, "disinterested" and "gratuitous"—that is, from an economic standpoint, "irrational"—love become the only legitimate reason and goal for marriage.[6] If love has indeed become rationalized, we must be able to account for this process. How is the legitimation of a rational institution (marriage) by an irrational feeling (romantic love) to be understood within the general process of the rationalization of subjectivity?

The beginning of an answer can be found by looking at how the association between romantic love and marriage became during the first decades of the century the object of public scrutiny by self-appointed "experts" on the human psyche such as sociologists, psychologists, and marriage counselors. As marriage became increasingly "romantic" rather than "realist," it was perceived as increasingly fragile, as indicated by sharply rising divorce rates. In response to this crisis the number and prestige of "scientific" experts claiming the authority to discuss, manage, and ultimately remedy it grew apace.[7] To a public in search of advice, these new experts offered what I suggest calling "parascientific discourse," that is, a popularized version of scientific modes of analysis, geared to a broadly educated lay public. Although endowed with less prestige and authority than one aimed at a community of experts, a parascientific discourse is invested with the semiotic and institutional marks of symbolic competence. Since the first decades of the century, these experts have become arbiters of "emotional health," their voices increasingly prominent in the larger cultural arena, in magazines and self-help books, on radio and television.

Through these parascientific discourses we can question the opposition between the rationalization of love and the legitimation of irrational erotic impulses. What forms of discursive consciousness and normative orientation of the romantic personality are promoted by parascientific discourses? This question has become especially pressing as the authority of these discourses has sharpened the trend toward the "scientization" of love, subjecting love to rationalized, "scientific" scrutiny in a wide variety of public forums. In my analysis of women's magazines, it became clear that Weber's conclusion about the growing separation between the "erotic sphere" and the rationalized spheres of the market, science, and bureaucracy is questionable. "Instrumental reason" has penetrated domains hitherto beyond its reach and, in the process, has rationalized the psyche itself. This is manifest in the themes, metaphors, and normative logic of the romantic discourse of women's magazines.[8]

CHARTING THE HEART

Most of the thirty-five magazine articles I analyzed can be categorized according to three general thematic orientations: (1) *prescriptive* articles giving "recipes" for attaining a successful relationship, rejuvenating romance in a marriage, obtaining a date, or imbuing a "stale" relationship with passion; (2) *normative* articles dealing with relationships with forbidden or unsuitable persons, such as a boss, a married man, an older man, or the ex-boyfriend of one's best friend; (3) *analytical* articles aimed at providing an understanding of how love starts, the difference between a good and a bad relationship, or how the "magic of love" is to be explained, based on polls and popularized sociological or psychological works. These categories go hand-in-hand with problems women face in finding a mate, identifying whether or not he is suitable, and keeping the romance in marriage alive.

To the first problem, the recommended solution runs counter to the myth of predestination. The articles advise organizing the search for a soul mate like a job search, offering tips, for example, on places where one is likely to meet men. In other words, these articles explicitly and forcefully advise women to actively take their romantic destiny into their own hands.

To the problem of a prospective mate's suitability, the magazines offer a variety of solutions, for example, comparing checklists of his assets and defects. The romantic conception of love is explicitly replaced by more realist discussions on socioeconomic and psychological compatibility. Numerous quizzes are provided to help women evaluate compatibility and to draw the delicate boundary between "suitable" and "unsuitable" mates. For example, differences in religion or large age differences are considered acceptable, while dating married men is deemed highly problematic.

As to keeping romance alive, the magazines surveyed provide two types of answers: make efforts to enhance romance by a variety of innovations, and accept that good relationships are based on negotiation and undergo occasional conflicts. For example, *Woman*'s "recipes" for creating or maintaining passion include writing love notes and putting them on the refrigerator, giving unexpected, creative presents, and preparing a romantic, gourmet dinner to be eaten by candlelight. The message conveyed is that lack of romance is caused by lack of effort. With the right will and a little calculation, such essential ingredients of romance as spontaneity can be restored to any relationship. Other articles prescribe a more ambiguous strategy in which "recipes" for romance are subordinated to more psychologically oriented strategies for rejuvenating love. For example, observing that "we resist the idea that negotiation and romance can coexist," one magazine columnist asserts that "romance and negotiation are not only compatible but necessary in an adult relationship."[9] Carried further, this logic suggests that romance and marriage do not necessarily coincide. "Conflicts and even occasional doubts are normal in marriage—especially in the early years, when you must learn to compromise and adjust your own needs and expectations to harmonize with those of your mate. Marriage means compromise, conflict, sharing and inevitably surprise."[10]

While the discourse of these articles implicitly suggests that the hedonist romance is the only valid ideal, it discredits that ideal as well by prescribing an alternative model of relationship, based on realism, mutual understanding, and communication, that normalizes and legitimates the absence of romance in marriage. In other words, here also, two models of relationship seem to be advocated at the same time: one holding routine, labor, and calculation as the enemies of true romance, and another prescribing regular applications of effort and skillful management as necessary conditions for a long-lasting relationship. The idealist and realist narratives analyzed in chapter 5 are embedded in root metaphors of "intensity" and "work," examined in the following section. Such an analysis of the root metaphors of love enables us to grasp what an analysis of narratives cannot deliver, namely, that there is an affinity between metaphors of the workplace and the contemporary realist model of love.

PASSION WITHIN REASON, REASON WITHIN PASSION

Two broad metaphorical fields correspond to the two models of love that predominate in American society and culture: love as an all-consuming intense force and love as hard work.

LOVE AS PLEASURE

The metaphor of love as an all-consuming force is one of the most familiar ones in the romantic tradition. It has several metaphorical subfields. It may be a burning force; the metaphor of love as fire is one of the most ancient and pervasive in the rhetoric of love: "There were *sparks* between them" or "Passion: How to Ignite It, Reignite It, Make It Last."[11] A related, more modern metaphor is that of love as a magnetic force, as in "there was a magnet pulling them together" or "there was an irresistible attraction between them." Another culturally central metaphor is that of magic. This metaphor may have its roots in ancient folk practices in which magic was actually employed to help someone gain the heart of another.[12] In modern discourse, however, this metaphor indicates love's mysterious, sweeping power. For example: "Truly passionate love can magically transform us into fuller, richer persons," and "When you stop focusing your attention on your relationship you forget how much you enjoy the magic of love."[13]

A common conceptual thread runs through the metaphors of love as fire, as a magnetic force, and as magic: love is conceived as an autonomous agent, acting with a force of its own, independent of the will or control of the lover. Grammatically and semantically, in phrases like "love pierced her heart" love is conceived as an entity in itself, detachable from the person and acting on its own: what sparks and maintains love is beyond conscious and rational understanding. Consequently one cannot predict love; one can only wait to be enraptured by it.

However, although such metaphors are consistent with the tradition of love as an intense force, the activities and the values promoted by this model differ from those that make up the idealist tradition of love. For example, according to an article analyzing what begins, sustains, and terminates love, the most important ingredients for keeping love alive are "heroic adventures, secret getaways, the moving bed, dining au naturel, a picnic in the train, snoozes and snuggles, love notes, sex on the dining-room table."[14] The paradoxical values promoted in this list of ingredients of a happy love are a scripted originality and a calculated spontaneity; they appeal to the "anti-institutional" and hedonist definitions of the self that have increasingly characterized romantic practices since the turn of the century. Emphasis on the ability to deliberately create spontaneous moments of pleasure, with hedonism as an implicit goal, conflict with the Romantic notion of love as an uncontrolled and overwhelming passion with an absolute, spiritual significance.

LOVE AS WORK: THE ROMANTIC ETHIC AND THE SPIRIT OF CAPITALISM

As we saw in chapter 5, the cultural model of love as an intense force coexists with the opposing model of love as work. In the latter, effort replaces the magic spark, commitment the overwhelming force of passion, relativity the absoluteness of love, and conscious monitoring the spontaneous outburst. "Work" has thus become one of the most widely used metaphors for relationship. One works at a successful relationship by "laying its foundation" and then "building" it. Partners are "coworkers" involved in "teamwork"; one "invests" in a relationship in order to "benefit" from it, and so on.[15]

As developed by these magazines, the metaphor of love as work indicates a transfer from the discursive arena of market exchange to that of interpersonal relationships. For example: "As in business or social contract, the parties [to a love relationship] govern themselves by whatever definitions and limits they have agreed on."[16] And: "Love is a feeling but a relationship is a contract. While falling in love can just happen, a loving relationship requires certain skills in order to be sustained."[17] The distinction between "feeling" and "relationship" is an interesting one, for it preserves the "mystique" of love while making it at the same time subject to the metaphors of the marketplace. These metaphors have two broad implications: (1) love is controllable by our thoughts, and we are therefore responsible for its success or failure; and (2) love is a commodity susceptible to the strategies of market transactions and bargaining.

In a broad sense, this discourse derives from "utilitarian individualism," which stipulates that one must evaluate relationships by weighing their costs against the extent to which they satisfy one's needs.[18] Such a view can be detected in this example: "No matter how much he loved me, my partner couldn't intuit my needs in some mystical fashion. He had his own needs to worry about. It was up to me to see that my needs were met and the way to do that was to negotiate with him for what I wanted."[19] Contrary to the Romantic or organic vision of love, in this approach the bond is not viewed as the merging of two bodies and souls but as one in which each partner has a distinct set of needs that, if incompatible, can only be satisfied through a process of bargaining. Contrast the utilitarian premise of the above citation with the vision of love as an organic bond also present in some women's magazines: "The very best I-love-you's come with no ifs, ands, or buts attached. They come in the kitchen as well as in the bedroom. They are spontaneous expressions of affection that don't hide silent assumptions or demands."[20] The contrast between these two examples cogently illustrates the premises of the utilitarian ethos, namely, that the main goal of relationships is to satisfy both partners' needs and interests and that this is achieved through control, negotiation, and compromise. Gone is the Romantic vision of two lovers passionately longing for the fusion of their souls, in life or even, as was often the case, in death. Instead, these articles offer forms of reasoning promoted in the public sphere of market transactions. In the first place, they propose that individuals freely choose their relationships from a pool of possible partners. An article in Self magazine calls seeking a partner like looking for a job and explains in detail that one must be decisive and systematic in the search for a "soul mate."[21] Secondly, they foster the same values required for success in business: independence, self-reliance, aggressiveness, and the ability to project one's personality and needs. Another article in New Woman magazine extends this list: "Negotiators . . . assume equality and do themselves and their partners the service of stating their needs clearly, hearing out their partners, and compromising with them in those places where the two diverge."[22] Above all, the utilitarian ethos advances the notion of relationships as a transaction in which the couple must be partners in an equitable and fruitful exchange. Here is a rather glaring example of how economic jargon is used within the romantic sphere: "Love is like a marketplace transaction . . . lovers are content with their relationships to the degree that what they're giving is in line with what they're getting. The weighing of contributions (inputs) to profits (outcomes) can trade off personal attributes such as beauty or personal warmth against power or riches."[23] Metaphors of business have thoroughly pervaded the discourse of love and romance used by laymen and laywomen and by experts such as psychologists, sociologists, and economists.[24] As Daniel Goleman puts it: "In recent years, the mainstream of psychological research has looked at love almost as if it were a business transaction, a matter of profit and loss."[25] The semantics of "romantic entrepreneurship" even rely on the same vocabulary that Norman Kohn found characteristic of middle-class values toward work: self-directedness, a sense of responsibility, and self-monitoring.[26] Echoing the powerful cultural idiom of the sphere of production, women's magazines suggest that instead of being "stricken" or "smitten" by love, a woman is responsible for her romantic successes and failures, that she must "work hard" to secure a comfortable emotional future for herself, and that she should guarantee that a relationship will provide an equitable exchange. One may therefore conclude that for middle-class women the values of romance are intertwined with the kind of self-reliance and values that are demanded by the workplace.[27]

The penetration of culture and love by the values of capitalism betrays a rationalization not only of interpersonal relationships but of the self as well. Jackson Lears has argued that at the end of the nineteenth century, "in the interdependent marketplace, the fragmented self became a commodity like any other, to be assembled and manipulated for private gain." Lears goes on to propose that "rationalization of our inner life promoted other subtle forms of rationalization—forms that accommodated to rather than opposed the corporate system which emerged in the late nineteenth century."[28] Thus, far from being above, outside, or beyond the sphere of capitalist production, modern discourses of love are suffused with the self-reliance, individualism, and utilitarian outlook derived from this sphere.

In Weber's terminology, the romantic ethic promoted by these magazines is analogous to the ethic instrumental in the formation of the capitalist entrepreneur. Like the Protestant ethic, this ethic promotes an instrumental, rather than affective or value-laden, rationality by viewing the romantic relationship as a goal attained through the systematic implementation of controlled and planned procedures. The "romantic ethic" is fully consistent with the capitalist credo that relationships should be evaluated using the same logic of profit and loss common to the business world.

THE UNCERTAINTIES OF THE HEART

In the terminology of anthropology, the metaphorical field of love as an intense force depends on an economy of the gift, while that of love as work is based on the same contractual exchange model underlying capitalist markets. Although the cultural motif of love as pure "waste and gift" is withering away, the various metaphors of love as an intense force are anchored in social and economic practices of waste, a pure expenditure of self and wealth for the sake of an organic bond. On the other hand, the love-as-work model is rooted in the mutually profitable exchange of contractual relationships. The aim of the organic bond of love is to achieve the fusion of two individual selves regardless of their position in a relation of power and of any potential losses or benefits. Therefore, women's magazines and media with similar audiences are promoting two antithetical emotional (and for that matter, economic) cultural models.

How are we to explain the continuing coexistence of these two equally powerful repertoires of love, the "organic" and the "contractual"? Why and how are relationships to fulfill two contradictory requirements, one affective-gratuitous and the other instrumental-utilitarian? Traditionally, sociologists explain this contradiction by suggesting that romantic love and marriage promote different values and that the incorporation of love into marriage creates a symbolic contradiction between the values espoused by romantic love (intensity, idealization of the other, interest-free emotion) and those necessary for a successful marriage (sharing daily life, coping with a less-than-perfect other, envisioning love in the "long term," integrating love with the responsibilities of a family and work). According to Ann Swidler, this incompatibility translates into "tensions between . . . partially conflicting conceptions of love and marriage endemic in our society today." These tensions result from the fact that the need for "spontaneity" and "personal intimacy" is not "anchored in objective patterns of roles and social institutions."[29] Pursuing Swidler's argument, I propose that these tensions are the result of a structural contradiction between marriage as an institution of social reproduction and marriage as a unit for the expression of the individual's emotions.

The family was conceived as an economic unit of production until the eighteenth century, when the economic function of marriage was gradually replaced by a view of marriage as the altar of private life and affectionate sentiments.[30] Individuals became free to choose their partners on the basis of moral and "personal" merits rather than social status or family fortune. In contrast to the traditional marriage, romantic love stood as the "disinterested bond" par excellence: transcending the barriers of class, it presumably could unite people otherwise separated by a multiple array of social boundaries. While the notion of interest became progressively legitimized in the public sphere (most noticeably in the political and economic spheres), it was suspect in the private sphere of human relationships. In the currently dominant ideology, marriage can be legitimately entered into only under the auspices of the irrational, gratuitous, and disinterested emotion of romantic love.

Nevertheless, marriage remains a powerful, though unacknowledged, channel for social mobility and by extension, for maintaining social inequalities. As economists and sociologists of the family claim, and contrary to our popular myth, love is rarely blind. Under capitalism, social relations are characterized by class stratification and individual competition; marriage bonds are formed in this context and sustain rather than disrupt it. One of the primary functions of marriage is to reproduce social class through the encounter and choice of social "likes." Although love seems to be "interest free," marriage follows strategies of investment that aim at maintaining or enhancing one's social position ("Does he make enough money?" "Is he intellectual enough for me?" "Is she interested in the same cultural activities?"). Marriage is often still a search for a partner with the "best available assets," and the affectionate marriage has, paradoxically enough, instituted a "market point of view" in romantic relationships.[31] The conflict between "idealist" and "realist" or "organic" and "contractual" approaches to marriage thus mirrors the conflict between the ideal of "interest-free" love and marriage's function of social reproduction. The language of the marketplace, of "homo economicus," furnishes a "natural" cultural frame to articulate this conflict. As we will see in the next chapter, in handling the tension between the choice of a "socially desirable" partner and a choice made on purely emotional considerations, my respondents use the purposive and utilitarian rationality of the market.

At this point, traditional analyses of the mass media would probably conclude that the two metaphorical fields we have delineated unconsciously reflect and reproduce the contradictions in marriage bred by the culture of capitalism, but women's magazines—and self-help literature in general—display an interesting feature: namely, they not only reflect this contradiction but reflect *upon* it. Far from being unconscious, the contradiction between the "ideal romance" and the "realistic working out of relationships" is endlessly articulated, commented upon, and explained in these publications. Even more importantly, women's magazines offer symbolic tools to manage these contradictions, through the implementation of a new epistemology of the self, the "therapeutic ethos." While utilitarian individualism brings the interpersonal sphere under the sway of purposive rationality (*Zweckrationalität*), the therapeutic ethos submits it to cognitive rationalization. By promoting self-reflexive and formal modes of reasoning, this ethos fosters a rational attitude toward the self.

THE SCIENCE OF LOVE

THE THERAPEUTIC ETHOS

In their study of the American cultural traditions that form the backbone of middle-class value orientations, Robert Bellah and his associates point to therapeutic discourse as an important source of the formation of the self. They further suggest that because the therapeutic ethos evolves from the utilitarian individualism that has pervaded American social relationships, it is ill-equipped to provide a basis for commitment.[32] In my view, however, although they use convergent models of self and social relationships, the therapeutic ethos is distinguished from utilitarian individualism by its use of self-knowledge and reflexivity.

As it emerges from the articles used in this study, therapeutic discourse revolves around the following core propositions:

Relationships can be divided into "healthy" and "unhealthy."

The bond uniting a man and a woman is open to study and can be evaluated by experts according to objective criteria.

Just as people can acquire knowledge about any other area, they can control their romantic relationships through work and the application of appropriate strategies and techniques.

The key to romantic failure lies in early life experiences.

Understanding past experiences will lead to healthy relationships.

Romantic success thus depends upon self-knowledge and the ability to implement this knowledge in one's life.

The therapeutic ethos functions on two ideological levels: on the first, the authority of experts and the use of science in interpersonal relations are legitimized; on the second, forms of rationality are instilled by "epistemic devices," through which one comes to "know" something. The therapeutic ethos not only relies heavily on the discursive style and authority of scientific discourses but utilizes the same epistemic categories as social scientists who study the emotions. The first claim concerns the use of science as a way of asserting the symbolic authority of romantic discourses, while the second concerns the modes of self-understanding conveyed by the therapeutic ethos.

THE LEGITIMATION OF EXPERTS

When women's magazines cite experts on love, it is usually either to explain what "sparks, maintains and ends love" or to prescribe specific romantic behavior. The normative dimension consists in defining the boundaries between normal/healthy and pathological/unhealthy relationships, while the explanatory dimension provides women with a framework within which to account for their success or failure in finding a partner and sustaining romance.

THE NORMALIZING FUNCTION OF THE THERAPEUTIC ETHOS

The therapeutic ethos is heavily represented in the magazine articles analyzed, which make frequent mention of "scientists," including psychologists, physicians, and the generic "researchers." Indeed, in the articles surveyed, I found an impressive number of references to experts of various types (thirty-four); the overwhelming majority were psychologists, and the rest "sociologists," "anthropologists," and "researchers." As one article puts it with typical breathlessness: "For thousands of years the question [of love] has been explored by poets, philosophers and songwriters. More recently, scientists have joined the inquiry."[33] The invocation of experts is used to unveil and explain what the title of a *Cosmopolitan* article calls the "sweet scientific mystery of love."[34] Many

articles introduce a specific argument with the phrase "in a study. . . . "
And romantic articles rely heavily on statistics and polls to "prove" the
validity of their analyses and advice. For example: "Researchers have
come up with information and insights gleaned from studies on what attracts us to someone of the opposite sex, how lasting bonds between men
and women are forged, how personality and early childhood experience
affect our capacity for and success at love."[35] Far from being a medium
for the reproduction of fictions or mythologies, women's magazines are
a forum for the popularization of academic research. However, these
magazines use social-scientific research not only for its descriptive but
also and more importantly for its normative functions, the most notable
of which is defining "healthy" as opposed to "pathological" behaviors.
In other words, they utilize scientific discourse to legitimate a particular
vision of normality. And they fulfill this function in such ritual phrases
as "it is perfectly normal to" or "while it is healthy to. . . . " For example: "Conflicts and even occasional doubts are normal in marriage."[36]
Or: "When a friend dates an ex-boyfriend of yours it's normal to feel
jealous, competitive and left out. . . . The healthy thing is to walk
away."[37] Normalization serves to convert moral statements into truth
statements validated by the signs of "scientific" expertise. Such normalization is presented in impersonal judgments ("it is healthy") rather than
in the personal form ("*I* consider it healthy"). Such a discourse thus jus-
tifies the intervention of experts through the use of medical metaphors
in which human relationships are discussed in the same terminology as
"sick" or "healthy" organisms.

THE EXPLANATORY FUNCTION OF THE THERAPEUTIC ETHOS

The explanatory function of the therapeutic ethos lies at the heart of its
symbolic power. From an ideological standpoint, explanatory systems
are crucial because they provide justifications (i.e., ideologies) for why
things are the way they are, and justifications are essential to the ideological arena because they entail corrective strategies. For example,
blaming a romantic failure on male chauvinism, an unresolved Oedipal
conflict, or the general deterioration of human relationships under capitalistic society will yield very different curative strategies.

   Like many psychological textbooks, women's magazines maintain
that the reasons for romantic failures may be sought in early childhood. By so doing they imply that such failure results from a personality problem inherent in the woman herself. But whereas Freud of-

fered a tragic vision of man and woman as enslaved by the masked and unruly forces of their unconscious, these magazines hold those who fail at romance or marriage responsible for these failures. (They often suggest, for example, that women may "resist" successful relationships.) Whereas in classical psychoanalysis, the determinism of the unconscious could be overcome only through the long and painful process of the analytical cure, women's magazines promote the view that, like the self-made man, a woman can rise above the pattern of her failures through "self-help," diligently taking to heart the right advice. This ethic of responsibility is ambiguous, however. Since it locates the original reason for romantic failure in circumstances beyond the control or even awareness of the subject, experts of the psyche become necessary. Experts become the intermediaries between the different parts of our divided selves, thus partially discharging us of responsibility. But at the same time, the therapeutic ethos fully reinforces and extends the credo of the Protestant ethic by making one responsible even for one's emotional destiny.

The historical encounter between the ideology of romantic love and the rising influence of experts in the domains of private life has given birth to another paradox: now that it is no longer ruled by reason, calculation, and planning but is seen rather as consecrated by the irrational and intense emotion of love, marriage has become an object of scrutiny by scientific rationality.

THERAPEUTIC DISCOURSE
AND REFLEXIVE DISCOURSE

This development calls into question a well-established view of women's magazines as fostering "irrational," "mythical," or emotional approaches to love. Instead, as may be seen by examining the forms of rationality and reflexivity they promote, these magazines offer a diluted form of social science, inviting their readers to adopt a proto-scientific attitude toward themselves and their romantic relationships. This transfer of scientific into romantic discourse is achieved by a metadiscourse that dwells upon itself and fosters self-reflexivity.[38]

THE LABELING FUNCTION

Naming and defining are formal procedures of thinking fundamental to the discursive and ideological arena. As Marc Angenot puts it,

"Defining is also a way of arguing. It means taking a stand from the outset."[39] For example, whether we label the physiological response that follows our attraction to someone "a crush," "love at first sight," "sexual desire," "lust," or "the neurotic enactment of past desires" connects us with very different cultural repertoires. Women's magazines explicitly ask their readers to focus on the names of emotions and to become aware of the labels they use and misuse. A typical example: "The 'go-crazy kind of love,' [a psychologist] contends, is often nothing more than a mad, passionate mislabeling of your emotions."[40] Such discursive strategy parallels the cognitive therapies that attempt to modify behavior by showing patients how they have wrongly labeled their emotions. Metadiscursive discussion of the "appropriate" naming of emotions is likely to increase awareness of the labeling strategies used to classify emotions. Women's magazines dwell on this classificatory function of language, which consists in consciously drawing semantic boundaries between concepts and/or events. Consider the following example: "Falling in love on vacation can be hazardous to your heart if you expect to love happily ever after. Romance, on the other hand, can be a delightful adventure that you revel in while it's happening."[41] Such symbolic boundaries give different meanings to what may appear to be the same experience (a romantic/sexual encounter) and imply different consequences depending on how such an event is labeled. That is, rather than expressing the nature of an experience, a label can determine that nature. In doing so, as in this example, labeling articulates the boundary between "safe" and "hazardous" romantic encounters, which is to say, between behavior that is acceptable or otherwise according to the conventional morality of prudent calculation. Consider some other examples: "Passion is more than just sexual desire. It is also characterized by the powerful emotions of love, hate, and rage, of lust, zeal, jealousy and possessiveness. Passion encompasses the myriad expressions of aliveness and intensity in a relationship."[42] Or: "Often the men with whom we have the strongest sexual chemistry are the men with whom we would be the least able to form a compatible marriage."[43] In these examples, the boundary has the function of circumscribing zones of "allowed" and "forbidden" behavior. More importantly, by insisting that the reader reflect on the boundaries between "real" and "ephemeral" feelings, such discussions invite a reflexive posture toward the self.

In fact, women's magazines treat the heart as a text that women have to decipher and interpret correctly if they are to be happy. "Watch out for anyone who happens to walk into your life when you're having a bad day—that's not love, that's a spillover of feeling from one realm to another."[44] Thus women's magazines convey not only a normative content but also a mode of hermeneutic self-reflexivity in which readers are advised to routinely question the "true meaning" of their emotions. Such activity promotes a self-reflexive scientific attitude toward romantic relationships and self in general.

SELF-ANALYSIS AS SCIENTIFIC ANALYSIS

To remedy romantic failure, women are further encouraged to adopt a pseudo-scientific attitude toward the self and self-knowledge.

First, they are asked to view themselves as objects of study, for the magazines suggest that the problem is not the failure to find or sustain romance in itself but the repeated pattern of failure. For example, in an article (written by a psychologist) "on falling in love with a man everyone (including you) thinks is wrong for you," the reader is advised, before reacting to other people's disapproval of her relationship, to study herself for signs of a general "pattern of going against the tide."[45] The pattern, more than the behavior itself, is the problem, and women are advised to become aware of such repetitive patterns through self-observation. Once they discover a pattern to their romantic failures, they can recognize new instances and—with will power and the right advice—break the pattern.

Furthermore, the magazines implicitly ask women to perform on themselves the same mental operations that define social-scientific inquiry: take a subject (herself) as the object of study, identify behavioral patterns, establish correlations, find a causal variable, and unveil the reasons behind the behavior.[46] What Philip Rieff has written about "psychological man" can be applied even more pointedly to "psychological woman": "[She] takes on the attitude of a scientist, with [herself] alone as the ultimate object of [her] science."[47]

One of the most interesting features of articles proffering such "self-improvement" programs is that, like many sociological studies, they denounce the falsity of mass media representations. "Marriage is not always the romantic fantasy you see played out in advertisements for honeymoon getaways. Few, if any, have such an idyllic relation and you should not measure your own marriage against impossibly high standards."[48] The claims to superior knowledge made by these articles thus includes the unmasking of illusions produced by the media. By attacking the falsity of the media and decrying their power, they invite women to examine and question the cultural sources of these representations. Here also we find expressions of the postmodern suspicion that media cultivate images and stories that substitute for the "real" experience of love, but this suspicion is here invoked in order to empower women with a *critical* consciousness rather than to revel in the ironic semiotic cynicism that so often characterizes postmodern consciousness. This form of reflexivity invites women to critically examine the foundations of their representations and ground them instead on the "unglamorous reality" of "real relationships." The increased self-reflexivity encouraged by therapeutic discourse thus promotes both criticism and self-criticism.

What are the political implications of the penetration of the rationalized discourse of the market and of science into the romantic discourse? Does this rationalized discourse debase the romantic bond, or does it have, as it claims to, an emancipatory potential?

LOVE AND THE RATIONALIZATION OF THE LIFE-WORLD

Women's magazines reveal that romantic discourse has undergone the same process of cognitive and practical rationalization that Weber deemed characteristic of the cultural logic of capitalism.

Adorno and Horkheimer's critical theory of capitalism rests on the utopian premise that intersubjective relationships and economic exchange ought to remain in two separate spheres.[49] The foregoing analysis apparently confirms Adorno and Horkheimer's claim that in capitalistic societies processes of commodification and reification have penetrated all spheres of life and that "instrumental reason" has undermined all of modern culture, a process Jürgen Habermas has called the "colonization of the life-world." As one commentator puts it, "In contemporary capitalism, areas once separate from exchange and commodification, such as sex, love and culture, [are] becoming integrated into the system of exchange, and [are] increasingly dominated by exchange values and relationships."[50] Because of the depth at which rationalization processes seemed to have invaded modern subjectivity, Adorno and Horkheimer were pessimistic as to the possibilities for emancipation in capitalist society.

Michel Foucault has provided the most powerful critique of the various instruments of control of the psyche developed by modern psychoanalysis and psychology. Therapeutic discourse is part of what he calls "bio-power," the collaboration of science, capital, and the state to mold individuals into "disciplined" subjects, that is, objects of their own observation and control.[51] In this view, the encroachment of scientific rationality into romantic love has made women into their own "panopticon": in monitoring their emotions and behavior according to norms of social science and capitalist exchange, women are made subject to what Foucault sees as the vast technology of control deployed by modernity.

Rejecting Foucault's assessment and departing somewhat from his predecessors at the Frankfurt School, Habermas is reluctant to see rationalization of the interpersonal or "communicative" sphere as having the same negative effects as rationalization of the economic and political spheres ("system rationalization").[52] He holds that rationalization of the latter has the potential to counter the deficiencies inherent in system rationalization and is thus emancipatory. Since rationalized therapeutic discourses are primarily geared to women, the most obvious way to evaluate Habermas's claim is to frame the question in the terms of feminist emancipation. How has the rationalization of love reinforced the traditional association of women with a sphere of sentimentality and emotion? Any answer to this question can only be speculative and tentative.

As Francesca Cancian and others have argued, in nineteenth-century America, as the family ceased to be a unit of production and men and women more and more took their respective social identities from the now-separate spheres of economic production and domestic life, the realm of feeling, which seemed to have no place in the increasingly competitive and "masculine" world of the capitalist economy, came to be viewed as the territory of women alone. As Cancian puts it, love was "feminized," and women were equated with the expression of love.[53] In Helen Lewis's summary, "Nineteenth-century notions held women as naturally emotional and men as naturally rational."[54]

This analysis would lead one to expect that the vocabulary and values of the women's magazines would convey the "traditional" female values of "irrationality and emotionality." Instead, the romantic discourses of these magazines promote utilitarian and therapeutic ethics consistent not only with the logic and values of the public sphere but also with feminist discourse of the last century. Far from encouraging an irrationally romantic view of love, many nineteenth-century feminists promoted traditionally "masculine" values of control, assertiveness, and more "rational," that is, utilitarian and contractual, forms of thinking.[55] These discursive strategies continue to play a large role in feminist thought. By embracing "masculine" values of autonomy and instrumental reason and a contractual view of relationships, women have achieved a measure of equality in the male-dominated economic arena, and many women have transferred this discourse to the traditionally "female" sphere of emotions in order to articulate their claims to equality in this realm as well and to achieve power and control in relationships that too often have disempowered them.[56] Similarly, therapeutic discourse makes available to women "masculine" values such as rational self-criticism and the capacity to know, control, and modify one's emotions, abilities with obvious emancipatory potential.

Anthony Giddens has recently defended a similar claim. According to him, the "pure relationship," in which two people are together for the sake of emotional intimacy and sexual fulfillment, is a contract similar to that at the basis of the public, democratic sphere. The pure relationship is predicated on the autonomy of the person, a principle Giddens defines as the capacity "to deliberate, judge, choose and act upon different possible courses of action."[57] In the realm of personal life, such autonomy implies the freedom, based on self-knowledge, to choose the partner with whom one can further one's self-realization, a project to which therapeutic discourse has much to contribute. The principle of autonomy entails open discussion about the respective rights and obligations of the partners, and the contract may be renegotiated or voided if the relationship is perceived as unfair or oppressive. As Giddens convincingly puts it, rights and obligations are the stuff contemporary intimacy is made of. Thus the pure relationship is based on a communicative rationality that assumes that two persons are equal to each other, can make claims about their needs, and base these claims on agreed-upon norms of equality and reciprocity.

The rationalization of love points to emancipatory features, framing romantic relationships as equitable contractual exchanges within which women can assert themselves as equal partners. It has dangers as well, however. Women have long been regarded as the primary "caretakers" of romantic relationships and of the realm of feeling in general, and the transfer of values from the realm of economic production to the private sphere may simply redefine this traditional function in terms of "work." Women could easily be at a disadvantage in using this discourse if all the work of relationship is seen as their responsibility. This hypothesis receives partial confirmation in the present study: women are more likely to use metaphors of "work" when describing their relationships than men, who tend to view relationships in terms of "play" and "relaxation."

Furthermore, the rationalized vocabulary of rights and obligations and needs may actually undermine the emotional bond it is meant to strengthen. This discourse is separated only by a fine line from a utilitarian ethos that makes of others only a means to reach one's own satisfaction or "self-realization." As Fromm observed, in this ethos "modern man has been transformed into a commodity, experiences his life forces as an investment which must bring him the maximum profit obtainable under existing market conditions."[58] In this context, basing interpersonal relationships on principles of individual rights and autonomy may infect them with the competitive self-interest of the market. While it has played an important role in helping legitimate women's claims to self-realization and emancipation, this mix of utilitarian and democratic contractualism can thus undermine men and women's common search for a way to transcend their struggle for power.

Of equal concern, the pseudo-scientific self-reflexivity promoted by the therapeutic discourse may have "disenchanted" romantic love (in Weber's famous, poignant sense of the word) by subjecting it to the neutral and dispassionate gaze of reason. Undoubtedly, the rationalization of the romantic bond has broken many of our romantic idols and has substituted abstract norms of reciprocity and equality for the mystical halo in which women and love had hitherto bathed.

CHAPTER 7

The Reasons for Passion

"Could anyone in the world be more lovable than Miss
Osmond?" "No one, possibly. But love has nothing to do
with good reasons." "I don't agree with you. I'm delighted to
have good reasons." "Of course you are. If you were really in
love you wouldn't care a straw for them."

Henry James, The Portrait of a Lady

Romantic love, we are endlessly told by novelists, poets, and folk wisdom, defies "good reasons." The popular image of Cupid blindly striking people with the arbitrary arrows of love illustrates the notorious
scorn of love for reason. Mighty love defeats will, control, and even self-
interest.[1] This experience has been aptly captured by Lawrence Durrell:
"How many times have you tried to love the 'right' person in vain, even
when your heart knows it has found him after so much seeking? No, an
eyelash, a perfume, a haunting walk, a strawberry on the neck, the smell
of almonds on the breath—these are the accomplices the spirit seeks out
to plan your overthrow."[2] Yet, despite our bewildering incapacity to fall
in love with the "right" person and our frequent attraction to less desirable mates, the contemporary sensibility is not ready to proclaim love
an irrational, arbitrary, and uncontrollable passion. Unlike Henry
James's heroine, we care about "good reasons" and call for explanations
of when and why love arises or persists. As we have seen, the romantic
sentiment has become a highly rational affair, an emotion that we feel
can and must be managed deliberately and skillfully. In this chapter, I
pursue this line of inquiry by examining the claim made by economists
and sociologists that marriage, including the love marriage, is an important element in our strategies of social mobility and that most of
us "spontaneously" love and marry people who are socially and economically compatible with us. If correct, this claim suggests that love
and marriage can be causally explained by the properties of rational economic action: self-interest, calculation, weighing of costs and benefits,
and maximization of predefined utilities.

The economists' claim that the romantic lover is a rational actor contradicts one of our most cherished and deep-seated beliefs, namely, that love is a response to ineffable, inexplicable, and unique qualities of another person. Writing to her lover Abelard, twelfth-century Heloise illustrates this idea forcefully: "God knows, I have ever sought in thee only thyself, desiring simply thee and not what was thine."[3] Indeed, Heloise's address to Abelard's innermost self intimates a love that our cultural sensibility recognizes as indisputably superior to the attachments described by sociologists and economists. Unless we assume that romantic love is an ideological mask concealing rational self-interest and calculations, it is difficult to understand how such love connects with our strategies to maintain or increase our social position.

In sociological studies, love is the most frequently cited reason for marriage, and this trend has actually accelerated with the intensification of the capitalist labor market. A study undertaken in the mid-1960s by William Kephart, for example, found that women were significantly "less romantic" than men, that is, they were more likely to say they would marry someone whom they were not in love with but who had "all the other qualities [they] desired."[4] When this study was revisited some twenty years later, women were found to have grown significantly more romantic and on this scale had closed the gap with men.[5] The authors offered a number of reasons for this, the most important being women's entry into the work force: less dependent on the institution of marriage for their economic survival, women could now "afford" to marry for purely romantic reasons. A similar argument has been made by the historian Edward Shorter, who, taking a macroscopic view of the changes undergone by the Western family, observed that women's access to the labor market has emancipated marriage from its economic mission.[6] In this view, then, it is the access to economic independence provided by the market that frees romantic attachments from economic pragmatism. But instead of providing an explanation, the idea that economic independence frees passion from self-interest is part of the phenomenon needing explanation.

Also contradicting the idea that a purely romantic marriage prevails, another battery of surveys found that the choice of a marriage partner involves considerations of status and prestige.[7] Even the more casual relationship of dating appears to be based on status and prestige. The well-known 1937 study by Willard Waller found that among college students, dating was based on a highly competitive system of stratification in which students were rated according to looks, popularity, membership in fraternity houses, and so on. According to Waller, dating is a mechanism of mate selection in which those who rank highest are the most desired by everybody else.[8]

However much we believe love to be above considerations of social class, other findings suggest that romantic love does not fundamentally undermine class endogamy (marriage between "likes"): most people marry members of their own class. Laumann's study of urban networks of solidarity found, for example, that 71 percent of all those surveyed married someone of their own class or of an adjacent class fraction. He also found that class endogamy was especially marked among the upper fractions of the middle class. More recently, Kalmijn found that education is an important factor in class endogamy. That is, college attendance is a far better predictor of marriage than religion, ethnicity, or even income.[9]

One possible explanation for the coexistence of romantic and more practical motivations as competing norms for marriage is that people simply lie, to others and perhaps to themselves, and that marriage is indeed a matter of a careful weighing of the prospective partner's social standing and the "exchange" or "bargaining" of perceived qualities.[10] But this thesis is counterintuitive and eludes what is at the center stage of cultural analysis, namely, that the social world is constituted and maintained through the active and willful choices of people who are at least *somewhat* aware and knowledgeable about the reasons for their actions.

A more convincing explanation for these phenomena is that people do fall in love sincerely and disinterestedly but they do so with the people most readily available to them, namely, coworkers or neighbors. Since residences and workplaces tend to be segregated by social strata, people fall in love with people of their own class. Class is not a prerequisite of love, but people of the same class just "happen" to be most readily available. In this view, social reproduction is based not on individual decisions but on the extrinsic conditions that structure the geographical and social distribution of encounters. This explanation problematically presupposes that there are no connections between the meanings people attribute to their actions and the outcomes of their actions, between a seemingly irrational emotion and the patterned reproduction of social classes.

The view I would like to defend is that the meanings people give their actions can and must explain some of the outcomes of those actions. In this chapter, I offer and discuss some tentative hypotheses in answer to these difficult questions. How do we come to love the personal qualities, rather than the market value, of our mates and yet make choices that are congruent with our social and economic positions? Do we view the object of our affection as a unique and irreplaceable entity or as a set of attributes that can be traded off, bargained, and compared? In other words, when faced with the prospect of making enduring choices, do people choose between two competing and ultimately irreconcilable forms of social relationships, one gratuitous, disinterested, and irrational (romantic love), the other self-interested, calculating, and rational (marriage as a socioeconomic investment)? Or is there rather a cultural mechanism that accounts for (and makes possible) the fact that the romantic sentiment carries, translates, and reproduces the social structure while simultaneously unleashing the disorderly passions of the heart?

AGAPIC AND EROSIC LOVE

When examining the cultural and philosophical history of love, it appears that the romantic sentiment itself exhibits an antinomy similar to this sociological dilemma. In their normative attempt to decide what love ought to be, philosophers have distinguished between "erosic" love, based on reason, and "agapic" love, which owes nothing to reason but is freely bestowed.[11] Although traditionally associated with Christian theology, agapic love has the attributes of the romantic passion: it is irrational and inexplicably bestowed on someone. It cannot be grounded on the qualities of the person loved and therefore cannot be held accountable. In the words of Roland Barthes, "I love the other not according to his (accountable) qualities, but according to his existence. What I liquidate in this movement is the very category of merit."[12] Loving someone solely because of his or her existence is precisely what defines agapic love, love bestowed on someone in virtue not of what she or he has but rather of what she or he is. This is the meaning we invoke when trying to explain why we do not fall in love with someone who has otherwise "all the required qualities." Echoing Henry James on the "good reasons" of love, Robert Burch observed: "If you love someone, you cannot say, 'I love her because . . . ' referring to anything. If you can correctly give any reason for that tender attitude you have toward her, then that attitude you have is not love but something else, be it admiration, respect, pity, selfish interest, or what not."[13] But if love does not derive from reasons or causal principles, it is ineffable, incommunicable, and irreducible by the scrutiny of analysis.

Another aspect of agapic love is that it is not motivated by the preservation of one's own self-interest. We can love someone in defiance of our social or emotional interest. Agapic love, then, seems to belong to the domain of social bonds that Bataille identified as "waste," oriented toward neither utility nor maximization of personal preferences but consisting of the ostentatious and sacrificial consummation of self (for example, consummation of one's time, riches, personal values, and family or national loyalties.)

Finally, an additional aspect of agapic love is loss of self-control. Whatever our conscious decisions, love is beyond our monitoring or control. It spontaneously overflows the person.

By contrast, erosic love is easy to clarify: it is causally explainable in the sense that it is grounded in identifiable properties of the person loved. The person in love is aware of his or her reasons and can enunciate them. Furthermore, love does not undermine one's social, moral, economic, or psychological welfare but on the contrary enhances it. Last, love can be released, stopped, or increased, according to rational appraisal and decision. Although erosic love per se is not necessarily self-interested or calculated, it lends itself more readily to a view of love as rational and self-interested, for it has the cognitive properties of rationally induced emotions.[14] It certainly seems compatible with choosing to love someone from one's own class.

However, as becomes clear in the analysis of my interviewees, agapic and erosic love do not line up in a simple-minded opposition between "rationality" and "irrationality," or "interestedness" and "disinterestedness." As we know from Weber, rationalities are multiple and are to be explained by the properties of a given situation; "irrationality" appears to be so only from the standpoint of a conflicting rationality. Thus, while agapic and erosic love may seem to be analytically incompatible, they are sociologically reconciled in the practice of love. My interviewees draw as needed from the cultural repertoires of erosic and agapic love to account for different aspects and stages of their relationships and sentiments. This in turn implies that we cannot find one-to-one correspondences between properties of the romantic sentiment (say erosic) and strategies of social reproduction. Instead, we must understand irrationality and rationality as coterminous properties of the romantic bond.

Such an approach contradicts common sense and even conventional histories of love and marriage, which maintain that mechanisms of social reproduction and romantic attachment run on opposing principles, with capitalism witnessing the triumph of the latter. The triumph of the bourgeoisie based marriage on emotions rather than on economic rewards. However, although this ideology favored an emotionally fulfilling love marriage over a socially advantageous alliance, lovers were not to follow the capricious whims of their hearts. As with economic reward, attachments to others were to be grounded in merit. The popular eighteenth-century novel by Samuel Richardson, *Pamela*, is an example of the bourgeois idea that virtue simultaneously brings love and upward mobility: for her moral merit, the servant Pamela is loved and eventually wed by her master. But as Jane Austen's novels illustrate, in the bourgeois ideology fortune and social status are the *unintended* results of love motivated by inner merit and character.[15] Social status and upward mobility are seemingly accidental rewards, not conditions of love.

In and of itself, the notion of merit was not new to the idea of love. In twelfth-century courtly love, both men and women proved themselves worthy of love by their virtue. However, the courtly tradition was an aristocratic one: before factors of virtue, honor, or individual excellence, personal superiority was intrinsic in the fact of "noble" birth. The bourgeois notion of merit presupposes that persons are sets of nameable, identifiable, and ultimately quantifiable properties, which can be compared to and traded for other attributes or persons with the purpose of matching each individual's idiosyncratic personality and merit. In bourgeois meritocracy, love addresses neither the irreducible uniqueness of a person, as in the Christian theology of agapic love, nor the glorious manifestation of noble character. Instead, love is based on qualities that must correspond to and satisfy one's preferences and that potentially can be found in a number of individuals. The ideal of "personal compatibility" carries with it the ideas that people are comparable and exchangeable with one another and that love must satisfy some preestablished preferences. Although the eighteenth-century bourgeois ideology forcefully distinguished between passions and interests, its notion of merit opened up the possibility of reducing people to a set of tradable assets.

But even among the bourgeoisie, marriage remained in practice a financial bargain until at least the end of the eighteenth century.[16] According to Jean-Louis Flandrin, the romantic view of marriage could not take hold until the structure of wealth and property changed. He has argued that the bourgeois, "emotional" conception of marriage was a literary fantasy that started shaping actual conjugal practices only when wealth became less a matter of land or other forms of real property and more one of cultural capital. Only then would the love marriage cease to threaten the social order.[17] Flandrin thus links the institutionalization of romantic love in marriage with the new centrality of cultural capital, and so we would expect the love marriage to flourish in an age of "postindustrial capitalism" based on information, expert knowledge, and "human capital" rather than on material property.

According to Pierre Bourdieu, such society reproduces itself not through the monitored and conscious choices of economists' rational actors but through the invisible hand of "habitus." Habitus is a "matrix of perception, appreciations, and actions" acquired during socialization, slowly inculcated and accumulated in the body and expressed in opinions and aesthetic tastes and everyday, "micro" behaviors, such as table manners, accent or way of speaking, way of drinking wine, or aesthetic appreciation of a can opener.[18] Habitus is the ensemble of habits, ideas, and dispositions subjectively lived and communicated as personal identity and taste but objectively determined by position in the hierarchy of cultural and economic capital. Through habitus, people come to desire only what they can objectively have, thus "making a virtue of necessity." Despite the functionalist overtones of the notion, habitus is neither static nor monolithic, for it also accounts for the ways in which particular individuals cope and "play" with the particular conditions of their life chances. That is, two people of similar social positions will not necessarily maximize their capital in the same way because they will manifest a different habitus. Habitus, then, accounts for how a macroscopic process (social reproduction) is sustained through the microscopically variable practices of individuals. Bourdieu's theory also accounts for the transformations of the structure of capital in late capitalist societies. By making cultural and educational capital central to the formation of habitus and thus to social reproduction, Bourdieu incorporates within his theory the historical transformation of the bases of social class, from tangible wealth to knowledge, credentials, and cultural taste.

In *Distinction,* his now-classic study of French cultural practices, Bourdieu offhandedly remarks that the working of habitus is nowhere more apparent than in love, precisely because habitus allows people to experience romantic love as a spontaneous and free emotion while simultaneously assigning them partners who are compatible with their social positions and trajectories. People unconsciously and inadvertently harmonize their romantic desires with their objective chances to pair with others. As Bourdieu puts it, "a happy love, that is, a socially approved and success-bound love, [is] the same thing as *amor fati,* love of one's own social destiny, which brings together socially compatible partners by way of free choice that is unpredictable and arbitrary in appearance only."[19] Thus, Bourdieu implicitly suggests that the open system of class stratification conceals what was previously overt, namely, the strategies and calculations to increase or maintain social standing through marriage. From Bourdieu's viewpoint, then, romantic and marital choices are made in a "market"; but unlike Gary Becker's "marriage market," Bourdieu's is neither voluntarist nor rational but instead operates through the spontaneous harmonization of people's desires and of their resources.[20] Although people are not avowedly self-interested, are not conscious of the causes of their actions, and do not behave like rational actors, they nevertheless produce rational, self-interested outcomes, choices of a mate consistent with their social and economic interests. In short, people unconsciously want only what they can get.

Like Weber, Bourdieu views social action as driven by interest, where interest is a general category that becomes sociologically operational only when articulated within particular cultural worldviews. But despite its centrality in Bourdieu's cultural theory, the notion of self-interest has remained undefined, partly because the theory stipulates that the concept must be specified according to the field under study. The political economist Albert O. Hirschman, however, has offered a definition of self-interest suited to the kind of noneconomic behavior that occupies us here. For him, interest is defined by two features. The first is self-centeredness: "the predominant attention of the actor to the consequences of any contemplated action for himself." The second is rational calculation: "a systematic attempt at evaluating prospective costs, benefits, satisfactions, and the like." The first aspect pertains to a personality orientation, while the second deals with the cognitive style of a self-interested action.[21]

A VERY REASONABLE MADNESS

As Bourdieu would have warranted, the antinomy between emotion and social reproduction is analyzed here in the context of an empirical sociology of cultural practices. The question of how romantic relationships and sentiments are initiated by one's habitus can be answered only by examining the cognitive categories used by people to explain how and why each came to love someone, to stop loving someone, or to reject someone.

The "merit" looked for in a partner is twofold. First, the other person must conform to some abstract standard of excellence based on aesthetic, moral, and intellectual criteria: the other person must be "attractive," and "intelligent," and occasionally "good." Second, the partner be "compatible." The last requirement is so well rooted in popular conceptions of love that much of the self-help literature revolves

around the crucial problem of deciding whether someone is truly compatible with oneself. For example, in the popular self-help book *If I Am
So Wonderful, Why Am I Still Single?*, Susan Page provides a series of
experiments designed to help the reader achieve the goal of meeting not
just any mate but the right mate:

EXPERIMENT #6

a.   On paper, describe your ideal mate. List all the qualities, talents, propen-
sities you'd like him or her to have. "Brainstorm" with yourself. Take your
time and include everything. There is no need to be "realistic." Don't censor.
b.   Now go back over your list and place either "E" for essential or a "D"
for desirable next to each item.
c.   List all the "E" qualities on a separate page in the order of their importance to you.
d.   Draw a line under the top 5 items on the "E" list."

EXPERIMENT #8

If you are trying to evaluate a specific relationship, whether new or of long
duration, one or more of the following may be useful for you:
1.   How does your partner measure up to the top five items on your essentials list? (see Experiment #6).
2.   Write down your long-range life goals. If you could have *everything* you
want, what would you most like your life to look like in five years? In ten?
In twenty? Will staying with this partner help you to achieve these goals? Will
staying with this partner keep you from achieving these goals? (If you aren't
at all certain what your long-range goals are, think about your immediate
goals, your present life. Is this partner helping or hindering you from having
the life you want now?)
3.   List all the qualities you like about your partner. Now list all your areas
of dissatisfaction with him or her. Now, on both lists, put a 5 next to your
extreme likes and dislikes, a 3 next to your medium-level likes and dislikes,
and a 1 next to your mild likes and dislikes. Finally, rewrite the list in order
with 5s on the top and 1s on the bottom.

Which list is longer?
Which total score is higher?[22]

The approach to love advocated here is clearly erosic. It invites people
to conceive of themselves and others as a collection of discrete, identifiable positive or negative attributes that can be matched against one's
own personality and ultimately exchanged with those of others. Such a
view of romantic relationships demands that one scrutinize and clarify
one's own preferences, tastes, and life orientations and choose a partner

according to these factors. As we began to see in the preceding chapter, this approach is rational to the extent that it adheres to the ideas that the self is purposive and goal-directed, that life is organized and monitored according to a preconceived "life-plan," and that the romantic relationship should be integrated within this plan. The emphasis on the ideal of compatibility stems from the widespread idea that romantic love must precede the decision to share life with another, in contrast to the belief of traditional societies that both compatibility and love emerge only after the couple has shared life together.[23] Thus, paradoxically, the insistence that love precede marriage makes the romantic bond more likely to be rational, as it puts pressure on the person to find, choose, and love a "compatible" partner.

It is difficult to judge the validity of such "experiments" as indicators of actual practices, but they do suggest that an important segment of our society, the middle class, subscribes to and forcefully promotes a rational approach to romantic relationships, basing choices on a careful analysis of one's own personality attributes in order to satisfy one's needs and goals.

Asked whether they were looking for specific attributes in the other person and, if so, for which ones, most respondents answered by referring to personality and moral attributes. With varying degrees of articulateness, many respondents spelled out a set of "desirable qualities." Many seemed to have already thought about these questions and answered them with ease, invariably offering a list of good reasons to choose an imaginary "ideal partner." Furthermore, respondents weighed and evaluated their partners' assets and drawbacks. For example, a married woman told me about her encounter with her husband, some fifteen years earlier:

Was it love at first sight?

I don't really know. I am such a realist, it could have been love at first sight but I always tend to weigh off things, I won't let myself just go like that. See, I met him in a very unusual situation, I was definitely very very attracted to him when I first met him but I don't really know that it was, uh—

When you say you are "such a realist," what do you mean?

Well, I am. I think about things; I weigh things out and whether or not. . . . Well, my husband is younger than me, so that was a very big factor so I would try to hold back my feelings because of the fact he was younger than me. I guess I was trying to check myself. (Homemaker, interview 17)

"Realist" is opposed to romantic and is apparently a synonym for "rational" or "practical." By her own admission, this woman was able to keep her feelings in check and release them only when she had come to the rational conclusion that her partner's age would not pose a problem to their relationship.

Thus, the idea of compatibility, incessantly put forward by popular culture, demands that one be aware of one's needs and preferences and then evaluate another person accordingly. Where premodern calculative rationality stressed the economic and social assets of the person and was often voiced by parents rather than by the person in love, contemporary romantic rationality claims to apply only to the personal qualities of the prospective partner. In contemporary culture, rationality is psychological rather than economic and is borne by individuals themselves rather than by formal agencies of mate selection. Consider another example from my interviews. A female artist explained what happens when she meets somebody she is "interested in." "So you want to know something about him, I think. What he does for a living. What his interests are. That he's interested in you. Why he is interested in you. . . . Usually you find out about their background. It's like having references" (artist, interview 35). Clearly, for this woman knowledge of the other person's interests, motives, and history should precede, or at least accompany, the romantic sentiment. She uses a comparison with the workplace ("it's like having references") to evoke the process of gathering information in order to the costs of incompatibility.

From their accounts of past relationships or choice of partner, many if not most of the respondents engaged in the process of weighing positive or negative attributes in order to maximize satisfaction. Few respondents evoked an agapic view of love but instead conspicuously engaged in the process of naming, ranking, and weighing personality attributes. Such an attitude was cogently summarized by one respondent, a thirty-five year-old single male who expressed the desire to be in a long-standing relationship and explained his and others' difficulties in committing themselves.

> I think that people are hesitant to give up their freedom and their independence unless they are absolutely sure it is going to work, it is a lack of faith. "I will be with you now, but if somebody better comes along, that will be it."
>
> *"Somebody better."*
>
> Somebody better.
>
> *What is "somebody better"?*
>
> Somebody who is willing to give me more what I need than you are. (Male actor, college education, interview 29)

At the center of this psychological vocabulary of "needs" is the motive of self-interest. The rational assessment of personal attributes has clear economic overtones, for it is used to shop in the supermarket of relationships for the partner most likely to satisfy personal preferences.

That such an approach is culturally and historically specific can be illustrated by the contrast with one of Proust's early short stories, written at the turn of the century. A woman of great distinction has fallen in love with a man who is intellectually, morally, physically, and socially her inferior. The narrator states that "if she had loved [him] for his beauty or for his wit, then one could have looked for a brighter or more handsome young man. If it had been his goodness or his love for her that had bound her to him, then another one might have tried to love her more faithfully. But Mr. de Laleande is neither handsome nor intelligent. He did not have the opportunity to prove to her if he is tender or tough, neglectful or faithful. . . . It is therefore him she loves and not the merits or charms that could be found in others. It is him she loves despite his imperfections, despite his mediocrity. She is destined to love him, after all."[24] In this story, love addresses someone's unique individuality and not his merits; for merits are interchangeable, while the person is not. Clearly, such an approach negates the possibility that love is contingent on psychological, cultural, or social "utilities" and skirts the very ideal of compatibility. Love is here bestowed arbitrarily and even against the self-interest of the lover.

Although such a view of love was virtually nonexistent in the middle-class and upper-middle-class respondents in my sample, it was present in somewhat different form among the working-class men. They were the most likely to view story 2 (the whirlwind romance; see chapter 5) as the one closest to their real-life experience, and they had difficulty explaining the origins of their own past romantic attachments. The quality most often invoked to explain how and why their feelings started was "looks," which explains sexual attraction but hardly implies an elaborate weighing of needs and preferences against assets and liabilities. As Kephart found, men are more likely than women to hold a romantic view of relationships.[25] My interviews suggest that this trend is even more pronounced among working-class men than among middle-class men. Although they subscribed to the romantic view, the latter nevertheless held to a detailed script of the qualities sought in a partner, whereas the former filled this script with very few attributes and instead usually "followed their hearts" or their "impulse." Furthermore, middle- and upper-middle-class respondents subscribed to the widespread ethos that love is a merit-based emotion, grounded on (real or imaginary) properties of the other person that must satisfy utilitarian criteria of self-satisfaction. This ethos was virtually absent from the responses of working-class men.

At this point I venture an hypothesis: an agapic conception of love is more likely to be encountered among those for whom marriage does not represent a significant asset in their social position or strategy of mobility. These individuals are the most likely to approach love as unpredictable and unaccountable whims of the heart. By contrast, the people most likely to use the rational conceptions of love promoted by popular culture are upwardly mobile and concerned about maintaining and maximizing their social status. This would explain why the middle-class and upper-middle-class respondents, women especially, among my interviewees held very detailed scripts of their partners' desirable attributes. But which attributes qualify or disqualify someone as a potential partner, and how do they connect to social position?

Trying to understand the process by which people define someone as "worthy" or "unworthy" and its relation to the process of social reproduction, Michele Lamont suggests that we distinguish among three categories of symbolic boundary: moral, socioeconomic, and cultural. Lamont criticizes Bourdieu for making cultural boundaries a priori central to social identity and to the formation of social bonds and for not identifying inductively the people's actual definitions of worth. By contrast, she suggests, for example, that moral boundaries—evaluations based on moral attributes such as honesty, generosity, "goodness"—are also, like money or cultural taste, important determinants of a person's informal network of friends.[26] Lamont's argument can be enlisted in support of the view that some social interactions evade the self-interested mechanism of social reproduction. If people choose others on the basis of personal moral merit rather than social assets, this implies that social reproduction, distinction, and exclusion are not the only mechanisms at work in the formation of social bonds. To clarify the connection of love and social reproduction, we will examine the role of Lamont's three types of boundary in the evaluation of potential romantic partners.

SOCIOECONOMIC BOUNDARIES

When asked to address the issue explicitly, most respondents vehemently rejected the notion that they would choose someone for his or her social and economic assets, frequently referring to the sacrosanct norm that money and sentiment are distinct categories. Some of the respondents even invoked the classic stereotype that money spoils sentiment as it brings boredom and dissension to the couple. Self-interest was disavowed in favor of the implicit model of a disinterested, organic, and gratuitous bond. Belief in romantic love is apparently sustained by a belief in its disinterestedness.

Despite the pressure exerted by this residual norm to disavow self-interest, we can approach more obliquely the role of socioeconomic values in romantic relationships. When reviewing the reasons behind disputes or rejection, some respondents, men especially, denounced the way they had felt evaluated according to a monetary scale, something they resented and felt diminished their sense of self-worth. One male respondent distinguished between love and affection by observing that love has an "irrational side to it," while "affection is based on very solid reasons." He suggested that in order to get married, he would like to have the "eyes meet" and a "little magic." Words such as "magic," "spark," and "mystical side" are threads of the emotional and cultural fabric that supports love without the need for reasons or explanations. When asked why his most long-lasting and meaningful relationship ended, however, the same man explained that money played a significant role in the breakup. His girlfriend, a frequently unemployed actress, expected him to provide for her, something he was not willing to do on his limited salary because of his desire to save money. This expectation subsequently kindled tensions, resentment, and ultimately separation (physician, interview 8).

A distributor of noncommercial films, also with a limited income, viewed his prospects of finding a mate as follows:

Do you feel that money is important for love?

No. I mean, I think no, I don't. The answer is no. But money is important for the ability of a relationship to endure I think.

What do you mean?

Because, for example, someone my age, a woman my age in New York, certainly, would probably not be very serious about starting a relationship with somebody who didn't have any money or wasn't likely to have any money in the near future. That is, they would be concerned about their economic security, their economic well-being in the future, and perhaps rightly so. (Male movie distributor, college education, interview 34).

This man found himself caught in an uncomfortable social position, one in which he readily perceived what was at stake in his market of relationships: his relatively high cultural competence put him in the position of meeting professional women, but, with his low income, he was at a competitive disadvantage in finding a mate of his own status. He moved unhappily between the norm that money should not be important for love and his resignation at not being wealthy enough to offer a prospective partner economic security.

Echoing the disenchantment of this man, an actor with a low-to-average income declared that money did not play any role in his romantic relationships, but then added angrily that for certain people money plays a very important important role:

> *Do you know people like that, who would not fall in love with you if you don't have money?*
>
> Yes, I just went out with a girl who has a lot of money from commercials. She didn't fall in love because I didn't have money but she, uh, after she broke up with me she said, "I didn't feel we were dating anyway" and I said "Why?" She said "Well you only paid for me once," and I said "That's a philosophy that I don't subscribe to and I won't be intimidated by."
>
> *What did she mean?*
>
> She meant that if we were really serious about being boyfriend and girlfriend, I would pay for her all the time. Even though she has more money than I do, and I am not that poor, but I felt like what she was revealing to me was, if you couldn't pay for her, she wasn't interested. I think this is what she was saying to me. (Male actor, college education, interview 29)

This story points up the ambiguous meaning of money in romantic relationships. The woman's equation of "paying" with "being serious" is not necessarily proof of her crude self-interest but may indicate that, ironically, she confers on money emotional rather than economic significance. The ostentatious spending of money on a date is a display of social status, but it can also be taken as a "sacrificial" and voluntary waste of goods for the purpose of creating and expressing romantic solidarity and commitment. The display of money as a sign of social power is articulated in terms of the moral economy of waste in which the strength of attachment is measured by willingness to give up wealth. Pushing the separation of passion and interest to its end, however, my interviewee suspected that the moral economy of waste implicitly invoked by the woman gave voice to the less honorable morality of self-interest, of which he felt a victim. Opposing the self-interested evaluation of economic assets, the man insisted that women assume an equal share of the cost for dating, thus stripping money of its ritual and sacrificial meaning and legitimating the norms of equitable exchange at work in the market.

An economically more secure male respondent expressed greater resentment about the fact that women expected him to pay for dates.

What would be unromantic to you? What would be a put-off?

One of the things that puts me off—but I think this is my own problem. I often have problems about money in that I feel like there should be some type of mutuality about it. It's partially my problem, I think about it more than I should, I know that, but what puts me off, not so much on a first date but over a period of time, if a woman assumes that, for some reason, maybe she gets the impression that I am totally loaded or maybe because of the different roles that we are supposed to play, that the man, that whenever we go out, I am supposed to pay for everything, she feels that it's not her area, that's something I find off-putting. (Male corporate banker, graduate education, interview 20)

This man, like the previous one, resented what he perceived to be women's "testing" of his financial power via date expenditures. But even though these complaints were formulated in the name of the "legitimate" norm of equality, these men still revealed embarrassment and felt compelled to justify themselves for demanding financial reciprocity. Their embarrassment stemmed less from their evasion of the traditional male role than from their departure from the expectation that love must transcend economic considerations. On the other hand, their resentment at being evaluated on their ability to pay for dates can be traced to their perceptions that they were "rated" against a market value and did not score highly enough.

In my sample, three of the five men advocating that romantic relationships should satisfy the rules of equitable exchange were in artistic professions. Their fluctuating incomes and professional and economic insecurity made it likely that they competed with men of higher and more reliable incomes for the same women. Resisting downward mobility, these men wanted to meet women with cultural and educational assets comparable to theirs, yet their low rank on the income scale put them at a disadvantage vis-à-vis other potential competitors. Their insecurity paired with their instability made them particularly prone to denounce, with varying degrees of resignation and resentment, the value of the male's economic security, stability, and capacity to "provide for the woman." As Bourdieu found in the domain of art, people on the margins of a field are the most likely to denounce what is at stake in it.

The connection between uncertain socioeconomic status and perceptions of being treated as tradable goods might be further supported by the
fact that in my sample these anxieties and resentments were never voiced
by working-class men who subscribed more readily to the norm that men
"pay for the date" and had not adopted the egalitarian ethos characteristic of higher socioeconomic brackets. According to Bourdieu, working-
class males derive a positive sense of identity from their domination over
women. Hence, the same financial security demanded of women by these
middle-class men can pose a threat to working-class men. Indeed, the contrast between the previous accounts and the following is striking:

Do you think that money is important for love?

No I don't think that money is important for love.

Do you think that money can make love better and easier?

It can, but money isn't important for love as far as, I don't think that
should be your first, uh, the first thing you notice in someone, I don't think
that should be someone's main interest.

Do you think that lack of money can bring problems?

A lot of arguments and fightings. It can also bring jealousy.

Have you seen that around you?

Yes.

Who?

Myself. I am in a better job than my ex-fiancé. I have more things. I have a
car, he doesn't. Things like that. And he became very jealous because I was
very successful and he wasn't.

What kind of job does he do?

He is a file clerk for a law firm, a messenger. (Female legal secretary, interview 18).

In ironic counterpoint to the preceding examples, this woman's professional and financial success caused her lover so much jealousy that she
eventually broke off the relationship. This account indirectly supports
the claim that for the working classes, the morality of equitable exchange
is far less prominent than among middle-class men, because the sacrificial waste of money usually performed by the working-class male sustains and is sustained by his domination over the woman.

On the basis of these and other examples, I venture another hypothesis: the denunciation of the economic stakes of romantic relationships

is expressed in the egalitarian morality of exchange by men whose social position is insecure, who fear downward mobility, and who compete with men of superior economic status for the same women. Similarly, those attempting upward mobility through marriage might be more prone to acknowledge the economic considerations and carefully monitor their romantic interactions. This might explain, for example, why women are more likely than men to acknowledge self-interest in their choices and to use the rational logic of bargaining: because women are still in a more precarious economic position than men and remain more dependent on marriage for social status, they are more likely to try to control their position in this relationship by drawing on the rational cultural repertoire of love.

In my sample there were four such people, three women and one man, who feared downward mobility and admitted that economic stability had been or would be important in their choice of a mate. All three women explicitly cited money as an important criterion in selecting a mate, as illustrated by this middle-class woman.[27]

Do you think that money is important for love?

It is in a way, because when I think of the kind of guy I would like to marry, he has to be making a living, a nice living. The nicer the better, I have to admit it. I don't like to tell everybody that because it makes me sound like a materialistic person and, I just think it is nice, like a girl at work the other day said she knew a guy who was single and would I like to meet him, and he was a carpenter, and he's like an apprentice, a carpenter's apprentice, and without even wanting to learn about the guy I said "No thanks." (Female advertising designer, college education, interview 30)

This woman behaved like a rational economic actor. Not only did she attach to the potential partner an "index" of economic value but her financial preferences determined in advance whether she would be willing even to meet a potential partner. Despite her forthrightness, she was apologetic and aware that she broke the norm of disinterestedness.

When respondents acknowledged a rational, self-interested approach to choosing a partner, they usually also showed signs of discomfort and felt the need to do face-saving work. A freelance cameraman with a low and irregular income "confessed" only after the interview was over that he wanted to meet a "strong, independent woman, with lots of money, who would not depend on me for anything." He said this in a joking tone, as if to underplay his breach of the norm of disinterestedness. His economic insecurity and the ethos of self-determination demanded by his freelance work are mirrored in his insistence that his partner be "independent" and able to provide for herself. In a less apologetic style, a working-class woman said the following:

Would you have married someone [other than you husband] who has less money?

No.

Why?

Because I like my lifestyle and I am very comfortable with it and I couldn't see myself having less than I have now. I would never be happy. (Female homemaker, high school education, interview 28)

As a final example of the rational, self-interested approach, I cite a woman, an artist, who had married an extremely wealthy man. When the interview ended, I asked her for her impressions of the interview.

Did you find my questions difficult to answer?

No, but I felt bad, I felt bad to say, well, it wasn't just that I was madly in love with the person I married. There were a lot of other considerations and maybe I should be the kind of person, you know, like the story number one, just to know right away on the bus and get married and that's that, instead of thinking it through, what I wanted.

And that's bad?

Well, because it's not romantic. It's, I feel like, in picking a partner, I think I was much more, ah, conscious of what it was I wanted and I did not, ah, it was not, ah, it was much more conscious thing. I knew what I wanted and I was going to stay on course. I wasn't going to fall for, ah, I don't know, I wasn't going to fall for men, I was just, love at first sight kind of thing or attraction, I was just going to wait beyond that, I was a little bit cynical about it.

Cynical.

Yeah

To get what you want is to be cynical.

Yeah, cynical is that I just didn't trust my feelings this time around. I didn't trust my feelings and I think in romantic love you just *know* you're in love. This is *it*. And I didn't go about it that way and I was much more, in a way, I was much more calculating. I didn't trust my feelings. I just, I thought I'm going to wait and see how I feel later about this, and, ah I'm not in a hurry.

And you didn't like saying that during the interview?

Yeah, it doesn't go along with the magazine ads of what it should be like. I felt much more, almost like I was buying a house or something, that I was really looking at the whole thing and I wasn't going to be very impulsive about it and I planned not to be impulsive about it. I wasn't out to change my whole life or have somebody who was going to turn everything I have ever thought around. I wasn't looking for somebody like that. (Female artist, interview 35)

As an artist, this woman was economically insecure and consciously chose a partner who would enable her to devote herself to her art without the worries of survival. Her behavior exemplifies that of the rational economic agent; she maximized preferences (at the time her artistic work) and traded passion for economic security. The woman compared her choice with "buying a house" and insisted that she did not let her feelings control her decision making in order to evaluate "the whole thing." But here also she was apologetic and appeared embarrassed by her behavior. To behave in a rational, calculated, and self-interested fashion was highly inappropriate, for, as she said, such behavior is traditionally opposed to the ideal of love as irrational and disinterested. In this approach to love, one does not think; rather one just "knows" that this is it. In other words, she dismissed the economic rationality of her behavior by contrasting it with a form of love that is organic, immediate, and based not on reasoning but on an intuitive grasp of one's emotions.

Thus, despite the strong norm of disinterestedness and the sacrosanct separation of money and sentiment that pervaded most answers, some of the respondents, anxious about social mobility and economic security, articulated most clearly the rational process of choosing others. Whether they evaluated others or felt evaluated by others according to "economic value," these respondents offered cogent examples of a self-interested rationality.

MORAL AND PERSONALITY BOUNDARIES

The fact remains, however, that most people do not admit that economic considerations and strategic thinking are central to their choices. While our culture endorses rational choice based on moral or personal qualities, it forcefully denies the legitimacy of such a choice based on socioeconomic factors. In *If I'm So Wonderful, Why Am I Still Single?* it was suggested that qualities such as "thoughtfulness, generosity, self-assurance, physical warmth, sexiness, and the ability to listen and to express affection are more important than things like social status."[28] In my interviews, when asked to describe their "ideal mate," educated middle-class respondents made many more demands in regard to intellectual qualities and cultural compatibility than did their working-class counterparts. They demanded that their mates be "intelligent," "thoughtful," "communicative," "original," "creative," "interesting," that they have "curiosity," "the same ideas," "the same values," "the same lifestyle"—qualities related in one way or another to familiarity with the forms of cultural capital. While working-class respondents did speak about "being able to share ideas" or "explore new things together," they never mentioned being interesting, creativity, or even curiosity as necessary or important criteria in selecting a mate. Working-class respondents (mostly women) instead used a vocabulary with heavily moral overtones. Besides a high school education, they wanted their "ideal partner" to be "considerate," "honest," "dependable," "stable." These were not virtues such as charity or loving-kindness but rather qualities a mate needed in order to be a reliable provider and parent, to value work discipline, and to keep within the boundaries of legality.[29] This emphasis of working-class respondents reflects the relatively greater financial insecurity of working-class households. In contrast, because they already had security and stability, middle- and upper-middle-class respondents made many more demands on the personality characteristics of their partners and used cultural or aesthetic criteria to evaluate them.[30]

This was elucidated *a contrario* in responses professing indifference to formal education. These interviewees claimed that qualities such as "intelligence" and "ability to discuss ideas" express another person's personality and worth better than education does and are more important than education per se. Listen, for example, to a woman whose father and husband are both tenured professors at prestigious universities and who was herself educated at an equally prestigious private school:

Would you marry someone who was much less educated than you?

I don't care about the credentials of an educated person, I just care that the person has an interest and curiosity about the world. And if they do, if they read and look into things, then we have something in common. But if somebody has no interest in reading, I would have a hard time having a relationship with this person because literature and books and ideas are very important to me and I wouldn't be able to talk about something very important to me. (Artist, interview 13)

Although this woman discounted the importance of formal education, she attached a great deal of importance to activities usually associated with high educational competence. Talking, reading, going to art galleries, sharing ideas about art and politics, these constitute the habitus of those who have attended universities and consider "culture" to be an integral part of their identities. Because these activities seem gratuitous and divorced from the social benefits at stake in them, this respondent saved the appearance of disinterestedness. She converted cultural capital into a personal quality such as "curiosity" or an activity such as the "sharing of ideas."

The following example is the kind of answer never given by working-class respondents:

What is your ideal mate?

> It would have to be somebody with interests and beliefs that I share. Because I don't think that among two people that are involved, intellectual or political disagreement should be a source of conflict. There are plenty sources of conflict and that one may as well not be there! Somebody who enjoys similar recreations, like good music, films, things like that. I would hope that the person would be very warm and understanding. (Male Ph.D. student, interview 24)

This response eloquently illustrates that for people in the most educated brackets, "moral" attributes are so intertwined with cultural ones as to be hardly distinguishable. "Warmth" goes with "understanding," which refers to the ability to share the complex and sophisticated tastes and opinions that form the basis of these respondents' social identity. Acquired intellectual qualities that have everything to do with educational capital are converted into intrinsic personal, moral qualities.

The moral qualities expected in a partner are thus grounded in people's differing life conditions, working-class emphasis on reliability and upper-middle class emphasis on curiosity and taste. These findings appear to contradict Lamont's contention that moral boundaries are autonomous in relation to economic or cultural ones. Although we both found that cultural specialists are more likely to use cultural boundaries to choose their associates, I would suggest that moral boundaries are subordinate to respondents' relative sense of economic security or the importance of education. In other words, as criteria for romance or friendship, moral, economic, and cultural boundaries are distinguised only fuzzily.[31] The following section will show even more clearly that for middle- and upper-middle-class respondents moral attributes are implicitly grounded in educational and cultural capital.

EDUCATIONAL AND CULTURAL BOUNDARIES

When asked if they would marry someone less educated than themselves, working-class men said only occasionally that education was not important, but more than half of the upper-middle-class respondents and *all* the working-class women said they would not marry such a person. Clearly, education is considered necessary in a partner. It is explicitly acknowledged as a preference and appears to infringe on the norm of disinterestedness less than money does. In contrast to economic capital, education is more readily viewed as reflecting personal characteristics (such as intelligence or perseverance) and, when directing romantic choices, is therefore more likely to be converted into moral attributes that are congruent with the norm of disinterestedness. As Bourdieu writes: "Practice never ceases to conform to economic calculation even when it gives every appearance of disinterestedness by departing from the logic of interested calculation (in the narrow sense) and playing for stakes that are non-material and not easily quantified."[32]

The importance of cultural capital is also seen in respondents' accounts of how relationships ended. A woman lawyer who had attended two of the top law schools in the country but who did not want to be labeled with "Ivy League" stereotypes (she came from the lower segments of the middle class) spent three years with a man who had no formal education and whose main professional activity was hunting. She eventually ended this relationship on the grounds that the man was not "communicative enough," and she later married a successful graphic designer with an income and education similar to hers as well as a predilection for the "unconventional" lifestyle she was looking for.

Another professional woman, a graphic designer working in advertising, somewhat downwardly mobile, expressed a distaste for "educated nerds" in favor of "real masculine men." She went out for a few years with a "pizza guy" but eventually broke off the relationship on the grounds that, since she didn't intend to marry a "pizza guy," the relationship "was not going anywhere."

Trying to explain why he broke up with a woman who had all the "objective qualities to be an ideal partner," a third respondent, a thirty-

year-old music conductor, said that he could not fall in love with her because "I need a mystical side which I can't explain." The same man, however, was very clear in the qualities he wanted in a partner. For him, the
ideal mate was "someone who has a certain decorum, a certain refinement, it's very hard to find the combination. Either people tend to be
very open and I think a little gaudy, a little bad taste, or they tend to be
very refined but boring" (music conductor, interview 33). Drawing from
the agapic cultural repertoire of love, this musician required a "mystical" feeling to fall in love, yet he could articulate the specific attributes
of the "ideal partner" and point to trade-offs in different qualities. His
vocabulary was unambiguously aesthetic; he expressly disqualified the
"vulgar" manners of "too open" people and made "refinement"—the
ultimate attribute of class distinction—the key characteristic of his ideal
partner. In contrast to the other respondents, this man did not engage in
the script of "good reasons." His mystical love instead relied on the tacit
recognition of invisible cultural attributes.

A final example of the importance of cultural capital was provided by
a woman who had dropped out of college and was about to enroll in a
police academy at the time of the interview. She had been in a relationship that seemed to be leading to marriage but ultimately ended. She recalled their dating:

> We liked to read together, we liked to read a lot, listen to music, sight-
> seeing, just taking walks, not too much involved with other people, like
> parties. I like going to museums and stuff like that, maybe operas, plays,
> and stuff like that. We went to see a few concerts together, and we went to
> impressionist museums.
>
> *Which museums?*
>
> I don't remember the name. That was his hobby. (Female, college drop-out,
> interview 21)

While it is doubtful that they engaged as frequently and intensively in
those activities as she claimed (she could not remember any music or
books or museums they shared together), this relationship acquainted
her with a cultural lifestyle she otherwise would not have been familiar
with. Her boyfriend finished college and became a lawyer. He broke off
the relationship because of her refusal to continue her college education.
And although she did love him, she did not yield to his request that she
stay in college rather than seek a career in law enforcement. The force
of habitus was clearly stronger than their feelings for each other.

As these examples show, people can choose *not* to be with somebody because of incompatible cultural and educational backgrounds; sometimes this choice is conscious, but most often it is hidden under personal attributes such as "curiosity" or "creativity."

To summarize, then, I found that the downwardly mobile or the "strained" upwardly mobile respondents for whom marriage was an important factor in achieving a certain social status were the most likely to acknowledge an economically rational approach to love and marriage. Even those who subscribed to the norm of disinterestedness revealed in their responses the cognitive and psychological properties of a self-interested rationality: mates are chosen on the basis not of a blind and uncontrollable romantic passion but rather of a more-or-less careful and controlled evaluation of personal and moral qualities. These qualities are translations of assets associated with various levels of education. The moral boundaries usually invoked by working-class respondents to evaluate prospective partners were defined in terms of commitment to work and family. As Bourdieu found in France, a moral vocabulary is more evident among the working class and the lower fractions of the middle class. My upper-class respondents, especially those with high cultural capital, emphasized a battery of personal qualities that directly relate to cultural rather than moral resources and reflected "highbrow" tastes. Both social groups, then, translated the particular exigencies of their social positions into moral or personal attributes or both.

I TALK, THEREFORE YOU LOVE ME

This analysis still leaves unanswered the central question presented at the beginning of this chapter: what is the cultural mechanism invisibly reconciling love as the outcome of a self-interested choice of a socially compatible partner with love as pure emotion?

To begin answering this question, I offer the case of a working-class man who had dated for several months a woman with significantly higher income and education. He recalled their dating as follows: "I dated only one woman who had a lot of money and we had a great thing going." Despite the difference in their socioeconomic status, they had a fulfilling relationship. Although his income was limited, he was able to "take her places" and fulfill the cultural script of the "man treating the woman." He was able not only to compete successfully with other men of higher socioeconomic status but also to make use of the virility and sexual boldness often valued by working-class men (his partner often asked him to make love in unconventional places, for example, near a statue in the park of a large city). But she eventually broke off the relationship because of his lack of formal education. Talking like a lay sociologist, he viewed education as a more important factor than his income in explaining their separation.

> I've only dated one person who had a lot of money and we had a great thing going, but one thing that killed us. She could come down to my level, but I could not go to her level or class. She made better than $150,000 a year. . . .
> She was around lawyers, doctors, professional people who always wore a three-piece suit, always went out with a tux on, always drove a limousine or had a limousine pick 'em up, where, even though I, at the time, had a Caddie and I took her to nice places, but I could not go to her office parties or her boss's house when she got invited out there.

Why?

> She thought I wouldn't fit because I didn't have the higher education that she wanted to have, like a B.S. or a double E behind their name: electrical engineer or a doctor or a lawyer or somethin' like this and she married a professional person. But I wasn't hurt when she left and I analyzed it afterwards and I realized that I enjoyed her company and I had a very strong like-love for her and it was almost love-love and I think what made me come to my senses is the fact that there's different type of people in classes. There's rich class, professional class, working class, even low-life class. You, to me, you cannot mix a rich class with a working class. It don't mix. You cannot mix a professional who makes better than a $100,000 with a working person. They don't mix.

What do you think was the biggest obstacle in what you say, money or education?

> Education is the biggest obstacle, although some people who have a working-class, they are more educated than the people who have a professional-class. They have more sense. They have more knowledge, where a professional person has that degree behind their name, even though they went to school and they took all the courses and they know all the proper words to say and everything, but they don't have the smarts. They don't have that knowledge.

When you say education is an obstacle, what do you mean exactly?

> Oh, uh, say, for instance, you met a person. You say, for instance, I had my doctor's degree in sociology, Okay? Most of the people you would talk to are in your category. If you happen to go down into a lower class or into a working class, you may find a very bright person who is smart and can hold a conversation and can talk in their sense of their class of intelligence, of knowin' the fancy words, of the right pronunciation of the words, of the right, to me, the four, ah, the four-dollar words that are so long that some people have to look up in the dictionary to find out what the meanings are. (Male electrician, interview 36)

Although they were of different social and economic backgrounds, the man took the "$150,000 lady" to "nice places," thus suggesting that there is some degree of class interaction, even if not enough for marriage. Dating, as we saw earlier, allows for more class interaction than courting, calling, or keeping company, that is, getting to know somebody with the express purpose of marriage. Because it is relatively noncommittal, dating favors class interactions, but in the short rather than long term. In this man's story, both money and education divided them, although ultimately education was the more important reason for their parting. The fact that he "was not hurt" illustrates Bourdieu's claim that people adapt to the chances they objectively have; that is, people desire only what they can objectively get, or, as was the case here, they do not mourn what they objectively cannot get. In choosing their mates, people unconsciously adapt their choices to their objective assets and chances. Finally, and perhaps most noteworthy, the man indicated that verbal communication was one of the important avenues, if not the most important, through which his educational inadequacy or incompatibility was made visible. This provides us with an important clue as to the nature of the cultural mechanism "translating" emotion into social reproduction.

The model of emotional communication that has pervaded the portrayals of love in the mass media presents ideal love as an eminently *talkative* love. We are indeed endlessly told that communication is not merely an important feature but the defining feature of good and loving romantic relationships. Many studies of love and marriage agree that communication, self-expression, self-disclosure, and verbal intimacy are prerequisites of a successful relationship and are crucial in eliciting and maintaining romantic feelings.[33] The historical and cultural situatedness of this emphasis is evocatively illustrated by the twelfth-century *Treatise on Love and Its Remedies,* in which Andreas Capellanus warned that too many opportunities to see the beloved and too many chances to talk to each another actually decrease love. Furthermore, unlike the seventeenth-century aristocratic French ideal of sharing tastes through the refined art of conversation, the aim of contemporary communication is not to engage in sophisticated seduction games, in which the self is as often veiled as it is disclosed, but rather to expose and express, as authentically as possible, one's inner thoughts and self. Soap operas, popular psychology, self-help books, and women's magazines have been the main vehicles for the elaboration, codification, and popularization of the principle that romantic communication is a way to attain self-knowledge, mutual understanding, and ultimately emotional fulfillment. The ideal of communication is presented and lived as an ideal of emotional self-disclosure and intimacy.

However, as we saw in the previous chapter, the communicative rationality that strengthens and enriches the romantic bond verges on an economic rationality that makes the other person a tradable good. Conversation and other forms of expression function as indicators of the cultural capital on which they are so dependent, so that for my middle- and upper-middle-class respondents, talking and listening aid in selecting a mate from a compatible habitus. Two examples help clarify this. In a popular book with the self-explanatory title *How to Marry the Man of Your Choice,* the author, Margaret Kent, advises, "Once you have started dating a particular man, how do you determine if he is a potential husband for you? How do you know if he is that special one man in a hundred—or in a thousand—who is your ideal mate?. . . . 'Interview' him for the job of husband before you 'audition' for the role of wife."[34] The author proceeds to list topics and questions one can and should address during these interviews to determine in a man is compatible: for example, questions about values and goals and questions such as "Do you believe in heaven and hell?" and "How often do you like to go on vacation?" and "What would your dream house be like?" and "What are your attitudes toward capital punishment?" The golden rule of the interview is that a good atmosphere must prevail: "Let him talk." "Show interest and remember what he says." "Avoid censorship." "Avoid criticism and ridicule." The "romantic interview" makes the romantic encounter focus on the conversational exchange at the same time that it makes conversation the tool through which one identifies the truly compatible partner.

The second example is provided by a twenty-five year-old male respondent in my sample.

What kind of things would be unromantic on a first date?

I would mostly pay attention to the conversation that she initiated.

Which means—?

The sort of subject she is interested in talking about.

So what would be a romantic subject?

I think art or politics or just very typically beautiful things, talking about spring or swimming or something like that. I enjoy comparing notes about things that we think are enjoyable.

Would you marry someone less educated than you?

No.

Why not?

Because the principle that I like to do with the person I am with is to talk, discuss, and argue, and if somebody can't do that, I would not really know what to do.

What attracts you in somebody?

More than anything else, somebody that I am able to talk to easily, feel very comfortable with. . . .

Can you describe your ideal mate?

It would have to be somebody with interests and beliefs that I share. Because I don't think that among two people that are involved, intellectual or political disagreement should be a source of conflict. There are plenty of sources of conflict and that one may as well not be there. Somebody who enjoys similar recreations, like good music, good food, films, things like that.

How would you like to meet your partner, ideally?

I think in the context of work, I would like to meet somebody who is interested in the same sorts of commitments and pursuits that I have and who also is interesting and fascinating in their own right, but I think that having common intellectual and political interests is a good and important thing. I think you can build a lasting partnership on something like that. (Male Ph.D. student, interview 24)

The cultural ideal of talking gives voice to the ethos that communication prevents and resolves conflicts, brings a better knowledge of oneself and others, binds two people emotionally, and serves as the basis for true intimacy. This ethos in turn expresses a belief in the redemptive value of language, its capacity to represent the person, to know the world, to act on it, to steer emotions, and to bind people in their mutual openness. It fits perfectly the "new middle class" for whom signs are the paramount reality of their work and who view the world as a generalized system of communication. The more one is likely to work in the professions that demand a manipulation of signs and language (advertising, media, publishing, academia), the more likely one is to value verbal communication for its own sake. Thus for a well-established New York editor in my sample, talking was the very essence of the romantic. Asked what she would do if she wanted to have a romantic moment with someone, she replied succinctly, "Talk! Talk! Talk!" (female editor, interview 3). And, in fact, when asked to remember one of her most romantic moments, this woman mentioned having met someone and having talked to him for "two days and two nights in a row, without getting any sleep."

What we call a successful date is a mix of pleasure and utility. The intimacy of kindred souls is an effect of social compatibility, the product of similar tastes in leisure, the tacit recognition of one's own ways of talking, thinking, and relaxing. For middle- and upper-middle class couples, the ability to experience simultaneously the pleasures of leisure and those of conversation guarantees a compatibility that a good sexual relationship comes to confirm and epitomize. Such a harmonization is the result of a subtle correspondence between modes of consumption, class membership, tastes, talk as symbolic capital, although it claims to be the effect of the happy, chance union of kindred souls.

The "logocentrism" of the new middle class has permeated the standard definitions of romantic relationships. Communication is important to the romantic interactions of the new middle classes because it contains not only the possibility of intimacy and emotional openness but also the possibility for mutual assessment of educational and cultural compatibility. The self is revealed, in this view, through the statement of opinions, tastes, and personal experiences. A shared belief in the importance of conversation can even overcome other personal differences, as seen in the case of one of my respondents, a seventeen-year-old high school student, daughter of two publishers and possessing substantial cultural capital.

> *Can you pick one or two significant relationships and tell me what was significant about them?*
>
> One was interesting because we would fight all the time.
>
> *About what?*
>
> About anything, but usually it was more like having a debate on anything, politics or a movie, anything.
>
> *How did you end up being together?*
>
> That's what led our relationship, fighting and debating. (High school student, interview 30)

Even if this teenager went on to acknowledge that she had no romantic experience, her cultural habitus clearly gave her a predilection for verbal communication. For her, "debating" or "intellectual challenge"— core components of the culture of the classroom—are privileged modes of communication to establish a romantic relationship.

Asked if education was important in a partner, a woman lawyer who has been married for ten years responded, "To me education is too important, although I may fall in love with a painter tomorrow who you know makes zero for a week. Again that's the money but if I love the painter, if I thought he was wonderful, maybe I would. Education is important, to me to find someone who is uneducated might not be challenging intellectually" (interview 7).

People with a high cultural competence do not talk simply for the sake of talking: through the prevalence of debate and challenge in their conversation, they carry into personal life the work ethic of the new service class. As we will see, for the working classes talking is a matter not of debating but rather of the ability to express needs and solve problems. While the middle-class concept of communication contains the two ideas of problem solving and the "sharing or debating of tastes," for working classes conversation is almost exclusively the former.

For middle- and upper-middle-class respondents, then, conversation is a form of romantic pursuit, but one that helps determine the cultural and educational compatibility of their partners. Because talking most often means talking about topics that require from the two partners similar amounts of cultural competence and educational capital, it is an effective way to choose partners of similar background.[35] Communication is thus an informal mechanism to gather initial information about each other. Linguistic capital is central to cultural and educational capital. As Bourdieu puts it, "The laws of the transmission of linguistic capital are a particular case of the laws of the legitimate transmission of cultural capital between the generations, and it may therefore be posited that the linguistic competence measured by academic criteria depends, like the other dimensions of cultural capital, on the level of education (measured in terms of qualifications obtained) and on the social trajectory."[36]

The modern ideal of communication is presented under the guise of a pleasurable pursuit that arouses emotion and encourages bonds. To use Parsonian terminology, the instrumental dimension of communication is intermingled with its expressive dimension. Talk fulfills its instrumental function only to the extent that it also fulfills the expressive function of providing warmth and intimacy.

We no longer live in an era in which, as Durrell observed, a "perfume or a walk" haunts us. What excites the imagination and the emotions of modern people is their ability to share verbally their opinions, tastes, and lifestyle. D.H. Lawrence described this excitement over seventy years ago in *Lady Chatterley's Lover:* "Neither was ever in love with a young man unless he and she were verbally very near: that is, unless they were profoundly interested, talking to one another. The amazing, the profound, the unbelievable thrill there was in passionately talking to some really clever young man by the hour, resuming day after day for months. . . . "[37]

Sociologists of the contemporary family have suggested that marriage has become a "lifestyle enclave," with marital choices based on personal compatibility and lifestyle, but they have not specified the subjective mechanism through which this is accomplished.[38] In an economy where lifestyles and cultural competencies are distinctive markers of social stratification, the notion that love evolves from communication, from the sharing of common tastes, feelings and ideas, incorporates under the guise of an ideal of intimacy the idea that one's mate should be culturally, educationally, and linguistically compatible. The centrality of education to the choice of a partner is congruent with Bourdieu's (and more tangentially Gary Becker's) claim that education is a new form of capital in which people (and states) invest.

Thus, at least one of the mechanisms through which people experience their love subjectively as a disinterested emotion and yet, at the same time, reproduce patterns of social class is mediated by a communicative habitus, the expression of identity through conversation and verbal self-disclosure. The process of mate selection takes the form simultaneously of an exchange of tradable goods and a pooling of resources through the sharing of common tastes, leisure activities, and values.[39] From my sample, it is difficult to determine which aspects are "traded" and which are "shared." Rather, these apparently correspond to different stages of the romantic relationship, the former manifesting itself at the earlier stages of the relationship and the latter coming into play slightly later. The cultural model of communication plays an important role in the second stage of the process and has both instrumental and expressive functions. Through it people both evaluate one another's cultural and educational standing and forge and continuously renew the emotional bond per se.[40] Hence, even if, as Lamont correctly argues, "high" culture does not play the critical role it plays in France in the formation of associations, other forms of cultural capital and distinction, such as the ability to carry on an "intelligent conversation" and the ability to display the forms of "common sense" and understanding that are part of one's habitus, are central to the choice of a mate.

Transformations in middle-class cultural definitions of romantic love and marital relationships, in which these come to be viewed as constituted and maintained by communication, explain therefore, at least in part, how people can choose a linguistically, educationally, and culturally compatible mate while maintaining the face of disinterested irrationality. This ideal of communication allows us to understand how apparently "disinterested" emotions and norms coexist with strategic action. The personal qualities that rational-action theorists claim underlie the preferences of actors are in fact social qualities that are not acknowledged as such but are formulated and subjectively lived in the broad cultural ideal of communication. In keeping with Bourdieu's criticism of these theorists, my findings suggest that interests are neither universal nor preconstituted.[41] Their particular forms emerge from historical transformations of the cultural and economic spheres. As Weber argued, culture provides the particular languages and frames of thought within which interests "move on the tracks of history."

This analysis thus partially conflicts with that of Lamont in arguing that moral, cultural, and social boundaries are blurred and porous. Like Lamont, I find that high culture per se does not play the central role in the reproduction of American society that it does in France, but I would argue that more abstract, less content-driven forms of cultural capital, such as the general ability to communicate thoughts, opinions, and emotions, play an important part in romantic associations. As Bourdieu would expect, I found respondents sometimes to be conscious strategists with a clear sense of "investment" and sometimes to make romantic choices by using semiconscious judgments guided by habitus. This conclusion, however, is more relevant to the beginning stages of a relationship than to its subsequent stages, during which the phenomenology of the romantic bond changes.

LOVE FOR FREE

The paradox of the romantic bond is that although it can be motivated by self-interest, it is fully convincing only if at a certain point the individual proves his or her disinterestedness. Once the choice has been made and the romantic bond established, what people view as the most loving acts are those that are ostensibly indifferent to their "market value" but instead display disinterestedness and gratuity.[42]

> *Can you remember a moment in your relationship with your husband that stands out in particular?*
>
> One very special moment—I don't even know why this comes to mind—but it was Valentine's Day, it was the first Valentine's Day that I knew him.

And he called me to see if I was home and if he could come over and I told
him not to, because I had something, something had happened to my eyes,
they were all swollen, I really looked like a freak, I had gotten something, I
still don't know what it was, but my face was all popped up and I told him
not to come over because I didn't want him to see me like that. And a while
later he was up at the door with a dozen roses and it did not offend me that
he came over, it made me feel good because it did not matter to him that I
looked that way. He still wanted to spend time with me. (Female secretary,
interview 16)

This incident, which seemed so clearly to evade the logic of calculation,
was vividly recalled after fifteen years by the same woman who had
weighed so carefully getting involved with someone younger than herself. What made the event stand out was that her boyfriend showed that
he loved her for "something else" other than what was then probably
one of her only assets on the marriage market, her beauty. He manifested
a disinterested behavior and a concern for her rather than for the immediate benefits he could garner from meeting her on Valentine's Day.

To fully convince, romantic love must be an ostentatious manifestation of disinterestedness and appear to short-circuit the economic rationality of profit and loss. For example, a working-class woman, who earlier in the interview had said that she would not have married someone
with an income lower than that of her husband, recalled why one of her
love relationships did not work out: "I am thinking back [on] someone
I dated for a long time, maybe that's why I didn't stick it out with him.
Because I loved him, he was a very successful-type person, every woman's
dream, but I guess he didn't have that spark, the romance" (female legal
secretary, interview 18). This woman implicitly opposed two kinds of relationship, one motivated by the fact that he was "very successful" and
"every woman's dream," the other based on an ineffable "spark." In this
relationship, in other words, the woman could not switch to a thoroughly disinterested and gratuitous bond. This woman eventually married a man who, by her own account, was as successful as her former
boyfriend but for whom she felt "that spark." This second relationship
thus contained both the conscious and calculated elements of economic
investments and the irrational mystique that makes the romantic
bond different from purely economic behavior and shrouds it in a
halo of disinterested emotionality. Another of my respondents openly
acknowledged having pursued a woman because he found out her family owned an island, but then confessed, "When I started going out with
her, it clearly wasn't going to happen, the island became irrelevant. It's

like 'Who needs the island?' I would rather not go to the island if I have to go with her" (male actor, interview 29). Even though the island sparked his initial interest, it was not sufficient to maintain it in the absence of other, nonmaterial elements. Echoing the women in the preceding examples, he suggested that an interest that cannot be converted into sentiment cannot provide the ground for an enduring bond.

Thus, contrary to popular myth, the initial attraction is mixed with, if not steeped in, the self-interested rationality of the market, while later stages of the romantic bond lend themselves more readily to the gratuitous gift of oneself and irrational love for someone else.[43] Lamont's attempt to establish moral boundaries as autonomous from the mechanism of social reproduction fails to take into account the role of *time* in the development of relationships. At some point, or during some of its privileged moments, the couple shifts to a mode where gift rather than exchange value binds the two. This aspect of the romantic bond is befittingly apparent in the practices of gift-giving reported by my respondents.

The gift has ambiguous properties. On the one hand, it seems gratuitous, disinterested, and beyond the rationality of economic exchange, but on the other, the norms of reciprocity that constrain the circulation of gifts make them socially binding. Receipt of a gift usually calls for a reciprocal gift, and the prestige or honor of the giver depends on the value of the gift.[44] In other words, the gift seems to be at one and the same time gratuitous, because it is a waste of economic capital and evades the rationality of market exchange, and binding, because it puts pressure on the giver to give a gift appropriate to the code of honor and pressure on the recipient to give back a gift of equal or superior value. Pursuing and extending Mauss's insights, Bourdieu suggests in his study of Kabylia that in the system of gift-giving power is simultaneously affirmed and disguised. By giving generous gifts that cannot be reciprocated, the giver creates a debt that is in effect an imposition of power.[45]

Not all the gifts circulated in the romantic relationship exhibit the power dimension discussed by Bourdieu, however. On the contrary, for a certain category of gifts, pressure is put less on the recipient to reciprocate than on the giver, in the obligation that the gift must express sentiments, intimacy, and shared experiences that negate market value and status. When asked what sort of gifts people like to give or receive, many respondents answered in a single voice: "Little things, little cards, little flowers, like little things" (interview 11). "We like small [inaudible] of affection, he would bring me flowers, but it does not have to be expensive flowers" (interview 28). "I tend to buy little garbages, like cheap toys, or, I have a hard, I am not the type to buy flowers and candy" (interview 14). "I like to be given small, not very valuable things" (interview 24). "I used to buy Laura lots of things, like tee-shirts, just little chachkas" (interview 8). These examples, given by males and females of different ages and social classes, reveal a common theme: romantic gifts are "little," "small," "cheap," of no economic value. The smallness of these gifts functions as a conspicuous sign of intimacy. Removed from more stereotypical expressions of romance, they can take on a private meaning shared only by the couple. They are, as one respondent put it, "garbages," that is, that which cannot be recycled, the surplus to which everyone else is indifferent.

There seem to be, then, two parallel scales to measure the exchange of gifts, one in which bigger is better and one in which sentiments are expressed by inverting the logic of the market or the ostentatious display of prestige. The romantic gift points to all that cannot be commodified or indexed to social status: spontaneity, originality, intimacy, effort, creativity, and authenticity. The smallness of the romantic gift inverts the rules of gift giving. The solidarity expressed by the gift is all the more convincing in that it is condensed into an economically worthless object. Where one would have expected the romantic bond to be most commodified, it appears, on the contrary, to evade the logic of the market and to retain as valuable only those actions and objects that signify neither by their economic value nor by the prestige attached to them, but by their capacity to communicate feelings.[46] For example, a male janitor in my sample recalled that the most loving present he had received was "a card. A very loving card. Presents are nice. Somebody is thinking about you. It's nice to give presents when there is no occasion for it" (interview 40).

Why is giving a present "when there is no occasion for it" considered romantic? Precisely because it is an ostensible manifestation of the fact that the action is not constrained by the rules of gift giving; the recipient releases the giver from these rules so that the gift may come from the free desire to give and thereby to express love. For every respondent, a gift given unexpectedly was deemed much more romantic than a gift given on its "due date" (such as an anniversary or birthday). The romantic gift transcends the system of reciprocity and thereby appears to be an act of pure will and love.

Another respondent also characterized a card she had received as a very romantic present: "My husband did something very romantic. When we first met, he drove down to this parking lot where I would park and of all the cars that were there, it was huge parking, he found my car and put a card on my window. When I came there was a love card. That he went out and found my car, that was romantic" (female lawyer, interview 23). This card was memorable to the woman because its giving demanded effort and was not given as a routine token of affection. The gift thus conceived is culturally constructed as more than an obligatory ritual of social interaction and solidarity. It is rather, an expression of one's innermost feelings.

When asked to choose between an expensive present and "a rose with a poem," respondents with few exceptions preferred the rose, on the grounds that it is a more "natural symbol" of feelings. "It's a love relationship. The expensive object, unless it is connected to something deep in my life that the lover noticed, I associate with other things. It's not how expensive is the object, it's how it relates to my life. The rose with the poem will always relate because that's the feeling. The rose isn't even as important as the poem if she makes it up. So it would be the rose" (male lawyer, interview 5). The noninstrumental character of the ideal romantic gift is a precondition of its capacity to express the uniqueness of the relationship by imbuing it with particular, unrepeatable life history. The ideal romantic gift is defined by its capacity to signify an experience and an emotion reflective of the unique intimacy shared by the couple, an intimacy located out of the reach of public display and public attribution of value.

> *Were you ever given a present that you liked?*
>
> Yes, that sounds stupid, but I had an orange comb for years. In fact, I found it again. I've had it for about fifteen years now, twelve years. A comb. It's real stupid of me, fifty cents, and I lost it, and this lady that I was in love with went to stores all over the place. She lost it, and she went to stores all over the place trying to find me an orange comb, so she bought me one. She bought me—I mean, it's stupid, but it sounds stupid, but just putting all that time and effort and thought over such a little thing, that meant a lot. It was the thought behind it. (Male boxer, interview 15)

Another man remembered a similar gift:

> Somebody once gave me a toy car, really a wonderful thing, not a fancy one, it was in plastic.
>
> *What did you like about it?*
>
> It was funny, and also it was whimsical, it just set emotions when I looked at it. Memories of times when [inaudible] nearby or something about the person. (Male Ph.D. student, interview 24)

These two gifts are romantic because they serve a "private" code that isolates the lovers from the outside world. Such gifts evade the order of public meaning by signifying a particular and private event of the life story of the couple.[47]

Luc Boltanski has offered an account of gratuitous and disinterested behaviors, suggesting that we include within the realm of sociology relationships based on "agape," a state of peace in which one gives oneself without any aim of control, struggle, power, or even reciprocation.[48] In a state of agape, people stop desiring or fighting for recognition, stop conceiving of others as a set of exchangeable attributes that can be traded and bargained over, and switch to a mode of sociality where the self gives itself with no intention of defending or increasing an interest, but rather with the sole purpose of giving selflessly to another. The concept of agape may seem to be a minor variation on the major theme that underlies Durkheim's sociology, namely, social solidarity, but unlike solidarity it is not motivated by the functional purpose of maintaining the cohesion of the social bond. It is a category of bond that evades utilitarianism and is the uncompromised affirmation of relationships that affirm nothing but themselves.

The findings discussed in this chapter offer partial, tentative, and preliminary evidence of such states of agape. Although many of my interviews point to the fact that considerations of social class, prestige, and power enter into the equation of love and gifts, other elements also indicate that during certain privileged moments romantic relationships are lived in the mode of agape, as a free and disinterested bestowal of one's love on another.

CONCLUSION

While Engels and the critical theorists of the Frankfurt School posited the theoretical possibility and empirical existence of a "real" (agapic?) love outside the realm of private property, Bourdieu has remained silent as to whether a disinterested romantic sentiment can exist at all or whether *all* romantic sentiments are to be understood primarily in terms of class interests and habitus.[49] In an early analysis of marriage strategies in the French region of the Bearn, he suggested in his concluding remarks that the antinomies between sentiment and duty and between individual and kin strategies are invisibly reconciled through well-incorporated habitus.[50] In his later work he has apparently moved to the more radical position that emotions are the disguising veils of class reproduction and that class reproduction occurs not despite but precisely within and through the "blind" and "irrational" emotion of love.

My own findings affirm Bourdieu's argument to the extent that, whether people make choices based on the invisible and tacit mechanism of the habitus or whether they monitor their choices consciously by using the commodified languages of the market, the *initial* stages of a relationship are likely (but not necessarily) to be based on the social, cultural, and economic assets of their partner. I part company with him, however, in claiming that at different stages of their development, romantic attachments involve different categories of love and modes of binding. An enduring bond spans adult life by alternating between a rational and self-interested bond and an agapic one. The same relationship that can be initiated by interest-driven considerations and a sense of investment can and in fact must later be transformed into a selfless and disinterested one. It seems as if, once a self-interested bond is established, it can be maintained only if it is lived and shared, at least periodically, in the mode of a disinterested emotion, an emotion that is expressed through the economy of the "little gift." Thus disinterestedness and pure emotion are imbricated within, rather than antinomic with, the economic rationality that structures romantic encounters.

CHAPTER 8

The Class of Love

When winter came and there was little to eat, they were still
content. They found a cave and told each other love stories
and sang and played the harp in turn. They loved each other
as their hearts prompted. How did they love? Their love was
a part of the cave, and the cave was round and high and
broad. As their bodies weakened, for there was little food,
their loves soared, filling the expanse of the cave, exploring
the depths of their hearts. In the roundness of the cave, they
came to know the tender curves of love's inner circles.

Tristan and Iseult (as retold by Diane Wolkstein)

Tristan and Iseult illustrate a motif that haunts our love mythology: love
flourishing where riches have fled. As hunger weakens the body, the radiant light of love fills the lovers' hearts (as well as, we are led to presume,
their stomachs). Not only is love blind to status and wealth, it ultimately
transforms poverty into abundance, hunger into satiation, lack into surplus. Reversal of identity is the theme par excellence of love, ugliness transformed into startling beauty, poor shepherds into kings, frogs into princes.
But this alchemy of love is primarily social, for it expresses the hope that
lowly conditions can be transmuted into noble ones and that love can unite
people otherwise separated by barriers of class, nationality, and birth.

Parallel to this classless mythology, the courtly and gallant ideal that
was to shape Western romantic consciousness has promoted the very
forms of expression of the literate and propertied classes: poetry, music,
and songs are the consecrated and seemingly "natural" expressions of
love.[1] Although these literate ideals have less currency today, the cultural
forms within which love is expressed are those of various factions of the
dominant classes. As Herbert Lantz suggests, historians tend "to view
romantic love as handed down from the affluent classes to the poor."[2]
He gives three reasons for the origin of love among the literate elites.
First, these classes were more likely to be influenced by the liberalizing
effects of "macro" economic and political events. Given their relatively

secure economic existence, such groups could afford to experiment with new lifestyles. Second, because the poorer classes spent their energies on matters of economic survival, their family environment was harsh with competition for resources. Finally, literacy is a necessary precondition of romantic love: "people have to be able to read and discuss feelings before feelings can become part of their experience."[3]

Lantz's observations suggest three elements important for a sociological understanding of the relationship between love and class. (1) Mechanisms of symbolic domination, that is, cultural standards flowing from the top to the bottom, can structure how romantic love is perceived by various social groups. (2) The practice of romantic love demands availability of time and distance from material necessity. The expression of romantic love may vary according to one's economic capital and resources in leisure time. (3) Although it is doubtful that romantic love intrinsically demands reading skills, as Lantz implies, his observations suggest that romantic practices might be related to what Bourdieu calls "cultural competence," that is, to forms of talk, taste, and aesthetic evaluation, themselves related to standards of romance.

As argued in earlier chapters, advertisers, cultural entrepreneurs, parascientific experts, and members of the new service class have contributed to definitions of love that promote modes of expression of relatively affluent and educated segments of the middle class. The therapeutic model of love discussed in chapter 6 privileges forms of self-awareness and expression that ultimately depend on the linguistic and cultural capital of people with college education. Similarly, the hedonist model of romance, which demands an efficient use of the leisure market, depends on the requisite income and lifestyle. Thus, the ability to enact the romantic ideal in the twin domains of communication and consumption demands a *romantic competence* marked by access to linguistic, cultural, economic, and time resources. This in turn implies that people with less access to these resources are at a disadvantage and are romantically "less competent." At the heart of this chapter lies the claim that the notion of "cultural capital," which has been recently under attack, is relevant to understanding differences in romantic practices.[4] However, as we saw in chapters 2 and 3, the commercialized formula of romance addresses and includes disparate social groups.[5] Differences of income, education, and culture are ultimately circumscribed within the *common* arena of the market.[6]

THE ELEMENTARY FORMS OF ROMANCE

Working-class and upper-middle-class respondents share a common "blueprint" of romance, consisting of activities such as going to a movie or restaurant, having a candlelight dinner, going to the beach, taking a vacation or just "getting away," being in nature. On the other hand, their romantic practices diverge most significantly in the case of cultural activities, whether these demand consumption (going to the opera, say) or not (writing love poems). Examples of the blueprint among working-class and upper-middle-class respondents in my interview sample are abundant:

> *What would you do if you wanted to have a romantic moment with your partner?*
>
> It would be at home. If I had my ultimate place. A very nice long dinner. Discussing things at candlelight. I am very attracted by candlelight. And very beautiful music.
>
> *What kind of music?*
>
> Beautiful classical music. Bach, Monteverdi. (Male orchestra conductor, interview 33)

> What I would do is like, ah—okay, the first thing I would do is probably have a nice, romantic dinner at my apartment, candlelight and soft music and stuff like that, plus—that's what I have done. That's romantic to me. Very soft music and just be into each other with not a lot of distraction and things like that.
>
> *What kind of music?*
>
> Real soft, soft music. Easy listening music.
>
> *Do you have some at home? Can you name names?*
>
> Ah, let me see. I like Barry Manilow. I like soul, very light soul music. (Female security officer, high school education, interview 37)

Although these two respondents used different linguistic, cultural, and economic capitals, they both referred to a common cultural script of romance: the "nice" dinner at home, the candlelight, the beautiful music—all essential elements of romantic rituals.

Other examples show a similar pattern. Asked what he would do to have a romantic evening, a male university professor replied, "I'd say I had a pretty romantic evening one night recently. Is that reasonable to describe? I went to a formal dance, so you get dressed up really nice and you go to a pretty place, you do some dancing, and then I think we came back here for the dessert" (interview 1). Similarly, a male janitor with a grade-school education said, "Have a nice dinner with some wine, quiet, dancing, I don't know, go back to her place" (interview 40). Although formulated by two men at opposite ends of the economic and cultural spectrum, these answers enact a similar script of romance: eating a "nice" dinner, dancing, and going back to the man's or woman's place.

Activities taking place in nature also follow a common script. Responding to the same question, a female university professor said, "It would always be in a place in nature. Like either in the woods having a picnic or in the mountains hiking or at the beach. I think I would pick the beach as the most, like being at the seashore, maybe in the evening and eating a dinner, a picnic dinner there, and just listening to the waves and going for a walk on the beach, that's to me very romantic" (interview 19). And a male electrician with a high-school education said, "It would be a couple places I would like to be. One is the beach early in the morning or late at night, when nobody else is around, either seeing the sunrise or the sunset, with somebody, even if you're in [inaudible] or whatever, you're warm, you're snugly and, if you could build a fireplace, a fire and have a fire there and maybe have some hot chocolate or coffee or even have some diet drinks, since I don't drink" (interview 36). Here again, the two answers articulate a common cultural scenario: both people chose the beach as the most romantic place and mentioned a picnic, the building of a fire, and having drinks as symbols of seclusion, tranquility, and romance.

As we would expect from our findings in chapters 3, 4, and 5, respondents from different cultural and economic backgrounds invoked similar meanings of love as a liminal ritual and an invisible act of consumption.[7] Even if working-class people participate in the market of romantic leisure *less* than their middle- and upper-middle-class counterparts, and even if they do not manifest the same proficiency at manipulating the symbols of the romantic formula, it remains that many of the formula's distinctive components have pervaded romantic practices at all levels of society. Far from being excluded from the market-based romantic formula, working-class people consume and enact the same "elementary forms of romance" as members of higher social strata.

This represents a break from the premodern period, when working-class and middle-class romantic practices differed significantly. During the nineteenth-century, middle-class people interacted within the protected boundaries of the home, while members of the working class, who often lived in crowded apartments, were forced to meet outside their living space and were excluded from the practice of "calling."[8] The commodification of romance has provided a formula that, if it does not unify the romantic practices of different classes, is at least accessible to most of them. This development is not surprising since from the nineteenth century onward capitalist markets of consumption have grown by assimilating previously marginal groups, such as children and adolescents. In a similar vein, David Gartman suggests that advanced capitalist societies possess both a class culture and a mass culture and that these work conjointly rather than against each other. The homogeneity of products consumed in the leisure sphere does not cancel class relationships but translates and obscures them in a common language of consumerist solidarity.[9] Social differences resurface in the ways in which cultural capital orients people's choice and appreciation of romantic commodities.

LOVE AS DIFFERENCE

In their romantic practices, middle-class respondents extended the limits of the blueprint of romance by making greater use of what is offered by the market, whereas the latter remained within these limits. Working-class respondents rarely mentioned activities frequently reported by their middle-class counterparts, such as reading together (a book, a newspaper, poetry), going to art galleries, dining or strolling in a remote and exotic place, eating luxury goods (caviar or salmon), attending formal dances (which require formal attire), traveling somewhere on the spur of the moment, and finally, experiencing romance in the most mundane situation. To put these examples in broader categories, middle- and upper-middle-class respondents (1) display a broader range of romantic practices, which include directly consumptive, indirectly consumptive, and nonconsumptive activities; (2) consume more expensive goods more frequently; (3) consume more culturally legitimate goods; (4) are more likely to reject the idea of romance altogether and praise the category of the "mundane."

As Bourdieu has suggested in *Distinction,* we can learn more by examining the how of consumption, the styles or codes under which consumption is practiced, rather than the what of consumption. That is, the meaning of a given commodity depends on the context of its usage and not on any intrinsic signification. Bourdieu thus invites us to examine the interpretations accompanying the use of romantic commodities, the structure of these interpretations, and their link to class position.

The differences between the social strata represented in my sample can be captured succinctly: whether they reported their romantic practices or commented on the props of the interview, middle-class and especially upper-middle-class respondents displayed an elaborate anticonsumerist ethos, whereas working-class people uncritically adhered to the content of mass-manufactured romantic commodities. By "anticonsumerist ethos" I mean a combination of several elements: an explicit rejection of goods manufactured expressly for "romance"; an emphasis on originality and creativity; and an emphasis on anti-institutional values such as spontaneity, informality, and authenticity. The following examples clarify the nature of these differences.

When asked to remember one of their most romantic moments, two working-class respondents mentioned trips to "romantic resorts," catering solely to couples and abounding in highly conventional symbols of romance (heart-shaped furniture and accessories, love poems hung on walls, etc.). As a working-class male respondent said that during these weekends, "everyone else around are also couples." Although I did not solicit respondents' opinions about such romantic resorts, middle-class and upper-middle-class respondents would have mocked such "organized romantic weekends," for one of the recurrent traits of their responses was disdain for "manufactured," "cheap," and "clichéd" expressions of romance. This was made particularly clear in their reactions to the three greeting cards shown during the interview.[10] A Hallmark card containing a love poem and an image of a sunset elicited reactions such as the following:

Which of these three cards would you give your partner?

Ah, well I hate these things, the first [card] certainly would not be that, I hate these things, they're just so, they're just trashy, they're just these poems that someone writes, they're a dime a dozen, they're so meaningless, I'd never give anybody one of those. (Female editor, interview 48)

I think number one is a very sappy card and I wouldn't be caught dead sending a card like that, just—

"Sappy"? What is "sappy"?

Sappy. Sentimental. It's like overkill, you know. I just find I have a hard time getting into it. I don't even like the colors they have used. (Female artist, interview 35)

Middle- and upper-middle-class respondents nearly unanimously described card 1 as "ugly," "trashy," "corny," "nauseating," "silly," "sappy," "cliché," and "tacky." Asked why they would not give such a card to their lover, people with the highest cultural competence used the same vocabulary that, according to communication scholar Larry Gross, is used to evaluate art.[11] The card was "not original enough," was "not creative," was "stereotypical," and showed poor "colors" or "design." In Gross's terms, respondents invoked values of originality, sincerity, effort, and creativity to express their disdain and bristled at the fact that "someone else would have written it for [them]."

Which one of these cards would you pick?

This one [card 3].

Why?

I think it looks nicer. It's Matisse, right? I liked it visually, it's an attractive card. Also what I liked about it is that I could write what I wanted and be sort of the message I wanted it to be.

What about the other two?

Well, they're both somebody else doing the talking for me which is not something [inaudible] as an idea. I think one should say what one has to say oneself, you know, having it written for you does not seem you're really saying it to them. (Female artist, interview 13)

The criteria of originality and creativity invoked by middle-class respondents are viewed as aesthetic equivalents of "spontaneity," "sincerity," and "authenticity." Because the Hallmark card uses highly conventional symbols of love, it is perceived to be insincere and exaggerated. The word "sentimental," often used to mock this card, expresses the scorn for forms of expression that are both too conventional and too emotional. In keeping with this viewpoint, card 2 was often chosen as a "card they would give" because its humorous message ironically deflates the mass cultural clichés of romantic pathos. Scorn for convention and consumption is also scorn for emphatic expressions of emotion, and according to Bourdieu emotional distance characterizes the attitude of people with high cultural capital to aesthetic forms.

By contrast, for the least formally educated classes the Hallmark card chosen most frequently precisely because it is the most emotionally expressive and therefore the most "romantic." Where middle- and upper-middle-class respondents made aesthetic evaluations, working-class respondents made emotional evaluations. Because of these criteria, they viewed card 3, an abstraction, as "meaningless." "I think it's very nice but it does not say anything about love. If I was giving my husband a card, I want him to know how I felt" (female homemaker, no high school, interview 28). The Hallmark card, on the other hand, did express and convey the full emotion of love. Asked why he picked that card to give to his partner, a male janitor explained, "To me it expresses love, the words—." Asked about the others, he said of card 3, "I don't like that one" (interview 40).

The Hallmark card expresses forcefully what working-class people felt they could not otherwise express themselves. For example:

Which one of these cards would you give your partner?

This one

Number one.

I've given 'em and I like those.

Why?

'Cause they express how I really feel. Some cards express how you really feel inside and sometimes you can't say that. I've given those out.

What about two and three? What do you think of them?

Two is okay, if you want to be comical, but, uh—

What about three?

It's wild. I don't like that style. That's not me. (Female security officer, high school education, interview 37)

While for the upper-middle-class respondents the expressive sentimentality of the Hallmark card was "inauthentic," "cheap," and "manufactured," for the working-class respondents the same card was the most authentic because it uncompromisingly expressed the full intensity of their feelings.

In extending the scope of this observation to romantic gifts in general, I found the same differences among respondents. When asked to choose between a rose with a poem and an expensive object, *none* of the working-class respondents would have answered the way this female artist did:

As a romantic present, would you prefer to get a rose with a poem or an expensive object?

Neither of them is appealing.

Why?

Because roses are very declassé and only if the poem is nice and felt. If it is an expensive gift, it doesn't really matter, if I like the design. There are a few things at Tiffany's that I like but it has nothing to do with money. If I like the design and I think it's pretty, then it can be five cents or five million dollars, I don't care. (Female artist, interview 6)

This respondent simultaneously distanced herself from the emotional code attached to roses and from the material value of expensive gifts. Her double scorn has the main function of emphasizing the importance of her idiosyncratic sense of good taste ("if I like the design"). In a similar vein, a male Ph.D. student recounted his reaction to a poem written by a woman in love with him:

As a romantic gift, would you prefer to get a rose with a poem or an expensive object?

That's a hard one. I was involved with a person who used to write me poems and send me notes all the time, and at the time I thought it was nice but also kind of raise my eyebrow at it, I mean this is cute and clever but maybe a little too cute.

What do you mean?

Forced or formal. But then I was going through these things, I was going through my boxes and found those and realized that she really loved me. I hadn't thought of that in those terms then, it was more of a game, more of a formalized sort of thing. (Interview 24)

The "raised eyebrow" betrayed his sense of cultural distinction, activated even by someone else's love. People with the highest cultural competence were the most likely to characterize roses and poems as "stereotypical," "forced," "declassé," and thereby "inauthentic." This man's suspicion, although not typical of most middle-class answers, underscores that the attribute of "stereotypical" opens an emotional distance from manufactured representations of love and more generally from any conventional (in their view, hackneyed) expression of love. In contrast, this secretary's explanation of her preference for the rose and the poem is typical of women working in the pink-collar sector: "That's romantic, I like romance. If the poem was, uh, if he wrote the poem that would mean a lot to me" (interview 16). Instead of viewing presents as opportunities to express one's own good taste and creativity, she values them in terms of their ability to directly signify emotions. Compare this answer to what an upper-middle-class woman remembered as a very romantic gift:

One night we were walking together and we were by a storefront and they had models with plastic around them, sort of like a dress, and we were laughing that was a new style of dress and that was a very romantic night.

And on my birthday, it was about three weeks later, I opened this beautiful package and it was the plastic and he had gone to the store and asked them to please give him the plastic, that was very romantic.

What was romantic about it?

It was taking something that we did together, doing something creative to remind us of that and putting some effort and thought into that. (Female lawyer, interview 23)

This present stood out in her memory because it had no conventional meaning of love. Instead, its romantic meaning was created by the shared experience of a singular moment and by the effort, creativity, and originality of the giver. The emotions conveyed by this present were thus mixed with aesthetic criteria.

Such upper-middle-class, aesthetic romantic ethos insists on its own autonomy from clichéd or manufactured practices and images of romance.[12]

Let's imagine you wanted to have a romantic moment. What would this moment be like?

No!

Why not?

Because I think it varies with every person, I don't have one image of romance, it changes according to the person.

OK. Then give me several examples of romantic moments you have had with several people.

Being at the beach at night, anything by the beach, by the ocean, it's difficult for me to be specific about romantic.

Then don't be specific. I just want you to pull out from your memory some moments that were romantic to you.

By the beach at night, usually you are able to concentrate on the situation I am in as opposed to worrying about other things. . . .

When you say you can't think of a general definition of romance, does it mean—I mean, I want to understand if you are rejecting the idea of romance or if you are saying it is more specific.

I personally cannot define romance because it is too varied in my experience. Pictures like this [figures 1, 2, 3, and 4; see appendix 3] don't intimate romance, they intimate people posing. (Male artist, interview 25)

This man's first reaction was to deny that he had a single (read, stereotypical) image of romance. Rather, as he suggested, his images varied

with the identity of his partners. However, when prompted to give examples of romance, he answered with one of the most conventional images of all, the beach at night. Although his representation of romance
was as stereotyped as those of others, he felt compelled to mark a distance between it and himself, a strategy rarely encountered among the
working-class respondents.

Let's listen to another voice, very similar to the previous one:

> *If you wanted to have a romantic moment with someone, what would this
> moment look like?*

> You know, I may be a very bad person for this survey just because in a way
> the idea of romanticness is already to me sort of embedded in a prejudicial
> thing. To me, when something is moving or something involving love or
> something involving sex or anything, whatever it is, it is not something that
> I have an image of before it occurs. It is something special enough that you
> know if you plan it in a way, I mean the whole idea of "let's have a roman-
> tic dinner like candles and blah, blah, blah," that's never what happens. I
> mean it can be a time where you are with somebody in any kind of situa-
> tion, it can be in an incredibly unromantic, traditionally unromantic set-
> ting, what makes it romantic for me is the interaction with the other person
> and the combination of moods you are in and things that happen, it is not
> something I would construct. (Female artist, interview 13)

This quote condenses many of the practices of distinction characteristic
of the most culturally competent respondents. Prefacing her answer with
"I may be a bad person for this survey," she singled herself out from the
mass of people who are "good for the survey." She rejected the idea that
romance can follow a script that she herself has not written, thereby affirming her ability to improvise, to create new versions of romance in a
variety of situations. Similarly, a young Ph.D. student prefaced his response with "I pursue romance in a nontraditional sense." Another respondent of the same socioeconomic category suggested that "romance
is this bullshit Park Avenue restaurant, wine and roses and flowers type
of concept." The most educated classes vehemently asserted their distance from stereotypes of romance, thus affirming the autonomy of their
thought from commercial influence ("no one dictates to me what to
think"), the validity of their representations ("I am not as mystified as
others are"), the originality of their self ("they all follow the same model,
I am original"), their creativity ("I can create my own scenarios"), and
the authenticity of their feelings ("Their feelings are manufactured, mine
are authentic"). These ideas are inscribed within larger ideological practices of cultural specialists, who view themselves as modern iconoclasts

who can dispel the mystifications that baffle others.[13] More than any other class, educated, upper-middle-class people cultivate the "third person" effect, or the belief that others ("they") are victims of deficiencies from which they themselves are exempt.[14]

These findings confirm Bourdieu's observations that popular classes tend to identify emotionally and in a participatory mode with cultural products, while the most educated classes cultivate distance, either by disparaging cultural products or by focusing on their formal, aesthetic features. Upper-middle and, to a lesser extent, middle-class respondents valued highly autonomous and creative self-expression independent of the props provided by the market. More exactly, while they held as legitimate the "creative manipulation" of commodities (furniture, clothing) for expressing a genuine but hidden self, they spurn the use of mass-marketed commodities when unmediated by an original "self."

> Romance seems to me something where you take your time and create something. When you are not creating something and you are just living your daily life, it's not romantic.
>
> *When you are living your daily life.*
>
> Yeah, when you just day in and day out—but there is a certain fun living in New York, having a nice place, coming home. If you didn't go out, if you didn't put anything romantic in it, if you didn't make these moments where you both realize how much one loves another, how attracted you are to one another, then I think you become unattractive to that person and they become unattractive to you. (Female lawyer, interview 23)

A romantic moment must express not only one's personal creativity but also one's total inner being. Asked why he would prefer staying home to going out, the orchestra conductor replied, "Because I could create an environment that I like, with the right music and the right, you know. . . . In my ideal, in my fantasy, my home would express myself, and it would be a certain environment" (interview 33). He described at length how he would arrange background music, food, and clothes to create a romantic atmosphere. It is difficult to know whether in actuality working-class people indeed spend less time and effort to "create" their romantic moments, but clearly, for middle- and upper-middle-class respondents, a romantic atmosphere results from an expressive and individualistic conception of the self.[15]

The ethos of spontaneity echoes that of creativity. Listen, for example, to two men relate how they would go about having a romantic moment. First, an investment banker: "Have dinner in a real romantic restaurant. On the spur of the moment pick up a flight and go to the South of France. Something like that" (interview 4). An actor: "I suppose it would involve a certain amount of surprise and spontaneity. . . . It might involve, 'let's get in the car and drive to the beach and have a picnic'; in the middle of dinner say 'let's go away for the weekend,' that kind of element of spontaneity" (interview 33). Male working-class respondents never referred to spontaneity in this fashion. While upper-middle-class men easily articulated this ideal of spontaneity, it was not self-consciously spelled out by working-class men. But even if working-class men and women never referred to the value of spontaneity, they were not necessarily any less spontaneous about their feelings. Rather, such spontaneity presupposes availability of and total control over one's time and money, as indicated by a male electrician.

> *What do you think are the consequences, if any, on romantic relationships of having a lot of money?*
>
> Actually, I'd love to have a lot of money, but [laughs] I don't think, uh—
>
> *Do you think it would change anything in your relationships to have a lot of money?*
>
> Well, I'd be able to do a lot more things than I do now.
>
> *Like what, for example?*
>
> I'd love to go to Jamaica, love to go to Hawaii, love to go to Japan, love to say to somebody, "Pack your clothes. Let's go. We're going for a weekend or we're going for a week." Something like this. If I had the money, I'd love to. (Interview 36)

For this man, money meant the ability not only to travel but to do it on the spur of the moment. The ideal of spontaneity was rooted in and made possible by objective resources of time and money.

Class differences were apparent as well in the interview situation itself. Working-class respondents were hesitant and sometimes reluctant to answer my questions, whereas upper-middle-class respondents, both men and women, talked at great length. The average length of a working-class interview was one hour; for middle-class and upper-middle class respondents, interviews frequently lasted over two hours. Working-class people gave short and matter-of-fact answers; the tone of middle and upper-middle-class answers was chatty, light, and often confidential.

Part of the working-class resistance to the interview stemmed from their feelings of incompetence. They answered for example, "That's a hard question," "You're taxing my mind," "I don't really know," "I don't have the words for it." On the other hand, if and when middle- and upper-middle-class respondents resisted the interview, it was because they felt *too competent*. They reacted to the props used during the interview with the same scorn that they expressed for manufactured romantic objects in general.

> *You said before you don't like any of the stories [see chapter 5 for the stories], but still, I was wondering if you can say which one of the stories you like best.*
>
> Let's skip that question.
>
> *I would prefer not to, if you don't object to it too much.*
>
> I am afraid we have to. Because I am an art reader and I write rather well. It would be very difficult to develop any good story out of any of these stories. It would be, I suppose, a sort of Harlequin novel.
>
> *You see, none of these stories has by any means any ambition or pretension to be what you call a "good" story. It is not supposed to be aesthetic. In each story, there is a different ending. Here people fall in love immediately, here it takes them more time, here they meet through their parents. The style is dry because it has to be readable by everybody. I am simply interested in how you interpret these stories. (Interview 6)*

This interview with a well-established New York artist condensed the scorn that often accompanies the cultivation of "distinction" characteristic of the highest segments of artistic bohemia. Another respondent also expressed this scorn in a more subtle form:

> *Which picture do you find the most romantic?*
>
> In my terms of romance?
>
> *Yes.*
>
> These are very loaded pictures. I have a little trouble because I see them all cliché. So, in a way I have a hard time relating to them, as identifying with them because they look so constructed by somebody's ideas. I mean they are from advertising but you know that they're all alike. . . .
>
> Because to me they are like another kind of Hallmark cards and they are very much keyed into fashion. This one a stereotype of sensitivity and married couple, so I don't really relate to them.

Do you know more specifically what you find clichéd in them?

Actually, when I look at this one, for example [figure 1], that one is the least extreme, I suppose all of them in some ways but you know for some reason I can't help seeing as someone who has done this photograph to appeal to a group of people who would be maybe more mature and going out to dinner. I keep thinking of the person making the photograph rather than, I am blocked identifying with them.

Thus, this is the cliché of what?

Um, married couple going out to dinner, you know, family life is not excluded from this image. (Female artist, interview 13)

This interviewee also refused the terms set by the interview and rejected the photographs on the grounds that they were commercially and institutionally manufactured and thereby not even worth reacting to.

Several studies have argued that "creativity" and originality are particularly prized by the middle- and upper-middle-class, but why?[16] Bourdieu would argue that these values actually depend on cultural capital, in a more or less explicit fashion. When asked why he would not choose card 1 (the Hallmark card), a respondent put the point bluntly: "Because I am an educated person, I have my own words. I wouldn't take somebody else's" (male university professor, interview 1). For this man, writing a love note demanded the same verbal facility as succeeding in college does: a cultivation of "personal" tastes and opinions and an ability to articulate them clearly and effectively. Only someone comfortable with verbal self-expression will feel at ease with the ethos of creativity advocated by upper-middle-class respondents.

In contrast, in the course of their socialization, working-class people have been led to consider such verbal competence as outside of the reach of their capacity and identity. Not having attended college, they are less familiar with the formal exercise of self-expression, and they viewed Hallmark cards as useful aids for overcoming difficulties in expressing love. As a working-class man said, "I have the feelings, but I don't have the words for it." This does not mean that working-class respondents were less competent at expressing love than their upper-middle-class counterparts. It does mean, however, that working-class people *perceived themselves* as incompetent in domains traditionally related to school performance. Because romance is culturally constructed as an essentially linguistic form of expression, the feeling of linguistic incompetence spills over into the domain of romance.

The class differences displayed in romantic practice parallel not only differences in education but differences in work as well. Not only do upper-middle-class jobs often require a mastery of grammar and vocabulary, these jobs are also likely to require creativity and autonomy.[17] Working-class jobs, on the other hand, are less likely to engage linguistic skills or the autonomous and creative self. This would suggest a more straightforward relationship between the sphere of work and that of romance than has usually been assumed.

The notion of cultural capital has recently come under criticism by American sociologists who argue that it is problematic to illuminate the reproduction of inequalities in American society because in American society, high culture is not as valued as it is in Europe, France in particular.[18] My own findings do not support these critiques. Although in my respondents' answers cultural capital does not always take the straightforward form of "high" culture, as is more likely to be true in Europe, abilities such as choosing a tasteful greeting card, writing a love note in clear but moving prose, carrying on an "intelligent" conversation, avoiding clichés, and so on are equally forms of cultural capital, ones that appear almost exclusively in the romantic practices of people who have earned degrees beyond the college level, professionals as well as cultural specialists. Although it is difficult to say just how central these forms of distinction are, it remains that middle-class and upper-middle-class respondents, women in particular, are receptive to such euphemistic expressions of cultural taste, which they interpret as manifestations of romance.

The greater attention they pay to individual "taste" and self-expression might imply, on the surface, that middle-class respondents are less dependent on the industry of romantic culture than working-class respondents. However, although middle-class and, especially, upper-middle-class people often derided commercialization, I found that not only were they avid consumers of romantic commodities but also they were likely to experience the *stereotypical* romantic moments they otherwise often deride. For example, a university professor with an income above $70,000 suggested that "a romantic night would be getting dressed up and going out, I guess champagne always makes it more romantic, coming back and being together and doing something intimate at home, after we went out" (interview 1). Describing a romantic evening with her husband the day before the interview, a female lawyer with a combined income over $100,000 said, "We had a really romantic afternoon yesterday, we went to see a movie, *New York Stories*, we came back in a cab, we came home, and I made champagne cocktails, and we had the champagne and we made love and we had dinner and we watched a video and we just stayed home together" (interview 23). Dressing up, drinking champagne cocktails, riding in a taxi, taking a long time (afternoon and evening) during a "normal" week to engage in leisurely and intimate activities require relatively large amounts of time and money and full participation in the market of luxuries.[19]

Class differences go beyond sheer expense, however, for working-class experiences of romance seem much less dependent on commodities:

Can you give me an example of an actual romantic moment you have had?

Recently, someone came over to have dinner. That was very romantic.

What was romantic about it?

I was happy to see her. It couldn't be enough to prepare for the meeting. We talked about what she was doing. (Male private investigator, interview 22).

Can you describe an actual romantic moment you have experienced?

Well, we were at Hane's Point and there's a really, really—ah, it was the Fourth of July, ah, fireworks and everything, just, you know, we were really together. I don't know. It just came on me in impulse.

What was romantic about that moment?

We were just close together, real close, I guess, it just, it looked like it was coming right at us.

You mean the fireworks?

Yeah, just—you know, he just grabbed me real close and it just felt really warm at that time. (Female security officer, interview 37)

Can you give me an example of an actual romantic moment?

This library [in a] law office where she worked as a secretary brings one to mind, with a coworker putting up books and setting things up and organizing and touching hands, something like that to me would be very romantic. (Female secretary, interview 18)

What was a romantic moment you have experienced?

I was walking on the street and he came behind me and he said "Hi, it's me!" and he held my hand, it was intimate, it was just like no one was around even though it was a busy street, there was like no one existed. (Female police officer, interview 21)

For these people (only one of whom was educated two years beyond high school), romance was grounded in physical and emotional intimacy

(holding hands in the office or the street, being together watching public fireworks, etc.) and not in an elaborate atmosphere saturated with romantic meanings and supported by various expensive "romantic" props.
Compare the simple response cited above of the working-class man who
found it romantic that "recently someone came over to have dinner,"
with that of a college-educated movie distributor: "I remember once,
some years ago, just off the top of my head, having dinner with a young
woman in a sushi restaurant and I found that very—she had never eaten
sushi before and, ah, sort of the, for the first time experienced how sensual that food can be, because it's raw flesh, I suppose, ultimately. I remember very much enjoying that, that moment, that extended moment
of sharing that food, and there is a real sort of physical connection, you
know, the food between us, and that sort of thing" (interview 34).
*Middle- and upper-middle-class respondents dwelled much more on the
physical, material, and atmospheric components of the romantic moment than did working-class respondents,* who rarely mentioned the role
played by beautiful, expensive, or rare objects in their romantic moments.[20] Furthermore, middle- and upper-middle-class respondents not
only tended to make greater use of commodities, and of expensive commodities, in romance, but also tended much more than members of the
working class to *spiritualize* commodities, making them the carriers of
romantic atmosphere and, at times, of their feelings as well.

The commodity-centered character of the upper-middle-class romantic
experience goes hand-in-hand with the fact that this experience is more
stereotypical than that of the working class, that is, it corresponds more
closely to the clichés codified by mass culture. This can be seen again in the
kind of travel associated with romance. While more than half of the middle-class respondents mentioned a romantic moment in a foreign country
or in some other faraway place, working-class people tended to escape from
their urban environment by going to parks (like Hane's Point in Washington, D.C.) or to places less than a day away by automobile (like New Hope
or the Poconos from Philadelphia). One reason for this difference is rather
straightforward: working-class respondents have little surplus income and
time to go on vacations in foreign countries. Tourism and the paraphernal-
ia of monuments and prepackaged sites occupied a central place in the romantic memories of middle- and upper-middle-class respondents:

What was a very romantic moment you have experienced?

It has been a while, um, probably when I was traveling with someone
through Italy and we were at the Spanish Steps in Rome. The moon was

out, we bought some wine, and we sat on the steps. We were a little older, everybody around was students, and I started to sing, I was an opera singer, and a whole group came and surrounded me, was applauding me. When they left, it was just the two of us, it was a very special moment, a very special feeling. (Male investment banker, interview 4)

This answer evokes ready-made images of romance that have been incessantly conveyed through the clichés of Hollywood cinema and advertising. Consider another example: "Finally, one evening in Paris, it has snowed, we walked for a long time, we ended up on the Eiffel Tower and we kissed each other, it was the first night I ever was with anyone and because for so long I had dreamed about that, it was wonderful" (male orchestra conductor, interview 33). This scene evokes the familiar imagery of romance we examined in chapter 3: Paris, for Americans the exotic, romantic city par excellence (just as the Eiffel Tower is the symbol par excellence of Paris), the "special" atmosphere of nighttime and snow. Both memories mix exotic travel settings, symbols of distinction, and commodities.

In my interviews, the very "scripted" character of the scenes evoked by upper-middle-class respondents was readily discernible. This is not surprising since the ideas and ideals at work in mass culture usually represent the practices, values, and interests of the upper segments of society. What makes the finding noteworthy is that the upper-middle-class romantic discourses were explicitly geared *against* the mass cultural and stereotypical practices of romance. The same respondents who most vocally rejected the commercial and codified character of romance were also those who reported the most stereotypical and the most deeply market-based practices of romance. As Mike Featherstone puts it, "The wealthy have always been able to display style by demassifying and individualizing commodities."[21]

LOVE AND SYMBOLIC DOMINATION

These findings still leave unanswered the question at the heart of this chapter: do romantic practices follow a logic of class domination? As one working-class man in my sample asked rhetorically, "So you give a dozen flowers, instead of one, so what difference does it make?" He suggests to sociologists that even if we can demonstrate that romantic practices differ along dimensions of income, education, or both, we cannot yet claim that certain groups are at a disadvantage when experiencing romance. In other words, the problem is to determine whether and how we can make the transition, so often taken for granted, from an *analysis of patterns of consumption* to *a sociology of "class domination."* The argument about cultural domination makes several distinct claims: (1) cultural practices differ along class lines; (2) the dominated classes define and posit their own cultural practices in reference to upper-class definitions of romance; (3) the cultural standards adopted by the dominated groups reflect the particular positions and interests of the dominant classes; and (4) because they recognize as legitimate cultural practices that in effect exclude them, the culture of dominated groups is a culture "by default," deprived of a positive content of its own.[22] The remainder of this chapter, then, will be concerned with questions raised by the hypothesis of cultural deprivation. Are the lower segments of society romantically less competent than their upper-class counterparts? Is the standard middle-class formula the only legitimate formula of romance?

From my interview data, I contend that the commercial formula of romance is easily accessed and experienced by the working class and the middle class when both groups are dating. Even if choices of consumption remain different, these differences have no consequences for the lovers' ability to "have a good time together," to express and live their love. It is when people get married that the qualitative romantic experiences of the two groups start to diverge significantly. Following Scitovsky, one may say that once people start sharing daily life, they move from an intense feeling to a comfortable one, and that the phenomenology of their love changes: the challenge of the dating period is to experience intensity and to bring this intensity to the "comfort" of intimacy; on the other hand, during marriage, the problem is to bring a comfortable, familiar and sometimes dull relationship to the renewed experience of intensity.[23] Although my working-class and upper-middle-class respondents coped equally well with the first challenge, the former seem definitely more ill-equipped to cope with the problem of creating intensity within the daily bond of marriage. It is precisely at this point, that is, where intensity must be voluntarily and skillfully created, that differences of income, leisure resources, and education play an important role in the political economy of love. A working-class woman, a secretary, recalled from her early days of dating, "We would do many things, we would go to the movies, flea markets, we used to rummage a lot, we would travel together. . . . We traveled a bit together, out to dinner, spend a lot of time with friends" (interview 16). A working-class homemaker had similar memories:

Can you remember a romantic moment [in your relationship with your husband]?

I would drive to his house—this is back to the gasoline crisis and we would drive together to work. Naturally, he was always dressed with a shirt and tie. This particular day he had no tie and his shirt open, and there was, I thought, wow! It seemed like Robert Redford walking in the street, like that feeling when you see somebody you like in a movie. Anyway, there was that time when we went down to the shore, no, I was sick, scrap that time. It must have been when we spent the weekend together, just spend the weekend together, it was just that spending time together.

Did you use to spend time together?

Yes we spent a lot of time together.

What would you do?

Go shopping, or look at things, go to movies maybe, a lot of times at home, maybe that's what we did, spend time together, all that starts falling apart when kids come along, that messes up your schedule. (Interview 9)

In the dating situation, middle-class standards of romance do not put working-class people at a disadvantage and do not create an incompetence. Having neither children nor mortgage, the dating working-class couple has the surplus income and time to engage in inexpensive leisure pursuits. Even if participation in the realm of leisure is more limited for the working class than for the middle or upper middle class, this does not affect the quality and intensity of their romantic feelings. In the dating situation, the need for intensity is met "naturally" by the beginning stages of love; the couple is thereby functionally less dependent on the leisure market to satisfy this need. Furthermore, working-class respondents' autobiographical accounts indicated that they were more likely to fall in love intensely and quickly than their middle- or upper-middle-class counterparts, who by contrast often seemed to move more slowly and cautiously. One possible reason for this difference is that, being less worried about social mobility than their middle- and upper-middle-class counterparts, working-class respondents have less at stake in falling in "love at first sight" and are less likely to conceive of their bonds in rationalized terms.

At the beginning of a relationship, then, the frequency, object, and mode of consumption have little bearing on the competence necessary feel romance. From my respondents' accounts, nothing indicates that differences in income or education hampered their ability to form exalting or interesting romantic bonds. This implies that we cannot deduce class domination or exclusion from class consumption: while in the dating situation, different patterns of romantic consumption do not interfere with the lived experience of love; these patterns become obstacles to love only within the framework of the daily life of those who have the least resources to carry on the leisure-based formula of romance.

When romance becomes integrated within the daily life-world and lifestyle of people, that is, when its intensity fades away and it no longer occupies the spare time of the couple, it becomes intertwined with the inequalities and lack of resources inherent to working-class lives. These inequalities take two forms: (1) Married working-class people practice the commercial romantic formula significantly less often do than their upper-middle-class counterparts, who, even after marriage, continue to be full members of the leisure market. (2) The working class and the up-per-middle class have different patterns of romantic communication: while upper-middle-class people share many forms of companionate leisure (which is itself related to their broader cultural habitus), work-ing-class men and women communicate less than their middle- and up-per-middle-class counterparts.

CLASS, ROMANCE, AND
THE STRUCTURE OF EVERYDAY LIFE

Frequency marks another class difference in romance. In my interviews, romantic memories were typically more distant in time for working-class than for upper-middle-class respondents. For example, a working-class man cited an experience "twelve years ago," whereas upper-mid-dle-class respondents referred to romantic moments that had taken place a few days or even the day before the interview. None of the working-class-respondents said that they had had a romantic evening in the week prior to the interview. In fact, many elements of their responses indicated that the working-class people struggled much more than upper-middle-class respondents to experience romance in their daily lives. The most obvious explanation for this is shortage of money.

When asked to reflect on the "problems that people in general en-counter in their relationships," the *only* people in the sample who men-tioned lack of money came from the ranks of the working class.

> You need money to survive, the more money you have, the easier . . . it is to get along in life. Money problems can be a real hardship on marriage.
>
> *Do you think that love alone can make a couple happy?*

Initially yes, but after a relationship, no. It's not reality. You have to have money.

Why?

Because it allows you to have, to do this extraspecial thing that keeps the love going. Like going to dinner together, going out, going anywhere together, possibly taking a trip, only the two of you, it all takes money to do that. Aside from that, just to be able to get through your monthly payments, your bills, you're paying for your apartment and whatever it may be, without worrying. It all helps make things easy.

If you had been richer, do you think this would have changed your relationships?

I think we have less stress in our relationships, if we had more money. (Female secretary, interview 16)

In 1974, Andrew Levison observed that despite their apparent prosperity, working-class people are caught in difficult financial struggles because, after paying for the mortgage, the car, and other expenses, there is not much surplus income for leisure: "Many workers, in the elation of the first days after their honeymoon, lock themselves into a lifetime of debt when they buy a house and furniture to add on the payments they are already making on their car. From then on, their freedom to travel, or to try a new job, or just engage in a range of activities outside work is taken from them by the structure of debt in which they are enmeshed."[24] This is undoubtedly even more the case today because of the progressive erosion of real income that has characterized the last decade.[25] As Collins and Coltrane put it, for working-class people "the most serious source of . . . unhappiness . . . is simply economic pressure."[26] Such pressure is particularly acute during the first years of marriage, precisely during the transition from steady dating to a settled married life.

By contrast, only when probed did middle-class and upper-middle-class respondents admit that lack of money could be—theoretically—a problem. Rarely did they spontaneously refer to it as a concrete problem in their own relationships or even in those of people they knew.[27] Instead, they framed problems in relationships in psychological or moral categories pertaining to the self, typically in terms of the "genuineness" or "authenticity" of their feelings. For example, the male orchestra conductor cited, as "the problems most people encounter in their relationships, "Having illusions about the other one. And not accepting the other one's feelings and judging the other one's feelings instead of trying to accept them" (interview 33). Contrast this answer

with the following response from a janitor: "The only problems that I
have ever had is financial problems. . . . That causes problems. That's
why I say if two people really love each other, you really get through
these problems. And maybe that's why we both get along, because
money doesn't really mean that much to us. If you have it, it's fine, if
you have enough to survive, it's fine, but it's not really important" (interview 40). This man denied and at the same time acknowledged the
effects of money on his marriage.

When asked to talk generally about their romantic lives, working-
class people rarely referred to money-related difficulties, instead characterizing their lives as unconducive to romance. However, asked to
talk more specifically about the difficulties they had encountered in
their relationships or to reflect on the role of money in romantic relationships, working-class answers differed from those of the upper-
middle-class. A secretary with a high-school education thought that,
for "most people,

> the number one problem is money. Maybe the man doesn't make enough
> money to give the girl what she wants or take her out as many times as she
> wants and the girl can resent that. Or jealousy, one partner is more success-
> ful than the other or. . . . [inaudible] about "we should do this fifty-fifty,"
> there is a lot of fights about that, I think. Money is the biggest problem.

Was this also your problem?

Yes, it was. (Interview 18)

A man with a high-school education and a working-class background,
but who was upwardly mobile, gave the following response:

Do you think that money is important for love?

Yes. Everybody says if you really love somebody, your money doesn't matter. You can be poor and all that. But I've seen too much. I've seen money,
or rather the lack of money, drive families apart, because if you love somebody but you don't have any money, then you're spending all your time
working, trying to get money, and it causes resentment and they're not going to be in the greatest mood if you don't have the kind of food they want.
They can't spend that kind of time on their relationship because you've got
to worry about the money. So it caused a lot of stress and problems and
worries and all that. . . . But if you have money, I am sure that gives you
the time, you can be with the person as much as you want, spend the kind
of time you want, not time working, but time getting to know each other
and having fun with each other and concentrating on the relationship. So
money definitely plays an important role. (Male boxer, interview 15)

Money was seen to affect romance in two ways: through the pressures produced by daily worries about bread-and-butter issues and by creating stress
and competition between working-class men and women. But as indicated
in the quote above, the importance of money was seen to lie not only in the
commodities it could buy but also in the leisure time it made available.[28]

The different role attributed to money by different social groups was
also apparent in the respondents' interpretations of story 3: the *only* people who dismissed this story as "boring," "dull," "mediocre," or too
"calculated" and "yuppieish" were middle- and, especially, upper-
middle-class respondents. Working-class respondents typically liked the
third story because they interpreted it as a love story with "financial security." The janitor, for example, thought that "this couple has probably a better chance than the other two."

> *Why?*
>
> Well, they had more time to know each other, and they both seemed secure
> in what they were doing. Because I think, today in the world situation, you
> have to have some kind of security to make a marriage work.
>
> *Do you think they are right to wait for the promotion?*
>
> I don't know, I guess so, I guess today maybe I would have. In the world
> economy, maybe to be a little more secure. You don't have any kind of se-
> curity today. That's hard and that creates problems. (Interview 40)

By contrast, upper-middle-class respondents criticized the "calculated"
aspect of the story in the name of an ethos of disinterestedness and spontaneity. The more one is removed from material necessity, it appears, the
more one is likely to denounce calculation and the struggle for security
in romantic bonds.

When middle-class respondents talked about their shortages of
money, they reverted to a vision close to that of the working class, but
with many hedges. For example, a music conductor who had lived in
Paris for a few years—unemployed—reflected on the financial difficulties that arose in his relationship with a French woman there:

> *Do you feel that money is important for love?*
>
> Surprisingly, I do.
>
> *Why surprisingly?*
>
> Because I am an artist and artists are supposed to be very idealist. Only
> love exists.

Artists are supposed to be idealists.

Artists are supposed to be so idealistic that love is the only important thing. Money is horrible. I think that money itself is not important, and it's not a reason to, to love someone, but I think money is important, is important in that without it you can't really do what you want to do, you can't really express, it's very hard to express what you have inside and this I have experienced, being in a relationship and not having money, you automatically, there is an imbalance. You can't do things you would like to do, there is an inequality.

Did she have money?

Yes, she didn't have a lot, but she had money.

What kind of things did you want to do that you couldn't?

First, there is the problem, each time we went out there was a problem, we were always very careful, which I never liked, because that's not the way I am. I would like to just be, just not worry about that. I like inviting people to do things, like get little gifts to someone, if I see something that I like I like to get it. That's a problem, living with someone and not being able to pull my share. I think that in that way money is important. (Interview 33)

This man experienced the lack of money as a double source of problems: not only did it affect his sense of self-worth (he did not fulfill his alleged role of provider), but it also prevented the couple from engaging in enjoyable leisure pursuits. Despite his—admittedly temporary—experience of strained economic circumstances, this man repeated the ritual middle-class expression of repugnance to money ("money is horrible"), an aversion never expressed by working-class respondents.

But even when the romantic interchange did not demand large expenditures of money or time and took place inside the home, the romantic practices of married working-class and upper-middle-class respondents differed a great deal. Let us listen to two voices, the first of a working-class homemaker:

What would you do if you wanted to have a romantic evening?

I think that a romantic evening at this point in my life would be simply going out. We are talking about someone who has been married fourteen years and has two kids and . . . because my husband and I have been married so many years, just going out, going to dinner, or even going to a movie and stopping at the [inaudible] to do something, that would be romantic. It would have to be without worrying about coming home at a certain time. . . . I am just saying there is no room to even think about being romantic, you know what I mean? Our lives are not like they are on television. (Interview 9)

The second belongs to a successful female lawyer, married and well educated:

> [After describing a romantic restaurant.] There are different kinds of romantic evenings.
>
> *What, for example?*
>
> You just decide that you are going to make love that night and you do nothing but just make love, that would be a different kind of evening, or we would sit together and look at old photographs and talk about what happened a few years ago. That would be romantic.
>
> *Do you often have romantic moments like that?*
>
> Yes, I think so.
>
> *You mean, you devote a lot of time to it?*
>
> Well, I try to. I think we both get the urge for it, after we work so hard and we come home and you are tired during the week. But the weekends or when we are on vacation or even some weeknights when we get home early, we try to do something nice, romantic together, kind of quiet, the two of us and loving. (Interview 23)

Romance was not experienced as frequently by the working-class woman as by the upper-middle-class one. Are these differences due to the length of her marriage and the presence of children, or are there other reasons? As we will see, the differences are related to their leisure and financial resources as well as to the mode of interaction between wife and husband, that is, in the respective role they assume and their patterns of communication.

Several married working-class women in the sample suggested that the home was not a romantic place because of the burden of domestic chores. For these women, who could not afford outside help and whose husbands were less likely to help, the house was more work than for upper-middle-class women, who were more often able to pay for outside help and also were more likely to be married to men who shared domestic duties.[29] Moreover, as Randall Collins argues, working-class women invest a particularly high amount of time in domestic labor because a neat and clean home is a source of status.[30]

> *Do you often have [romantic] moments like that?*
>
> Not often enough, when we have children, it changes romance in marriage.
>
> *In what way?*

> Well, you don't have the time, you're too preoccupied taking care of your
> family to have a lot of time for romance. There is always some type of ro-
> mance in a good marriage but you don't get the time to go to the beach just
> the two of you, which would be an ideal situation. (Interview 16)

For this woman, time more than money deprived her of the more frequent
romantic moments enjoyed by the upper-middle-class women inteviewed.

One could argue that, more than either money or time, children are the
real obstacle to a frequent experience of romance. David Halle, for example, has shown convincingly that the leisure activities of the
working-class man are significantly curtailed when he marries and has children, but that these patterns change again when the working-class couple
has finished taking care of children. Thus, we should not "mistak[e] one
stage in the life cycle, a stage when leisure is particularly restricted, for the
essence of leisure among the working-class."[31] This view implies that the
presence of children, more than class, accounts for the fact that working-
class people rarely experience romance. Halle's sensible argument explains
to a great extent the differences in leisure and romance found in my study,
but it does not account for two other findings. First, the married upper-
middle-class respondents who had children did not seem hampered by
them in their pursuit of romance, as working-class couples often were.
Middle- and upper-middle-class women who had children and worked
outside the home (most of the working-class mothers stayed at home) usually did not mention the presence of children as a hindrance to romance.
When they did acknowledge that children made romance more difficult,
these women maintained that romance was always possible "if one puts
enough time and effort into a relationship," by focusing on weekends, for
example, or making "a special effort." Transferring the work ethic into
their personal relationships, they viewed the creation of romance as under
their control, a result of willed and skillful effort.[32] Thus, lack of leisure
time is only partly explained by the presence of children.

The other finding is that even romantic moments demanding little
leisure time were reported significantly less frequently by working-class
respondents than by upper-middle-class respondents. Contrast, for example, the responses of working-class women cited above with the following one from an about-to-be-married, upper-middle-class man:

So you think that romance lasts after marriage?

Obviously, I don't have marriage experience, but from experience of going
out with someone for a long time, it can last if you keep it alive. But again,

if you do things once in a while that you consider very romantic, you can keep it going.

How would you keep it alive?

That was an example of a romantic evening [dressing up, drinking champagne and going out to a formal dance], so by making sure you get dressed up even though sort of no courting anymore, make sure you do things out of the ordinary once in a while. (Male university professor, interview 1)

As this answer shows, the ability to "rekindle" (as the women's magazines put it) moments of passion by creating the conditions for romantic rituals is grounded in the middle-class belief that routine is not inevitable but can be avoided by skill and effort.

The middle-class ideal of communication also shows how the ability to maintain romance in daily life depends on one's class ethos. As we have seen, people with higher cultural capital tend to place a higher value on verbal communication in relationships, and this affects the experience of intimacy.

My husband and I had read something, by the time you are married *x* number of years, you say only *x* number of words, maybe something like fifteen or twenty, and I said, "That would never happen." It happens, it happens.

Is it good or bad?

It forces you sometimes to stop and say, "You wanna talk?" When a question pops into your head, you just know the answer. . . . If there are things in his work, or the people he works with, he does not talk about them. I would be more inclined to talk about the people that I know, let's say that are volunteering at school, I would be more inclined to say, "Oh! So and so did such and such," you know, that sort of thing, and I am not going to say it just to keep the conversation going but because it's my life. His work is his life. He does not come home and tell me about the problems that they had, something with another department, because that's nice, he knows I [inaudible] care. He knows he does not need to talk about it. If he wants to talk about specific people or specific events or something that happened at work, that's different, you know, but it depends, what interests me, what interests him, and if what interests me doesn't interest him, and there are so many things that don't—I am very careful about choosing my words—so therefore what I am saying is that it would be a great put-off to him if I started talking about the other things that I do. (Homemaker, interview 9)

Asked if she found it romantic just to talk with her partner, another working-class woman said, "At times I could, but my husband is really not a good talker. He is not a talker at all. There have been times when we have talked and it was a romantic talk but that does not happen very often at all" (secretary, interview 16). For working-class respondents, "communication" is a means to share information in order to fix problems. For upper-middle-class respondents, it intensifies their bond not only through the resolution of conflicts but by the exchange of ideas and tastes and the avowal of emotion.

Furthermore, this class difference was more pronounced for men than for women in my sample. While in upper-middle-class couples, both men and women placed a high value on "talking," among the working-class couples it was only women who did so (without, however, the stress on debating and intellectual challenge). For example, in response to a question about his most memorable romantic experience, a working-class man answered:

> I don't know how I would start it. As far as—I don't know how I would start it. I tended bars years and years ago, and a nice French girl, I spent, I don't know how to describe. I don't know, it was a very passionate woman, it's all I could say. It was very nice experience because it was very romantic, winter, and we really did a lot of things together. I don't know how to put it into words. But it was a very nice thing.

> *Can you describe the feeling of being in love?*

> That's hard to put into words. I guess when you really love someone it's a nice feeling, because they're always there for you. When it's both ways. It's nice to know no matter what you do, you're going to have somebody there to back you up no matter what you do. To me love is a two-way street. You can overcome everything if you love somebody no matter what, it always works out. To me. (Janitor, interview 40)

This man's difficulty expressing himself, his own perception that "he does not have the words for it," contrasts with the verbal facility of upper-middle-class respondents, who talked with an obvious ease, dwelling at length on various shades of feeling.[33]

The gender gap in communication is much wider for the working class than it is for the upper middle class. In his update of the study of Middletown, Theodore Caplow confirms these findings (without, however, elaborating on them). He observes that in the late sixties and seventies there was an upsurge of advice literature advocating "communication" in marriage. Despite these models, however, working-class couples still were having difficulties communicating with each other.[34] And in her study of working-class marriage, Lillian Rubin concluded that "the role segregation and the consequent widely divergent socialization patterns for women and men become clearly dysfunctional. And it is among the working class that such segregation has been more profound."[35] In the 1992 reissue of her study, she found that this had not changed. The following exchange from my interviews illustrates this difficulty:

Do you often have [romantic talks] with your wife?

No. Very rarely.

Why? Do you want them?

Yes, but I have to force myself to it.

Why?

Because I like to keep a lot of distance to myself, you know, you have to take these things out of me. I keep a lot of things inside me. It builds up until [inaudible], sometimes I want to, sometimes I don't, so it's like something in the way that is stopping me.

So you don't like to talk about your feelings?

Right, I keep them inside me.

Most men around you, do you think they are romantic or not?

Around me? Naaaaah!

How do you know they are not romantic?

They just seem like they joke a lot.

Joke about what?

Anything, they just joke. Jokers.

They joke about their wives?

They just joke, jokers. When you joke like this every day, you're just not yourself.

So why do you joke?

Just to make friends, to be with more friends and to be with, uh, and to get your bad feelings out, like sometimes you get bad feelings and you just joke and you just take it away, you know. If you joke with your friends, it takes that moment [away] for a while, but it comes back after you joke. (Male supermarket worker, interview 32)

As this man suggested, the reluctance of working-class men to express their emotions is an extension of their patterns of communication in the workplace. The "jokes" are ways of venting indirectly feelings that, if expressed directly, might make them seem emotional and therefore weak.

The nature of most blue-collar work can further deprive men of the opportunity or resources to engage in romance. An extreme illustration of this was provided by one of my male respondents who explained why he divorced his wife:

> I had a terrible job, I had to work sometimes twelve hours a day.
>
> *What were you doing?*
>
> I was lugging pigs, carrying pigs on Fourteenth Street. The idea was, I was supposed to learn and make money, but it was damaging the relationship, then I quit. But I think it's more important, you can always get a job, it's a hard thing to talk about.
>
> *When you say it was damaging the relationship, what do you mean?*
>
> Well, if you are working all these hours, sometimes you can't speak, you just collapse, and if the person wants some romance perhaps you are practically unconscious, it's not conducive to nurturing a romantic situation. (Private investigator, interview 22)

As this example potently illustrates, the sheer physical exhaustion that often characterizes working-class men's work is an obstacle to casual conversations, intimacy, sexual play, and romance after work.[36]

In general, working-class men tend be more controlled and less emotional than their middle-class counterparts.[37] Gender roles tend to be more traditional and rigid in working-class households, and male domination of women is more pronounced.[38] The work of middle-class men typically gives them a degree of autonomy and power over others, which can translate into a psychological security at home not enjoyed by working-class men. A more subtle explanation, however, has been proposed by some Marxist scholars. Because of the demands of most blue-collar work, working-class men tend to base their identities and sense of worth on their physical strength, prowess, and stamina.[39] To be asked to share in activities and attributes associated with women's sphere, such as emotional sensitivity and "talkativeness," is experienced as a threat to their virility. This gap is increased by the fact that working-class women, in charge of the "status work" of the family, are exposed to middle-class "romantic style" and are likely to adopt elements of middle-class cultural identity,[40] thus making them even more estranged from the masculine, untalkative ethos of their spouses.

An example will usefully recap the discussion.

It seems that once we got married the romance went out the window. That's very important to me. After years of fighting, I finally got my point to him, that our marriage was not going out to survive.

What happened before?

Coming home from work and falling asleep on the sofa and just saying hello to me and doing short conversation when I would want an arm around me and a real passionate kiss, something to show me that you are still interested in me. Or he would never bring me flowers, he would never take me out to dinner, it all stopped! All these are romantic gestures!

Why do you think it all stopped when you got married?

I have no idea! I think there is a false idea where a lot of people, once they get married, you no longer have to please that person anymore, to make that person feel special anymore, because now you are married, now you have each other for the rest of your life. But it still counts! (Homemaker, interview 28)

As I have suggested, in the dating stage working-class people show the same romantic competence as their upper-middle-class counterparts, and we see here that, before they got married, this couple was enacting the "correct" script of romance (he was buying flowers, taking her out to dinner, etc.) After marriage, however, living up to the standards of romance became more difficult, not only because of time and money, but because working-class men and women have different expectations of marriage. While the man expects wife and home to provide him with comfort and emotional security, the woman expects romance, passion, and communication to continue. If there is a gap in romantic competence, it is between working-class men and women, a gap that was opened by the middle- and upper-middle-class models of communication and intimacy that have been disseminated through popular culture and that are consistent with women's socialization at large.

By contrast, verbal communication is part of the social identity of both men and women of the upper middle class, a part of the an exercise of cultural competence that is important in both their education and their work. As Randall Collins again puts it: "Probably male/female cultural differences are minimized for upper-middle-class men who themselves work in the culture-production sector; their own class positions are already involved in culture-laden activities that match those of their wives, whether the latter are employed or not."[41] Moreover, the talk exchanged by upper-middle-class men and women during their romantic interactions is instrumental in *furthering* their work activities, as illustrated by the answer of a well-established artist asked what she talked about with her husband.

We often tell each other interesting things that happened to each other when
we are not together, or ideas that really interest each other. Sometimes I would
just read something that I think is wonderful, I would tell him to read it and
talk about it. Vice versa. Sometimes I would be working on something and I
would have a really good idea and I would just share it with him and he would
give me his criticism. Sometimes when I write something or when he writes
something, we edit each other's writing. And we're kind of as brutal as possible because like sometimes it's hard because neither of us get overcome by
hurt feelings. We can usually deal with it and take criticism and use it and
even hold on to—in the end if I really feel he is right about it, I will make the
change. And he is pretty much the same way. So you know we definitely share
our work with each other and ideas we have and things that happen to us.
(Interview 13)

This answer helps us understand one reason why upper-middle-class
couples converse more intensely and frequently than working-class
couples. Upper-class couples are likely to hold jobs demanding similar intellectual and personal qualities and can therefore use their partners as
"critics" or as an audience on whom to test ideas. Or if they work in corporations, conversations about work can help them plan moves, decipher
the "boss's" cues, and prepare strategies. This has the double effect of
transferring their professional ethos into the private sphere (thereby im-
proving their professional performance) and of increasing their communication with their partners. This intermingling of work and romance
does not hinder or jeopardize their capacity to communicate with each
other but rather increases it. Bryan and Alsikafi studied the leisure patterns of university professors (and by extension, the "intellectual" professions in general) and found that leisure and work greatly overlapped.
Leisure was used to derive benefits directly recyclable for work, and vice
versa; work provided many reasons to engage in the sphere of leisure.[42]
Middle-class and upper-middle-class couples enjoy more companionate
leisure than do working-class couples, who tend to be more segregated.[43]

How do working-class women cope with the fact that their husbands
do not conform to middle-class models of communication? The evidence
of my sample is mixed. In my interviews, women seemed to hold lower
standards of communication than those advocated by mass culture, thus
suggesting that they had adapted to their husbands' identity.

Television sometimes shows people that have been married for a real long
time, having heart-to-heart talks about their deep feelings and holding each
other. I don't know anybody who talks that way.

What do you mean, "that has deep talks"?

> My husband and I, we have a very good communication, but it is very
> brief, we are not going to get that deep, like you see people talking in the
> soap operas or on the TV shows. I don't think that anybody does that.

What do you mean by "that"?

> Let's take the soap operas. It seems that the same couple can sit there for
> one week, even though they have been married for many many years, and
> sit there and hold hands and look in each other's eyes and say "I love you"
> a million times and "You are the only person." Married people do talk that
> way but it is not on a daily basis. Maybe we will reflect on these things
> once a year, on an anniversary or on Valentine's day . . . but it's not on a
> day-to-day basis. (Homemaker, interview 28)

Echoing other working-class women, this respondent suggested that the
the ideal of communication set by soap operas and mass culture generally was excessive for her own needs.

Working-class women's familiarity with new models of intimacy and
masculinity conveyed by mass culture have nonetheless made them expect something different from their relationships. As Lillian Rubin has
suggested, "The daytime soap operas, watched almost exclusively by
women, do picture men who may be more open and more available for
intimacy. But the men on the soaps don't work at ordinary jobs, doing
ordinary things, for eight, ten, twelve hours a day."[44] Rubin notes that
popular culture in general, and television especially, are closer to a middle-class experience. Consequently, working-class respondents are confronted with models that do not reflect their own circumstances but are
powerful enough to make women expect their marriage to fulfill them.[45]

The differences in leisure and communication entail different attitudes
toward the home among working-class versus upper-middle-class couples. For my working-class female respondents, and for working-class
women generally, the home is viewed as boring and the site of chores
rather than leisure.[46] This viewpoint in turn seems to define different
attitudes toward the role of romance in daily life. When we examine how
romance is enacted and lived inside the home, linguistic and cultural
competence as well as the availability of leisure time appear to be very
important factors in explaining why domestic romance is so different for
the middle and working classes. Recalling what was romantic about her
marriage, a woman in my sample, a social worker with a master's degree in education, said: "For example, on Sunday morning, we just used
to read *The New York Times* together" (interview 44). In response to
the same question, a working-class woman said that "the opportunity

to be with your husband, let's say sit in a bedroom reading a book, that does not happen in our life, that does not happen" (interview 9). Activities like reading the *Times* together or "doing a crossword puzzle" together use the home as a place of relaxation; by exercising together their cultural competence upper-middle-class couples make their daily domestic interactions romantic.

In my sample, only the upper-middle-class respondents intentionally defined romance in ways that explicitly reversed the traditional or standard conception. When expressing their scorn for romantic stereotypes, many respondents claimed, for example, that a romantic moment can be "very mundane." A man who had lived for many years with a woman said that one can "find romance in the most mundane situations, just being with the person makes it a wonderful rosy situation, just sitting around, reading together." The same man, asked what kind of things he usually likes to do with his partner, answered, "Going to the movies, going out to dinners, taking trips. I also like a lot of evenings at home, watching television together, fixing dinner together, even cleaning up together afterwards" (interview 29).

Not only are middle- and upper-middle-class romantic practices more varied than those of the working class, but they are also more inclusive, admitting activities usually excluded from traditional attitudes to romance ("just sitting at home," "watching television," "cleaning up together"). The more affluent respondents suggested that love does not take place in preconceived romantic places and that it can in fact occur within mundane or traditionally unromantic places. As has often been noted about the realm of culture, once upper-middle class people establish cultural standards, they engage in a more or less reflexive distancing from these same standards and are consequently able to opt for "nonstandard," alternative cultural practices.[47] Thus the idea that the mundane can also be romantic is an upper-middle-class cliché that aims precisely at the "sentimental" clichés favored by the working class:

What would be an unromantic thing to do?

That's a tough question. You could say, doing laundry, but if in the middle of doing laundry you start hugging each other and kissing each other, that would be romantic. (Female lawyer, interview 12)

Another woman, a married, successful artist, after explaining that love can happen in traditionally unromantic settings, opposed the traditional idea of romance in the following way:

What do you mean by traditionally unromantic settings?

What I mean is something pedestrian, like you fill up your car with gas, although I mean on the flip side you can have a stylish image of a gas station that can turn into anything. But traditionally when people think of romantic settings, it is not often at a truck-stop diner or, you know, on the highway, but those locations to me are not excluded from something that would have a sense of romance in it. (Interview 13)

Another respondent, an editor, said that "Romance to me is not really giving roses or going to a restaurant. It is not events or props. It is not setting up certain situations and being in them. It's more of a feeling that comes naturally from what you do *day-to-day*. . . . I am much more likely to do something like to be in a store, see something he would like, and buy it for him. That's much more *mundane*" (interview 45).

Contrast those previous answers with the following ones given by working-class women:

What would be something unromantic?

Almost everything that goes on generally. I guess what I am saying is all of the distractions that are in my life, all of those. I am not going to say it's a put-off. I am just saying there is no room to even think about being romantic, you know what I mean? Our lives are not like they are on television. (Homemaker, interview 9)

Or also:

Do you think that romance is important to keep love going?

Yeah, definitely.

Why?

I don't know, just—it makes you realize you're in love with each other. You know, day-to-day is not easy at all for any couple, especially in the long-term relationship, you need some romance to rekindle that spark that first brought you together. (Homemaker, interview 16)

Or also:

Did you use to do a lot of things together?

Yes, we spent a lot of time together.

What would you do?

Go shopping, or looking at things, go to movies maybe, a lot of times at
home, maybe that's what we did, spend time together, all that starts falling
apart when kids come along, that messes up your schedule. (Homemaker,
interview 28).

For the working-class woman, everything that goes on usually is unromantic; for the upper-middle-class woman the reverse is true, namely,
everything that goes on usually *could* be romantic. In fact, the people
who are most likely to say that something mundane can be romantic are
those whose daily lives are the least burdened by chores and duties and
who have, objectively and subjectively, the greatest sense of freedom. *The
more one is objectively distanced from necessity, the more one is likely
to say that a mundane or ordinary moment can be romantic.* Because
laundry or housecleaning or child rearing is less oppressive for middle-
class or upper-middle-class women, they are more likely to consider these
tasks as potentially romantic. Thus, although the middle- and upper-
middle class are the most likely to withdraw most thoroughly from daily
chores, they are also the most likely to view daily chores as romantic.

Positions in the work process explain why daily life is likely to be more
romantic for upper-middle-class people than for the working class. The
categories and scripts used to evaluate and construct romance are rooted
in objective resources such as nature of work, equality between men and
women, educational competence, available leisure time, and income.
Not surprisingly, the ability to subvert, invert, or twist conventional tax-
onomies of love also varies with possession of these resources. Because
the "life-world" of upper-middle-class people is more congenial to romance, they are functionally less dependent on commodified forms of
romance, and their chances to experience romance, in both traditionally
romantic and traditionally nonromantic settings, is thereby increased.

The middle-class models of love elaborated through the mass market
and mass culture have created tensions in the working-class romantic experience. To put it differently, middle- and upper-middle-class people
have two ways of coping with the threat of boredom.[48] First, they can
acquire novelty and stimulation by purchasing new leisure goods. Second, they have at their disposal a communicative competence that can
substitute for and complement the model of intensity. Once they reach
the level of comfort that follows the initial level of excitation, upper-
middle-class people can avoid boredom by getting stimulation from the
market, by sustaining relatively intense patterns of communication, and
by incorporating their romantic experience within the very texture of the
mundane.[49] *The inescapable conclusion is that the upper-middle class is*

better equipped to cope with the cultural contradictions between defini-
tions of love that demand continuity and longevity and definitions of
love as an intense and pleasurable bond. They can and do switch easily
from being hedonist consumers to being the communicative "managers"
of their relationships.

To summarize, married working-class respondents found romance
less often than the upper-middle-class respondents, in the realms both of
consumption and of communication. This difference can be explained
by the combination of several factors: limited surplus income to invest
in leisure or romantic pursuits; limited leisure time, the result both of
limited income and of the more tiring character of their work (men's
blue-collar occupations and women's lack of assistance in housework);
gender differences in patterns of communication; the sharp separation
of the men's and women's spheres, which translates into leisure activities and spills over into romance; and, finally, the different positions of
men and women in the realm of work and culture.

CONCLUSION

The standard definition of romance demands a middle-class cultural
competence and lifestyle. Lacking these resources, the working-class
marriage can be considered deprived in several ways. First, as we have
seen, in contemporary culture the experience of romance affords a secular access to the experience of the sacred, and without this experience
or some analogue of it daily life becomes oppressive in its continuity, reg-
ularity, and necessity. The experience of the sacred is important in and
of itself, but it also introduces into daily life an "organized disorder," a
rhythmic alternation between "hot," passionate times and "cold," pragmatic, profane ones.[50] Second, whether communal or interpersonal, human bonds are constituted through shared memories and the shared narratives that sustain them. I have argued that the liminal nature of
romantic experience lends itself more readily to the "writing" of such
bonding narratives of shared memory. Insofar as working-class couples
engage less often in romantic practices, their lives are less likely to provide the raw material for such narratives.

Other kinds of narrative are also at stake here. The ideal of intimacy
promoted by the therapeutic worldview entails a narrative of progress:
as it moves forward in time, a relationship brings to its participants an
ever-increasing understanding of self and other that carries emancipatory potential. This narrative provides the relationship with a structure

of meaning that not only strengthens the bond but makes differences and conflict more intelligible and therefore more acceptable and manageable. Insofar as therapeutic discourse and the therapeutic worldview are not part of the cultural capital of the working class, the members of this class, particularly the men, are less "romantically competent." This implies that for working-class couples, the category of the "profane," the day-to-day routine of relationships, does not have the rich texture offered by the therapeutic narrative of progress.

By contrast, because of their education, income, and position in the work process, middle-class and upper-middle-class respondents enjoy numerous advantages. For one thing, their contradictory attitude toward the stereotyped, mass-market version of romance is actually a source of strength. Their understanding of common romantic scripts and their ability to enact the more "upscale" ones (those requiring greater expenditure) provide the sense of security derived from the "fit" between actions and cultural standards. At the same time, their disparagement of "clichés" provides them with the psychological certainty that their experiences were "special," "creative," "unique." They therefore had the comfort of living up to culturally prescribed standards while enjoying a sense of autonomy and individualism.

The success of a romantic moment, its capacity to draw the couple out of the routines of daily life, depends largely on its degree of ritualization and liminality, and in postmodern culture, as we saw in chapter 4, ritualization is achieved with the help of commodities. Access to luxury commodities, including expensive travel and vacations, enables partners to renew the feeling of love more frequently and to further intensify and solidify the romantic bond.

The common cultural competence upper-middle-class people exercise in their romantic communication has two positive consequences. First, it provides an experience of romance alternative to that promoted by the public sphere of consumption, making romantic even those moments that do not depend on the market of leisure. Second, shared cultural communication strengthens the organic bond between the couple.

Finally, because the daily life of the middle and upper-middle class contains fewer burdens or financial constraints than that of the working class, it is much easier for the former to view even the most mundane moments or situations as romantic. The better educated and better off thus have the easiest access to the commercial-ritual formula of romance but at the same time are functionally least dependent on it and can extend the scope of what they define and live as romantic.

We can see now that the intersection between class and romantic love is not transparent and can be understood only after a painstaking reconstruction of the subjective meanings contained in the experience of romance. Furthermore, dating and marriage are phenomenologically different and reproduce the culture, values, and social relationships of late capitalism in different ways.

The crux of this chapter, as well as that of the preceding two, is found in the ambiguous, contradictory properties of the therapeutic ethos. On the one hand, in providing a language of self-direction, self-knowledge, and egalitarian self-assertion, therapeutic discourse helps enable women to formulate and assert their needs and conceive of themselves as equal partners, with "rights" and "duties" formulated in the abstract, contractual language of the sphere of work. This, of course, has emancipatory potential for men as well as for women. On the other hand, the therapeutic ethos risks commodifying relationships in two ways. The practice of self-understanding it promotes encourages people to conceive of themselves as a list of preferences and needs and to evaluate relationships in terms of the other's abilities to satisfy these preferences and needs. Furthermore, by making "communication" so indispensable to intimacy, the therapeutic view discriminates against those men and women—but most often men—who feel uncomfortable, incompetent, or otherwise uninterested in articulating their emotions. Again, however, for those in possession not only of therapeutic discourse but of other, material advantages, this contradiction brings benefits. The middle and upper-middle classes are the most likely to use the rationality of economic transactions in their self-conceptions and in their relationships, yet they are also the most likely to form marriages on the basis of what Anthony Giddens calls the "pure relationship," a relationship for its own sake. In other words, they get to have their cake and eat it, too. In my conclusion, I examine what this and other paradoxes have to tell us about the contemporary romantic condition.

Conclusion

A Happy Ending?

And there is a dignity in people; a solitude; even between husband and wife a gulf; and that one must respect, thought
Clarissa, watching him open the door; for one would not
part with it oneself, or take it, against his will, from one's
husband, without losing one's independence, one's self-
respect, something, after all, priceless.

Virginia Woolf, Mrs. Dalloway

To the still skeptical reader, the emotional oscillation described in this book might seem to have nothing to do with capitalism, for the oscillation between passion and reason, between states of emotional exaltation and the routine of everyday life are universal phenomena. Thus the ultimate question that needs to be addressed is precisely this: what difference does it make that the languages, the goods, and the worldviews of the market are those used to make sense of the romantic bond? After all, why should we care to know that the naggingly persistent contradictions of the romantic sentiment have assumed the cultural forms and languages of the market? The answer to this question will take the form of a recapitulation of the main findings of this book.

THE STORY OF LOVE

The popular view of love, often repeated in social psychology textbooks, is that it is "blind" at its inception but usually recovers its reason as the initial infatuation subsides. Because it has focused on the shifting *meanings* of love, this book sees a different, more complicated love story as typical of contemporary society.

The model of love as an intense and spontaneous feeling has lost its power, partly because it is now subsumed under a model of liberated sexuality, partly because a slow and progressive knowledge of the other is thought to be the only reliable way to build romantic attachments. Because sexuality need not be sublimated in a spiritual ideal of love, and because "self-realization" is perceived to depend on experimentation with a variety of partners, the absoluteness conveyed by the experience of love at first sight has faded away into the cool hedonism of leisure consumption and the rationalized search for the most suitable partner. The pursuit of pleasure and the gathering of information about potential mates now constitute the initial stage of romance, codified in the practice of dating. Dating is the institutionalization of romantic encounters without the goal of commitment. It can take the form of short-lived "affairs" undertaken for their own sake or of a search for the right mate through successive partners. In both cases, the initial romantic interaction frequently takes place in the anonymous and pleasure-driven sphere of leisure consumption.

Dating thus contains three cultural and emotional experiences, which are often intertwined but can also assume an independent and "pure" form: (1) The increasing legitimacy of sexual pleasure for its own sake, for both men and women, often makes the romantic encounter a primarily sexual one, the occasion for sexual experimentation, sometimes justified in terms of "self-realization." Its pure form is the "affair." (2) Whether the romantic bond is oriented toward long-term commitment or has the fiery brevity of an affair, the sphere of consumption provides the framework within which the bond is forged through the cyclical consumption of formal or liminal rituals of leisure. (3) Finally, the formation of the romantic bond can express interest-driven behavior that seeks to match one's own needs and preferences to the assets and liabilities of another person, either rationally and self-consciously or through the semiconscious mobilization of habitus in the mutual sharing of leisure activities, cultural tastes, and forms of talk. From my data, it is difficult to determine which, if any, of these three forms of romantic bond—the sexual, the ritual-consumerist, or the rational-economistic—is the most central. Instead, dating seems to demand that a person be able to shift skillfully from one mode to another. In dating, pleasure and utility, gratuity and profit, rationality and irrationality, chance and social destiny are so closely imbricated that they become confused with each other. In this respect, dating is a typically postmodern form of romantic interaction.

As Mike Featherstone has suggested, the apparent disorder of postmodern experience points to a "more deeply embedded integrative principle, for there are rules of disorder which permit swings between order and disorder, status consciousness and the play of fantasy and desire, emotional control and decontrol."[1] The hedonism that Daniel Bell saw as stemming from an "adversary Bohemian culture" does not contradict the spirit of contemporary capitalism but, on the contrary, marks a new, more advanced discipline of the self, for it is undergirt by an intensive rationalization of the personality and the cultural sphere, integrating both into the economic logic of advanced capitalism.

While dating blurs and confuses the boundaries between the rational pursuit of a compatible other and a hedonist consumption of leisure and sexual pleasure, married life is structured by a more rigid alternation between the ongoing routine of daily life and periodic rituals of romantic fusion. Contrary to popular laments that marriage is threatened by the fading of the emotional intensity of the "beginnings," my analysis suggests that the everyday—monotonous, wearing, "pedestrian"—is the symbolic pole from which moments of romantic exaltation draw their meaning. Such moments are significant precisely because they are short-lived and unsustainable in daily life. Far from marking a "dwindling" of love, the entry into the "profane" realm of daily life (usually the realm of marriage) begins a rhythmic alternation with "sacred" romantic modes of interaction. The stability of married life depends on sustaining this rhythm.

However, as I suggested in chapter 5, this motion is not a simple to and fro between the sacred and the profane. Because our culture presents a ceaseless flow of highly stylized images and stories of the "eruptive" version of love, the profane is also set against the background of the sacred, so that everyday life must be continuously "justified" in terms of this romantic ideal. This task, I have argued, is performed by the middle-class therapeutic ethos, which, in reformulating the romantic bond in more mundane terms like "companionship," "friendship," "compatibility," bestows something of the exaltation of romance on the everyday. Further, although the therapeutic ethos often seems to offer only palliatives to the shortcomings of daily life ("know how to compromise," "accept the other as he is"), it also offers a powerful narrative of emancipation, based on self-knowledge, gender equality, and open-ended communication. While the realm of everyday life is often seen as devoid of the intense ritual meanings lived in the realm of leisure, it recuperates "meaning" through a narrative of progress that makes the success of a relationship depend on self-knowledge and unconstrained communication.

Like dating, love in daily life has many cultural layers. One consists in the pragmatic coordination of a couple's activities, the mundane "business" of daily life. In an era where intimacy must increasingly reconcile the conflicting needs of men *and* women, the threat of conflict always lurks. Intimate everyday life is now structurally threatened by conflicts, the necessary and natural outcome of women's greater equality. And with the inevitability of conflict in contemporary definitions of intimacy comes the practice of conflict resolution through communication, a now necessary component of intimacy,[2] especially among middle- and upper-middle-class couples. Such a practice not only restores the couple's smooth practical functioning but also promotes a communicative rationality, which assumes that two autonomous selves can achieve understanding and love through the communication of their needs and the acceptance of the legitimacy of those needs. Communicative rationality stands at the indeterminate boundary between an economistic language of needs satisfaction and an agapic intimacy, the gratuitous love given to another person simply because of who he or she is, a uniqueness irreducible to a list of attributes.

Does this story have a happy ending, then? Does it represent an advance over the earlier vision of love, or have we lost more than we have gained? This question raises the further question of the criteria we might use to answer it. According to much sociological and moral thought, the values and attitudes of private life are starkly opposed to those of the realm of commodity exchange; the private sphere borrows from the economic sphere only to its own detriment. By this norm, the story I tell of love seems to augur its demise. Instead, I hope my story will lead readers to reassess the sacrosanct character of the norm itself.

One argument for the present-day decay of love, asserting an opposition to consumer culture at once Marxist and elitist, claims that the love depicted in Romantic literature is more authentic because the lovers affirmed their passion against an oppressive social order. But if modern (or postmodern) love seems domesticated by comparison, its strivings encouraged rather than denied by the surrounding culture, this is because the social order itself has changed, acknowledging the claims to freedom, self-realization, and equality contained in the utopian vision of love. It was precisely for these values that romantic lovers suffered, and present-day romantic culture, hedonist and "weightless" as it sometimes seems, nevertheless represents these lovers' posthumous victory. It cannot be denied that modern love empowers its lovers, giving them greater control over their romantic destinies.[3] To discount the significance of this runs the risk of glamorizing the defeat and death that premodern martyrs to love—mostly women—typically suffered and of viewing their stories of struggle and suffering with nostalgia and envy.

A more serious objection comes from the pessimistic Weberian view of the "disenchantment" of capitalist society, developed in Habermas's contention that the realm of human relationships must be kept separate from the instrumental rationality of the economy, technology, and the state. I am not in fundamental disagreement with this thinking, but I argue that the sociologist must make a more nuanced and empirical use of these categories. The goods and values of commodity exchange can either reinforce or undermine the romantic bond, depending on the context. For example, the therapeutic ethos can strengthen the romantic bond in middle-class couples, but it can divide men and women in working-class households. The instrumental vocabulary of needs and preferences can make persons and relationships into tradable goods, but it can also help women assert their equality. An elegant restaurant can function both as a status marker and as an element of the ritual renewal of the romantic bond. My point may seem a simple one, but it is crucial for sociology. We cannot presume a priori how the sphere of commodity exchange and the private sphere will interact, or what the outcome will look like. Rather, this interaction must be systematically and empirically investigated in particular contexts of class, ethnicity, and gender.

There are no absolute or universal norms for evaluating the forms assumed by love. The criteria I have adopted come from a particular tradition, the legacy of the Enlightenment and of modernity. This tradition values self-knowledge, autonomy, equality, and tolerance of difference. The question then becomes, does modern love actually live up to these values? Does it promote equality and tolerance, or does it perpetuate inequities of power and frustrate the need for openness and understanding? Just what kind of self-knowledge and how much of it is made available by authorized romantic discourses and practices? How and to what extent does modern love give life meaning?

As we have seen from the interviews documented in this book, the middle and upper-middle classes are the most likely to fulfill the potential of the romantic utopia because they possess the necessary economic and cultural prerequisites; modern romantic practice is attuned to their social identities in general and their work identities in particular. Paradoxically enough, although the affluent have an easy access to its utopian meanings, romantic love fails to provide them with a fixed sense of values and identity, something religion often provided in the past. The reason for this is not, as a prominent conservative thinker suggests, that contemporaries suffer from an amoral relativism.[4] Rather, they are committed simultaneously to *too many* values, institutional and anti-institutional, driven by economic interest yet affirming the creative power of emotions and spontaneity. We acknowledge more openly the multiplicity of our desires and the inevitability of power struggles within romantic relationships. We enjoy greater freedom in choosing a partner but also encounter a much greater number of potential partners. At stake is the personal welfare, conceived as economic well-being, satisfying intimacy, and opportunity for self-realization, that is paramount to middle-class identity. This pluralism of emotions and values has made romantic feelings less intelligible and more open to an anxious questioning of what it means to "be in love." Indeed, if overwhelming passion and a quasi-religious sentiment are not reliable signs of love, if we must fight for equality in the innermost privacy of our daily lives, then what is love on a daily basis about? Our passion is now confused by and confused with our self-interest. Marriage and love are subject to the sobering prudence of economic action and to the rational search for self-satisfaction and equality, a far cry from the amoral relativism presumed to have destroyed our relationships and our "family values."

Romantic passion has been further "disenchanted" by its very triumph in the mass media and consumer culture. Because of the ubiquitous use of romance to sell commodities, romance in real life has become an empty form, acutely conscious of itself as code and cliché. We have become deeply aware that, in the privacy of our words and acts of love, we rehearse cultural scenarios that we did not write. The formulas of romance now compel the belief only of the culturally deprived. Greater cultural capital leads to greater cultural alienation: the educated postmodern lover treats her romantic beliefs with the skeptical irony of a post-Marxian and post-Freudian consciousness.

The therapeutic ethos makes its own contribution to this alienation. As therapy, its aim has always been to "cure," and there is a long tradition viewing romantic passion as a sickness. What the therapeutic ethos proposes to cure us of is anything in the psyche that escapes or subverts rational self-control. Growing out of the Freudian "hermeneutics of suspicion," it proposes a regime of self-knowledge that is fundamentally skeptical, testing all experience for signs of irrationality and illusion. In postmodern culture, "romantic faith" is celebrated throughout the mass media even as it is deconstructed by the therapeutic ethos.

The conjunction of these elements—emotional pluralism, consumerist rituals of romance, and the critical self-consciousness cultivated by the therapeutic ethos—generates a crisis characterized by a deep-seated suspicion of love, confusion between its rational and irrational expressions, and difficulty interpreting one's feelings. For the more affluent and educated, moreover, romance has been rationalized in that consumerist "lifestyle choice" has become the basis of their relationships and social identity. This crisis in the meaning of love epitomizes the crisis of meaning that Weber identified as the hallmark of modernity. As we try to control our lives through the rational management of our relationships, experiences that transcend rationalization become more elusive and our longing for them all the more urgent.

The exertion of control in private life, however, may have an emancipatory character. In an era of giant corporations and transnational capital, private life is one of the last arenas in which the individual can experience a measure of control and autonomy. That this autonomy is framed in the languages of the market is only one of the many ironies of capitalism that Marx himself wrestled with when he confronted industrial capitalism. The current disarray in our romantic attitudes is also the outcome of what Stephen Kern calls a more "authentic" consciousness of the meaning of love, a higher self-knowledge, a greater ability to exercise our freedom and autonomy in the domain of love, and a greater awareness of the existential difficulty in loving another.[5]

I suggest that the capacity to live an authentic meaning of love is reserved for those whose lives are not determined by "necessity." The emotional repression and distrust of verbal expression demanded of working-class men by their jobs is at odds with the middle-class ideal of intimacy and expressiveness adopted by working-class women; their life conditions, limitations in income, leisure time, and education, further hinder the working class's access to the "romantic dream." By contrast, for the middle class and, more especially, the upper-middle class, the focus on self-knowledge and on expressive and interpersonal skills, as well as the recent gains in the workplace made by the women of this group, mitigate gender differences and help their relationships live up to the romantic standards promoted by the media.

From this, three general conclusions may be drawn: *the spheres of private life and commodity exchange intersect in different ways for the middle class and the working class; romance is a good unequally distributed in our social structure; love provides personal freedom only to those who already have a measure of objective freedom in the workplace.*

This book, then, has a number of implications for the warnings, from the right or the left, about the decline in family values and in the sense of community. One is that the disappearance of Victorian values so self-righteously mourned by conservative apostles of doom is caused to a great extent by the same economic forces they are otherwise eager to celebrate and unleash. One cannot promote the claims of the individual against all forms of collective solidarity in the sphere of economic exchange and yet lament the triumph of these claims in the realm of the family.

Furthermore, insofar as it encourages individuals to find their greatest emotional satisfaction in private experiences linked to rituals of consumption, romantic love probably contributes to the breakdown of local networks and the sense of civic responsibility lamented by communitarian critiques of liberalism.[6] Any program to "reconstruct" the social fabric must face the fact that the conjunction of love with postmodern consumer culture is deeply ingrained in the psyches of the most educated and skilled members of society and exerts a power that will not be dispelled quickly or easily. However uncomfortable we are with this fact, it should spur us to new reflection on the role of the private sphere in the democratic ideal of citizenship, a task that has been undertaken by Robert Bellah and his associates.[7]

Some feminist scholars have recently held that liberalism itself is partly to blame for the declining participation in civic life. Stephanie Coontz, for example, argues that liberal political theory has excluded values of care, need, and dependence from political discourse, and insofar as these values have been relegated to the private sphere and to women, it has discouraged women from political life.[8] But as I hope to have shown, the abstract and impersonal discourse of the public sphere has been incorporated into private life, helping women achieve, however imperfectly, the autonomy feminists claim they have been denied as caretakers. It is true that this autonomy is problematic, as it rests on the discourse and values of consumer culture, and in its emphasis on rights it has dramatically failed to articulate duties.[9] Nevertheless, the commodified language of individualist self-realization is, at present, the only language we understand well enough to open our relationships to a project of autonomy, equality, and emotional fulfillment. I do *not* deny that this language is an impoverished one or that we will eventually need to transcend it. But in the commodified society in which we in fact live, women can use this language to subject relationships to the forms of egalitarian negotiation and accountability legitimated in the realm of commodity exchange.

While I began interrogating the meaning of love in contemporary culture under the auspices of Emile Durkheim, my conclusion belongs to the intellectual legacy of Max Weber. In the analytic style he gave to sociology, Weber has poignantly conveyed the fact that the gains of modernity are also losses and that sociology cannot help adjudicate between conflicting values. Modernity has brought irretrievable losses in the meaning of love, most notably the connection between love and moral virtue and the dissolution of the commitment and stability of premodern love, but these losses are the price we pay for greater control over our romantic lives, greater self-knowledge, and equality between the sexes. Whether or not we are willing to pay this price is an important yet an idle question, for we have already paid it. For the foreseeable future, the ideals of equality and autonomy may survive in the society at large only at the price of their continuing association with the hedonist and utilitarian idioms of postmodern culture. It is my hope that a better understanding of the losses and gains brought by the postmodern condition of love can empower us to choose and control both our romantic and our social destinies.

A Few Words about Methods

THE SAMPLE: DEFINITIONS AND PROCEDURE

I have used income, occupation, and educational level as the critical dimensions along which I compare the working and middle classes and also individuals within the middle classes.

Traditionally, the working classes have been defined by their position in the process of production (i.e., they sell their labor but do not own the means of production); by the nature of their occupation (in the "production" rather than service sector); and by a common lifestyle. Although this definition is still accurate to a great extent, it has been called partially into question because some of the traditional segments of the middle class also fall into the category of working class. Clerical workers and salespersons belong to the category of working class because these occupations do not require any college attendance and have been considerably devalued. Computers have made their work even more routine than task-oriented, thus even more boring and alienating. The lower fractions of the middle classes labor in a hierarchical system similar to the strict division of labor in factories.[1] Moreover, they live in working-class neighborhoods and have lifestyles similar to those of their working-class counterparts. Thus, the working classes are made up of the "traditional working class" (that is, factory workers) and "all clerical workers and *all* sales workers with the exceptions of advertising, and insurance agents, stock and bonds salesmen, sales representatives, and related groups whose position in the labor process and more affluent lifestyle would make their inclusion in the working class somewhat ridiculous."[2]

Working-class membership is defined by an educational level of high school or less and a low-prestige occupation. Typical working-class occupations among my respondents included cleaning person, salesperson, secretary, electrician, security guard, babysitter, and doorman. The ratings from these dimensions were not always consistent. For example, two men in my sample had not completed high school; though their incomes were low, they worked in middle-class professions, one as a private investigator (formerly an insurance representative) and the other as a professional boxer.

The middle class is notoriously difficult to define. Once the lower fractions are taken out, three subcategories remain. The first are managers, who direct and control the productive process and are least likely to be supervised. This subclass does not necessarily own the means of production but directly assists those who do. The second subcategory comprises "cultural specialists," such as mathematicians, scientists, social scientists, researchers, artists, journalists, university professors, and editors, and cultural intermediaries such as nurses, paramedical workers, elementary-school teachers, and people working in advertising, public relations. The third subgroup is made up of persons commonly called "professionals": lawyers, doctors, and financial consultants.

My sample of middle- and upper-middle class respondents held college and advanced degrees. Annual income ranged from $40,000 to $100,000. The sample includes professionals (doctors, lawyers, investment bankers, executives) and people whose main income derives from participation in the production of culture (actors, musicians, painters, filmmakers, movie distributors, cameramen, editors, academics, advertising executives, high-school teachers). Here also, some interviewees occupied contradictory positions. For example, a cameraman/filmmaker who dropped out of college and earned a low income had a very high cultural competence, manifest in his expertise and practice of art forms. One lawyer had average-to-low cultural competence, low income, and friends from the working classes, and did not participate in the arts.

INTERVIEWEES

N = 50.[3] Number of women = 25; number of men = 25.

Symbols: M = male; F = female; S = single; MA = married; D = divorced; C = college; C + = graduate education; C − = two years of college or less; HS = high school.

In addition to income, education, and profession, I have evaluated respondents' class position and cultural capital with variables such as parents' profession (social origin); profession of close friends; neighborhood; and type and frequency of cultural activities.

UPPER-MIDDLE-CLASS RESPONDENTS (N = 20)

All respondents had undergraduate degrees, and many had graduate degrees as well.

Interview 1: M. S. C + . University professor; $70,000–100,000.

Interview 4: M. MA. C + . Investment banker; above $100,000.

Interview 5: M. S. C + . Lawyer; $20,000–40,000.

Interview 6: F. D. C + . Artist; $60,000–100,000.

Interview 7: F. MA. C + . Lawyer; $60,000–80,000.

Interview 8: M. S. C + . Physician; $40,000–60,000.

Interview 12: F. S. C + . Lawyer; $60,000–80,000.

Interview 13: F. MA. C + . Artist; $60,000–80,000.

Interview 14: M. D. C + . Physician; $60,000–80,000.

Interview 19: F. MA. C + . University professor; above $100,000.

Interview 20: M. S. C + . Corporate banker; $60,000–80,000.

Interview 23: F. MA. C + . Lawyer (husband: graphic designer); above $100,000.

Interview 27: F. MA. C + . Homemaker (husband: economist); income $40,000–60,000.

Interview 30: F. S. High school student (parents: publishers); parents' income: $80,000–100,000.

Interview 35: F. MA. C + . Artist; above $100,000.

Interview 43: M. D. C. Art dealer; $40,000–60,000.

Interview 44: F. D. C + . Social worker; $40,000–60,000.

Interview 45: F. S. C + . Collagist; $20,000–40,000.

Interview 49: F. S. C. Advertising designer; $40,000–60,000.

Interview 50: M. S. C + . Scientist; $40,000–60,000.

CULTURAL SPECIALISTS WITH AVERAGE TO LOW INCOME (N = 10)

Interview 2: F. S. C. Avant-garde filmmaker; $10,000–20,000.

Interview 3: F. D. C + . Editor; $30,000–40,000.

Interview 24: M. S. C + . Ph.D. student; $20,000–40,000.

Interview 26: M. S. C. Cameraman; $20,000–40,000.

Interview 29: M. S. C − . Actor; $20,000–40,000.

Interview 33: M. S. C. Music conductor; $10,000–20,000.

Interview 34: M. S. C. Movie distributor; $10,000–20,000.

Interview 41: F. S. C + . Historian; $4,000–10,000.

Interview 47: F. D. C + . Kindergarten teacher; $20,000–40,000.

Interview 48: F. S. C + . Editor; $20,000–40,000.

LOWER FRACTIONS OF THE MIDDLE CLASSES (N = 4)

Interview 21: F. S. C − . Police officer; $20,000.

Interview 10: F. MA. C − . Preschool teacher (working-class husband); combined income $20,000–40,000.

Interview 22: M. D. C − . Private investigator; $20,000.

Interview 42: M. MA. C − . Salesperson; $10,000–20,000.

WORKING CLASS (N = 14)

None of the respondents had finished college; some had not finished high school.

Interview 9: F. MA. HS. Homemaker (husband: accountant; working-class parents); household income $40,000.

Interview 11: M. S. C − . Doorman; $4,000–10,000.

Interview 15: M. S. HS. Boxer; $10,000–20,000.

Interview 16: F. MA. HS. Secretary (husband: audio technician); combined income $40,000.

Interview 18: F. S. HS. Legal secretary (working-class parents); $10,000–20,000.

Interview 17: F. MA. Attended secretarial and horticultural schools. Word processor and secretary (husband: carpenter).

Interview 28: F. MA. HS. Homemaker (husband: project manager); $40,000.

Interview 32: M. MA. HS. Supermarket worker; $10,000–20,000.

Interview 36: M. D. HS. Electrician; $20,000.

Interview 37: F. S. HS. Security officer; $15,000.

Interview 38: F. MA. HS. Homemaker (husband: craftsman); combined income $20,000.

Interview 39: M. MA. HS. Automobile mechanic; $20,000.

Interview 40: M. MA. HS. Janitor (wife: waitress); combined income $10,000–20,000.

Interview 46: M. S. HS. Salesman; $20,000–40,000.

THE INTERVIEWING TECHNIQUE

I used a structured, open-ended questionnaire (the full text of the questionnaire is given as appendix 2). The interviews were not standardized, as I often asked questions in response to the answers given by the interviewees. Because of the highly private quality of emotions and love, ethnographic observation was not possible. As Critcher suggests, such subjects are difficult to study other than through interviews.[4]

I used my own personal knowledge of romantic practices to formulate hypotheses and to reflect on them. My approach to the interview subscribes to what Manning has called "existential fieldwork," which insists on the transaction between the subject and object and does not hesitate to use the researcher's own knowledge and even own circle of friends to make claims and hypotheses.[5] The main purpose of my interviewing technique was to create a climate of trust and to make my respondent confident that I was nonjudgmental. To judge from the number of people who said things like "it's embarrassing to say, but . . . " or "I hope no one sees this because my wife does not know about this," I believe I succeeded in my aim. This does not necessarily mean that respondents were always candid, but it does indicate that the interview managed to overcome *some* of the reserve that often characterizes the interaction between interviewer and interviewee.

The interview elicited three different types of answers. Some answers are *interpretative:* that is, they interpret motives, intentions, and personal qualities in the characters, events, situations, stories, and images offered as eliciting devices to respondents. Other answers tap into the *"folk theories"* by which respondents explain and justify the why's and how's of love or, as so many self-help books put it, its failures and successes. The third type of answer is *autobiographical,* elicited by asking respondents to recount diverse aspects of their romantic experiences. But these different categories were analyzed with a single intention: to grasp the fluidity of the cultural repertoires on which respondents draw to make sense of their shifting emotions. Most of my questions were designed to make respondents choose and then justify their choices between different love stories, gifts, greeting cards, and images. Choosing among different options would, I hoped, force people to spell out the rationale, the tacit assumptions, and the values upon which their choices rest. While in actual social interactions people do not always perceive that their behavior is the outcome of (conscious or unconscious) choices among many possibilities, when a crisis arises or when they are called upon to justify themselves, actions or choices are explained by invoking the meanings of a particular repertoire. The questionnaire aims at grasping the various cultural repertoires within which people understand and interpret romantic behavior.

Although I used an elaborate questionnaire, I did not follow it in a standardized way, preferring to pursue particular issues that emerged as more prominent or characteristic of a given respondent's romantic life. For example, I put more questions about marriage to a working-class woman who had married her first boyfriend and who seemed to have marital difficulties than I did to a woman who had had many boyfriends before marriage and did not indicate marital problems. Probing was done either by repeating a key sentence said by the interviewee and waiting for the respondent's reaction, by asking such questions as "What do you mean?" or "In what way?" or "How so?" or by telling them "I am not sure I understand."

I sometimes analyzed the responses to my interviews by following strict procedures of coding. For example, categories such as "consumption," "ritual behavior," "interest-driven" choice of a mate, "strategies of class distinction" were predefined and responses were coded accordingly. At other times, I resorted to less formalized interpretations of my data, trying to infer recurring patterns of meaning and connecting them to existing theory. Although I am aware that my analysis can be faulted for not always using replicable and falsifiable methods, I hope that my results, the recognizable and collective pattern and their systematic links to existing theory, will persuade the reader of the validity of my findings.

I used images from advertising as highly stereotyped representations of romance to examine the visual codes that make an image romantic or unromantic.

Figures 1, 2, 3, and 4 (see appendix 3) differ from one another along the following dimensions:

Setting: outside (2, 3) vs. inside (1, 4); urban (1, 2, 4, by inference) vs. natural (3).

Private vs. public space: Although the four pictures take place in settings with different degrees of privacy, they all tend to exclude the presence of people other than the lovers. Figure 2 is in a public space; figure 3 is in a secluded space; figure 4 is in a private space (home). Figure 1 is in a semiprivate space (a restaurant but apparently without other customers around). Although figures 3 and 4 are very different, they share one important trait: they both occur in very private and secluded settings (nature for 3, the home for 4). On the other hand, figures 1 and 2 occur in a half-public (restaurant) and completely public setting (the street). However, in figure 1 no one else is near the couple, while in figure 2 a car can be seen in the far background.

Mundane vs. unusual activities: I wanted to examine whether mundane activities are viewed as romantic and, if so, by whom. For example, the activity depicted in figure 3 (boating) is one liberated from the constraints of work and daily life. Figures 1 and 4 present activities that, although "out of the ordinary," are more integrated into daily life (eating at a restaurant or at home). Figure 4, however, also carries connotations of "celebration," since the characters, even though at home, wear elegant party clothes. Figure 2 does not fit easily into either side of this dichotomy because, although the couple seems to be strolling on a street, the man's kneeling position makes it an "extraordinary event."

Figures 5 and 6 are primarily a contrast in wealth. Figure 5 presents the image of a young and glamorous couple dressed in tuxedo and pearls; the other is a famous portrait by Walker Evans of a poor family during the Depression.

NARRATIVE PROPS

A narrative can be defined as a symbolic tool used to organize real or imagined events into a meaningful sequence and to communicate this to others. Semioticians have shown that the almost endless flow of seemingly heterogeneous stories circulating in the realm of popular culture can be reduced to a limited set of stable and predictable narrative structures. I distinguish between narrative *frame* and narrative *model*. A narrative model is the structure within which stories are organized, processed, understood, remembered, and retrieved; the narrative frame is the "mindset" within which we make sense of and communicate such structures. For example, contemporary Americans hold an ideal-typical (generic) narrative model of "love at first sight" that does not depend on each particular love-at-first-sight story encountered (e.g., the typical opening sequence of this generic narrative is the "eyes meet" sequence), and which can be alternately *framed* as the recognition of two souls predestined to each other (as in the Christian and neoplatonic tradition), as a hormonal disorder, or as sexual attraction.

Story 1 (see chapter 5 for the stories) conforms to the idealist tradition of love, the one most codified by popular culture.[6] Stories 2 and 3 present two different versions of the realist tradition: a "residual" version of the marriage of "reason" organized by families (story 2), and an "emergent" one, depicting a professional couple whose relationship combines emotion with financial and professional concerns (story 3). The television serial *Thirtysomething* provides many good examples of this last type of love story. None of the stories address whether and how much the protagonists actually love each other. They do, however, indicate the channels through which they meet and how long it takes them to get married. Stories 2 and 3 associate the relationships with attributes such as "feeling good," "health," and "solidity." In each story there is some obstacle that causes a delay in the final decision to get married, whether it be (1) parental consent, (2) the shyness and awkwardness of the protagonists themselves, or (3) a promotion. To keep the outcome of the narrative from affecting respondents' evaluation of the beginning and development of love, all three stories end with marriage.

I randomly changed the sequence of presentation to insure that the interpretations were not constrained by a specific order. I did not find any significant bias produced by the order of presentation.

QUESTIONS ABOUT GIFTS

Gifts have ambiguous economic properties: on the one hand they seem to evade the system of economic exchange. On the other, they are circulated within a binding system of reciprocity by which the social identity of givers and receivers is marked. It is precisely this duality I was interested in when I asked respondents which gifts they consider romantic and which greeting cards they would give someone. These questions would make them, I hoped, spell out the norms by which a gift is considered as appropriately romantic: for example, an expensive gift is usually considered less romantic than a gift expressing the giver's creativity.

Questionnaire

FACESHEET

Date:

Place:

Code #:

Sex: M   F

Age:

Currently married?   Y   N

Has been married before?   Y   N

If yes, how long?

Single: Y   N

Have you ever lived with somebody?

How long?

Religion: Protestant   Jewish   Catholic   Unaffiliated

Neighborhood you live in:

Formal education (diplomas and discipline):

From which institutions:

Current profession:

Profession before this one:

Profession of your parents:

Profession of the person you are married or involved with:

Profession of your close friends:

Please circle the category of income that corresponds to your yearly income:

$4,000–10,000 $10,000–20,000 $20,000–40,000

$40,000–60,000 $60,000–80,000 $80,000–100,000
$100,000–above

Do you have a lot of spare time?

When you have some spare time, what do you like to do?

Do you like reading?

What kind of books do you like to read?

Do you have many books at home? How many?

Do you buy books?

How many a year?

What is the last book you have read?

Do you read self-help books?

Do you read romances?

What kind of romances?

Do you read magazines?

What kind?

Do you go to the movies?

What kind of movies do you watch?

What is the last movie you have seen?

Do you watch TV?

How often?

What kind of programs do you like?

Do you ever go to art museums and galleries?

How often?

When was the last time you went? What did you see?

Are you affiliated to a group of any kind (religious, political, etc.)?

Do you consider yourself a feminist?

INTERVIEW

1. Look at the pictures and pick the one you find the most romantic [figures 1, 2, 3, 4; see appendix 3].

2. Why did you choose this picture?

3. Why do you find the others less romantic?

4. If you wanted to have a romantic evening with somebody, describe what this moment would be like. *(Probing)* Where would you go? What would you do? What time of the day would it be? Would there be people around?

5. Do you prefer to stay home or go out?

6. Can you give me an example of an actual romantic moment you have had recently? Please describe it.

7.   In general, what kind of things do you like to do with your partner? Do you like talking? Do you go to the restaurants, movies, theater? How often? Do you take weekend trips, vacations together? How often?

8.   Can you describe a romantic dinner?

9a.   Imagine you just met somebody, what would this person have to do or say to be unromantic to you?

9b.   Imagine the same but with somebody you would have been living with for a long time.

10.   In general, do you think that romance is important to keep love going between two people? Why?

11.   Have you ever had a relationship without romance? How do you describe the difference between a relationship with romance and a relationship without it?

12.   Do you think that for most people romance lasts after marriage? *(Probing)* Do you know couples for whom it has lasted? How do you know that it has lasted for them?

13.   Do you consider yourself a romantic person?

14.   Do you think that sex is important for romance?

15.   Would you say that a pornographic movie or picture romantic?

16.   Are there any scenes from a movie or a book you have read that you remember as being romantic?

Story 1

17a.   What do you think of this story?

17b.   Do you think they marry for love?

18.   Do you think they should have waited to get married?

19.   Do you think they were right to get married without the bride's parents' consent?

20a.   Do you believe in love at first sight?

20b.   Have you ever fallen in love at first sight? If yes, what happened?

20c.   Let's say, imagine you meet the man or woman of your dreams, would you like him or her to fall in love with you at first sight?

21.   Do you know how your parents fell in love?

22.   Which couples do you think have a better chance to succeed, those who fall in love with each other slowly or those who fall in love with each other quickly?

23.   In your own life, did you fall in love with other people quickly or slowly? Ideally, would you prefer your relationship to be or to have been slow or quick?

24a.   Is love more important than family, i.e., your parents?

24b.   Is love more important than your own family, i.e., with children?

25.   Do you think that love is more important than work?

Story 2

26.   What do you think of this story?

27.   Do you think that Robert and Theresa marry for love?

28a.   Would you like or would you have liked to meet or to have met the love of your life in the same way?

28b.   Would you mind if a friend rather than family set you up?

29.   How would like to meet or to have met the partner of your life?

30.   Do you think that if your parents had to choose someone for you, this person would be the same person you would choose for yourself? If no, how would it be different?

31.   Would you go to a matchmaker or an agency?

32.   What kind of men/women do you think go to a matchmaker or to an agency?

33.   How do you meet your partners most often?

Story 3

34.   What do you think of this story?

35.   Do you think they marry for love?

36.   Do you feel that money is important for love? In what way?

37.   Do you think that money can make love better and easier?

38a.   Would you marry somebody who was much poorer than you?

38b.   What do you think are the consequences for relationships, if any, of not having enough money?

38c.   What are the consequences, if any, of having a lot of money?

39.   Would you marry somebody who was much less educated than you?

40.   Have you ever had a relationship with someone who was much less educated than you? How did it work out?

41.   Do you think that rich and poor people experience love in the same way?

42.   In general, do you think that people make some kind of calculation when they choose a partner?

Comparing the Three Stories

43.   Which one of the three stories do you like best?

44.   Which one of the men/women of the three stories do you find the most interesting or appealing to you? Which one would you have liked to be?

45.   Which one do you find the most romantic?

46.   What differences do you see between these stories?

47.   Do you think that each story presents the same kind of love?

48.   What is the difference between them?

49.   What story presents the most passionate love?

50.   What story is the most likely to last?

51.   Is there a difference between love and passion?

52.   Is there a difference between love and companionship?

53.   Is there a difference between love and friendship?

54.   Which story, if any, is the closest to your ideal of love? Why?

55.   Would you change anything in it?

56.   Which one is the least appealing to you? Why?

57.   To which one were most of your relationships the closest?

58.   Which one of these stories is the closest to movies or novels?

59.   In which one of the three marriages is it most likely that there will be problems?

60.   What kind of problems would it be?

Difficulties Encountered in Relationships

61.   According to you, what are the problems that most people encounter in their relationships?

62.   What are the problems that you personally have encountered in your relationships? How did you deal with them?

63.   Do you usually fight in your relationship(s)? About what, usually?

64.   Can you describe for me a fight scene you have had in your relationships?

65.   What would make you end a relationship with someone?

66.   Can you remember one or several relationships you have actually ended? Can you tell me why you ended them? What was bad about it?

67.   How do you know the difference between a good and a bad relationship?

68.   Do you think that doing psychotherapy, that is, going to see a psychologist regularly, may help one in his or her relationships? Why?

69.   Have you ever sought professional help? Did you find it useful?

70.   Do you talk with your friends about your relationships/affairs? Can you describe a typical conversation with one of your friends about it? How do you talk about it?

71.   Do you talk with your own partner about your relationship? Do you find it useful? Important?

72.   Do you think of your emotions a lot?

73.   Do you show easily your feelings? Do you hug, kiss, say sweet words easily?

74.   In general, would you say that romantic relationships are easy or difficult?

75a.   Your own relationships, have they been easy or difficult?

75b.   Would you say that you have had a love story that corresponded to your expectations of what love should be?

Ideal Mate

76.   What attracts you in somebody?

77.   What repels you in somebody? Try to imagine someone whom you would be ashamed to be boyfriend or girlfriend with. What would this person be like?

78.   What is the most important quality you would require from your partner?

79.   Could you describe briefly the ideal mate?

80.   Would you require the same qualities from a lover and from a wife/husband?

81.   Have you ever met someone very close to your ideal mate? What happened with this person?

Autobiography

82.   What were the most memorable love affairs you have had in your life, if any? How did you first meet? What did you like about this person?

83.   Can you describe a moment in this relationship that was very special for you?

84.   (If several stories) what were the differences between these different but important stories you have just told me?

85.   How did you know that you were in love? Can you describe that feeling?

86.   If you wanted to show or say your love, what would you do or say?

Pictures/cards

87.   Look at these two pictures [figure 5 and and the Walker Evans photo of a Depression-era family]. What do they evoke to you?

88.   Which one is the most romantic?

89.   In which one is there the strongest love?

Gifts

90.   Look at these three cards (1, 2, 3). If you wanted to give one card to your partner, which one would you give?

91.   Which one would you like to be given?

92.   Is it important for you to buy presents for the person you are in love with?

93.   What kind of presents do you usually buy?

94.   Can you remember a present that you thought was very romantic?

95.   Would you rather be given a rose with a poem or an expensive object?

96.   Would you rather be given something for the house or a piece of clothing?

97.   Do you usually celebrate Valentine's Day?

98.   Do you celebrate any particular day related to the history you have or had with your partner?

99.   Look at [figures 7, 8, 9].[1] What do they evoke to you?

100.   Which one expresses love to you?

101.   Which one expresses more romance?

102.   Do you know couples who are very good couples? How do you see or know that they are very good couples?

103.   In general, how do you recognize among your friends or acquaintances good from bad couples?

104.   Among these three pictures, which couple would you rather be?

Sources of Love

105.   Where do you think that your ideas of love come from? Movies? Family? Friends? Novels?

106.   Do you think that your ideas of love have changed since you first started dating? How so?

107.   In general, how would you say that media portray love? Accurately? Falsely? Idealized or realistic?

108.   What, if any, are the love stories you have heard or read that you remember best?

AFTER THE INTERVIEW

Did you feel I covered everything that was important to you, or are they things that you would have liked to talk about more?

Before this interview, have you thought about most of the issues we talked about?

Did you find it difficult to answer my questions?

Images of Romance

Figure 1

Figure 2

Figure 3

Figure 4

Figure 5

Notes

INTRODUCTION

1. Abercrombie, Hill, and Turner 1986, 87. Although capitalist economic organization has been evolving since the sixteenth century, it first began to realize its full potential with the Industrial Revolution, from the early 1800s onward.

2. Bell 1976, 14.

3. Shorter 1977, 23.

4. Stone 1977.

5. Psychoanalysis has largely contributed to the "scientific" justification for such views by suggesting that emotions are the outcome of universal psychological mechanisms. Although psychoanalysis has given paramount importance to irrational unconscious emotions, it has operated on and reinforced the same opposition between the domain of collective norms (the superego) and that of emotions (located in the id).

6. Recently, there seems to be a return of the pendulum as various strands of the social sciences revert to a universalist view of romantic love. Psychobiologists, most notably, view romantic love as a universal emotion, transcending barriers of nationality, class, and ethnicity, by identifying the biochemical constituents of what the psychologist Dorothy Tennov (1979) calls "limerance," a state of intense physical excitement induced by attraction to another.

7. Bourdieu 1979a, 596–97.

8. Contrary to Weber's claim that "purely affectual behavior . . . stands on the borderline of what can be considered 'meaningfully' oriented" (1978, 1:25), I view emotion as a socially meaningful communication, which depends on collective cultural categories and scenarios. For example, although anger has physiological components (quicker heartbeat, sweaty palms, higher blood pressure), the causes for anger and the mechanisms to express and/or contain it vary greatly. An angry person can invoke different cultural scenarios such as "retaliate to

defend one's honor," "forgive others as Jesus Christ forgives you," "express anger because it is healthier for the psyche," etc.

9. Schachter and Singer 1962.

10. Dutton and Aron (1974) have documented this hypothesis empirically. By exposing male subjects to the sight of a frightening high bridge, and shortly afterward to a pretty woman, they were able to show that those exposed to the scary sight were more likely to ask the woman on a date, indicating that the fear-induced arousal was labeled and interpreted as sexual attraction.

11. Two features identify a cultural frame: (1) It is characterized by a set of semantically coherent propositions which people are only implicitly aware of but which they can articulate when asked to. For example, the cultural frame of "love at first sight" generates a series of propositions such as "love is sudden," "love is uncontrollable," "love is irrational." (2) Different frames may be used by the same person to interpret a single event, although usually not at the same time or in the same situation. For example, the "love at first sight" frame is incompatible with the frame of "love as developed from friendship," although one may use them alternatively to make sense of different aspects of the romantic sentiment.

12. Hochschild 1983.

13. Geertz 1973, 89.

14. As Robertson (1988, 5) aptly puts it, "there is something self-defeating in wanting to prove that culture is a more powerful explanatory variable in the duet between material and cultural structures."

15. Collins 1975.

16. Alexander 1989, 178

17. See in particular Alexander 1988c.

18. Marcuse 1963.

19. See Ann Swidler's chapter on love in Bellah et al. 1985.

20. Alexander 1989.

21. The core proposition of this book is in line, then, with the late Durkheim's attempts to found a religious sociology of the secular world (Alexander 1988b), that is, to identify those meanings that in the secular world are at once socially binding and sacred.

22. See Goode 1968.

23. To take several examples, Tristan and Isolde's story, which according to French historian Denis de Rougemont (1983) is the paradigmatic Western myth of love, boils down to the lovers' betrayal of the political and national order embodied in the person of King Mark. Heloise, the brilliant pupil and lover of the renowned twelfth-century scholar Abelard, has remained illustrious because she affirmed passionate and sensual love against the prohibitions entailed by vows of celibacy. Romeo and Juliet gained fame not so much because of the intensity of their love, as because they braved their family disapproval, thus affirming the supremacy and righteousness of an individual's passion against the abusive endogamic rules of the group. Contrast these with Virgil's Aeneas, who abandoned Dido to found Rome.

24. Lévi-Strauss 1949.

25. Goode 1968, 753.

26. While in the twentieth century the motif of the lovers struggling alone against the social order was considerably played down by commercial entertainment, such an idea found a powerful echo in Freud's scientific allegories. Like many other moralists, Freud held that, while the restraint of erotic bonds posed a problem for the individual's autonomy, release from such bonds was a problem for the social order. This view was shared by one of Freud's most illustrious and least Victorian contemporaries, Bertrand Russell, who held that "love is an anarchic force which, if it is left free, will not remain within any bounds set by law or custom" (1929, 87).

27. Lantz 1982; MacFarlane 1987.

28. Zeldin 1973.

29. Zeldin 1980, 335; my translation.

30. Turner 1967. The proposition that love is a symbolic exploration of the "liminal" overlaps the central tenet of sociologist Francesco Alberoni's analysis of *Falling in Love* (1983), in which he argues that romantic love has the phenomenological properties of revolutionary collective movements, albeit a collective movement "for two." For Alberoni, the life of the group as well as the life of individuals is punctuated by sudden and intense moments of transformation, during which the quality of experience is, in his word, "transfigured." It is during these moments that a strong and binding "we" emerges, whether at the collective or the individual level. To put it differently, love creates a social solidarity that at once binds the couple and isolates it from the surrounding environment. Extending Alberoni's proposition, I submit that this double movement of union and separation, of affirmation and transgression, contained in romantic love has the properties of liminal rituals, during which the rules of normal conduct are suspended, hierarchies are inversed, and energies otherwise controlled are released and consumed.

31. In this book, the "market" has three different meanings: it is the abstract sphere of commodity exchange, the organization of social relationships constitutive of the sphere of production, and the realm where consumption takes place.

32. See Bell 1976.

33. Details about media samples are provided in each relevant chapter. The reader wanting to know more about methods of data collection and analysis should consult the appendixes.

34. Most scholars locate the shift toward a postmodern culture in the period following World War II (Bell 1973, 1976; Jameson 1991; Baudrillard 1970, 1972; Kellner 1989; Lyotard 1984).

35. See Jameson 1984.

36. Following the position of Marxist scholars such as Jameson, I view postmodernism as the "cultural logic of late capitalism" and not as a radical transgression of forformer modes of cultural domination. But because the model of straightforward correspondence between culture and economy is notoriously problematic, the relationship between "techno-capitalism" and postmodernism is more fruitfully viewed as one of "affinity" than one of cause and effect (Lash 1990).

37. Examples of heroes would include Charles and Diana, Liz Taylor and Richard Burton; of genres, Harlequin romances, soap operas, photo-novellas; of theories, self-help books, talk-shows, advice columns. Artifacts such as greeting cards, love mugs, puppets, heart-shaped balloons, love tee-shirts, and Saint-Valentine's day gifts have become a profitable industry and have pervaded our practices of gift-exchange.

38. As sociologists of postmodernism Scott Lash and John Urry (1987, 14–15) put it, "post-modernism finds an audience when the boundaries which structure our identities break down; that is, during personal experiences of 'liminality' during which identity is unstable."

39. Lyotard (1984) calls the postmodern prevalence of the image "the figural," a mode of representation characterized by the preeminence of the visual over narrative, by its emphasis on "primary processes" over "secondary processes," and by the blurring of the boundary between life and art. Cinema is the most obvious example of the "figural" mode of representation. As Lash (1990) suggests, the cinema has much in common with the experience of daydreaming and puts into motion unconscious processes by defusing the controlling operations of the ego. The succession of images have the disjointed temporality of perceptions in the unconscious. Finally, film is the discourse of desire.

40. See Griswold 1994, 85.

41. See Denzin and Lincoln 1994.

42. Burke 1989.

43. See Schudson 1989.

44. Schudson 1992.

45. Although my analysis highlights the shifting uses of these repertoires, it ultimately gives a greater weight to the constraining power of culture. Culture is indeed a resource, but one that restricts us to doing only certain things with certain meanings.

46. See Hodder 1994.

47. I compare working-class respondents with various segments of the middle classes, ranging from the middle to the upper rings. Class has three dimensions: economic capital (measured by income), cultural capital (measured by level of education and familiarity with "high" arts), and occupation (to which an index of prestige is attributed).

48. See Bailey 1988; May 1980; Holland and Eisenhart 1990; Giddens 1992; Collins and Coltrane 1991.

49. See Rubin 1992.

50. My usage of "cultural capital" twists the meaning given to this expression by Bourdieu (1979b), who defines it as familiarity with high culture and art forms. I concur with the view of Halle (1984), Lamont (1992), and Collins and Coltrane (1991) that in the United States familiarity with high art is less central to status stratification than it is in Europe.

51. Lévi-Strauss 1988, 144.

52. Wuthnow 1987, 63.

53. As Schutz (1967) and Berger and Kellner (1981) have argued, even if the sociologist uses the same knowledge as the actor, she enjoys a specific position: contrary to the actor, the sociologist is not engaged in action and operates within

the relevance structure of science. This posture of "withdrawal" enables her to juxtapose and relate different practices, making for a privileged position from which to observe contradictions and self-deception.

CHAPTER 1. CONSTRUCTING THE ROMANTIC UTOPIA

1. One standard view holds that by upgrading the standard of living, early capitalism alleviated the concern with earning a livelihood. The concomitant decrease in mortality was a key variable in explaining the "affective revolution" that occurred in England at the end of the seventeenth century and in France in the eighteenth century (Ariés 1962; Stone 1977; Shorter 1975). Further, romantic love is thought to be part of the ideologies accompanying or even facilitating the rise of capitalism, "affective individualism," for example, which, according to Herbert Lantz, "was made possible by macro events such as the spread of early capitalism" (1982, 354). Historians and sociologists have commonly accepted that the "disruption of older patterns of social order" gave birth to "individualism and the isolation of the family" (Lewis 1983, 174). Yet another link is forged in the place that love came to occupy in the cultural ideals of privacy and the nuclear family, both central to the worldview of the capitalist entrepreneur.

2. E. May 1980; Bailey 1988.

3. I owe these two expressions to conversations with anthropologist Arjun Appadurai.

4. See Chandler 1977.

5. Blumin 1985.

6. See Dulles 1965.

7. Lears 1981; Marchand 1985; Strasser 1989.

8. See Lewis 1983.

9. See Fass 1977.

10. Fass 1977, 261.

11. See Rothman 1984; Gay 1984; Fass 1977; Seidman 1991.

12. See Peiss 1986.

13. See Peiss 1986; Kasson 1981; L. May 1980; Dulles 1965; Braden 1991.

14. See Gay 1984.

15. I studied articles from the following middle-class magazines: *The Saturday Evening Post* (hereafter abbreviated as *SEP*), *Cosmopolitan, Ladies Home Journal (LHJ), Harper's, Forum, American Magazine, Good Housekeeping (GH),* and *Woman's Home Companion (WHC).* These articles were selected from the entries "romance," "love," "marriage," and "courtship" in the *Reader's Guide to Periodical Literature.* I also studied the popular movie "fan" magazine, *Photoplay.* Since *Photoplay* is not included in the guide, I examined all the articles dealing with love, courtship, and marriage, selecting all those on love published from 1923 to 1931. Issues were drawn each year from the months of December to May.

16. Hart, L., "The Way to Win a Woman," *Cosmopolitan,* August 1903, 399.

17. Preston, A., "The Place of Love in a Girl's Life," *LHJ,* February 1908, 26, my emphasis.

18. Religious motives have long been intertwined with love. Twelfth-century French courtly love transferred cult worship from the Virgin Mary to the "Lady," who was worshipped by her knight as a quasi-divinity. In America, however, the influence of religion stemmed from Protestant asceticism rather than Catholic mysticism.

"Romantic discourse" refers to all expressions representing or discussing the nature, the forms, and the limits of love.

19. McCall, A. B., "The Tower Room: A Girl's Ideal of Love," *WHC*, February 1910, 4.

20. Gladen, W., "Who Should You Marry?" *GH*, April 1912, 489.

21. By the secularization of culture I refer to religion's no longer functioning as a collective system of salvation (see Bell 1976, 1980; Berger, Berger, and Kellner 1973).

22. Lystra 1989, 8.

23. Ellis 1960, 65.

24. See Swidler 1980; Rothman 1984.

25. "Little Stories from Real Life," *LHJ*, May 1931, 31, my emphasis.

26. Dulles 1965.

27. See Braden 1991.

28. See Gay 1984; Rothman 1984.

29. See Dulles 1965.

30. Smith, A., "Box Office Love: A True Story of a Studio Conference," *Photoplay*, January 1928, 37.

31. See Dulles 1965; Bordwell, Thompson, and Staiger 1985.

32. See Ewen and Ewen 1982, 99.

33. See Peiss 1986.

34. See Bailey 1988; E. May 1980; L. May 1980.

35. According to L. May, the most basic element of DeMille's movies was the resolution of marital conflict through the husband's and wife's mutual participation in the consumption of leisure and beauty products. May sums up the message of these movies as the "containment of sexuality in the leisure realm" (1980, 220). De Mille's most successful movies—*Old Wives for New* (1918), *Don't Change Your Husband* (1919), *Male and Female* (1919), *Why Change Your Wife?* (1920)—all open with a conflict between husband and wife over the too dull (i.e., too "Victorian") nature of one of them. Husbands are bored with their wives' excessive respectability, or wives are tired of their husbands' obsession with work. When the discontented partner embraces the colorful and adventurous world of leisure and fun, the disapproving other initiates divorce. The conflict is resolved when the "old-fashioned" partner ultimately accepts attractiveness, youth, leisure, and entertainment as desirable values.

36. Rogers St. Johns, A., "Is Matrimony a Failure in Hollywood?" *Photoplay*, October 1924, 28.

37. Waxman 1993, 23.

38. Rogers St. Johns, A., "The Married Life of Doug and Mary," *Photoplay*, December 1926, 35.

39. Biery, R., "Companionate Stardom," *Photoplay,* January 1928, 48.

40. To limit the scope of my study, I examined ads in fifty-four issues of the monthly magazine *Photoplay,* from 1923 to 1931, and used every image containing a heterosexual couple. Issues were drawn each year from the months of December to May. This sampling procedure yielded seventy-five advertising pictures of heterosexual couples. *Photoplay*'s readership was primarily working-class; I also drew ninety advertising images from more middle-class magazines such as *Cosmopolitan, Good Housekeeping,* and *Saturday Evening Post,* from 1900 to the 1930s. Issues examined were not sampled but were quickly skimmed to find different ads containing the image of a couple. I also examined sixty-five ads for automobiles. The total sample of advertising images studied in this chapter contained two hundred and thirty advertisements.

41. Darnton 1989, 41.

42. Peiss 1986.

43. See Susman 1984; Rieff 1966.

44. Susman 1984; Lears 1981; Fox and Lears 1983.

45. R. Turner 1976.

46. Bell 1976.

47. Throughout this work, "antimodernist" is used in Lears's (1981) sense. He found that a new *Weltanschauung* appeared at the end of the nineteenth century that was anti-urban, "natural," "authentic," in search of intense experiences, oriented toward the expression of an authentic self and a lifestyle of "fun living" (Lears 1984, quoted in Schudson 1986). Lears relates the emergence of antimodern themes to the emergence of the culture of consumption and the therapeutic discourse promoted by psychology.

48. Waller 1937.

49. Leiss, Kline, and Jhally 1988.

50. Rothman 1984, 267.

51. Binkley, R., "Should We Leave Romance out of Marriage?" *Forum,* February 1930, 72.

52. This 1929 ad in *Good Housekeeping* is very different from contemporary arguments to promote cereals, which would focus on benefits to health rather than to beauty and love. The images in the ad presented here seem incongruous to a contemporary sensibility: it is unlikely that cars, oil, cleaning products, washing powder, or cereal would be sold on the literal argument that they enhance the quality and intensity of romance.

53. An excellent example of such expansion is the advertising campaign for diamonds. Not only have diamond rings been promoted as symbols of "engagement" but they have recently been extended to the celebration of anniversaries, thereby extending the consumption of luxury items such as jewelry further into the life of the couple. A recent report by National Public Radio (February 14, 1995) suggested that the sale of jewels made up the highest revenues of presents bought on Valentine's Day.

54. For example, the widely popular 1940 movie *The Philadelphia Story,* directed by George Cukor, explicitly mocked the prospect of its heroine Tracy

(Kathryn Hepburn) marrying the industrious hard-working, and rigidly moral George. To the dull morality of George is contrasted the aristocratic and hedonistic Dexter (Cary Grant). In the end, the flamboyant Tracy decides to marry the wealthy, idle Dexter.

55. See Ewen and Ewen 1982; Marchand 1985; L. May 1980; Rosalind Williams 1982.

56. Leiss, Kline, and Jhally 1988, 180.

57. Rosalind Williams 1982.

58. See Barthes 1957.

59. See Waxman 1993.

60. I am not suggesting that the identification with love stories started with the culture of ads and movies. The narrative fiction of the nineteenth century exerted a very strong power of identification over its readers (see Sicherman 1989). The difference lies in the fact that movies exerted their power of fascination over all social classes and that their visual character may have intensified (rather than created) the mechanisms of identification already at work in narrative fiction.

61. I used songs from the Saint-Vincent Collection at the Archives of the National Museum of American History (Smithsonian Institution). The selection of songs was considerably facilitated by their being classified thematically. The songs included thirteen romantic ones dealing with movie-going and twenty-four with riding automobiles.

62. This hypothesis has been substantiated and explored by Caughey (1984), who, using in-depth interviews, analyzed the influence of media on the activity of daydreaming, interestingly enough in the realm of romance. Caughey found that the content of daydreaming activities was very much influenced by the characters and the stories of the media.

63. Blumer 1933, 67.

64. Blumer 1933, 47–48.

65. See Bandura 1969.

66. Stone 1977, 183.

67. Gladen, W., "Who Should You Marry?" *GH*, April 1912, 489.

68. These changes are well captured by Lary May: "Adults were now enhancing married life by purchasing victrolas, clothes, and cars geared toward leisure fun. What is more, they looked at youth as trend setters. In the youth-oriented items, they hoped to find a constant newness which might free them from the inhibitions of public propriety, or the restraints of the Victorian family" (1980, 204).

69. Lystra 1989, 51.

CHAPTER 2. TROUBLE IN UTOPIA

1. Consumer capitalism is characterized by the centrality of the sphere of consumption, the construction of national and transnational markets, and the generalization of consumption to all segments of the population. Traditional social classes, defined by their positions in the process of production, break into consumer groups or groups sharing a common lifestyle.

2. Peiss 1986; E. May 1980; Bailey 1988; Zelizer 1989.

3. George, W. L., "Women and Marriage," *GH*, January 1919, 115.

4. A somewhat different explanation can be found in Griswold's (1982) analysis of nineteenth-century divorce. Examining the increase in divorces between 1850 and 1890 in Santa Clara and Mateo Counties in California, Griswold argues that this increase may be explained by the emergence and consolidation of the ideal of companionate marriage, which reduced patriarchal power, elevated women's status, and stressed emotions and expressiveness. Griswold suggests that the ideal of companionate marriage, which evolved from republican ideals of autonomy and freedom, was supposed to bring stability but had the opposite effect. This was not only because women's new equality increased their self-esteem, but also because marital expectations increased as emotional fulfillment became more important. Griswold's view is partially confirmed by later magazine columnists, who attributed the changes to women's newfound independence and changes in expectations about marriage.

5. "Courtship after Marriage," *Atlantic Monthly*, July 1921, 652.

6. "Why Can't They Stay Married?" *Photoplay*, October 1927, 39.

7. This idea is not new. For example, in seventeenth-century France, La Rochefoucauld and many other moralists viewed fiction in general as guilty of cultivating false ideas about love. This theme is developed in chapter 5. For contemporary studies of the influence of movies on behavior, see Blumer 1933; Baber 1939.

8. Binkley, R., "Should We Leave Romance out of Marriage?" *Forum*, February 1930, 75.

9. Zelizer 1989, 354, 357.

10. May 1980.

11. McGee, L., "Nine Common Causes of Unhappy Marriages," *American Magazine*, March 1924, 29.

12. Binkley, R., "Should We Leave Romance out of Marriage?" *Forum*, February 1930, 75.

13. Dix, D., "And So You Are Married!" *LHJ*, February 1932, 12.

14. Dix, D., "And So You Are In Love!" *LHJ*, January 1932, 6.

15. Ibid., 51.

16. "After Forty Years," *LHJ*, May 1931, 31.

17. Historian Lawrence Stone (1977) traces it to seventeenth-century England; Mintz (1983) finds a clearly articulated ideology of companionate marriage in nineteenth-century America.

18. Van Wyck, C., "On Girls' Problems," *Photoplay*, June 1927, 88.

19. See chapter 6 for an analysis of the ramifications of such an ideal.

20. Zelizer 1989; L. May 1980.

21. *Webster's Ready-Made Love Letters*, 1873, 13. I have not sampled advice books as systematically as I did magazine articles, as I make only occasional references to etiquette books published in the 1890s, the 1920s, and the 1960s.

22. Lewis 1983; Whyte 1990.

23. See Bailey 1988.

24. For example, Bailey 1988; Waller 1937.

25. Braden 1991, 66–67.

26. Lutes 1923, quoted in Braden 1991, 67.

27. Lynd and Lynd 1957, 67.

28. See Fass 1977.

29. Sennett 1977; Lasch 1977.

30. Bailey 1988, 13.

31. Braden 1991.

32. Lewis and Goldstein 1983, 123.

33. E. Turner 1954, 237.

34. Cross 1992.

35. Braden 1991.

36. Cross 1992.

37. It was, in fact, one of the least expensive forms of entertainment: one ticket cost seven cents (see Peiss 1986).

38. Ewen 1976; L. May 1980; Peiss 1986; Braden 1991.

39. Couvares 1983.

40. Braden 1991, 166.

41. Post 1922, 293.

42. E. May 1980; Peiss 1986; Braden 1991.

43. Interestingly enough, dances such as the cakewalk became popular in high society in the 1890s, suggesting the same "bottom-up" cultural trajectory as with movies.

44. Braden 1991, 160.

45. Peiss 1986.

46. Rothman 1984; Peiss 1986; Bailey 1988.

47. Peiss 1986.

48. Bailey 1988.

49. See Kasson 1981.

50. Ibid., 50.

51. Peiss 1989.

52. This meaning of "political economy" is obviously not the one used by Marx, whose *Capital* was on the contrary a critique of the political economists who, in his view, were the supporters of capitalism.

53. E. May 1980.

54. "Old-Time Courting and a Red Hot Date," *Photoplay*, 1926, 36–37.

55. Connolly, V., "Happily Married," *GH*, 1930, 30.

56. Busby, Marquis, "Who Said the Woman Pays?" *Photoplay*, September 1930, 45.

57. Whitridge, A., "Changing Fashions in Romance," *North American Review*, August 1928, 226:195.

58. This form of interaction, centered on the man's ability to entertain the woman and to provide her with the newly available luxuries of the mass market, is well-illustrated in the widely popular 1925 novel by Theodor Dreiser, *An American Tragedy*.

59. "The Too-High Cost of Courting," *American Magazine*, September 1924, 27.

60. Unger 1960, 119.

61. It is interesting that the women's liberation movement criticizes the dating system in terms of "Who pays" and not "Why pay," thus being oblivious to the fact that gender divisions were subsumed under the new political economy of romance brought about by capitalism.

62. Duvall 1967, 140.

63. Kasson 1990.

64. The theme of awkwardness on a "first date" has become one of the clichés of American cinema. But the emotional awkwardness often masks the social awkwardness of two people who belong to two different classes.

65. See Dimaggio 1982; Levine 1988.

66. To be sure, the association of love with the acquisition of elite manners was a popular theme (see Shaw's *Pygmalion,* for example). But the modern version of the old theme, in which respectability and distinction are acquired through hard work and learning in the framework of the couple, incorporates the new modes of leisure consumption. For example, the 1990 box-office hit *Pretty Woman* features a prostitute (Julia Roberts) who is taken to fancy restaurants in fancy company by a rich millionaire (Richard Gere). In the process of falling in love with the millionaire, she learns the proper way of eating and behaving while dining.

67. Unger 1963, 171.

68. McGovern 1989, 82–83.

69. Finkelstein 1989.

70. "The Audience Speaks Its Mind," *Photoplay,* September 1931, 109.

71. See chapter 8 for more on this.

72. See Rubin 1992.

73. See Bailey 1988.

74. This is congruent with arguments made by Shorter (1975) on the liberating effects of capitalism on women, and by Schudson (1986) on the message of liberation promoted by cigarette advertising geared to women.

75. See Goody 1973.

76. A legitimate objection to this statement might be that indeed the members of the generation after World War II married at a much younger age than their Victorian predecessors, who presumably were not as fluent in the practice of dating. My claim does not imply that dating will cause postponement of marriage but that in general it favors the formation of relationships whose end is not necessarily marriage.

77. See Bell 1976. Chapters 5 and 6 explore precisely how these incompatible romantic ethics have developed in contemporary American culture.

78. This is a case illustrating Bourdieu's claim that goods are to be approached practically—to the extent that they reflect and reproduce social positions and relations—and *cognitively,* i.e., as symbolic devices that organize social and economic relations.

CHAPTER 3. FROM THE ROMANTIC UTOPIA TO THE AMERICAN DREAM

1. Marchand 1985, 235.

2. Schudson 1991, 29.

3. Ewen and Ewen 1982.

4. See Raymond Williams 1993.

5. Print images represent half the total output of advertising (Leiss, Kline, and Jhally 1988). They were preferred to television advertising because they are geared to more specifically targeted sociocultural segments and thus provide more evidence of how the romantic utopia is incorporated within the moral and economic values of specific consumer groups. Moreover, print advertising by its very nature offers not a flow of images but rather single vignettes that condense carefully chosen meanings.

I selected any image that contained a heterosexual couple apparently involved in some kind of romantic interchange. For example, a sales clerk serving a client with a businesslike expression on her face was not included in my sample. However, if the clerk and the client seemed to be involved in a flirtation (indicated by the characters looking at each other, smiling at each other, or touching each other or, sometimes, by the caption itself), the image qualified.

6. Following Leiss's typology, I analyzed the representations of persons, settings, and products as well as the accompanying texts (see Leiss 1983).

7. Some advertising images (albeit the minority) go so far as to picture the woman as more assertive than the man. For example, in 1989, an ad encouraging women to give diamonds to men pictured a spunky woman, dressed in business clothes, holding her man by his shoulders in a protective pose. Although this ad was discontinued, it still suggests a tendency in advertising toward the blurring of gender differences.

8. However, the behavior of men and women is not always interchangeable; for example, the man is seen driving more often than his companion; the woman more often rests her head on her companion's shoulder.

9. Birken 1988, 132.

10. Lystra 1989.

11. Barthes 1979, 4.

12. Schudson 1986, 214.

13. Bloch 1988.

14. Cross 1992, 176.

15. See Goffman 1967.

16. See chapter 4 for further development of this idea.

17. Green 1990, 131, 130.

18. Jameson 1984, 68.

19. See Machor 1987.

20. Marchand 1985.

21. Lystra 1989, 20.

22. Rothman 1984; McKinsey 1985.

23. Lystra 1989, 38.

24. See Lears 1981; Susman 1986.

25. See Jameson 1984.

26. However, the movement also celebrated nationalist themes, as in the paintings of Frederic Church.

27. Jameson, 1984.

28. Hebdige 1988, 197.

29. This idea is developed further in chapter 5.

30. To the extent, however, that these ad couples are white and heterosexual, they obviously exclude non-Caucasian ethnic minorities and homosexuals.

31. Green 1990.

32. Terry Eagleton (1986) has observed that the all-inclusive rhetoric of postmodern culture has affinities with transnational capitalism, which transcends boundaries.

33. Urry 1990.

34. Cross 1992.

35. See Gartman 1991.

36. Lash 1990.

37. Bourdieu 1979a.

38. Hirsh 1976.

39. Collins and Coltrane 1991.

40. Bloch 1988.

41. Lash 1990.

42. See Lyotard 1984.

43. Baudrillard 1972.

44. Marchand 1985, 235.

45. Leiss 1983, 15.

46. Cancian 1987.

47. Another reason why upper-middle-class respondents chose figures 1 or 4 more often than working-class respondents might be because they easily recognized in those images their own practices of frequently dining out or having a "special" meal at home (in fact, the products advertised are targeted to professional groups).

48. Kellner 1992, 147.

49. Ibid., 147–48.

50. Lash and Urry 1987, 14.

CHAPTER 4. AN ALL-CONSUMING LOVE

1. Durkheim 1973, 179.

2. See for example Goffman 1967; Wuthnow 1987; Moore and Myerhoff 1977; Alexander 1988a.

3. Although I agree with Goffman and Wuthnow that we should expand applications of the concept of ritual, I disagree with their contention that *any* strongly codified social behavior qualifies as ritual. Along with Goody (1977), I suggest that rituals point to those behaviors that are both formal and repetitive.

4. Zerubavel 1981.

5. *Woman*, April 1988, 27.

6. The couple among all my interviewees who seemed to be the most happily married had been celebrating for seven years the sixth of every month because they "had met on a 6th." This couple, who seemed to have an intense romantic bond, also had an intense ritual life.

7. One could speculate that this is one of the reasons for the wide appeal of Doisneau's picture "Le Baiser de l'hotel de ville," featuring a couple passionately kissing each other on a busy street, oblivious to the passersby and encapsulated in the private space of their embrace.

8. Even "open" couples such as Sartre and Beauvoir held a clear distinction between their "peripheral" affairs and their own "central" commitment to each other. When the distinction was blurred, conflict and resentment ensued.

9. Respondents were careful to draw this boundary. For example, as a female respondent put it, "your lover should be your best friend. Love is not friendship, it encompasses friendship, it is a much more complete kind of thing" (interview 49). When referring to a friend who may be confused with a lover, people say "he or she is just a friend." No one says, on the other hand "he or she is just a lover."

10. Although this man was the only one in the sample to have used such a clearly religious vocabulary, these metaphors are culturally pertinent in the modern romantic discourse.

11. See Otto 1923. The claim that the reverse is true can also be made, that is, that religiosity, and mysticism in particular, stem from (manifest or repressed) libido (consider for example Saint-Theresa's religious ecstasies during the sixteenth century). Because this issue is too complex to be addressed here, I am content to simply point to the affinity between religious and amorous discourses.

12. Durkheim 1985, 129.

13. Even this should be qualified, because to be romantic, making love needs to be separated from the routine act of making love. One obtains this romantic or special character of making love in the same way that one makes a meal romantic, that is, by creating an appropriate background and atmosphere.

14. Because cultural activities are based on cultural capital in more obvious ways than either gastronomic or touristic activities, I study them separately in chapter 8.

15. Bachen and Illouz, forthcoming.

16. In the research by Bachen and Illouz (forthcoming), children similarly most often characterized a romantic dinner in a restaurant in terms of candlelight and luxurious items.

17. Finkelstein 1989, 56.

18. This may explain a finding of the sociology of dining according to which "grazing" (going to different places for each part of the meal, e.g., having a cocktail in one place, the dinner in a second, and dessert in a third) is practiced mostly by couples. By fragmenting the activity of dining out, the couple can also keep renewing sources of pleasure and stimulation.

19. However, it is important to emphasize that the symbolic efficacy of these rituals can hold only if they are not repeated too frequently. In fact, because upper-middle-class respondents are likely to hold jobs that demand that they often eat out and dress formally, they value more highly the informal character of the romantic dinner at home. The reverse is true for couples who rarely have opportunities to go out.

20. Bourdieu 1973. It is irrelevant to my argument that this preference is a post-hoc rationale, which makes a virtue out of lesser economic means, and that ethnic restaurants are themselves instruments of distinction.

21. Sombart 1967. Following Douglas and Isherwood (1979), I define luxury as items that are first to be eliminated in times of economic crisis.

22. Veblen 1979.

23. Wuthnow 1987, 108.

24. Alexander 1988a, 190.

25. Bataille 1967.

26. For example, working- or middle-class couples who celebrate their anniversaries in a very expensive hotel or restaurant.

27. Leiss 1983, 15.

28. The travel literature from earlier in the nineteenth century reveals striking differences: travel was not for fun but for education; Tocqueville is, of course, the most famous example.

29. See Novak 1981; Lovejoy 1948.

30. Barbara Novak (1981) has found four themes characterizing the pictorial representation of nature in American painting of the nineteenth century: nature as primordial wilderness, as the garden of the world, as the original paradise, and as America awaiting the regained paradise attending the millennium. These themes are intertwined with the representation of romance.

31. Mandler 1984; Bartlett 1932; van Dijk 1980.

32. Leiss 1978; Scitovsky, 1976.

33. See Dutton and Aron 1974.

34. Turner 1974, 232, 14.

35. Turner 1977.

36. Jakle 1985; MacCannell 1976.

37. This view is shared by MacCannell in his analysis of the phenomenology of the tourist experience: "Sightseeing is a ritual performed to the differentiation of society. Sightseeing is a kind of collective striving for a transcendence of the modern totality, a way of attempting to overcome the discontinuity of modernity, of incorporating its fragments into unified experience" (1976, 13).

38. Turner 1967.

39. Jameson 1981, 110.

40. Featherstone 1983, 6.

41. Featherstone 1992b; Fiske 1989.

42. Alexander 1988a.

43. Csikszentmihalyi and Rochberg-Halton 1981.

44. In this perspective, Laski (1959, 119–22), Ewen and Ewen (1982), and Marchand (1985) fruitfully suggest that the culture of consumption, embodied for them in advertising, capitalizes on the need for the sacred and for "life-enhancing feelings," including love and marriage.

45. Ricoeur 1986.

46. Adorno and Horkheimer 1972; Marcuse 1963; Fromm 1956.

47. Kern 1994.

48. See McGovern, forthcoming. It should be noted that Marx himself saw capitalism as a revolutionary force with emancipatory powers.

49. Lukács 1971.

50. There is a distinction to be made here between luxury goods and travel goods. While the former were often viewed by respondents as a purely commercial ingredient to romance, the latter were never viewed by the respondents as "phony," "clichéd," "glitzy," or "fancy." The travel formula of romance is the most deeply mystified, i.e., perceived as autonomous from the market that produced it.

51. See chapter 8 for a fuller exploration of this question.

52. See Corcuff 1991.

53. See Elster 1985.

54. See ibid.; Leiss, 1988.

55. Elster 1985, 5. Although I do not advocate methodological individualism, I agree with Elster's insistance that we must explain the mechanism by which the macro level is produced and sustained in terms of actors' desires and beliefs. But contrary to Elster, I do not think that such explanation must *only* involve individual desires and beliefs.

56. Baudrillard uses the term "seduction." For him, what characterizes modern capitalism is that we have moved from a regime of oppression to a regime of seduction.

57. I thank Michele Richman for having read and commented on an early draft of this chapter.

CHAPTER 5. REAL FICTIONS AND FICTIONAL REALTIES

1. Shakespeare 1984, 104.

2. Flaubert 1874.

3. For example, in 1939 the sociologist Baber could write, in reaction to the movies and popular literature of his time, that "the literature of love has brought into being a cult of romance that dominates the thinking of both old and young. . . . It is a wishful cult, ignoring the basic realities of life and building its castles in the clouds of fancy, where none but knights and ladies, princes and princesses exist" (Baber 1939, 203). This theme is discussed in chapter 2.

4. Denzin, for example, contends that movies "shape real life, lived emotional experiences [such as] love, romance . . . " (1990, 97).

5. This remark applies to the character of Madame Bovary and not to Flaubert's writing, which, as Huyssen (1986) notes, prefigures high modernism.

6. Kellner 1989, 244.

7. Ellis 1960; Singer 1987.

8. Featherstone 1992b, 268.

9. Shuman 1986; van Dijk 1984; Gulich and Quastoff 1985; Gergen 1988.

10. MacIntyre 1984. The experience and communication of romantic love is embedded in narrative convention as such as the first encounter ("We met at a party and I liked her immediately"), the declaration of love ("He told me he loved me on Christmas Day"), the obstacles ("He was not religious" or "Her parents did not really like me" or "We didn't really have a good sexual relationship"), the outcome of the relationship ("We ended up getting married," "We finally split up," "We decided to become an open couple," etc.).

11. MacIntyre 1984. See also Lyotard 1984.

12. Featherstone 1992a.

13. The story is adapted from an actual story first published in the *San Francisco Chronicle* and quoted in Burgess and Wallin 1953, 151.

14. The respondents most likely to believe in love at first sight were men, of all social groups, and occasionally working women. Middle-class women were rarely prepared to believe this story. Chapters 7 and 8 offer tentative explanations for this.

15. See, for example, respondents' interpretations of figure 2 in chapter 3.

16. It is this tension between love and sex that informs ads like that for the 1991 film *An Indecent Woman:* "Between lust and love, she must choose." Although the 1980s witnessed a sharp increase in the representation of sex, "love" and "sex" are still recognized as separate domains.

17. For example, although it is legitimate to marry someone because he or she is "very smart" or "very interesting," few people would admit to marrying someone on the sole basis of sexual attraction or sexual talents.

18. Seidman 1991.

19. There are, of course, such examples in the past, as Casanova's *Memoirs* amply attest to. But by and large, a legitimate separation between the two categories of narrative, both for men and women (of course mostly for men), had to wait until after World War II.

20. For example, the Platonic tradition viewed the intense feelings accompanying love as ephemeral and as a disorder of mind and body (see Plato's *Symposium*). The Platonic opposition between "real" and "illusory" love is an instance of its more general suspicion of the realm of immediate sense as concealing "real" reality. Only through effort and knowledge can one discover the ultimate reality hidden behind the veil of appearances, and this was meant to apply to love as well as to metaphysics. This view of truth and self was amplified and reinforced by Christianity.

21. This last claim does not hold always true, as some respondents said that precisely because the protagonists of story 3 are too concerned with financial security, and because they are a two-career couple, they will be likely to divorce.

22. See Schutz 1967.

23. Common sense can be defined as "a body of knowledge common to a group, pertaining to nature, human nature, and social situations and thought to be rooted in a uniformity of human experience" (In van Holthoon and Olson 1987, 121).

24. Thomas Luckman defines "experience" as "those events in the stream of consciousness which stand out as topics to which the self attends, which are memo-rable rather than belonging to the flow of 'petites perceptions'" (van Holthoon and Olson 1987, 183). By asking for the respondents' own most memorable stories, one gains access to those events that are most significant for the romantic self.

25. Simmel 1984.

26. As Barbara Herrnstein Smith (1968) so acutely notices, a "closure" implies structure and differs from the mere ceasing of an activity.

27. Stone 1977, 191.

28. Luhmann 1986b, 8–9. Luhmann explains the pervasiveness of the romantic ideal in the novel by the fact that its internal structure fits the novel's semiotic temporality. Other explanations suggest that the theme of romantic love was codified in the novel because it is consonant with bourgeois psychological individualism and the linear conception of time; see Watt 1957.

29. Bruner 1987, 13.

30. Lyman and Scott 1975, 149.

31. Ibid., 151.

32. Lyman 1990, 217.

33. Scitovsky 1976.

34. Featherstone 1992a.

35. Featherstone 1992b.

36. Scitovsky 1976, 61.

37. Hirshman 1979, 27.

38. A psychological contradiction exists "when one individual simultaneously entertains beliefs and desires from which a contradiction can be logically derived" (Elster 1985, 44).

39. Goode 1968. Although this proposition obviously holds true more for women than for men, men by and large have also had to follow a norm of sexual restraint, if not total monogamy.

40. Examples abound. Among the most famous are Rousseau's *Julie, ou la nouvelle Heloise,* Goethe's *Werther,* Hugo's *Les Misérables,* Wagner's *Tristan und Isolde,* Verdi's *La Traviata,* and Puccini's *La Bohème.*

41. See Seidman 1991.

42. On "affinities," see Weber 1976; on "structures of feeling," Williams 1977. On the transience and ceaseless novelty of postmodern experience, see Scitovsky 1976; Leiss, Kline, and Jhally 1988; Lears 1980; Harvey 1989; Jameson 1984; Featherstone 1992b.

43. Scitovsky 1976, 58.

44. This does not mean that the affair has the anarchic and "disorganized" character often postulated by postmodern theorists. Quite the contrary: as the recent study on sexual behavior undertaken by Laumann and his associates (1994) suggests, despite the removal of barriers of locality, race, religion, most people chose sexual partners quite similar to themselves.

45. See Jameson 1987; Harvey 1989.

46. See Urry 1990 and Lash and Urry 1987.

47. Bell 1980.

48. I wish to thank Sigal Goldin for having brought to my attention the connection between "collage" and the postmodern experience of "romantic intensities."

49. As Koselleck puts it, "My thesis is that in modern times the difference between experience and expectation has increasingly expanded; more precisely, that modernity is first understood as a new age from the time that expectations have distanced themselves evermore from all previous experience" (quoted in Habermas 1990, 12).

50. Eco 1985, 17. I thank José Brunner for having brought this article to my attention.

51. An example is the popular 1993 movie *Sleepless in Seattle,* which can convince us of yet another love at first sight story only by quoting self-consciously and ironically the romantic Hollywood formula of romance.

52. However, one must qualify Baudrillard's analysis and add that these abstract and anonymous "masses" have clearly defined social identities: most of them are cultural intermediaries, academics, or artists. In chapter 8, I analyze at greater length how these postmodern semiotic "deconstructions" are grounded within specific cultural habituses. It is enough for the moment to observe that highly educated respondents are most prone to this type of "deconstructive" suspicion of media images of romance. Although working-class people do not manifest a similar deconstructive distance and do not use it for the same purposes (social and cultural distinction), they exhibit, albeit to a lesser degree, the same suspicion of mass media. Working-class respondents manifest such feelings as a sense of "hyperreality," "spectacle," and "simulation," but this is not an articulate and self-conscious ethos, as it is for respondents with more cultural capital.

53. I owe this last observation to Elchanan Ben-Porath.

54. Jameson 1981.

CHAPTER 6. REASON WITHIN PASSION

1. Bell 1976.

2. Weber, cited in Benhabib 1986, 183; Giddens 1971, 152.

3. Weber 1958. Although Adorno and Horkheimer (1972) modified Weber's concept of rationalization, they too held that processes of rationalization underwrote the project of modernity. They viewed "instrumental reason" as the main vector of social oppression, repression of desires, and domination of nature.

4. See Weber 1958; Gerth and Mills 1958.

5. Collins 1986, 78–79.

6. Rothman 1984; Lewis 1983

7. The Marriage Education Movement analyzed by Bailey (1988) was instituted to address "the why's and how's" of marriage on college campuses, in hopes of countering the threat that "modern life" posed to the structure and cohesiveness of the family.

8. I have analyzed all the articles pertaining to love and marriage in *Cosmopolitan* and *Woman* during a period of six months from January to June 1988. These two women's magazines were preferred over many others because they treat romantic relationships more frequently and in greater depth than magazines having a more domestic focus (e.g., *Woman's Day, Ladies' Home Journal,* and *Good Housekeeping*). In addition, I analyzed articles dealing with the same issues in such women's magazines as *Self, New Woman, Harper's Bazaar.* The total sample was thirty-five articles. I also occasionally refer to popular self-help books. The size and the time frame of this sample may be considered too narrow to adequately reflect the larger content patterns of the two magazines, but this objection can be skirted by suggesting that my study does not aim at validating a set of hypotheses quantitatively. Rather, its purpose is to generate hypotheses and explore connections between social theory, culture, and love.

The "theme" of an article is provided by what T. A. van Dijk calls the macrostructure of a text, "the semantic information that provides . . . overall unity to the discourse" (1985, 116). As van Dijk has amply demonstrated, "summaries" or "leads" reflect a text's macrostructures. (The summary corresponds to the few lines, usually in bold type, that appear before the article itself; these lines are supposed to capture the main gist of the article. The lead stands between the headline and the body of the article.) In this study, the theme of an article is equivalent to its summary or its lead.

Following theories of metaphors put forth by Lakoff 1987, Lakoff and Johnson 1980, and Krippendorff 1990, I analyze the dominant metaphorical fields within which romantic love is conceptualized. "A metaphor is a pattern, an explanatory structure, tied to a word or expression that is successful in a familiar domain of experiences and actions it thereby organizes and coordinates in its own way. Metaphors have entailments" (Krippendorff 1990, 11). Embedded in metaphors are explanatory models of the social world and logical conceptual structures. By "metaphorical field" I mean a set of metaphors that have similar logical entailments.

The "normative logic" is the set of assumptions that both underlie and exceed statements about a particular object. It is the structured but implicit, value-laden (axiological) dimension of discourses, the dimension most difficult to formalize and operationalize because it pertains to the tacit assumptions of discourse.

9. Raphael, B. J., "How to Talk with Your Lover," *New Woman,* February 1988, 45.

10. Arond, M., and Pauker, S., "Five Essentials to Keep a Marriage Together," *New Woman,* February 1988, 75.

11. Cowan, C., and Kinder, M., "Passion: How to Ignite It, Reignite It, Make It Last," *Cosmopolitan,* April 1988, 258–66.

12. See Gillis 1988.

13. *Self,* April 1988, 132; Dormen, L., " *Woman,* April 1988, 26–27.

14. Kelman, J., "What Starts Love," *Glamour,* 1987, 208.

15. Extending Herbert Marcuse's critique of subjectivity, Erich Fromm suggested in *The Art of Loving* that the problem of modern love was that it had come to be conceived in the same terms as capitalist economic exchanges. He noted that the modern ideal of the couple as a "working team" is tacitly based on the same calculation of gains and losses as capitalist ideology (Fromm 1956). Fromm was one of the first to articulate how the capitalist value system had come to frame romantic love. Like Marcuse, Fromm held a utopian vision of love and advocated a model of romantic relationships that would mark humanity's entry into an alternative social order.

16. *Cosmopolitan,* June 1988, 130.

17. *Self,* April 1988, 50.

18. See Bellah et al. 1985.

19. Raphael, "How to Talk with Your Lover," *New Woman,* February 1988, 45.

20. Druck, K., and Duey, K., "What Does It Mean When He Says He Loves You?" *Cosmopolitan,* May 1988, 48–49.

21. *Self*, April 1988.

22. Raphael, "How to Talk with Your Lover," *New Woman*, February 1988, 49.

23. Banks, A., "The Love Doctors," *Harper's Bazaar*, February 1988, 192.

24. See, for example, the model of "marriage markets" in Becker 1981.

25. Cited in Frank 1988, 186.

26. Kohn 1969. It was Marx rather than Weber who insisted on the pivotal role that language plays in the "commercialization" of human relationships. "For the bourgeois it is all the easier to prove on the basis of this language the identity of commercial and individual, or even universal, human relations, as this language is a product of the bourgeoisie, and therefore both in actuality and in language the relations of buying and selling have been made the basis of all others" (cited in Elster 1985, 82).

27. The consequences of this characteristic become apparent in chapter 8, when romantic practices are compared along the dimension of class.

28. Lears 1981, 37.

29. Bellah et al. 1985, 85.

30. See Degler 1980.

31. The second expression comes from Whyte 1990. This whole topic will be dealt with more fully in chapter 7.

32. Bellah et al. 1985.

33. Banks, "The Love Doctors," *Harper's Bazaar*, February 1988, 192.

34. Dranov, P., "Sweet Scientific Mystery of Love," *Cosmopolitan*, April 1988, 264–69.

35. Ibid., 264.

36. Arond and Pauker, "Five Essentials to Keep a Marriage Together," *New Woman*, February 1988, 75.

37. Ridge, J., "When Your Ex Dates (or Falls For) a Close Friend," *Woman*, February 1988, 16–17.

38. The reflexivity conveyed by the therapeutic ethos is brought about by formal procedures of speech rather than by "content." My focus on formal rather than content-based schemes of thought parallels Habermas's (1987) and Popper's (1972) view of science as constituted by a set of formal procedures rather than by a specific content.

39. Angenot 1982, 138, my translation.

40. Banks, "The Love Doctors," *Harper's Bazaar*, February 1988, 192.

41. Raphael, *New Woman*, August 1988, 56.

42. Cowan and Kinder, *Cosmopolitan*, November 1987, 259.

43. Dormen, "The Man Who Got Away," *Woman*, July 1989. 47.

44. S. Helm, "On Falling in Love with a Man That Everyone (Including You) Thinks Is Wrong for You," *Woman*, October 1988, 48.

45. Ibid., 48.

46. In suggesting a strong analogy between the therapeutic ethos and the rules of reasoning at work in the social sciences, I do not claim that women's magazines use this analogy explicitly and consciously. Rather, I suggest that self-observation according to such rules is implicit in the therapeutic ethos.

47. Rieff 1966, 50.

48. Raphael, "How to Talk to Your Lover," *New Woman*, February 1988, 45.

49. See Adorno and Horkheimer 1972.

50. Kellner, 1989: 53

51. Foucault 1975.

52. Habermas 1987. Positing an analytical distinction between market and state (what he calls "system integration") on the one hand and the lifeworld of interpersonal relationships ("social integration") on the other, Habermas distinguishes between "communicative action," defined as action oriented toward the maintenance of a shared intersubjective framework, and "instrumental action," or that aimed at securing one's goals and interests through the implementation of specific means.

53. Cancian 1987. See also Zaretsky 1973.

54. Lewis 1983, 199.

55. See Leach 1981.

56. It goes without saying that I am not suggesting that women's magazines as a whole promote feminist politics: as their fiction and advertisements amply attest, they are far from feminist ideals. The previous analysis does suggest, however, that the discourse of love in these magazines has changed in support of increasing equality between men and women.

57. Giddens 1992, 185. Giddens is here quoting David Held on models of democracy.

58. Fromm 1956, 86.

CHAPTER 7. THE REASONS FOR PASSION

1. The irrational nature of love has been indirectly reinforced by various social scientific theories. Psychoanalysis in particular claims that when falling in love, we reenact a past and unconscious conflict, thus suggesting that our romantic choices are arbitrary from the standpoint of reason, although explicable in light of the deeper and more obscure irrational forces of the unconscious.

2. Durrell 1982, 86.

3. Tierney and Scott 1984, 312.

4. Kephart 1967, 476. Scanzoni (1970) found similarly that women were more concerned about their prospective mate's social status than were men.

5. Simpson, Campbell, and Bersheid 1986.

6. Shorter 1977.

7. See Laumann 1966; Laumann et al. 1994.

8. Waller 1937.

9. Laumann 1966; Kalmijn 1991.

10. This position is taken, for example, by Scanzoni (1970) in his analysis of marriage and class.

11. The distinction between agapic and erosic love partially overlaps that between "realist" and "idealist" love, but it also contains different analytical categories that are more directly relevant to this chapter.

12. Barthes 1978, quoted in Soble 1990, 140.

13. Quoted in Soble 1990, 142.

14. The distinction between agapic and erosic bears a resemblance to Parsons's (1951) distinction between particularistic and universalistic roles.

15. See for example *Pride and Prejudice* (Austen 1949).

16. In eighteenth-century America, which was more liberal than Europe, Benjamin Franklin began courting a lady and wrote her parents, rather ingenuously, that he "expected as much money with their daughter as would pay off my remaining debt on the printing-house, which I believe was then above a hundred pounds" (quoted in Hunt 1959, 287).

17. Flandrin 1976.

18. Bourdieu 1977, 83.

19. Bourdieu 1972, 140.

20. See Becker 1981.

21. Hirschman 1986, 36. It should be noticed that the second aspect of Hirschman's definition is not compatible with the theory of habitus as a set of semiconscious dispositions by which agents tactically and strategically act in the world. One of the problems of the notion of habitus is that it does not enable one to distinguish between those actions that are the outcome of conscious and rational calculations and actions that follow the unconscious logic of incorporated habitus. Aspects of romantic practices conform to Hirschman's emphasis on "rational calculation," while others correspond more closely to Bourdieu's characterization of habitus.

22. Page 1988, 63, 89.

23. See Goode 1968; Linton 1936.

24. Proust 1993, 182–83, my translation.

25. Kephart 1967.

26. Lamont 1992.

27. It is instructive to note that working-class respondents understood this question as "Is *lack* of money important for love?"

28. Page 1988, 65. The conflict between personal and social merit has been an important theme of Hollywood cinema since at least the 1940s. Protagonists are often faced with a choice between potential partners, one of whom is of higher social standing while the other possesses such attractive personal qualities as honesty, simplicity of heart, or spontaneity.

29. One may object that these findings are artificial in that upper-middle-class respondents are more articulate about their expectations, but it is a strong premise of this research that actors, regardless of their position in the social hierarchy, are aware of their desires and goals and that they are able to formulate them.

30. These differences are consistent with the results of Kohn's (1969) study of patterns of socialization of working-class and middle-class children. He found that the parents of the latter valued and encouraged qualities such as curiosity, self-control, and happiness, whereas the parents of the former stressed honesty and obedience.

31. It should be clear, however, that my claim does not apply to moral behavior in general but only to the specific domain of the formation of friendships or romantic attachments.

32. Bourdieu 1977, 171.

33. Rubin 1976; Cancian 1988.

34. Kent 1987, 95.

35. In the 1991 movie *White Palace,* the hero, a rich and successful lawyer, has an affair with a working-class waitress. Their sex is passionate; the first sign that things will not go smoothly appears when he tells her, "Let's talk." It then becomes obvious that they do not share the same conversational style and references. But unlike Henry Higgins in Shaw's *Pygmalion,* he does not attempt to raise her above her low linguistic condition; instead, he leaves his own "hypocrite" educated milieu to live the simpler and more authentic life that she embodies. This movie articulates clearly the fact that so-called barriers of communication are quite often class barriers.

36. Bourdieu 1991, 61.

37. Lawrence 1962, 8.

38. See Bellah et al. 1985.

39. See DiMaggio and Mohr 1985.

40. The explanation given here does not, of course, cover the entire spectrum of social groups or romantic relationships, but it does provide preliminary directions for exploring how many middle-class Americans decide to engage in a relationship and unleash their passion.

41. Bourdieu 1980.

42. By "gratuity" I mean the performance of certain acts with no expectations of reward and material benefit. Giving money anonymously to a charitable organization and donating blood are in this category.

43. Research in the social psychology of love reinforces this myth by distinguishing between "attraction" and "attachment," the first being presumably blind and mindless, the second reasonable. My dichotomy covers an altogether different range of phenomena but, in the context of contemporary culture, views the beginning of a relationship as more rational than its subsequent phases.

44. See Mauss 1967.

45. Bourdieu 1977. In the next chapter, I elucidate how romantic gifts bear the mark of the giver's social identity and cultural habitus.

46. This inversion of market logic was ironically illustrated by the hesitant and apologetic way in which a respondent admitted that he preferred the "expensive object":

As a romantic present, would you prefer to be given a rose with a poem or an expensive object?

Honestly?

Yes. You can say whatever you want.

An expensive object. (Male physician, interview 8)

This man prefaced his answer as if acknowledging an important violation to norms of gratuity.

47. It is noteworthy that the market has exploited extensively the gratuitous character of the romantic gift by flooding the arena with inexpensive, "small"

objects expressly designed to convey one's inner feelings. Valentine's Day is celebrated in the United States by the mass production of greeting cards, teddy bears, coffee mugs, and innumerable heart-shaped artifacts.

48. Boltanski 1990.

49. Bourdieu 1972, 1979.

50. Bourdieu 1972.

CHAPTER 8. THE CLASS OF LOVE

1. For example, in his *Marriage and Morals* (1929), Bertrand Russell claimed that poetry and art are "intrinsic elements" of romantic love, thus ingenuously elevating his own cultural practices to universal standards.

2. Lantz 1982, 362. However, the reverse argument, that the propertyless classes were more likely to make choices based on personal inclination, has been forcefully advocated by E. P. Thompson (1966) and Edward Shorter (1977). Rejecting the claim that elite groups were the pioneers of romantic love, they suggest that romantic love flourished among the popular classes precisely because social or economic interests were less at stake than among the nobility. In a similar vein, Flandrin (1976, 1981) has suggested that in eighteenth-century France the elites' marriages mostly followed considerations of family alliances and economic interest and that the "popular classes," as he calls them, were more likely to perform love marriages. These views are all congruent with Engels's view of love.

3. Lantz 1982, 362.

4. See Lamont 1992; Lamont and Fournier 1992; Halle 1992.

5. While the "massification of culture" hypothesis claims that mass culture and mass consumption have leveled heterogeneous cultural practices, I suggest that the market intensifies inequalities but draws them into a common arena.

6. This claim differs from analyses of other domains of culture. For example, Paul DiMaggio (1982) and Lawrence Levine (1988) have convincingly showed that in the domain of art and culture the emergence of new elites has brought about a sharper division between the categories of art and nonart and the creation of "highbrow" culture.

7. As a corollary to this, and again as we might expect, it is noteworthy that the theme of nature has thoroughly pervaded the romantic imagination and romantic practices of both working-class and upper-middle class respondents.

8. See Bailey 1988. Theodor Dreiser's *An American Tragedy* offers a powerful illustration of these differences, as late as the 1920s.

9. Gartman 1991.

10. I enclosed in the interview schedule three greeting cards. Card 1 was a Hallmark card showing a pastoral landscape with love poem superimposed over it: "I will love you / As long as I can dream / As long as I can think. . . . " Card 2 is apparently intended to be humorous; its message, set in large capitals, reads, "I love you! I want you! I need you! You mean everything to me!" Card 3 reproduces, without any accompanying words, the abstract blue forms of Matisse's "The Pool." In choosing these three cards I assumed that each one would tap

into a different cultural habitus: the abstract card reflects the educated classes' proclivity for nonfigurative meaning; the Hallmark uses the traditional and presumably stereotypical rhetoric of romantic love; and the humorous card expresses love but with some distance.

11. Gross 1973.

12. This claim should be qualified since some working-class respondents did show such distance. Age and neighborhood seemed to be decisive factors: older respondents living in suburbs and working in "traditional" working-class jobs were less likely to deconstruct romance than were young, urban working-class respondents.

13. The self-proclaimed iconoclasm of these intellectuals is well described by Gouldner's (1979) notion of a "culture of critical discourse."

14. Although my examples here are mostly from "new cultural intermediaries," the same holds true for members of the wealthier segments, such as lawyers, investment bankers, and doctors. The last three professional categories showed the same deconstructive tendencies exhibited by artists and academics, although they tended to elaborate on them less.

15. It is interesting to observe how corporations have exploited the ethos of creativity when manufacturing romantic gifts. With the help of computer programs, for example, Swan Corporation manufactures and sells novels whose hero and heroine are given the names of the giver and the recipient. Each novel comes in three variations: "For $45, you choose the hero and heroine's name and get to insert a personal dedication. For $60, there is the ability to make additional choices regarding the couple's hair and eyes color, hobbies, special songs, etc. For $200, you get all the above plus, after filling out a questionnaire longer than the Harvard entrance application, a custom-tailored epilogue" (Streitfeld 1991, 5).

16. See Bernstein 1971; Kohn 1977.

17. See Kohn 1977.

18. See Lamont and Lareau 1988; Lamont 1992; Halle 1992; Hall 1992.

19. Although people with higher incomes use more expensive commodities in their romantic practices, it is important to remember that there is no consistent relationship between a high income and the cost of the romantic commodity. In other words upper-middle-class people who make over $100,000 do not necessarily go only to very "fancy" and expensive restaurants.

20. This finding was a surprise to me and actually contradicted an assumption I had made prior to the analysis, that because of their orientation toward "therapeutic discourse" upper-middle-class people would hold person-centered rather than commodities-centered definitions of romance. I also assumed that working-class people, being "deprived" of a regular practice of expensive romance, would define or recall such instances as the most romantic. While my expectations about the use of therapeutic discourse by middle-class people proved accurate, the remaining expectations did not.

21. Featherstone 1983, 8. Bourdieu (1973) also observed the capacity of people with a high cultural competence to transform mass cultural objects (e.g., Hollywood films) into objects of art (see, for example, the relationship between the French New Wave and the Film Noir). However, in the case referred to by Bourdieu, people with high cultural capital are aware of

the mass or commercial character of the cultural objects and modify it as such. Here, on the other hand, the anti-institutional ethos of the upper middle class is predicated on a denial of the clichéd character of their choices of consumption.

22. Bourdieu 1979.

23. Scitovsky 1976; see chapter 5 above.

24. Levison 1974, 106.

25. Rubin 1992.

26. Collins and Coltrane 1991, 204.

27. However, references to money problems did not occur within the more prosperous segments of the working classes, either.

28. This finding disconfirms the potent myth that busy upper-middle-class people experience romance less often than their working or middle-class counterparts because work has invaded their lives. As clarified in the next section, this is far from being the case.

29. Studies by Hochschild (1989), Kelly (1983), and Harris (1987) have largely demonstrated that working-class women enjoy much less leisure at home than their husbands and than their middle-class counterparts.

30. Collins 1992.

31. Halle 1984, 42.

32. According to an article offering tips on marriage in the upscale women's magazine *Redbook,* "'More relations are ultimately destroyed than enhanced over time,' says David Olson, Ph.D., of the University of Minnesota. 'You have to work at counteracting that by keeping your marriage a priority and investing time and energy in it like you would a job'" (Frank, C., "What's Your Marriage Style?" *Redbook,* May 1994, 93).

33. This finding echoes other studies comparing the working- and upper-middle-classes. In her study of working-class marriage, Lillian Rubin cites a particularly relevant example of a working-class woman who said: " I am not sure what I want. I keep talking to him about communication, and he says, 'Okay, so we're talking; now what do you want?' And I don't know what to say then but I know it's not what I mean" (Rubin 1976, 120).

34. Caplow 1982.

35. Rubin 1976, 116.

36. See Willis 1980.

37. See Rubin 1976.

38. See Komarovsky 1987; Rubin 1976.

39. See Willis 1977; Bourdieu 1979a.

40. See Collins 1992.

41. Ibid., 228.

42. Bryan and Alsikafi 1975.

43. See Rainwater 1965.

44. Rubin 1976, 121.

45. See Ehrenreich 1990.

46. See Rubin 1992.

47. Bourdieu 1979.

48. See Scitovsky 1976; also chapter 5 above.

49. This may explain the finding of the sociology of marriage that upper-middle-class couples, contrary to popular mythology, are much more stable than working-class married couples (Collins and Coltrane 1991).

50. See Zerubavel 1981, from whom I take the phrase "organized disorder."

CONCLUSION

1. Featherstone 1992b.

2. I did not have the benefit of Ulrich and Elisabeth-Gernsheim Beck's insightful analyses on the *Normal Chaos of Love* when I was writing this book.

3. See Kern 1994.

4. Himmelfarb 1995.

5. Kern 1994.

6. Sandel 1984.

7. Bellah 1985.

8. Coontz 1992.

9. See Elshtain 1995.

APPENDIX 1

1. See Mills 1951; Braverman 1974.

2. Wright 1978, 39.

3. Interview 25 was not used because the interviewee was discovered to be not of American origin. Interview 31 was inaudible because of technical problems.

4. Critcher 1980.

5. Manning, 1987

6. The narrative structure of the idealist tradition is characterized by the suddenness of its onset, the struggle of love against social or moral obstacles, the relentless affirmation of the lovers' intense feelings, the superiority of love over sex, and the final (moral) victory of love through death or marriage. It has pervaded elite as well as popular culture.

APPENDIX 2

1. Figures 6–9 (not reproduced) are black-and-white photographs. In figure 6, a Walker Evans photo, father, mother, grandmother, and children sit staring at the camera in a room of utter poverty. They are barely clothed, and the photo conveys a state of naked misery and hard work. Figure 7, Robert Doisneau's famous "Le Baiser de l'hotel de ville," shows a young woman and a young man, in public, in what seems to be a passionate and spontaneous kiss. Figure 8 shows a middle-aged couple sitting in a coffee house in physical proximity to each other, alone, in a private atmosphere, even though the setting is public. Figure 9 shows an elderly couple without physical contact.

References

Abercrombie, N., S. Hill, and B. Turner. 1986. *Sovereign Individuals of Capitalism*. London: Allen and Unwin.

Abu-Lughod, L. 1986. *Veiled Sentiment: Honor and Poetry in a Bedouin Society*. Berkeley: University of California Press.

Adorno, T., and Max Horkheimer. 1972. *The Dialectic of Enlightenment*. New York: Seabury.

Alberoni, F. 1983. *Falling in Love*. Translated by L. Venuti. New York: Random House.

Alexander, J. 1988a. *Durkheimian Sociology: Cultural Studies*. Cambridge: Cambridge University Press.

———. 1988b. *Action and Its Environment*. New York: Columbia University Press.

———. 1988c. "The New Theoretical Movement." In *Handbook of Sociology*, ed. N. Smelser, 77–101. Newbury Park, Calif.: Sage Publications.

———. 1988d. "Rethinking Durkheim's Intellectual Development: On the Complex Origins of a Cultural Sociology." In *Action and Its Environment*, 123–155. New York: Columbia University Press.

Alexander, J., B. Giesen, R. Münch, and N. Smelser, eds. 1987. *The Micro-Macro Link*. Berkeley: University of California Press.

Angenot, M. 1982. *La Parole Pampletaire*. Paris: Payot.

Angus, I., and S. Jhally, eds. 1989. *Cultural Politics in Contemporary America*. New York: Routledge.

Antaki, C., ed. 1988. *Analysing Everyday Explanation*. London: Sage.

Appadurai, A. 1986. "Introduction: Commodities and Values." In *The Social Life of Things: Commodities in Cultural Perspective*, ed. A. Appadurai, 3–61. Cambridge: Cambridge University Press.

Ariés, P. 1962. *Centuries of Childhood: A Social History of Family Life*. New York: Vintage Books.

Aronowitz, S. 1971. "Does the United States Have a New Working Class?" In *The Revival of American Socialism*, ed. G. Fisher, 199–216. New York: Oxford University Press.

———. 1981. *The Crisis of Historical Materialism: Class, Politics, and Culture in Marxist Theory*. New York: Praeger.

———. 1989. "Working Class Culture in the Electronic Age." In *Cultural Politics in Contemporary America*, ed. I. Angus and S. Jhally, 135–55. New York: Routledge.

Ashley, D. 1990. "Habermas and the Completion of 'The Project of Modernity.'" In *Theories of Modernity and Postmodernity*, ed. B. S. Turner, 88–107. London: Sage.

Austen, J. 1949. *Pride and Prejudice*. New York: Pantheon.

Averill, J. R. 1985. "The Social Construction of Emotion, with Special Reference to Love." In *The Social Construction of the Person*, ed. K. Gergen and K. Davis, 89–109. New York: Springer-Verlag.

Baber, R. E. 1939. *Marriage and the Family*. New York: McGraw-Hill.

Bachen, C., and E. Illouz. Forthcoming. "Visions of Romance: A Cognitive Approach to Media Effects." Paper presented at the International Communication Association, Dublin.

Bailey, B. 1987. "Scientific Truth . . . and Love: The Marriage Education Movement in the United States." *Journal of Social History* 20, no. 4: 711–32.

———. 1988. *From Front Porch to Back Seat*. Baltimore: Johns Hopkins University Press.

Bandura, A. 1969. *Principles of Behavior Modification*. New York: Rinehart and Winston.

Barthes, R. 1957. *Mythologies*. Paris: Seuil

———. 1978. *A Lover's Discourse*. Translated by R. Howard. New York: Hill and Wang.

———. 1979. *The Eiffel Tower and Other Mythologies*. Translated by R. Howard. New York: Hill and Wang.

Bartlett, F. 1932. *Remembering*. Cambridge: Cambridge University Press.

Bataille, G. 1957. *L'Érotisme*. Paris: Minuit.

———. 1967. *La Part maudite*. Paris: Minuit

Baudrillard, J. 1970. *La Societe de Consommation*. Paris: Gallimard.

———. 1972. *Pour une critique de l'economie politique du signe*. Paris: Gallimard.

———. 1983. *In the Shadow of the Silent Majorities, or the End of the Social, and Other Essays*. Translated by P. Foss, P. Patton, and J. Johnston. New York: Semiotext(e).

Beck, U., and E. Beck-Gernsheim. 1995. *The Normal Chaos of Love*. Translated by M. Ritter and J. Weibel. Cambridge, U.K.: Polity Press.

Becker, G. 1981. *Marriage Markets*. Cambridge: Harvard University Press.

Bedier, J. 1927. *Tristan and Iseult*. Translated by H. Belloc. New York: A. and C. Boni.

Belasco, W. J. 1979. *Americans on the Road: From Motorcamp to Motel, 1910–1945*. Cambridge: MIT Press.

Bell, D. 1973. *The Coming of Post-Industrial Society*. New York: Basic Books.

———. 1976. *The Cultural Contradictions of Capitalism*. London: Heinemann.

———. 1980. *The Winding Passage: Essays and Sociological Journeys, 1960–1980.* New York: Basic Books.

———. 1990. "Modernism, Postmodernism, and the Decline of Moral Order." In *Culture and Society: Contemporary Debates,* ed. J. Alexander and S. Seidman, 319–29. Cambridge: Cambridge University Press.

Bellah, R., R. Madsen, W. Sullivan, A. Swidler, and S. Tipton. 1985. *Habits of the Heart: Individualism and Commitment in American Life.* Berkeley: University of California Press.

Benhabib, S. 1986. *Critique, Norm, and Utopia: A Study of the Foundations of Critical Theory.* New York: Columbia University Press.

Berger, P. 1986. *The Capitalist Revolution.* New York: Basic Books.

Berger, P., B. Berger, and H. Kellner. 1973. *The Homeless Mind.* New York: Random House.

Berger, P., and H. Kellner. 1981. *Sociology Reinterpreted.* Garden City, N.Y.: Doubleday/Anchor.

Berger, P., and T. Luckmann. 1966. *The Social Construction of Reality.* Garden City, N.Y.: Doubleday.

Bernstein, B. 1971. *Class, Codes and Control.* London: Routledge and Kegan Paul.

Bernstein, R. 1976. *The Restructuring of Social and Political Theory.* Philadelphia: University of Pennsylvania Press.

———. 1985. *Habermas and Modernity.* Cambridge: MIT Press.

Billig, M. 1988. "Methodology and Scholarship in Understanding Ideological Explanation." In *Analysing Everyday Explanation,* ed. C. Antaki, 199–215. London: Sage.

Birken, L. 1988. *Consuming Desire: Sexual Science and the Emergence of a Culture of Abundance, 1871–1914.* Ithaca: Cornell University Press.

Bloch, E. 1988. *The Utopian Function of Art and Literature.* Translated by J. Zipes and F. Mecklenburg. Cambridge: MIT Press.

Blumer, H. 1933. *Movies and Conduct.* New York: Arno Press and The New York Times.

Blumin, S. 1985. "The Hypothesis of Middle-Class Formation in Nineteenth-Century America: A Critique and Some Proposals." *American Historical Review* 90, no. 2: 299–338.

Boltanski, L. 1990. *L'Amour et la justice comme competences.* Paris: Metaillie.

Boorstin, D. 1973. *The Americans: The Democratic Experience.* New York: Random House.

Bordwell, D., K. Thompson, and J. Staiger. 1985. *The Classical Hollywood Cinema: Film Style and Mode of Production.* New York: Columbia University Press.

Boudon, R. 1987. "The Individualistic Tradition in Sociology." In *The Micro-Macro Link,* ed. J. Alexander, B. Giesen, R. Münch, and N. Smelser, 45–70. Berkeley: University of California Press.

Bourdieu, P. 1972. "Marriage Strategies as Strategies of Social Reproduction." In *Family and Society,* ed. R. Forster and O. Ranum, trans. E. Forster and P. Ranum, 117–44. Baltimore: Johns Hopkins University Press.

———. 1977. *Outline of a Theory of Practice.* Translated by R. Nice. Cambridge: Cambridge University Press.

———. 1979a. *La Distinction: Critique sociale du jugement.* Paris: Minuit.

————. 1979b. "Les Trois Etats du capital culturel." *Actes de la recherche en science sociale* 30: 3–6.

————. 1980. *Le Sens pratique*. Paris: Minuit.

————. 1991. *Language and Symbolic Power*. Edited by John B. Thompson. Translated by Gino Raymond and Matthew Adamson. Cambridge: Harvard University Press.

Bower, G., and R. K. Cirilo. 1985. "Cognitive Psychology and Text Processing." In *Handbook of Discourse Analysis,* ed. T. A. van Dijk, 71–105. London: Academic Press.

Braden, D. R. 1991. *Leisure and Entertainment in America*. Dearborn, Mich: Henry Ford Museum and Greenfield Village.

Braverman, H. 1974. *Labor and Monopoly Capital: The Degradation of Work in the Twentieth Century*. New York: Monthly Review Press.

Brubaker, R. 1984. *The Limits of Rationality*. London: George Allen and Unwin.

Bruner, J. 1987. "Life as Narrative." *Social Research* 54, no. 1: 11–32.

Bryan, H., and M. Alsifaki. 1975. *The Case of University Professors*. Sociological Studies, no. 3. Tuscaloosa: University of Alabama Bureau of Public Administration.

Burgess, E. W., and P. Wallin. 1953. *Engagement and Marriage*. Philadelphia: Lippincott.

Burke, K. 1989. *On Symbols and Society*. Edited by J. Gusfield. Chicago: University of Chicago Press.

Callinicos, A. 1989. *Marxist Theory*. Oxford: Oxford University Press.

Campbell, C. 1987. *The Romantic Ethic and the Spirit of Modern Consumerism*. Oxford: Basil Blackwell.

Cancian, F. 1987. *Love in America*. Cambridge: Cambridge University Press.

Caplow, T. 1982. *Middletown Families: Fifty Years of Change and Continuity*. Minneapolis: University of Minnesota Press.

Capellanus, A. 1959. *The Art of Courtly Love*. Translated by J. J. Perry. New York: Ungar.

Caughey, J. 1984. *Imaginary Social Worlds: A Cultural Approach*. Lincoln: University of Nebraska Press.

Chambers, I. 1980. "Rethinking Popular Culture." *Screen Education,* no. 36: 113–18.

Chandler, A. 1977. *The Visible Hand: The Managerial Revolution in American Business*. Cambridge: Harvard University Press, Belknap Press.

Clarke, J., C. Critcher, and R. Johnson, eds. 1980. *Working-Class Culture: Studies in History and Theory*. New York: Saint Martin's.

Clifford, J. 1986. "On Ethnographic Allegory." In *Writing Culture,* ed. J. Clifford and G. Marcus, 98–121. Berkeley: University of California Press.

Clifford, J., and G. Marcus, eds. 1986. *Writing Culture: The Poetics and Politics of Ethnography*. Berkeley: University of California Press.

Collins, R. 1975. *Conflict Sociology: Toward an Explanatory Science*. New York: Academic Press.

————. 1981. "Micro-Translation as a Theory-Building Strategy. In *Advances in Social Theory and Methodology,* ed. K. Knorr-Cetina and A. Cicourel, 81–108. Boston: Routledge and Kegan Paul.

————. 1983. *Sociological Theory.* San Francisco: Jossey-Bass.

————. 1985. *Three Sociological Traditions.* New York: Oxford University Press.

————. 1986. *Max Weber.* Beverly Hills, Calif.: Sage.

————. 1992. "Women and the Production of Status Cultures." In *Cultivating Differences,* ed. M. Lamont and M. Fournier, 213–31. Chicago: University of Chicago Press.

Collins, R., and S. Coltrane. 1991. *Sociology of Marriage and the Family: Gender, Love, and Property.* Chicago: Nelson-Hall.

Coontz, S. 1992. *The Way We Never Were: American Families and the Nostalgia Trap.* New York: Basic Books

Corcuff, P. 1991. "Elements d'epistemologie ordinaire du syndicalisme." *Revue Française de science politique* 41, no. 4: 515–35.

Couvares, F. 1983. "The Triumph of Commerce: Class Culture and Mass Culture in Pittsburgh." In *Working-Class America,* ed. M. Frisch and D. Walkowitz, 123–52. Urbana: University of Illinois Press.

Critcher, C. 1980. "Sociology, Cultural Studies and the Post-War Working class." In *Working-Class Culture,* ed. J. Clarke, C. Critcher, and R. Johnson, 13–40. New York: Saint Martin's.

Cross, G. 1992. *Time and Money: The Making of Consumer Culture.* London: Routledge.

Csikszenmihalyi, M., and E. Rochberg-Halton. 1981. *The Meaning of Things.* New York: Cambridge University Press.

Darnton, R. 1989. "What is the History of Books?" In *Reading in America,* ed. C. Davidson, 27–52. Baltimore: Johns Hopkins University Press.

Davidson, C. 1986. *Revolution and the Word: The Rise of the Novel in America.* New York: Oxford University Press.

————. ed. 1989. *Reading in America.* Baltimore: Johns Hopkins University Press.

de Certeau, M. 1984. *The Practice of Everyday Life.* Translated by S. Rendell. Berkeley: University of California Press.

Degler, C. 1980. *At Odds.* Oxford: Oxford University Press.

D'Emilio, J., and E. Freedman. 1988. *Intimate Matters: A History of Sexuality in America.* New York: Harper and Row.

Denzin, N. K. 1984. *On Understanding Emotion.* San Francisco: Jossey-Bass.

————. 1990. "On Understanding Emotion: The Interpretive-Cultural Agenda." In *Research Agendas in the Sociology of Emotions,* ed. T. Kemper, 85–116. Albany: State University of New York Press.

Denzin, N. K., and Y. Lincoln, eds. 1994. *Handbook of Qualitative Analysis.* Newbury Park: Sage.

de Rougemont, D. 1983. *Love in the Western World.* Translated by M. Belgion. Princeton: Princeton University Press.

DiMaggio, P. 1982. "Cultural Entrepreneurship in Nineteenth-Century Boston: The Creation of an Organizational Base for High Culture in America." *Media, Culture and Society* 4, no. 1 (January): 33–50.

DiMaggio, P., and J. Mohr. 1985. "Cultural Capital, Education Attainment, and Marital Selection." *American Journal of Sociology* 90, no. 6: 1231–61.

DiMaggio, P., and M. Useem. 1978. "Social Class and Arts Consumption: The Origins of Class Differences in Exposure to the Arts in America." *Theory and Society* 5: 141–61.

Douglas, M., and B. Isherwood. 1979. *The World of Goods*. New York: Basic Books.

Dulles, F. R. 1965. *A History of American Recreation: America Learns to Play*. 2d ed. New York: Appleton-Century-Crofts.

During, S., ed. 1993. *The Cultural Studies Reader*. New York: Routledge.

Durkheim, E. 1973. *On Morality and Society*. Edited and translated by Robert N. Bellah. Chicago: University of Chicago Press.

———. 1985. *Readings from Emile Durkheim*. Edited by K. Thompson. London: The Open University.

Durrell, L. 1982. *Clea*. New York: Washington Square.

Dutton, D. G., and A. P. Aron. 1974. "Some Evidence for Heightened Sexual Attraction under Conditions of High Anxiety." *Journal of Personality and Social Psychology* 30: 510–17.

Duvall, E. M., with J. D. Johnson. 1967. *Art of Dating*. New York: Association Press.

Eagleton, T. 1986. *Against the Grain: Essays 1975–1985*. London: Verso.

Eco, U. 1975. *A Theory of Semiotics*. Bloomington: Indiana University Press.

———. 1985. "Reflections on *The Name of the Rose*." *Encounter* 64, no. 4 (April): 7–19.

Ehrenreich, B. 1989. *Fear of Falling: The Inner Life of the Middle Class*. New York: Pantheon.

Elias, N. 1974. "Avant-Propos." *La Societe de Cour*. Paris: Flammarion.

Ellis, A. 1960. *Art and Science of Love*. New York: Stuart

Elshtain, J. B. 1995. *Democracy on Trial*. New York: Basic Books.

Elster, J. 1985. *Making Sense of Marx*. New York: Cambridge University Press.

———. ed. 1987. *The Multiple Self*. Cambridge: Cambridge University Press.

Engels, F. 1985. *Origin of The Family, Property, and the State*. London: Penguin.

Eribon, D. 1990. *De prés et de loin: Entretiens avec Claude Lévi-Strauss*. Paris: Seuil

Ewen, S. 1976. *Captains of Consciousness*. New York: McGraw-Hill.

Ewen, S., and E. Ewen. 1982. *Channels of Desire*. New York: McGraw-Hill.

Fass, P. 1977. *The Damned and the Beautiful*. New York: Oxford University Press.

Featherstone, M. 1983. "Consumer Culture: An Introduction." *Theory, Culture, and Society* 1: 4–9.

———. 1992a. "The Heroic Life and Everyday Life." *Theory, Culture, and Society* 9: 159–82.

———. 1992b. "Postmodernism and the Aestheticization of Everyday Life." In *Modernity and Identity*, ed. S. Lash and J. Friedman, 265–90. London: Blackwell.

Finkelstein, J. 1989. *Dining Out: a Sociology of Modern Manners*. New York: New York University Press.

Fisher, C. S. 1990. "Changes in Leisure Activities in Three Towns, 1890–1940." Paper presented at the American Sociological Association, Washington, D.C.

Fisher, W. 1987. *Human Communication as Narration: Toward a Philosophy of Reason, Value and Action.* Columbia: University of South Carolina Press.

Fiske, D., and R. Shweder, eds. 1986. *Metatheory in Social Sciences.* Chicago: University of Chicago Press.

Fiske, J. 1989. *Understanding Popular Culture.* Boston: Unwin Hyman.

Flandrin, J.-L. 1976. *Familles: Parente, maison, sexualité dans l'ancienne société.* Paris: Seuil

————. 1981. *Le Sexe et l'occident.* Paris: Seuil

Flaubert, G. 1874. *Madame Bovary.* Paris: A. Lemerre.

Flink, J. 1988. *The Automobile Age.* Cambridge: MIT Press.

Foucault, M. 1966. *Les Mots et les choses.* Paris: Gallimard.

————. 1969. *L'Archeologie du savoir.* Paris: Gallimard.

————. 1975. *Surveiller et punir: Naissance de la prison.* Paris: Gallimard.

————. 1977. *Language, Counter-Memory, Practice.* Edited by D. F. Bouchard. Ithaca: Cornell University Press.

————. 1984. *Le Souci de soi.* Paris: Gallimard.

Fox, R. W., and J. Lears. 1983. *The Culture of Consumption: Critical Essays in American History, 1880–1980.* New York: Pantheon.

Frank, R. 1988. *Passions within Reason.* New York: W. W. Norton.

Franks, D. 1985. "Introduction to the Special Issue on the Sociology of Emotions." *Symbolic Interaction* 8, no. 2: 161–69.

Frazer, E. 1987. "Teenage Girls Reading Jackie." *Media, Culture and Society* 9: 407–25.

Freccero, J. 1986. "Autobiography and Narrative." In *Reconstructing Individualism,* ed. T. Heller, M. Sosna, and D. Wellbery, 16–29. Stanford: Stanford University Press.

Freud, S. 1962. *Civilization and Its Discontent.* Translated by J. Strachey. New York: W. W. Norton.

Fromm, E. 1956. *The Art of Loving.* New York: Harper and Row.

Gadamer, H.-G. 1975. *Truth and Method.* Edited by G. Barden and J. Cumming. Translated by W. Glen-Doerpel. New York: Seabury.

Gans, H. 1975. *Popular Culture and High Culture.* New York: Basic Books.

Garfinkel, H. 1967. *Studies in Ethnomethodology.* Englewood Cliffs, N.J.: Prentice-Hall

Gartman, D. 1991. "Culture as Class Symbolization or Mass Reification? A Critique of Bourdieu's Distinction." *American Journal of Sociology* 97, no. 2: 421–447.

Gay, P. 1984. *The Bourgeois Experience: Victoria to Freud.* Vol. 1, *Education of the Senses.* New York: Oxford University Press.

————. 1986. *The Bourgeois Experience: Victoria to Freud.* Vol. 2, *The Tender Passion.* New York: Oxford University Press.

Geertz, C. 1973. *The Interpretation of Cultures.* New York: Basic Books.

————. 1983. *Local Knowledge.* New York: Basic Books.

Gehlen, A. 1980. *Man in the Age of Technology.* Translated by P. Lipscomb. New York: Columbia University Press.

Gergen, K. J., and K. Davis, eds. 1985. *The Social Construction of the Person.* New York: Springer-Verlag.

Gergen, M. 1988. "Narratives Structures in Social Explanation." In *Analysing Everyday Explanation*, ed. C. Antaki, 94–112. London: Sage.

Gerth, H. H., and C. W. Mills, eds. 1958. *From Max Weber: Essays in Sociology*. Oxford: Oxford University Press.

Gibbons, M. 1987. *Interpreting Politics*. New York: New York University Press.

Giddens, A. 1971. *Capitalism and Social Theory: An Analysis of the Writings of Marx, Durkheim, and Max Weber*. Cambridge: Cambridge University Press.

———. 1979. *Central Problems in Social Theory*. Berkeley: University of California Press.

———. 1981. *A Contemporary Critique of Historical Materialism*. Berkeley: University of California Press.

———. 1984. *The Constitution of Society*. Oxford: Basil Blackwell.

———. 1990. *The Consequences of Modernity*. Stanford: Stanford University Press.

———. 1992. *The Transformation of Intimacy*. Stanford: Stanford University Press.

Giddens, A., and J. Turner, eds. 1987. *Social Theory Today*. Stanford: Stanford University Press.

Gillis, J. 1985. *For Better, For Worse*. New York: Oxford University Press.

———. 1988. "From Ritual to Romance: Toward an Alternative History of Love." In *Anger*, ed. C. Stearns and P. Stearns, 87–121. Chicago: University of Chicago Press.

Goertzel, T. 1979. "Class in America: Qualitative Distinctions and Quantitative Data." *Qualitative Sociology* 1, no. 3: 53–76.

Goffman, E. 1967. *Interaction Ritual*. New York: Pantheon.

———. 1976. *Gender Advertisements*. New York: Harper and Row.

Goode, J. W. 1966. "Family Disorganisation." In *Contemporary Social Problems*, ed. R. K. Merton and R. A. Nisbet, 467–544. New York: Harcourt, Brace and World.

———. 1968. "The Theoretical Importance of Love." *American Sociological Review* 33: 750–60.

Goody, J. 1973. *Bride Wealth and Dowry*. Cambridge: Cambridge University Press.

———. 1977. "Against `Ritual': Loosely Structured Thoughts on a Loosely Defined Topic." In *Secular Ritual*, ed. S. Moore and B. Myerhoff, 25–35. Amsterdam: Van Gorcum.

Gouldner, A. 1979. *The Future of Intellectuals and the Rise of the New Class: A Frame of Reference, Theses, Conjectures, Arguments, and an Historical Perspective in the Role of Intellectuals and Intelligentsia in the International Class Contest of the Modern Era*. New York: Seabury.

Green, N. 1990. *The Spectacle of Nature: Landscape and Bourgeois Culture in Nineteenth-Century France*. Manchester: Manchester University Press.

Grimsted, A. 1987. *Melodrama Unveiled: American Theater and Culture, 1800–1850*. Berkeley: University of California Press.

Griswold, R. L. 1982. *Family and Divorce in California, 1850–1890: Victorian Illusions and Everyday Realities*. Albany: State University of New York Press.

Griswold, W. 1994. *Culture and Societies in a Changing World.* Thousand Oaks, Calif.: Pine Forge Press.

Gross, L. 1973. "Art as the Communication of Competence." *Social Science Information* 12, no. 5: 115–41.

Gulich, E., and U. Quasthoff. 1985. "Narrative Analysis." In *Handbook of Discourse Analysis,* ed. T. A. van Dijk, 169–197. London: Academic Press.

Habermas, J. 1987. *The Philosophical Discourse of Modernity.* Translated by F. Lawrence. Cambridge: MIT Press.

———. 1989. *The Structural Transformation of the Public Sphere.* Translated by T. Burger and F. Lawrence. Cambridge: MIT Press.

Hall, J. 1992. "The Capital(s) of Cultures: A Nonholistic Approach to Status Situations, Class, Gender, and Ethnicity." In *Cultivating Differences,* ed. M. Lamont and M. Fournier, 257–88. Chicago: University of Chicago Press.

Hall, S. 1981. "Notes on Deconstructing 'The Popular.'" In *People's History and Socialist Theory,* ed. R. Samuel, 227–40. Boston: Routledge and Kegan Paul.

Halle, D. 1984. *America's Working Man: Work, Home, and Politics among Blue-Collar Property Owners.* Chicago: University of Chicago Press.

———. 1992. "The Audience for Abstract Art: Class, Culture, and Power." In *Cultivating Differences,* ed. M. Lamont and M. Fournier, 131–51. Chicago: University of Chicago Press.

Harré, R. 1986. *The Social Construction of Emotion.* New York: Oxford University Press.

Harris, L. 1987. *Inside America.* New York: Vintage Books.

Harvey, D. 1989. *The Condition of Post-Modernity.* Oxford: Basil Blackwell.

Hebdige, D. 1988 *Hiding in the Light.* New York: Routledge.

Heller, A. 1984. *Everyday Life.* Translated by G. Campbell. London: Routledge and Kegan Paul.

Heller, T., M. Sosna, and D. Wellbery, eds. 1986. *Reconstructing Individualism.* Stanford: Stanford University Press.

Himmelfarb, G. 1995. *The Demoralization of Society: From Victorian Virtues to Modern Values.* New York: Alfred A. Knopf.

Hirschman, A. O. 1979. *Shifting Involvements: Private Interest and Public Action.* Princeton: Princeton University Press.

Hirsh, F. 1976. *The Social Limits of Growth.* London: Routledge and Kegan Paul.

———. 1986. *Rival Views of Market Society and Other Recent Essays.* New York: Viking.

Hochschild, A. 1979. "Emotion Work, Feeling Rules, and Social Structure." *American Journal of Sociology* 85: 551–74.

———. 1983. *The Managed Heart.* Berkeley: University of California Press.

Hochschild, A., with A. Machung. 1989. *The Second Shift: Working Parents and the Revolution at Home.* New York: Viking.

Hodder, I. 1994. "The Interpretation of Documents and Material Culture." In *Handbook of Qualitative Analysis,* ed. N. K. Denzin and Y. Lincoln, 394–402. Newbury Park: Sage.

Holland, D., and M. A. Eisenhart. 1990. *Educated in Romance.* Chicago: University of Chicago Press.

Holland, D., and N. Quinn, eds. 1987. *Cultural Models in Language and Thought.* Cambridge: Cambridge University Press.

Holub, R. 1984. *Reception Theory.* London: Methuen.

Horkheimer, M. 1982. *Critical Theory: Selected Essays.* Translated by M. O'Connell. New York: Continuum.

Hunt, M. 1959. *The Natural History of Love.* New York: Alfred A. Knopf.

Huyssen, A. 1986. "Mass Culture as Woman." In *Studies in Entertainment,* ed. T. Modleski, 188–208. Bloomington: Indiana University Press.

Ignatieff, M. 1988. "Love's Progress." *Times Literary Supplement,* April, 15–21.

Illouz, E. 1991. "Reason within Passion: Love in Women's Magazines." *Critical Studies in Mass Communication* 8, no. 3: 231–48.

Izard, C. 1983. "Emotions in Personality and Culture." *Ethos* 11, no. 4: 305–12.

Jakle, J. 1985. *The Tourist: Travel in Twentieth-Century North America.* Lincoln: Neb.: University of Nebraska Press.

James, H. 1970. *The Portrait of a Lady.* New York: A. M. Kelley.

Jameson, F. 1979. "Reification and Utopia in Mass Culture." *Social Text,* no. 1: 130–148.

———. 1981. *The Political Unconscious.* Ithaca: Cornell University Press.

———. 1984 "Postmodernism and the Cultural Logic of Late Capitalism." *New Left Review,* no. 146: 53–92.

———. 1991. *Postmodernism, or the Cultural Logic of Late Capitalism.* Durham: Duke University Press.

Janus, N. 1981. "Advertising and the Mass Media: Transnational Link between Production and Consumption." *Media, Culture and Society* 3: 13–23.

Jay, M. 1973. *The Dialectical Imagination.* Boston: Little, Brown.

Kalmijn, M. 1991. "Status Homogamy in the United States." *American Journal of Sociology* 97, no. 2: 496–523

Kasson, J. 1981. *Amusing the Million: Coney Island at the Turn of the Century.* New York: Hill and Wang.

———. 1990. *Rudeness and Civility: Manners in Nineteenth-Century Urban America.* New York: Hill and Wang.

Keesing, R. 1987. "Anthropology as Interpretive Quest." *Current Anthropology* 28, no. 2: 161–76.

Kellner, D. 1983. "Critical Theory, Commodities and the Consumer Society." *Theory, Culture and Society* 1, no. 3: 66–83.

———. 1989. *Critical Theory, Marxism, and Modernity.* Baltimore: Johns Hopkins University Press.

———. 1992. "Popular Culture and the Construction of Postmodern Identities." In *Modernity and Identity,* ed. S. Lash and J. Friedman, 141–64. London: Blackwell.

Kelly, J. R. 1983. *Leisure Identities and Interactions.* Boston: George Allen and Unwin.

Kemper, T., ed. 1990. *Research Agendas in the Sociology of Emotions.* Albany: State University of New York Press.

Kent, M. 1987. *How to Marry the Man of Your Choice*. New York: Warner Books.

Kephart, W. 1967. "Some Correlatives of Romantic Love." *Journal of Marriage and the Family* 29: 470–79.

Kern, Stephen. 1994. *The Culture of Love*. Cambridge: Harvard University Press.

Knorr-Cetina, K., and A. Cicourel, eds. 1981. *Advances in Social Theory and Methodology*. Boston: Routledge and Kegan Paul.

Kohn, M. 1977. *Class and Conformity: A Study in Values, with a Reassessment*. 2d. ed. Chicago: University of Chicago Press.

Komarovsky, M. 1987. *Blue-Collar Marriage*. New Haven: Yale University Press.

Krippendorff, K. 1990. "The Power of Communication and the Communication of Power; Toward an Ethical Theory of Communication." Paper presented at the International Communication Association Conference, San Francisco.

Kristeva, J. 1983. *Histoires d'amour*. Paris: Denoel

Kuhn, A. 1984. "Women's Genres—Annette Kuhn Considers Melodrama, Soap Opera, and Theory." *Screen* 25, no. 1: 18–28.

Kupiec Cayton, M., E. J. Gorn, and P. W. Williams, eds. 1992. *Encyclopedia of American Social History*. New York: Scribner's.

Labov, W. 1972. *Language in the Inner City*. Philadelphia: University of Pennsylvania Press.

Lakoff, G. 1987. *Women, Fire, and Dangerous Things: What Categories Reveal about the Mind*. Chicago: University of Chicago Press.

Lakoff, G., and M. Johnson. 1980. *Metaphors We Live By*. Chicago: University of Chicago Press.

Lamont, M. 1992. *Money, Morals and Manners: The Culture of the French and American Upper-Middle Class*. Chicago: University of Chicago Press.

Lamont, M., and M. Fournier, eds. 1992. *Cultivating Differences: Symbolic Boundaries and the Making of Inequalities*. Chicago: University of Chicago Press.

Lamont, M., and A. Lareau. 1988. "Cultural Capital: Allusions, Gaps, and Glissandos in Recent Theoretical Developments." *Sociological Theory* 6: 153–68.

Lantz, H. 1982. "Romantic Love in the Pre-modern Period: A Sociological Commentary." *Journal of Social History* 15, no. 3: 349–70.

Lasch, C. 1977. *Haven in a Heartless World: The Family Besieged*. New York: Basic Books.

———. 1984. *The Minimal Self: Psychic Survival in Troubled Times*. New York: W. W. Norton.

———. 1992. "The Culture of Consumption." In *Encyclopedia of American Social History*, ed. M. Kupiec Cayton, E. J. Gorn, and P. W. Williams, 1381–90. New York: Scribner's.

Lash, S. 1990. *Sociology of Postmodernism*. London: Routledge.

Lash, S., and J. Friedman, eds. 1992. *Modernity and Identity*. London: Blackwell

Lash, S., and J. Urry. 1987. *The End of Organized Capitalism*. Cambridge, England: Polity Press.

Laski, M. 1959. "Advertising—Sacred and Profane." *The Twentieth Century* 165: 119–22.

Laumann, E. 1966. *Prestige and Association in Urban Community.* Indianapolis: Bobbs-Merrill.

Laumann, E., et al. 1994. *The Social Organization of Sexuality: Sexual Practices in the United States.* Chicago: University of Chicago Press.

Lawrence, D. H. 1962. *Lady Chatterley's Lover.* New York: Grove Press.

Leach, W. 1981. *True Love and Perfect Union.* London: Routledge and Kegan Paul.

Lears, J. 1981. *No Place of Grace.* New York: Pantheon.

————. 1983. "From Salvation to Self-Realization." In *The Culture of Consumption,* ed. R. W. Fox and J. Lears, 1–38. New York: Pantheon.

————. 1984. "Some Versions of Fantasy: Toward a Cultural History of American Advertising, 1880–1930." *Prospects,* vol. 8.

Leiss, W. 1978. *The Limits to Satisfaction: On Needs and Commodities.* London: Marion Boyars.

————. 1983. "The Icons of the Marketplace." *Theory, Culture and Society* 1, no. 3: 10–21.

Leiss, W., S. Kline, and S. Jhally. 1988. *Social Communication in Advertising.* Toronto, Ontario: Nelson.

————. 1963. *Structural Anthropology.* New York: Basic Books.

Levine, L. 1988. *High Brow/Low Brow: The Emergence of Cultural Hierarchy in America.* Cambridge: Harvard University Press.

Levinger, G. 1965. "Marital Cohesiveness and Dissolution: An Integrative Review." *Journal of Marriage and the Family* 27: 19–28.

Levison, A. 1974. *The Working-Class Majority.* Baltimore: Penguin

Lévi-Strauss, C. 1949. *The Elementary Structures of Kinship.* Translated by Rodney Needham. Boston: Beacon Press.

Levy, R. I. 1984. "Emotion, Knowing, and Culture." In *Culture Theory: Essays of Mind, Self, and Emotion,* ed. R. Shweder and R. Levine, 214–37. New York: Cambridge University Press.

Lewis, D., and L. Goldstein. 1983. *The Automobile and the American Culture.* Ann Arbor: University of Michigan Press.

Lewis, J. 1983. *The Pursuit of Happiness.* Cambridge: Cambridge University Press.

Lind, C. 1987. "Explanatory Systems in Oral Stories." In *Cultural Models in Language and Thought,* ed. D. Holland and N. Quinn, 343–65. Cambridge: Cambridge University Press.

Lindenberg, 1987. "Common Sense and Social Structure: A Sociological Perspective." In *Common Sense,* ed. F. van Holthoon and D. Olson. Lanham, Md.: University Press of America 199–216.

Linton, R. 1936. *The Study of Man.* New York: Appleton.

Lofland, J. 1984. *Analyzing Social Settings: A Guide to Qualitative Observation Analysis.* Belmont, Calif.: Wadsworth.

Lovejoy, A. O. 1948. *Essays in the History of Ideas.* Baltimore: Johns Hopkins University Press.

Luckmann, T. 1987. "Some Thoughts on Common Sense and Science." In *Common Sense,* ed. F. van Holthoon and D. Olson, 162–90. Lanham, Md.: University Press of America.

Luhmann, N. 1986a. "The Individuality of the Individual: Historical Meanings and Contemporary Problems." In *Reconstructing Individualism*, ed. T. Heller, M. Sosna, and D. Wellbery, 313–28. Stanford: Stanford University Press.

———. 1986b. *Love as Passion: The Codification of Intimacy*. Translated by J. Gaines and D. L. Jones. Cambridge: Harvard University Press.

Lukács, G. 1971. *History and Class Consciousness: Studies in Marxist Dialectics*. Translated by R. Livingstone. Cambridge: MIT Press.

Lutes, Della Thompson. 1923. *The Gracious Hostess: A Book of Etiquette*. Indianapolis: Bobbs-Merrill.

Lutz, C. 1983. "Parental Goals, Ethopsychology, and the Development of Emotional Meaning." *Ethos* 11, no. 4: 246–62.

———. 1986. "Emotion, Thought, and Estrangement: Emotion as a Cultural Category." *Cultural Anthropology* 1, no. 3: 287–309.

Lyman, S. M. 1990. "The Drama in the Routine: A Prolegomenon to a Praxiological Sociology." *Sociological Theory* 8, no. 2: 217–23.

Lyman, S. M., and M. Scott. 1975. *Drama of Social Reality*. New York: Oxford University Press.

Lynd, R., and H. Lynd. 1957. *Middletown: A Study in American Culture*. New York: Harcourt, Brace.

Lyotard, J. F. 1984. *The Postmodern Condition: A Report on Knowledge*. Translated by G. Bennington and B. Massumi. Minneapolis: University of Minnesota Press.

Lystra, K. 1989. *Searching the Heart*. New York: Oxford University Press.

MacCannell, D. 1976. *The Tourist: A New Theory of the Leisure Class*. New York: Schocken.

MacFarlane, A. 1987. *The Culture of Capitalism*. Oxford: Basil Blackwell.

Machor, J. 1987. *Pastoral Cities: Urban Ideals and the Symbolic Landscape of America*. Madison: University of Wisconsin Press.

MacIntyre, A. 1984. "The Virtues, The Unity of Human Life, and the Concept of a Tradition. "In *Liberalism and Its Critics*, ed. M. Sandel, 125–148. New York: New York University Press.

Maier, C. 1987. *In Search of Stability*. Cambridge: Cambridge University Press.

Mandler, J. 1984. *Stories, Scripts, and Scenes: Aspects of Schema Theory*. Hillsdale, N.J.: Lawrence Erlbaum Associates.

Manning, K. 1987. *Semiotics and Fieldwork*. Newbury Park: Sage.

Marchand, R. 1985. *Advertising the American Dream*. Berkeley: University of California Press.

Marcuse, H. 1963. *Éros et Civilisation*. Paris: Minuit

Marx, K. 1976. *Capital*, vol. 1. Translated by B. Fowkes. London: Penguin.

Marx, K., and F. Engels. 1967. *The Communist Manifesto*. Harmondsworth: Penguin.

Mauss, M. 1967 *The Gift: Forms and Functions of Exchange in Archaic Society*. Translated by I. Cunnison. New York: W. W. Norton.

May, E. 1980. *Great Expectations*. Chicago: University of Chicago Press.

May, L. 1980. *Screening out the Past*. New York: Oxford University Press.

McCarthy, T. 1985. "Reflections on Rationalization in the Theory of Communicative Action." In *Habermas and Modernity*, ed. R. Bernstein, 176–91. Cambridge: MIT Press.

McCracken, G. 1988. *Culture and Consumption: New Approaches to the Symbolic Character of Consumer Goods and Activities.* Bloomington: Indiana University Press.

McGovern, C. 1989. "Advertising, Consumers and American Culture, 1880–1930." Smithsonian Institution, unpublished manuscript.

McKinsey, E. 1985. *Niagara Falls: Icon of the American Sublime.* Cambridge: Cambridge University Press.

Medick, H., and D. Sabean. 1984. *Interest and Emotion.* Cambridge: Cambridge University Press.

Miller, D. 1987. *Material Culture and Mass Consumption.* Oxford: Basil Blackwell.

Mills, C.-W. 1951. *White Collar*, New York: Oxford University Press.

Mintz, S. 1983. *A Prison of Expectations: The Family in Victorian Culture.* New York: New York University Press.

Mischler, E. 1986. *Research Interviewing.* Cambridge: Harvard University Press.

Moore, S., and B. Myerhoff, eds. 1977. *Secular Ritual.* Assen: Van Gorcum.

Morley, D. 1980. *The Nationwide Audience: Structure and Decoding.* London: British Film Institute.

Murphy, G. 1987. "Media Influence on the Socialization of Teenage Girls." In *Impacts and Influences: Essays on Media Power in the Twentieth Century,* ed. J. Curran, A. Smith, and P. Wingate, 202–17. London: Methuen.

Murray, K. 1989. "The Construction of Identity in the Narratives of Romance and Comedy." In *Texts of Identity*, ed. J. Shotter and K. Gergen, 176–205. London: Sage.

Novak, B. 1981. *Nature and Culture: American Landscape and Painting, 1825–1875.* New York: Oxford University Press.

Ortner, S. 1984. "Theory in Anthropology since the Sixties." *Comparative Studies in Society and History* 26, no. 1: 126–66.

Otto, R. 1923. *The Idea of the Holy: An Inquiry into the Non-Rational Factor and Its Relation to the Rational.* Translated by J. W. Harvey. London: Oxford University Press

Page, S. 1988. *If I'm So Wonderful Why Am I Still Single?* New York: Viking.

Parkin, J. 1971. *Class Inequalities and the Political Order.* New York: Praeger.

Parsons, T. 1951. *The Social System.* New York: Free Press.

Peiss, K. 1986. *Working Women and Leisure in Turn-of-the-Century New York.* Philadelphia: Temple University Press.

———. 1989. "Charity Girls and City Pleasures: Historical Notes on Working-Class Sexuality, 1880–1920." In *Passion and Power*, ed. K. Peiss and C. Simmons, 57–69. Philadelphia: Temple University Press.

Peterson, R., and A. Simkus. 1992. "How Musical Tastes Mark Occupational Status Groups." In *Cultivating Differences*, ed. M. Lamont and M. Fournier, 152–86. Chicago: University of Chicago Press.

Popper, K. 1972. *The Logic of Scientific Discovery.* London: Hutchinson.

———. 1985. "The Defense of Rationalism." In *Popper Selections*, ed. D. Miller, 33–46. Princeton: Princeton University Press.

Post, E. 1922. *Etiquette in Society, in Business, in Politics and at Home*. New York: Funk and Wagnalls.

Proust, M. 1993. "Mélancolique villegiature de Mme. de Breyve. In *Écrits mondains*, 170–86. Paris: Collection 10/18.

Quinn, N. 1987. "Convergent Evidence for a Cultural Model of American Marriage." In *Cultural Models in Language and Thought*, ed. D. Holland and N. Quinn, 173–92. Cambridge: Cambridge University Press.

Quinn, N., and D. Holland. 1987. "Culture and Cognition." In *Cultural Models in Language and Thought*, ed. D. Holland and N. Quinn, 3–40. Cambridge: Cambridge University Press.

Rabinow, P. 1986. "Representations Are Social Facts: Modernity and Post-Modernity in Anthropology." In *Writing Culture*, ed. J. Clifford and G. Marcus, 234–61. Berkeley: University of California Press.

Rabinow, P., and W. Sullivan. 1979. "The Interpretive Turn: Emergence of an Approach." In *Interpretive Social Science*, ed. P. Rabinow and W. Sullivan, 1–21. Berkeley: University of California Press.

Radway, J. 1984. *Reading the Romance*. Chapel Hill: University of North Carolina Press.

Rainwater, Lee. 1965. *Family Design: Marital Sexuality, Family Size, and Contraception*. Chicago: Aldine.

Richardson, S. 1962. *Pamela, or Virtue Rewarded*. New York: E. P. Dutton.

Ricoeur, P. 1979. "The Model of the Text: Meaningful Action Considered as a Text." In *Interpretive Social Science*, ed. P. Rabinow and W. Sullivan, 73–101. Berkeley: University of California Press.

———. 1986. *Lectures on Ideology and Utopia*. Edited by G. Taylor. New York: Columbia University Press.

Rieff, P. 1966. *The Triumph of the Therapeutic*. New York: Basic Books.

Robertson, R. 1988. "The Sociological Significance of Culture." *Theory, Culture, and Society* 5: 3–23.

Rorty, A. O. 1987. "Self-Deception, Akrasia and Irrationality." In *The Multiple Self*, ed. J. Elster, 115–32. Cambridge: Cambridge University Press.

Rosaldo, M., 1984. "Toward an Anthropology of the Self and Feeling." In *Culture Theory*, ed. R. Shweder and R. Levine, 137–52. New York: Cambridge University Press.

———. 1980. *Knowledge and Passion: Ilongot Notions of Self and Social Life*. New York: Cambridge University Press.

Rothman, E. 1984. *Hands and Hearts*. Cambridge: Harvard University Press.

Rousset, J. 1981. *Leurs yeux se rencontrerent*. Paris: Corti.

Rowson, S. H. 1991. *Charlotte Temple*. New York: Penguin.

Rubin, L. 1976. *Worlds of Pain*. New York: Basic Books.

———. 1992. *Worlds of Pain*. New York: Basic Books.

Rumelhart, D. 1977. *Introduction to Human Information Processing*. New York: Wiley.

Russell, B. 1929. *Marriage and Morals*. New York: Bantam Books.

Sahlins, M. 1976. *Culture and Practical Reason*. Chicago: University of Chicago Press.

Sandel, M., ed. 1984. *Liberalism and Its Critics*. New York: New York University Press.

Scanzoni, J. H. 1970. *Opportunity and the Family*. New York: Free Press.

Schachter, S., and J. Singer. 1962. "Cognitive, Social and Physiological Determinants of Emotional States." *Psychological Review* 69, no. 5: 379–99.

Scheff, T. 1990. *Microsociology*. Chicago: University of Chicago Press.

Schmitt, P. J. 1990. *Back to Nature: The Arcadian Myth in Urban America*. New York: Oxford University Press.

Schudson, M. 1986. *Advertising: The Uneasy Persuasion*. New York: Basic Books.

———. 1989. "How Culture Works: Perspectives from Media Studies on the Efficacy of Symbols." *Theory and Society* 18: 153–80

———. 1991. "Delectable Materialism: Were the Critics of Consumer Culture Wrong all Along?" In *The American Prospect* 5: 26–35.

———. 1992. *Watergate in American Memory*. New York: Basic Books.

Schutz, A. 1957. "Common Sense and Scientific Interpretation of Human Action." In *Sociological Theory,* ed. L. Coser and B. Rosenberg, 233–46. New York: Macmillan.

———. 1967. *The Phenomenology of the Social World*. Translated by G. Walsh and F. Lehnert. Evanston: Northwestern University Press.

———. 1970. *On Phenomenology and Social Relations*. Chicago: University of Chicago Press.

Schutz, A., and T. Luckmann. 1973. *The Structures of the Life-World*. Evanston: Northwestern University Press.

Schwartz, B. 1981. *Vertical Classification*. Chicago: University of Chicago Press.

Scitovsky, T. 1976. *The Joyless Economy*. New York: Oxford University Press.

Seidman, S. 1991. *Romantic Longings*. New York: Routledge.

Sennett, R. 1977. *The Fall of Public Man: On the Social Psychology of Capitalism*. New York: Alfred A. Knopf.

Sennett, R., and J. Cobb. 1972. *The Hidden Injuries of Class*. New York: Vintage Books.

Shakespeare, W. 1984. *Romeo and Juliet*. Edited by B. Evans. London: Cambridge University Press.

Shorter, E. 1975. *The Making of the Modern Family*. New York: Basic Books.

Shuman, A. 1986. *Storytelling Rights: The Uses of Oral and Written Texts by Urban Adolescents*. Cambridge: Cambridge University Press.

Shweder, R. 1986. "Divergent Rationalities." In *Metatheory in Social Science,* ed. D. W. Fiske and R. Shweder. Chicago: University of Chicago Press.

Sicherman, B. 1989. "Sense and Sensibility: A Case Study of Women's Reading in Late Victorian Era." *Reading in America,* ed. C. Davidson, 201–25. Baltimore: Johns Hopkins University Press.

Simmel, G. 1984. *Georg Simmel: On Women, Sexuality and Love*. Translated by Guy Oakes. New Haven: Yale University Press.

Simpson, J., B. Campbell, and E. Berscheid. 1986. "The Association between Romantic Love and Marriage: Kephart (1967) Twice Revisited." *Personality and Social Psychology Bulletin* 12, no. 3: 363–72.

Singer, I. 1987. *The Nature of Love.* Vol. 3, *The Modern World.* Chicago: University of Chicago Press.

Smart, B. 1989. "Modernity, Postmodernity and the Present." In *Theories of Modernity and Postmodernity,* ed. B. S. Turner, 14–29. London: Sage.

Smith, B. H. 1968. *Poetic Closure: A Study of How Poems End.* Chicago: University of Chicago Press.

Soble, A. 1990. *The Structure of Love.* New Haven: Yale University Press.

Sombart, W. 1967. *Luxury and Capitalism.* Translated by W. R. Dittmar. Ann Arbor: University of Michigan Press.

Stearns, C., and P. Stearns. 1986. *Anger.* Chicago: University of Chicago Press.

Stone, L. 1977. *The Family, Sex and Marriage in England, 1500–1800.* New York: Harper and Row.

Strasser, S. 1989. *Satisfaction Guaranteed: The Making of the American Mass Market.* New York: Pantheon Books.

Streitfield, D. 1991. "Words to Love By, Chapter and Verse." *Washington Post,* February 14, 5

Susman, W. 1984. *Culture as History: The Transformation of American Society in the Twentieth Century.* New York: Pantheon Books.

Swidler, A. 1980. "Love and Adulthood in American Culture." In *Themes of Work and Love in Adulthood,* ed. N. Smelser and E. Erikson. Cambridge: Harvard University Press.

Tennov, D. 1979. *Love and Limerance: The Experience of Being in Love.* Briarcliff Manor, N.Y.: Stein and Day.

Thompson, E. P. 1963. *The Making of the English Working Class.* London: Gollancz.

Thompson, J. B. 1984. *Studies in the Theory of Ideology.* Berkeley: University of California Press.

Thompson, K. 1985. *Readings from Emile Durkheim.* Chichester, England: Ellis Horwood.

Tierney, B., and Scott, J. 1984. *Western Societies.* New York: Alfred Knopf.

Turner, B. S., ed. 1990. *Theories of Modernity and Postmodernity,* London: Sage.

Turner, E. 1954. *A History of Courting.* New York: E. P. Dutton.

Turner, R. 1976. "The Real Self: From Institution to Impulse." *American Journal of Sociology* 8, no. 5: 989–1016.

Turner, V. 1967. *The Forest of Symbols.* Ithaca: Cornell University Press.

———. 1974. *Dramas, Fields, Metaphors: Symbolic Action in Human Society.* Ithaca: Cornell University Press.

———. 1977. "Variations on a Theme of Liminality." In *Secular Ritual,* ed. S. Moore and B. Myerhoff, 36–52. Amsterdam: Van Gorcum.

Unger, A. 1963 *Complete Guide to Dating.* New York: Universal.

Urry, J. 1990. *The Tourist Gaze.* London: Sage.

van Dijk, T. A. 1980. *Macrostructures: An Interdisciplinary Study of Discourse, Interaction, Cognition.* Hillsdale, N.J.: Lawrence Erlbaum Associates.

————. 1984. *Prejudice in Discourse: An Analysis of Prejudice in Cognition and Conversation*. Philadelphia: Benjamins.

van Holthoon, F., and D. Olson, eds. 1987. *Common Sense*. Lanham, Md.: University Press of America.

Veblen, T. 1979. *The Theory of the Leisure Class*. New York: Penguin.

Volosinov, V. I. 1986. *Marxism and the Philosophy of Language*. Translated by L. Matejka and I. R. Titunik. Cambridge: Harvard University Press.

Waller, W. 1937. "The Rating and Dating Complex." *American Sociological Review* 2, nos. 1–6: 727–34.

Watt, I. 1957. *The Rise of the Novel*. London: Chatto and Windus.

Waxman, V. W. 1993. *Creating the Couple: Love, Marriage and Hollywood Performance*. Princeton: Princeton University Press.

Weber, M. 1949. *The Methodology of the Social Sciences*. Translated and edited by E. Stills and H. Finch. New York: Free Press.

————. 1958. "The Social Psychology of the World Religions." In *From Max Weber: Essays in Sociology*, ed. H. H. Gerth and C. W. Mills, 267–302. Oxford: Oxford University Press.

————. 1976. *The Protestant Ethic and the Spirit of Capitalism*. Translated by T. Parsons. New York: Scribner's.

————. 1978. *Economy and Society*. Translated by G. Roth and C. Wittich. 2 vols. Berkeley: University of California Press.

Webster's Ready-Made Love Letters. 1873. New York: Robert M. De Witt.

Wetherell, M., and J. Potter. 1988. "Discourse Analysis and the Identification of Interpretive Repertoires." In *Analyzing Everyday Explanation*, ed. C. Antaki, 168–83. London: Sage.

Whyte, M. K. 1990. *Dating, Mating and Marriage*. New York: Aldine de Gruyter.

Williams, Raymond. 1977. *Marxism and Literature*. Oxford: Oxford University Press.

————. 1993. "Advertising: The Magic System." In *The Cultural Studies Reader*, ed. S. During, 320–338. New York: Routledge.

Williams, Rosalind. 1982. *Dream Worlds: Mass Communication in Late Nineteenth-Century France*. Berkeley: University of California Press.

Willis, P. 1977. *Learning to Labor*. New York: Columbia University Press.

————. 1980. "Shop Floor Culture, Masculinity and the Wage Form." In *Working-Class Culture*, ed. J. Clarke, C. Critcher, and R. Johnson, 185–98. New York: St. Martin's.

Winch, P. 1958. *The Idea of a Social Science and Its Relation to Philosophy*. London: Routledge and Kegan Paul.

Wolkstein, D. 1991. *The First Love Stories: From Isis and Osiris to Tristan and Iseult*. New York: HarperCollins Publishers.

Wright, J. 1978. "In Search of a New Working Class." *Qualitative Sociology* 1, no. 1: 33–57.

Wuthnow, R. 1987. *Meaning and Moral Order*. Berkeley: University of California Press.

Zaretsky, E. 1973. *Capitalism, the Family, and Personal Life*. New York: Harper and Row.

Zeldin, T. 1973. *France, 1848–1945*. Vol. 1, *Ambition, Love, and Politics*. Oxford: Clarendon.

———. 1980. *Histoires des passions françaises, 1848–1945*. Vol. 1, *Ambition et amour*. Paris: Seuil.

———. 1981. "Personal History and the History of the Emotions." *Journal of Social History* 15, no. 3: 339–47.

Zelizer, V. 1989. "The Social Meaning of Money: 'Special Monies.'" *American Journal of Sociology* 95, no. 2: 342–77

Zerubavel, E. 1981. *Hidden Rhythms*. Chicago: University of Chicago Press.

Index

Compositor: BookMasters, Inc.
Text: 10/13 Sabon
Display: Sabon